ILLUSIONS

© The Photo Source, London

ILLUSIONS of GRANDEUR

MOSLEY, FASCISM and BRITISH SOCIETY, 1931–81

D. S. LEWIS

Manchester University Press

Published by MANCHESTER UNIVERSITY PRESS,
Oxford Road, Manchester M13 9PL, UK
and 27 South Main Street, Wolfeboro, NH 03894–2069, USA

British Library cataloguing in publication data
Lewis, D. S.
  Illusions of grandeur: Mosley, fascism and British society, 1931–81.
  1. Fascism – Great Britain – History
  I. Title
  320.5′33′0941   DA566.7

Library of Congress cataloging in publication data applied for

ISBN 0 7190 2354 8 *hardback*

Photoset in Linotron Century Schoolbook with Futura
by Northern Phototypesetting Co., Bolton
Printed in Great Britain
by the Alden Press, Oxford
and bound by Robert Hartnoll (1985) Ltd., Bodmin, Cornwall

CONTENTS

It is a great pleasure to acknowledge the many sources of assistance which I have received whilst writing this book, and without which its completion would have been very much more difficult, if not impossible. In particular I owe an immense debt of gratitude to Dr Peter Lowe of Manchester University. His kindness, encouragement, and advice have been as central to the writing of this book as any of the information contained within it.

My thanks are due also the staff of the many libraries and institutions within which I have worked over the last few years. These include the library at Balliol College, Oxford, (and here I must thank also W. Collins Sons and Co. Ltd, the publisher, for allowing me to consult the Nicolson papers); the British Library (especially the Bloomsbury and Colindale branches); the British Library of Political and Economic Science at the London School of Economics; the Institute of Historical Research; the John Rylands Library at the University of Manchester; the Labour Party Library; the Marx Memorial Library; Manchester Central Reference Library; the Public Records Office; the University of London Library, Middlesex south; and finally the Wiener Library, where I was furnished not merely with information but also with cups of tea and coffee.

I am indebted also to the many individuals who have assisted me in this project with their advice or recollections. Amongst these are Mr A. Excell and Mr 'J. G.' (whose identity I have promised not to reveal), both veteran anti-fascists; and ex-BUF members Mr E. J. Hamm and Mr R. Row of the Mosley Secretariat, who kindly received me and with whom I spent many hours in conversation. Also to Mr J. Hancock, whose advice on source material was extremely valuable; Mr B. Page, former editor of the *New Statesman*; Mr P. McNiven, who made available to me the extensive newspaper collection of the John Rylands Library; Mr S. Rawnsley, who was generous in his advice and who made available to me some of his unpublished work on fascism in north-west England; and Mr Jon Dyson for his advice on source material relating to Nazi Germany. A word of thanks must also go to the many residents of London's East End who shared with me their impressions of British fascism both past and present, and in particular to Mr B. Geller, veteran anti-fascist and member of the Socialist Party of Great Britain, and to Mr H. Berryman. Finally, my gratitude is extended to the late Sir Oswald Mosley and his wife Lady Diana Mosley, both of whom I met on several occasions. Sir Oswald generously granted me a lengthy interview in June 1980: even in old age he retained fascinating elements of his former magnificence and malevolence.

I am indebted also to those who have assisted in more practical ways. I include in this category my parents, family and many friends who have made moral, financial and miscellaneous contributions towards the successful completion of this book. Whilst it would be invidious to single out individuals in this respect I cannot but mention the assistance of Bill and Rosie, and the kindness of John and Monica Peberdy who provided me with a house in London whilst researching and writing this piece of work. I am grateful also to Mrs D. Keenan for her speed, co-operation and conscientiousness in typing the final draft of my manuscript. Finally, I am deeply grateful for the invaluable and versatile assistance and support of Joanna, who has lived with me throughout the writing of this book. Her gentleness and patience, her cheerfulness and her love have been unswerving and without limit. They transcend any words which I can assemble; but I shall remember them always. It is she to whom this piece of work is dedicated.

David S. Lewis
London, April 1986

ACKNOWLEDGEMENTS

The following abbreviations have been used throughout the text and notes:

BL	British Library
BM	British Movement
BNP	British National Party
BUF	British Union of Fascists
BUQ	*British Union Quarterly*
CAB	Cabinet Papers
CP	Communist Party of Great Britain
DPC	District Party Committee of the Communist Party of Great Britain
EEC	European Economic Community
FO	Foreign Office
FQ	*Fascist Quarterly*
GBM	Greater Britain Movement
HC Debs.	*House of Commons Debates, series 5*
HL Debs.	*House of Lords Debates, series 2*
IFL	Imperial Fascist League
ILP	Independent Labour Party
JPC	Jewish People's Council
LCC	London County Council
LEL	League of Empire Loyalists
LPL	Labour Party Library
LSE	London School of Economics
MEPO 2	Metropolitan Police Files, series 2
MS	Manuscript
NCCL	National council for Civil Liberties
n.d.	no date
NF	National Front
NLP	National Labour Party
n.p.	no pressmark or publication details
NSDAP	National Socialist German Workers' Party
NSM	National Socialist Movement
Nupa	New Party Youth Movement
PRO	Public Records Office
WDL	White Defence League
WL	Wiener Library

To JOANNA

Give it an understanding, but no tongue . . .
W. Shakespeare, *Hamlet*, 1, ii

Fascism defined

Fascism is the evilest spawn of capitalism and materialism, of the acquisitive society and war.
N. Thomas, *Fascism or Socialism? The Choice before us*,
George Allen & Unwin, London 1934, p. 62

We are . . . faced by the fact that a few people have misused the name of 'Fascism', in this country, and from ignorance or in perversion have represented it as the 'White Guard of reaction'. This is indeed a strange perversion of a creed of dynamic change and progress.
Mosley, *The Greater Britain*, BUF, London 1932, p. 15

. . . In substance fascism is a myth . . . a system of images defying logical definition or rational analysis, filled if submitted to either, with contradictions.
A. Hamilton, *The Appeal of Fascism:
A study of intellectuals and fascism 1919–45*,
Anthony Blond Ltd, London 1971, p. xix

It is ironic that fascism, through its common usage as a term of abuse, has itself become an abused term. It has been devalued and therefore blunted as a tool of analysis. For since 1945 fascism has been regarded universally as one of the most disreputable political creeds ever to have stalked the earth. Such sentiments have not assisted an understanding of what fascism is or why it prospers.

The aim of this book is to examine fascism in Britain. It concentrates upon the British Union of Fascists because throughout the 1930s the BUF provided a clear example of the strengths and weaknesses of fascism as the theoretical foundation of a political party. Indeed, the BUF remains the most successful fascist movement ever to have emerged within Britain. Its threat lay not in its eccentric extremism but in the potential appeal of its populist political stance which incorporated ideological currents from both the left and right of the political spectrum, and exploited the common desire (itself a product of the social problems of the inter-war period) to establish a government of national consensus.

In this respect fascism renders traditional political typographies inadequate and demands the application of a new terminology. As such it can be summarised as a form of authoritarian 'centrism': an attempt to achieve a consensus through the enforced mediation between and subsumation of the conflicting interests of competing social groups. What differentiates this from the consensus sought by liberalism (also an ideology of the centre of the political spectrum) is that fascism was prepared to achieve its desired end in an overtly authoritarian and collectivist fashion. For, as will be shown, it offered to hammer out a ruthless new synthesis within societies bitterly divided by conflicts of faction and class.

Although the impact of the BUF upon Britain was ultimately limited, it remains important because rarely has a fascist movement exposed its theory and programme to such detailed examination before assuming power. Furthermore, its philosophy, policies and evolution each reflected the movement's centrist perspective and therefore provide an important insight into the nature of fascism as a political phenomenon. For although these introductory remarks are related specifically to the BUF, they are of relevance also to the wider understanding of the appeal, the purpose and the problems of fascist movements elsewhere. The constraints of space prohibit any complete examination of this comparative theme, but an indication of the extent to which fascism in other countries has reflected this authoritarian centrism, as well as the position of post-war British fascist movements, will be explored in later chapters.

Arriving at a definition of fascism is difficult because of the internal contradictions both within the ideology itself and those movements which claim adherence to it. Far from acting as a deterrent, however, such difficulties have acted as a spur to the imaginative with the result that fascism has probably the dubious distinction of having been more widely defined than any other ideology. Attempts have been made to establish it upon the left of the political spectrum as a form of socialism operating within a strictly national context. Such a view relies upon a fundamental misconception of the differences between the aims of socialism and fascism, particularly with regard to economic organisation. Whereas any meaningful form of socialism aims at achieving the common ownership of the wealth-producing apparatus of a society, fascism seeks to rationalise the capitalist system whilst leaving its very essence (the private accumulation of capital) largely intact.

It is more usual for fascism to be defined as a movement of the right, although this involves a problem in ascertaining its relationship with traditional conservatism. The solution most usually adopted is to differentiate between the 'radical' fascist right which seeks to mobilise the population, and the 'traditional' conservative right which distrusts and discourages mass participation in the political process.[1] Whereas the former aims to create a new society populated by citizens with new moral values, the latter seeks to preserve the present. But attempts to fix a relationship between these two positions within a linear political spectrum remain uncomfortable.

Other interpretations have suggested that only through subdivision can fascism be understood. Ernst Nolte found four different types of fascism, each of which varied according to the social composition and ideology of individual movements and the nature of the societies in which they operated.[2] Others have distinguished between different species of fascism on a geographical basis, pointing to the obvious differences between fascism as it developed in the industrial democracies of the West and that which emerged in the more overtly reactionary agrarian states of eastern Europe.[3] The ultimate end of this process of fragmentation has been to shatter entirely the concept of fascism as a generic phenomenon.

It is undoubtedly true that fascism lacks a central theoretical source and is composed of diverse and often contradictory elements. Even when these are disentangled it is usual to find that they were disregarded by fascist regimes in the interests of expediency. The legacy of Hitler and Mussolini has led to suggestions that even the most basic elements of fascism were incidental to the opportunists who assumed the leadership of fascist movements and regimes. Whilst acknowledging these problems it will be shown that the concept of fascism as a single (if flexible) genus remains a legitimate one.

Amongst anti-fascists in the inter-war years there was certainly a broad degree of consensus as to the nature of fascism. It was agreed that fascism was the product of capitalism in crisis, an attempt by the ruling class to circumvent the laws of progress through which capitalism stood condemned to decay as a result of its internal contradictions. Survival demanded the raising of profits through the increased productivity of labour, which in turn required the establishment of a dictatorship, the destruction of trade unions and the prohibition of strikes as a prelude to lengthening working hours and cutting wages. Bereft of its rights and representative institutions, the labour movement would be fragmented and subjected to an ever-increasing level of exploitation whilst being denied any effective channel of protest. It was in this sense that Trotsky grimly described fascism as '. . . a razor in the hands of the class enemy'.[4]

There were minor differences concerning the degree of state complicity in the triumph of fascism, and the extent to which the ideology could be successful in producing permanent counter-revolution as opposed to merely providing capitalism with a temporary stay of execution. But the most striking aspect of any survey of the analyses and definitions of fascism by its opponents remains the high degree of consensus amongst them as to its essential nature. Almost all were unable to resist the temptation to oversimplify it as a political phenomenon. Accepting that fascism originated from a crisis of the capitalist system, and realising that the funds consumed by fascist parties originated in that system also, it proved too easy to make the illogical deduction that fascism was therefore, from the outset, a conspiracy by monopoly capital designed to facilitate the greater exploitation of the proletariat. The attractiveness of this analysis lay, as does the seductive qualities of all conspiratorial interpretations of history, in its simplicity. To see fascist movements as nothing more than gangs of thugs financed and controlled by the real enemy, the big capitalist, represented a refusal to accept that they could be political movements fired by the genuine protest of those whom the left had failed to attract. It was a distortion which avoided facing awkward questions concerning the development and role of the left, the echoes of which can still be heard today.

The greatest single offender in the creation and maintenance of this image of fascism was the Comintern. This, the theoretical brain of the international communist movement, rejected appeals from those such as Clara Zetkin whose analysis of fascism recognised it as a 'movement with deep social roots',[5] preferring the more simple conspiratorial approach of fascism as the paid creature of finance capital. The social democratic parties of western Europe were held directly responsible for fascism's growth by their betrayal of working-class demands and, therefore, it was unreasonably concluded that fascism and social democracy were different sides of the same coin. Consequently there could be no anti-fascist alliance between communists and the hapless social democrats who were condemned as 'social fascists'. Once again it was an error in an analysis distorted through oversimplification. It was to bear bitter fruit all over Europe, but none more so than in Germany. Not until 1935 was the 'social fascist' position reversed as the Seventh World Congress endorsed the formation of anti-fascist fronts with other working-class parties. By this time the Nazis had been voted into power, resulting in the prompt destruction of both social democratic and communist parties within Germany.

It is true that fascism rescues the capitalist system, intensifies the capitalist process, and uses capitalist funds to achieve this. It does not follow however that, from its very beginnings, a fascist movement is the servile creature of some well-orchestrated plot by big business. Rather than seeing a fascist movement as a lifeboat built and serviced by the upper echelons of the bourgeoisie in case it should be needed during the economic storm, it represents something more akin to a piece of driftwood which, although not fashioned by the drowning capitalist, is nevertheless grabbed gratefully by him in a crisis in a desperate attempt to stay afloat.

Inter-war British fascists portrayed their ideology as a higher stage in the evolutionary development of society. The nineteenth century had seen the triumph of liberalism and *laissez-faire* capitalism with all their attendant inequalities. In response had developed communism, a blind, angry and destructive reaction to such naked injustice. Thus the politics of individual greed were confronted by those of class envy. Both ideologies had been pursued without regard to the overall welfare of the nation and had been instrumental in the erosion of the economic and social foundations of European society.[6] Therefore, fascism was seen as the collective name for a common response to a common set of problems. This flexibility and rejection of dogma, it was argued, ensured that fascism could never be a foreign movement, for it was able to absorb the culture of its host nation and develop in harmony with national traditions.

It was a revolt by the young and vigorous against the old and lethargic; '. . . an explosion against intolerable conditions, against remedial wrongs which the old world failed to remedy'.[7] It was a refusal to accept the inevitable degeneration of Western civilisation as predicted by prophets such as Oswald Spengler in *The Decline of the West*.[8] Whilst agreeing with much of Spengler's diagnosis of the ills of Western civilisation, Mosley believed that fascism could affect the necessary cure. In this it was '. . . a movement to secure national renaissance by people who felt themselves threatened with decline into decadence and death and were determined to live and live greatly'.[9] It was a revolt also against the sterile materialism of the modern world, 'where there are no spiritual landmarks left, no theory unassailed by scepticism, no absolute moral concepts accepted by humanity, no essential truths left to teach to children'.[10] A world in which the young were encouraged to despise tradition and were '. . . reared to venerate metallic fetishes, factories and machines'.[11] Fascism promised a delivery from such heresies by a reversion to the old values and honoured traditions.

Each of these sources of revolt was connected in part to the 1914–18 war. The war had been a catastrophe for the liberal belief in the progressive advancement of civilisation, and had created an environment in which the doom-laden words of Spengler struck a nerve of truth. The war had also fostered a sense of unity in many nations which appeared to evaporate after the victory had been achieved. The problems and failures of the post-war world did not seem to justify the bloody sacrifices which had been made upon the battlefields.

The role of the war is crucial to any understanding of the origins of fascism as an ideology. The question concerning whether fascism developed from the nineteenth century or was solely the product of the war has been a matter of some debate. The issue has been complicated by the ideology's use of non-fascist sources. Sometimes this appeared as a cynical act whereby the work of scientists and philosophers such as Darwin, Malthus, Mendel, Hegel and Nietzsche (to name but a few) was systematically plundered to provide justifications for aspects of fascist theory. The work of many others required no such distortion. Racial theorists such as Houston Stewart-Chamberlain and Arthur de Gobineau, and social Darwinists such as Benjamin Kidd had ensured that by the early twentieth century there was already established a rich seam of work in areas such as eugenics and the organic nature of the state and of social evolution which was directly relevant to fascist theory.

But although fascist movements used such material directly or indirectly, fascism as a self-conscious and coherent ideology did not emerge until after the war. This was no coincidence. The war provided a dramatic demonstration of the failure of liberalism and the appearance of communism as an alternative. The war did not create fascism but it undoubtedly hastened its emergence. Thus, although some important strands of fascism's roots lay in the nineteenth century or beyond, as a complete ideology it was, nevertheless, truely a twentieth-century phenomenon.

Whilst Mosley accepted fascism as a post-war development he considered that it represented only the most recent appearance of a cyclical historical movement known as 'Caesarism'. When Rome had stood in danger from the mob on one side and the corrupt plutocrats on the other, it was Caesar, a man of superhuman qualities, who had restored authority. So had it been throughout history: unchecked crises produced representatives of Caesarism. In modern society the complexity of the state's mechanism required that the role of Caesar be filled collectivity by the fascist party. Unlike its previous appearances, however, the collective Caesarism of fascism had the means to end misery and poverty through the employment of modern science. Therefore, the very conditions which had periodically called forth Caesarism could be permanently eradicated. This was to be the historic destiny of fascism.[12]

This concept of Caesarism was not simply a euphemism for a government of reaction. For Mosley, Caesar was a symbol of strength emanating from the political centre,[13] preventing any single group or class from pursuing interests detrimental to the community as a whole. For Mosley, therefore, fascism was an ideology whereby a central course could be steered between capitalism and socialism and through which the benefits of each could be reaped. Whereas capitalism gave unchecked power to the owners of private capital without regard to the consequences for the welfare of society as a whole, socialism with its attendant state ownership resulted in inefficient bureaucracy. Between these two undesirable extremes fascism offered a system which retained '. . . the benefits of privately controlled capital and private enterprise' but prevented it from operating '. . . against the economic well-being of the community'.[14]

This declared rejection of unbridled capitalism and international socialism was an integral part of fascism's claim to reject the interests of any single class in favour of the nation as a whole. In this manner fascism aimed at the creation of a classless community where all were servants of the nation. The Great War was idealised in this fashion as a '. . . magnificent, classless union of the nation, in ordeal and struggle – the apotheosis of the people . . .'.[15] The extent to which classlessness was a practicable aim whilst the accumulation of private capital was to be allowed to continue almost unchecked is a point which is worth returning to at a later stage.

Thus, fascism was perceived by those who understood it as a process whereby disparate elements could be unified. A harmonious society could be achieved through national synthesis. The importance of fascism as an agent of synthesis was clearly visible within the composition of the BUF itself. Beneath the superficial unity of the disaffected who were drawn towards fascism were three major categories. Firstly, there were 'reactionaries': those who feared and despised modernity and longed to return to the security of an imaginary past based either upon prosperous capitalism or precapitalist forms of production. Secondly, there were 'crypto-socialists': those who felt hostility towards capitalism but, unlike the reactionaries, believed in change through a more equitable distribution of wealth. Fascism they perceived as a form of socialism made viable by its national context. Those within each of these categories understood different but equally limited aspects of fascism.[16] The moving spirit of the ideology was fully comprehended only by a third category of genuine fascists to whom fascism represented a means of riding above the adversary politics and economics of class war through mediation and enforced synthesis. It was this group who attempted to bind together the party by mediating between the conflicting interests of the others, and by reconciling incompatible aspects of fascist theory.

Too often the attractiveness of fascism has been examined only in terms of its irrational appeal to the emotions. Enforced synthesis, unity and mediation: these too represent essential components of the theoretical lifeblood of fascism. Herein lies a key to understanding the essence of the ideology. Fascism represents, in conception at least, a movement of the political centre. This is not the equate fascism with liberalism. But despite their obvious differences the relationship between the two is such that in a three-dimensional political spectrum fascism would appear as the mirror-image of liberalism. Fascism represents the *authoritarian* centre. It rejects left, right, and the liberal centre alike. In this rejection lies the potential strength of fascism in that it is capable of projecting itself as being external to the political process. It claims to stand above the politics of class or party and therefore has the potential to appeal to those of almost any political persuasion. In practice, however, this ideological position generates problems. For any mass movement which attempts to encompass a spectrum ranging from radical left to reactionary right cannot but produce policies rent with internal contradictions. The resulting inconsistency manifests itself through a tendency for the party to oscillate between radicalism and reaction. This in its turn means that attempts at reconciliation through synthesis are frequently followed to seemingly absurd lengths. As supporters and policies are drawn from all parts of the political spectrum fascism finds itself forced to swallow countless contradictions. Attempts to digest these through synthesis not infrequently stretch its theoretical credibility to breaking point. An appeal upon an emotional plane to popular desires for the restoration of national unity, pride and grandeur play an essential role in concealing the seriousness of the theoretical cracks.

Adherents of fascism believe implicitly that class conflict is detrimental to the interests of the community at large. A failure to grasp that it is the direct result of the incompatible demands of capital and labour leads them to suppose that such conflict can be reconciled through the creation of mediatory machinery, and ultimately through a synthesis of class interests. But the professed aim not to destroy capitalism but to control it means that the very forces which gave rise to class conflict cannot be significantly altered. This desire to eradicate class conflict whilst refusing to address its causes illustrates not merely a flaw in theory but also shows how fascism can be represented as a response to capitalism in crisis in that it preserves the essence of the capitalist system. As suggested earlier, however, it would be quite wrong to deduce from this that fascism is nothing more than a conspiratorial response to the needs of business. Fascism does harness a genuine desire to harmonise society's warring factions, but such naivety leaves it vulnerable. As it moves nearer to the threshold of power the pressures generated by its internal contradictions (and the influence of its financial backers) are sufficient to ensure the sacrifice of those who see fascism as a vehicle for genuine social change. Upon achieving power, or shortly thereafter, fascism as an ideology of the centre ceases to exist. Rather than seeking compromise (even enforced compromise) between capital and labour it invariably becomes a thinly disguised conservative regime. Under its dictatorial rule it allows freedom for capitalism to regenerate itself, through the greater exploitation of a work-force stripped of defences.

That fascism in practice becomes synonymous with dictatorial conservatism should not obscure the important differences between them on a theoretical level. As a doctrine of the centre fascism advocates not merely the suppression of class conflict but its eradication through the construction of corporate machinery through which conflict can be reconciled. Although in practice such machinery may never be built, or if built will prove incapable of succeeding in its task, its theoretical existence illustrates a desire (or the remnants of one) for each side to be treated fairly and firmly by the state in its attempt to produce national synthesis. Dictatorial conservatism has no need of corporate machinery.[17] Rather than desiring compromise it seeks victory, achieved by disarming the working class through the prohibition of strikes, trade unions and political parties. When a fascist government becomes a conservative dictatorship this indicates a failure on the part of fascism to construct a durable regime in accordance with its avowed principles, rather than the synonymity of fascist and conservative ideologies.

This analysis of fascism is given further credibility by the observation that a high proportion of fascist recruits tend to be *petit bourgeois*, for it is they who have most to lose through class conflict. Caught between those above whose wealth he envies, and those below whose poverty he fears, each class with its own institutions and political parties to defend its interests, the *petit bourgeois* feels isolated and vulnerable. He longs for a non-political state strong enough to deal with the unscrupulous capitalist and greedy worker in the same non-partisan fashion. Thus fascism reflects both the fears and aspirations of the *petit bourgeois*, and serves as a vehicle through which he can try to assert his political independence.

In summary it should be said that although fascism represents a movement of the authoritarian centre, desiring greater unity in society and a termination of class conflict, it fails to provide an economic formula through which this end might be realistically achieved. To do so would require a full-scale assault upon the very essence of the capitalist system and this fascism has never been prepared to undertake. This inhibition ensures that rather than harmonising class conflict through mediation and enforced synthesis, fascism is driven instead to rely upon the suppression of its superficial manifestations. Therefore, although fascism as an ideological concept arises from the centre of the political spectrum as the mirror-image of liberalism, the achievement of this end has proved impossible in practice.

NOTES

1   For further details of such a differentiation see H. Rogger & E. Weber (eds.), *The European Right: A Historical Profile*, Weidenfeld & Nicolson, London 1965, p. 9. See also R. De Felice, *Fascism: An Informal Introduction to its Theory and Practice*, Transaction Books, New Jersey 1976, p. 55.

2 E. Nolte, *Three Faces of Fascism: Action Francaise, Italian Fascism, National Socialism*, Weidenfeld & Nicolson, London 1965.

3 S. J. Woolf (ed.), *Fascism in Europe*, Methuen, London 1981, pp. 4–15.

4 L. Trotsky, 'The turn in the Communist International and the German situation', 1930, as reproduced in L. Trotsky, *Fascism: What it is and how to fight it*, Pathfinder Press Inc., New York 1969, p. 14.

5 'Aus den Referat der Genossin Clara Zetkin Uber ben Faschismus', *Imprekorr*, 27 June 1923, as reprinted in T. Pirker, *Komintern und Faschismus: Dokumente zur Geschichte und Theories des Faschismus*, Stuttgart, 1966, as quoted in *Science and Society*, XXI, spring 1967, p. 151.

6 O. Mosley, *Fascism in Britain*, BUF Publications Ltd, London 1934?, pp. 3–4.

7 Mosley, *My Life*, Nelson, London 1968, pp. 13–14.

8 O. Spengler, *The Decline of the West*, 2 vols., George Allen & Unwin, London 1926–9, first published in Germany in 1918.

9 Mosley, *My Life*, p. 287.

10 *Blackshirt*, 1 May 1933, p. 4.

11 *Action*, 12 February 1938, p. 7.

12 Mosley, *My Life*, pp. 323–4.

13 *Ibid*, p. 324.

14 *Blackshirt*, 1 June 1934, p. 9.

15 *Action*, 12 February 1938, p. 7.

16 It should be stressed that these labels are a form of shorthand which refer to general attitudes rather than to clearly defined ideological positions and, therefore, should not be interpreted too literally.

17 Some conservative regimes appropriate fascist trappings for reasons of expediency. See Chapter 8.

CHAPTER 1

Antecedents

There was a Birth, certainly,
We had evidence and no doubt. I had seen birth and death,
But had thought they were different: this Birth was
Hard and bitter agony for us, like Death, our death.
T. S. Eliot, 'Journey of the Magi'

Better the great adventure, better the great attempt for
England's sake, better defeat, disaster, better far the end
of that trivial thing called a Political Career than stifling
in a uniform of Blue and Gold, strutting and posturing
on the stage of Little England, amid the scenery of
decadence, until history in turning over an heroic page
of the human story, writes of us the contemptuous
postscript: 'These were the men to whom was entrusted
the Empire of Great Britain, and idleness, ignorance and
cowardice left it a Spain'. We shall win or at least we
shall return upon our shields.
Mosley, Action, 31 December 1931, p. 2

The crowd was violently hostile to Mosley and the New
Party. It roared at him, and as he stood facing it,
he said to me 'That is the crowd that has prevented
anyone from doing anything to England since the war.'
At that moment British Fascism was born. At that
moment of passion, and, of some personal danger, Mosley
found himself almost symbolically aligned against the
workers.
J. Strachey, The Menace of Fascism,
Victor Gollancz, London 1933, p. 161.

The definition of fascism suggested in the previous chapter is borne out
by the development of the BUF, particularly in its evolution from its

predecessor, the New Party. Despite a considerable amount of writing on British fascism in recent years, the New Party remains an area of study curiously neglected. Too often it has been mistaken as an attempt by Mosley to import fascism into Britain under a false label, or has been dismissed merely as a strange aberration which detained Mosley temporarily on his journey into fascism and political oblivion. By refusing to give sufficient consideration to the New Party, or by analysing it incorrectly where it has been considered, students of British fascism have all too often spurned the opportunity to observe the evolution of a fascist perspective and a fascist party. For although the New Party was not a fascist party when it was founded in March 1931, it did provide the chrysalis within which British fascism developed, and from which the BUF emerged in October 1932.

Having entered the House of Commons as a Conservative in the general election of 1918, Mosley soon resigned from the party and defended his seat successfully in the elections of 1922 and 1923 as an Independent. In March 1924 he joined the Labour Party and became Chancellor of the Duchy of Lancaster in the Labour Government of 1929. He resigned his office in May 1930 to protest over the government's refusal to implement any of the measures which he had suggested for reviving the economy, and remained on the back benches until his departure from the party in March 1931.

Mosley's interest in economics began in the early 1920s, and by 1925 he had developed the *Birmingham Proposals* which, with the assistance of his friend and fellow Labour Party member, John Strachey, were expanded into a book entitled *Revolution by Reason*. The crux of the argument proposed was that a socialist programme concerned merely with the re-distribution of wealth was not sufficient to restore economic prosperity. Overall demand was too low to produce full employment, it was argued, and measures designed to restore the economy to pre-war normality (such as the return to the gold standard) were deflationary and therefore only served to aggravate the existing problem. The solution proposed by Mosley was to create new wealth rather than simply to redistribute existing wealth, and this was to be achieved by the planned expansion of credit, which in turn would stimulate domestic demand. The fact that this expansion was to be planned and directed primarily towards the needs of the working class was really the only socialist aspect to what was, in essence, a Keynesian solution to the problems of inter-war capitalism.[1]

As Chancellor of the Duchy of Lancaster, Mosley expanded this Keynesian package and produced in 1930 the *Mosley Memorandum* which was an all-embracing plan for national reconstruction and the eradication of unemployment. It was this which was to lie at the heart of Mosley's economic thought throughout the 1930s. The *Memorandum* was submitted to the cabinet which rejected it after only the most perfunctory of examinations on the advice of Chancellor Snowden, whose timid conservatism made him unwilling to renounce his firm belief in the concept of a self-regulating market in which government intervention had no part to play. The road to renewed national prosperity, for Snowden and the Treasury, lay in the rationalisation of Britain's pre-war export industries. Although it was acknowledged that this would lead to unemployment in the short term, it was conceived as an unpleasant necessity in order for Britain to recapture lost foreign markets upon which her long-term prosperity depended.[2]

Following this rejection Mosley resigned from the government and eight days later won a rousing ovation in the House of Commons when he justified his resignation with a brilliant exposition of the policy contained within his *Memorandum*. He insisted that in order to deal with unemployment there had to be '. . . a revolution in the machinery of government', just as there had been during the war. Rather than Germany, however, on this occasion unemployment was the enemy to be fought and, therefore, he recommended the establishment of a special executive committee as a type of war cabinet, consisting of the Prime Minister and his leading ministers liaising with a body of economists and scientists in an effort to deal with economic matters. He recognised that the war had merely accelerated the process whereby the struggle for international markets was intensifying, and that Britain could never again reap the advantage which she had enjoyed in the previous century by virtue of becoming the first industrial nation. Consequently he saw the future in terms of the creation of new industries assisted by government credit, rather than solely in the rationalisation of the old export industries which served only to drive steadily higher the number of unemployed. In Mosley's view

> . . . this hope of recovering our position through an expansion of our export trade is an illusion, and a dangerous illusion; and the sooner the fallacy is realised, the quicker we can devote ourselves to a search for the real remedy. . . . We have got to get away from the belief that the only criterion of British prosperity is how many goods we can send abroad for foreigners to consume.[3]

Whilst this long-term strategy was being implemented Mosley suggested immediate short-term relief, to be provided by the reduction of the age of retirement to sixty, the raising of the school-leaving age, and the beginning of a public works scheme which would include slum clearance, land drainage, and a massive road-building programme. Such measures, he estimated, could provide work for up to 800,000 of those presently unemployed. He concluded his speech with a grim warning to the government '. . . that the days of muddling through are over, that this time we cannot muddle through. This nation has to be mobilised and rallied for a tremendous effort and who can do that but the government of the day. If that effort is not made then we may soon come to crisis, to a real crisis. . . .'[4]

Such a Keynesian approach meant a complete departure from the under-consumptionist analysis prevalent on the Labour left, which saw the slump as a result of excessive savings, and advocated therefore a reduction of savings by the transfer of wealth from the savers to the consumers. Since this in effect meant the redistribution of wealth from rich to poor its implications in terms of class analysis were obvious. That Mosley rejected this model and its in-built class hostility is not surprising, for his was never the socialism of class conflict. In fact it is doubtful whether Mosley ever understood socialism in any realistic or meaningful sense. He believed, as did many others of the Labour leadership, rather than an alternative to capitalism, socialism was the balm to soothe the injustices and expiate some of the inhumanities of capitalist society. But Mosley also went further and saw in socialism a means of substituting '. . . a general idea of unselfish service for unlimited and unfettered competition',[5] leading ultimately to the establishment of a '. . . collectivist state',[6] – an ideal organism not torn and rent by competition or conflict. Thus, rather than eliminating class conflict by redistributing wealth and replacing the capitalist system, Mosley's 'socialism' envisaged a more efficient capitalist economy where conflict was replaced by harmony, a sense of common purpose, and of 'unselfish service'. Furthermore, the replacement of 'unlimited and unfettered competition' applied not merely to the capitalists in search of greater profits, but also to the working class itself in 'competition' with its employers. Rather than seeing the triumph of the workers over their oppressors as the means to end class conflict, Mosley was proposing that it could be ended by a government strong enough to reconcile the classes by instilling within them a sense of duty and service to higher objectives. Rather than a victory of the left, this was a formula for the triumph of the centre.

Through such a solution overall production could be increased within a regenerated economy, which in turn would increase the general prosperity of the working class without necessitating the dispossession of the capitalists. Indeed, implicit within Mosley's analysis was the Keynesian concept of a community of interest between capitalist and worker. As early as 1923 Keynes had shown that during a deflationary period wealth was shifted from the community as a whole to financiers, and during a period of inflation (as long as wages kept pace with prices) then the community benefited at the expense of financiers. As the concept of the community included both capitalists and workers Keynes tended to dismiss any analyses of society which stressed the divisions between capital and labour. Instead he preferred to see an identity of interest between these two groups of producers, each of whom had a common enemy in the financier.[7] This was an approach which, by rejecting the concept of an irreconcilable conflict between capitalist and worker, was particularly well suited to Mosley's political analysis. He drew upon it extensively and it was to provide the principal component of his fascist ideology.

Following his resignation from the government and his unsuccessful attempts to persuade the Labour Party to accept his rejected proposals (culminating in a narrow defeat at the party conference in October) Mosley came increasingly to personify the vital forces of the political centre. He drew support from the young of all three political parties and included in his informal group of followers MPs on the left of the Labour Party such as Aneurin Bevan and John Strachey, Liberals such as Sir Archibald Sinclair and Henry Mond, and Conservatives including Bob Boothby, Harold Macmillan, Oliver Stanley and Walter Eliot.[8] The one common factor between these diverse elements was their urgent desire for action to alleviate the economic crisis, for by January 1931 unemployment had passed 2,600,000 and was still rising. Mosley's programme promised to meet that desire, and if its implementation demanded changes in the machinery of government then this was considered a small price to pay. He was in close touch also with influential parliamentary mavericks still hungry for power such as Lloyd George and Churchill, as well as with those barons of the press such as Beaverbrook and Rothermere who believed it their privilege to dispense power upon their chosen sons.

Using such disparate political elements as his base, between October 1930 and March 1931 Mosley attempted to achieve '. . . a national consensus to secure action'.[9] He appealed to his fellow MPs to place the welfare of their country before their allegiance to any political party on the grounds that '. . . we have to face modern problems with modern minds, we should then be able to lift this great economic problem and national emergency far above the turmoil of party clamour and with national unity could achieve a solution adequate to the problem and worthy of the modern mind'.[10] This attempt to produce a realignment at the very centre of governmented failed, however, because of the power of the old party machines, the reluctance of many young MPs to risk their political careers, and a degree of personal mistrust of Mosley himself.

Undeterred by this failure Mosley decided to build a new party on the basis of national consensus emanating from the grass roots. He broke from the Labour Party, taking with him five Labour MPs including his wife Cynthia, John Strachey, Robert Forgan, Oliver Baldwin, and W. J. Brown. All but Brown joined him in the New Party along with W. E. D. Allen, Mosley's only parliamentary recruit from the Conservatives. The resignations were to be announced in a piecemeal fashion in order to cause maximum embarrassment to the Labour leadership. But this stratagem was also the cause of a considerable degree of chaos and bitterness. It was amid this wealter of confusion and vicious recrimination that the New Party emerged from its womb to be founded formally at a meeting in early March. Mosley, who was billed as the star speaker, was lying too ill with pneumonia even to attend. His wife, aided by Strachey and Baldwin, deputised gallantly and attempted to inspire an audience which was at times rowdy but for the most part was merely curious. It was an inauspicious inauguration.

The New Party as it existed in March 1931 was not a fascist party. It was, however, an ill-defined appeal to the centre asking for an end to the class conflict and seeking a mandate to implement a package of measures designed to restore general prosperity to the British economy. Mosley was appealing to the masses for the sort of co-operation which had been denied to him by those at Westminster. The New Party was in this sense an attempt to circumvent the old men who were lodged in the higher echelons of all the political parties. These constituted the 'Old Gang': those who had frustrated any attempt to solve the crisis in favour of allowing orthodoxy to prevail, unemployment to rise, and the slump to deepen. In creating the New Party Mosley forsook the frustrations of the House of Commons and returned to the masses who had served him so effectively in the past. For, as he was reported to have said to Harold Nicolson back in November, he believed that if he could have £250,000 and the support of a press magnate, then he could '... sweep the country'.[11]

Nor was Mosley alone in his desire to seek a centrist solution to the nation's economic problems. Political and Economic Planning (a pressure group composed of businessmen, civil servants and academics founded in the spring of 1931) also stated its contempt for the 'Old Gang' and advocated the conquest of contemporary problems through the impartial application of intellect and planning, and the rationalisation of the country's political and economic structure.

The New Party programme as published in March 1931 was drawn largely from the *Mosley Memorandum* of the previous year. Overseas competition employing sweated labour and operating behind protective cartels was condemned, and an urgent appeal was made to abandon declining export industries and to concentrate instead upon the scientific expansion of the home market. This expansion was to be achieved through a combination of planning and insulation, the former being conducted through a National Investment Board and a National Planning Council, whilst the latter was to include selective tariffs on industries subject to foreign competition, being assessed by commodity boards, the constituents of which were to include representatives from a broad cross-section of the relevant industry and trade unions. Also proposed was a miscellaneous package of measures designed to stimulate the economy, including a public works programme, aid to the agricultural sector, and the progressive reduction of taxation. The implementation of such measures was to have been made easier by reforms in parliamentary procedure whereby government was to be conducted by a cabinet of five or six, and parliamentary debate was confined to the discussion of governmental strategy in general terms only.[12]

This programme was no more fascist than the party itself, but both contained the essential components of fascist ideology. On a political level the New Party arose from and appealed to the political centre, but not in the same way as liberalism represents an appeal to the centre. The New Party programme advocated government by a small strong executive with little accountability to a parliament stripped of many of its rights and functions. Mosley's refusal to analyse society in class terms led him to see parliamentary opposition as a nuisance in that it obstructed the implementation of policy chosen by the majority at a general election. Rather than see the nation inevitably divided by class hostility with parliament as an institutional device designed to sublimate such a conflict and thereby prevent it from destabilising the regime, Mosley preferred to see a community whose sense of corporate identity had been destroyed by liberal and democratic politics and *laissez-faire* economics. A sense of identity which could be restored only through the destruction of liberalism, and the forced conclusion of factional strife inside parliament and class conflict within the nation. Thus the New Party was anti-liberal and the centrism it offered differed profoundly to that advanced by traditional liberalism.

The same trend was visible in the sphere of New Party economics where the replacement of *laissez-faire* capitalism by an economy with a high degree of planning and control, and the substitution of economic nationalism for free trade, underlined the party's rejection of the principle economic tenets of liberalism. Particularly interesting amongst these measures was the suggested establishment of commodity boards. Mosley had defined these as early as October 1930 as a compromise between free trade and a tariff, neither of which offered the specialised protection needed in confronting the problems of the twentieth century. They were to be composed of representatives from both management and the employees of a particular industry, as well as representatives of the consumer, and of other related industries. Protection from foreign competition would be given to industries provided that they struggled to increase their productivity. Those refusing to co-operate in this manner would be re-exposed to foreign competition by the government and allowed to founder.[13] In essence, the commodity boards represented the machinery of a voluntary form of corporate state where co-operation between the various components of the industrial process was requested and encouraged, rather than demanded.

Thus, although a movement of the centre, the New Party was espousing a creed radically different from that of liberalism. Its proposed changes in the machinery of government and in particular the strengthening of the executive at the expense of the legislature, foreshadowed the full-blown dictatorship of party and leader as later advocated by the BUF. Similarly the New Party's support for a planned and controlled capitalist economy, its economic nationalism, and above all its proposed commodity boards reconciling workers, bosses, and consumers within a given industry all hinted at the autarchic corporate state which Mosley was to plan in such detail, and which was to become the foundation of the BUF's programme. The New Party was an attempt to break the class deadlock by appealing to the nation as a whole, or as John Strachey retrospectively described it, '. . . an entirely Utopian appeal for social compromise'.[14] That such a compromise was being sought within the capitalist system, together with this complete repudiation of liberalism, meant that the New Party, regardless as to whether its leadership realised it, had, even at the moment of its own creation, embarked upon a journey which was to take it laterally across the centre of the political spectrum bringing it even closer to fascism.

This movement was accelerated by the hostility of the left towards Mosley's new creation. Mosley's proposed economic remedies were ridiculed by the Labour Party, whilst he himself was the object of a series of vicious personal attacks, employing that special brand of venom which the Labour Party reserves for those who defect from its own ranks.[15] The usual charge was that he had betrayed the interests of the workers and had reverted to the class from whence he had come because of his inability to control his personal ambitions.[16] In April the New Party was denounced as a non-socialist organisation, and Ramsay MacDonald, the Labour Prime Minister, assured Labour voters that every seat held by the defectors would be fought and won back by the Labour Party at the next general election.[17]

Another important factor in assisting the New Party in its journey towards fascism was the Ashton-under-Lyne by-election. Initially the New Party had decided to concentrate upon building electoral machinery at constituency level before attempting to fight any elections[18] but when this Labour seat fell vacant the party's national executive revised its earlier decision and announced that it would be contested.[19] With its high level of unemployment, the constituency was thought to offer a good testing ground for the appeal of the New Party's economic formula. The campaign was hampered, however, by the complete lack of any grass-roots organisation in the constituency, and the resignation of the entire Manchester branch of the New Party as a protest against the national leadership foisting upon them a candidate about whom they had not been consulted.[20] Furthermore, Mosley was unable to participate in all but the final days of the campaign as he was still convalescing from his bout of pneumonia. Although the party's candidate, Allan Young,[21] was ably assisted by Strachey, Cynthia Mosley, and a battery of hired speakers, Mosley's powers of oratory were sorely missed.

The result of the contest was that Young polled sixteen per cent of the votes cast and saved his deposit but the seat itself changed hands with the Labour majority of 3,407 being replaced by a Tory majority of 1,415.[22] It would appear likely that the absence of a Liberal candidate (who had polled 6,500 votes in 1929) was largely responsible for the size of the New Party vote.[23] The Labour supporters, however, saw the result as a clear case of treachery, whereby Mosley and the defectors had split Labour's vote and thus ensured a Conservative victory. This belief resulted in an angry crowd venting its fury and disappointment upon Mosley, Strachey, and the other New Party representatives at the count. After gazing at this display of hatred[24] Mosley turned to Strachey and remarked 'This is the crowd that has prevented anyone from doing anything in England since the war.' This, claimed Strachey, was the moment when Mosley fully adopted fascism as he found himself aligned symbolically against the working class.[25]

This was a gross oversimplification (for Mosley remained as much a populist after the events of Ashton as he had been before them), but Strachey was correct in so far as the Ashton by-election did mark a watershed in the development of the New Party. Not only did it illustrate to the leadership that the winning of elections by a new party was a momentous task, but it also provided an important lesson which was to hasten the New Party's descent into fascism. It showed the sort of hostility which the party would have to expect from the left, which suggested that there could be no voluntary suspension of class warfare in order to allow the reconstruction of the British economy. Ashton, therefore, had exposed the weakness of the New Party's centrist position. This evidence was interpreted differently by the Party's two leading theoreticians. For Strachey it meant that the New Party should return to the left-wing roots from whence he believed it had sprung. Mosley, however, saw it as an illustration of the necessity to build an organisation capable of meeting force with force which, whilst countering the violence of its opponents, could also facilitate the imposition of the sort of national unity for which the New Party had initially appealed.

Two weeks after Ashton Mosley announced that the New Party was to form an active force of young men designed to defend free speech by protecting New Party meetings from disruption by political opponents. He gave assurances that such a force would not carry weapons but would instead '. . . rely on the good old English fist'.[26] Mosley attempted to justify the creation of this corps, to be known as Nupa (an abbreviation of 'New Party'), by arguing that the New Party's only channel of communication to the public was being jeopardised by organised left-wing hooligans. Therefore, he reasoned, it was a choice between closing down the party or physically defending its meetings.[27]

Superficially there was some credibility in this explanation. New Party meetings had indeed been attacked and disrupted by opponents from the left over the previous two and a half months. Even the introductory meeting to launch the party back in March had been interrupted continuously by an enraged Labour Party supporter until he was removed after a struggle with stewards whom some in the audience denounced as fascist thugs.[28] Organised opponents disrupted meetings in Liverpool,[29] and Manchester[30] (also in March) and succeeded in enforcing the termination of meetings in Dundee and Hull.[31] The trend continued in April with police being called to restore order after fighting had broken out at a New Party meeting in Hammersmith.[32] The violence worsened after the formation of the youth movement culminating in October 1931 during the general election campaign. In Glasgow organised chanting from sections of the audience was supplemented with volleys of stones and an alleged razor attack upon New Party representatives.[33] A month later in Birmingham Mosley and his followers were involved in a pitched battle with members of the audience in the course of which clubs and missiles were used in such profuse quantities that by the end almost every chair in the entire hall had been smashed.[34]

The protection of New Party meetings, however, was not the only function of Nupa, it was also designed as the embryo of a force able to take control in a revolutionary situation by defeating the forces on the left and restoring order as had been done in Italy. It was, as Mosley described it, an '. . . iron core . . . around which every element for the preservation of England will rally', when the crisis finally broke.[35] In this sense the Youth Movement was little short of a paramilitary force in both its conception and its organisation, fostering a level of patriotism and discipline rarely found outside the ranks of a professional army.[36] Mosley admitted this many years later when he wrote of how, after Ashton, 'we had to develop a different character to meet an entirely new situation. Newer men came to us who were ready to fight for their beliefs, in type the dedicated blackshirt'.[37]

The rise of the youth movement was not an isolated aberration, but was indicative of the New Party's drift towards fascism. As early as May 1931 Harold Nicolson, Mosley's friend and colleague on the New Party executive, recorded the observation that recruits to the new movement were displaying characteristics which were '. . . distinctly fascist'.[38]

sympathetic to the youth movement and the values for which it stood, but there is no clear evidence to suggest that at this stage he had forsaken the parliamentary road to fascism. It was, after all, through parliament that he had made his reputation, and he was still an MP at this point in his career.

This deadlock between the two sides of the party was finally broken by the general election of October 1931. The national political re-alignment which had occurred in late August when MacDonald and several senior members of his cabinet collaborated with the Conservatives and elements of the Liberal Party to form the inaptly named National Government undoubtedly damaged the New Party's potential appeal. Squeezed between the National Government calling for national unity and the Labour Party posing as the traditional champion of the working class now rid of its treacherous leadership, the New Party found itself without an original political message or a class to whom such a message could be directed exclusively. A shortage of credible candidates meant that the Party's original desire to fight over 400 seats was reduced gradually until eventually only twenth-four were contested. As polling day grew nearer Mosley's pessimism increased,[58] and attempts to secure a pact whereby a number of New Party constituencies would not be contested by National Government candidates failed despite a clandestine meeting which he was alleged to have had with Neville Chamberlain.[59]

The Party campaigned upon a platform almost identical to those policies announced at its inauguration six months earlier. It called for the reform of parliament, selective protection, national economic planning, greater economic co-operation with the Dominions, and a general powers act to give government the power to implement its chosen programme. The '. . . petty intimidating and bullying . . .' aspects of foreign fascism were condemned as unintelligent and inhumane, and little mention was made of the corporate state. *Action*, the New Party newspaper, however, did advocate the creation of what it referred to as the 'modern' or 'organic' state: a planned and ordered society where merit and initiative reaped due reward and yet all contributed to the common good.[60]

The election results were catastrophic. The New Party was swept away by a landslide victory for the National Government. All twenty-four of its candidates were defeated. Although Mosley came a respectable third in Stoke (the constituency which his wife had held for Labour) most of the results were humiliatingly poor. At Ashton only 424 votes were received as the reintervention of the Liberals made nonsense of the four and a half thousand which the New Party had polled there in April.[61] Even the Communist Party, standing candidates in only two more constituencies, managed a total vote almost twice that of the New Party.[62] New Party representatives blamed this decisive repudiation by the electorate upon the inequitable nature of the British electoral system.[63] They also bolstered their morale by arguing that their defeat was not so great as that suffered by the 'modern movement' abroad, and yet from such defeats their European counterparts had returned with fresh strength to triumph over their opponents.[64] In this sense, it was claimed, the New Party had made better progress in less time than any comparable party on the continent.[65]

This oblique identification with European fascism coincided with sweeping internal changes instituted by Mosley following the election fiasco. The dismissal of individuals on charges of corruption and incompetence heralded the complete and rapid destruction of the more orthodox side of the party. This included the closure of its headquarters, the disbanding of the remaining regional organisations, and the sacking of almost all of its paid officials,[66] with the result that by the end of the year the New Party had ceased to exist in all but name. The party newspaper (edited by Nicolson) survived until the end of December, losing over £1,000 per month with a rapidly falling circulation, until Mosley abruptly terminated it in an effort to preserve the little that was left of party funds.[67] Such steps represented the triumph of the youth movement over its rival faction, and were no more than the logical result of the election. The function of the electoral side of the party had been to secure influence, and ultimately power, in parliament and, therefore, the very completeness of its defeat at the polls had removed its *raison d'être*.

This destruction of the electoral side of the party was symbolic of Mosley's rejection of electoral politics. Similarly his careful nourishment of the youth movement illustrated how he had come to see it as the distillation of all that was worthy and pure within the New Party. By the end of December he was writing quite openly of the type of organisation which he saw as the necessary instrument with which communism could be defeated and order, discipline, and dynamic patriotism restored from the chaos soon to engulf British society. Such a movement, he wrote, '. . . must differ fundamentally from the old political parties in both ideology and organisation. It must be a movement of youth which willingly and gladly accepts the discipline, effort and sacrifice by which alone great executive purposes can be achieved, and by which alone the modern state can be built'.[68] It illustrated the extent to which Mosley had become convinced (or had convinced himself as a means of coming to terms with his own failure), that electoral politics were no longer relevant. In short, he was waiting for the development of a revolutionary situation and conceived of a political party as an instrument designed solely to extract power from such a situation. It was for this reason that the BUF took no serious interest in electoral politics until the mid-1930s when partial economic recovery made the crisis seem less imminent.

In January 1932 Mosley and a retinue of followers visited Mussolini's Italy to view the inspirational source of fascism at first hand. Mosley was already planning the style of his own future fascist campaign and distressed Nicolson by his inability to '. . . keep his mind off shock troops, the arrest of MacDonald and J. H. Thomas, their internment on the Isle of Wight, and the roll of drums around Westminster'.[69] The formal closure of the New Party followed in April 1932, but it was decided that the youth movement was to remain active, much to the anguish of those like Nicolson who wanted Mosley to return to parliament rather than become further embrangled with 'fascist bands' and identified with 'Hitlerism'.[70] Two weeks later Mosley informed his colleagues that despite offers from the Labour and Conservative parties, he had no wish to return to parliamentary politics. Instead he desired

> . . . to coordinate all fascist groups with Nupa and thus form a central fascist body under his own leadership. He is convinced that we are entering a phase of abnormality and that he does not wish to be tarred with the brush of the old regime. That he thinks, as leader of the fascists, he could accomplish more than as a party back-bencher, and . . . is prepared to run the risk of further failure, ridicule and assault, rather than allow the active forces to fall into other hands.[71]

This meeting prompted the final departure of those, like Nicolson, who had sought to restrain Mosley, for he was now entering a wasteland into which they dared not follow him. They believed still in his genius, they desired still his leadership, and they even accepted still his vision of a corporate state but they could not accept fascism in all its organisational nakedness. They chose instead to leave him.

In the summer of 1932 Mosley began expanding his vision of the fascist state and produced *The Greater Britain*, the first of his fascist textbooks, which analysed Britain's economic problems and offered solutions in the form of a detailed plan for a corporate society. Thereafter there followed negotiations with existing fascist groups in Britain, particularly aimed at the British Fascists[72] with whom an amalgamation was proposed. The ruling council of the British Fascists rejected these overtures against the advice of their leader who responded by immediately defecting to Mosley and taking with him their entire membership lists.[73] On 1 October 1932 Mosley announced the formation of a new political party which would include all of the remnants of the New Party. It was to be known as the British Union of Fascists.

Mosley's refusal to retreat to parliamentary politics and his insistence on attempting to forge a fully-fledged fascist party was linked undoubtedly to his genuine belief in the approaching crisis. The basis of this belief and the destruction of his political career within the British establishment which it engendered are subjects to be speculated upon by his biographers. The New Party episode, however, goes far beyond the personal tragedy of any single individual in that it illustrates the essence of fascism and explains its potential for mass appeal.

To understand fascism is to understand the desire of those who wish to see an end to class conflict. The left offered this only through the maiming of the capitalist order and the bourgeois society which it created. The solution of the right was to drive such conflict underground through clumsy and overt oppression which could only be sustained by increased levels of oppression and would eventually produce an unstable society permeated with subterranean discontent. The liberal centre has always accepted class conflict as an integral part of society, allowing it to manifest itself through strikes, demonstrations and other forms of controlled protest which do not threaten the fundamental authority of the regime. This it calls freedom. The New Party rejected all of these political philosophies. It wished to retain capitalism and therefore rejected any solution which included its destruction. Its genuine belief in improving the living standards of the masses (primarily through a general increase in prosperity although also to an extent through the limited redistribution of wealth) similarly alienated it from the reactionary right. Most interesting of all, however, it rejected entirely the liberal centre which it condemned as the source of a society obsessed with internal bickering, and which lacked the ability to produce rapid or decisive action.

Those who founded the New Party, and many of those who joined it, were seeking some other way forward. They sought a means of combining greater social justice, a prosperous capitalist economy, and a permanent end to the internecine fighting of a society deeply rent by bitter social divisions. Any answer to this hopeless riddle was perceived to lie beyond the boundaries of the established British political spectrum, and, as the quest continued, the New Party broke new ground as it travelled in a lateral traverse towards the authoritarian centre. The speed at which it proceeded was variable but the direction was assured, and, providing the party survived the rigours of the journey, its destination could only be fascism.[74]

Increasingly it became clear that there could be no voluntary inter-class armistice and consequently the party came to reflect in its policy a belief in coercion. It came to believe that the interests of left and right, of worker and capitalist must be subdued to, and if possible synthesised with, the greater interests of the community and the nation as a whole. Having arrived at this theoretical position all that was needed was the instrument with which this process could be realised. The theoretical position was fascist and the necessary instrument was a full fascist party.[75]

The difference between fascism and the orthodox right is illustrated by the gulf which separated the New Party from the 'fascist' parties which existed in Britain before 1932. These organisations, which grew like mushrooms in the decade after 1923 under the shadow of Mussolini, included the British Fascisti (later the British Fascists), the British Empire Fascists, the Fascist League, the Fascist Movement, the National Fascisti, the Kensington Fascist Party, the Yorkshire Fascists, the Empire Fascist League, and the Imperial Fascist League. Each had two common characteristics, neither of which was shared by the New Party or later by the BUF. They were all small and lacked any mass base for their membership, and they were all right-wing in political philosophy. The British Fascisti was the largest of them and although it claimed a membership of 400,000[76] it certainly never exceeded a few thousand at most, many of whom were inactive. The decline which the organisation suffered from the mid-1920s onwards was accelerated by the defection of many of its remaining members to Mosley in 1932. By 1934 Home Office estimates considered its membership to be around only 300.[77] The tiny size of such organisations reflected their own elitism and inherent fear of the masses. This in turn was the product of their political philosophy and it was this more than any other characteristic which cut them clean apart from the self-conscious (if only partially successful) populism of the parties created by Mosley. For without exception the fascist parties which existed in Britain before 1932 were rabidly right-wing, believing not in fascism but in authoritarian reaction. Without even a pretence at impartiality on the issue of class conflict, such parties spent what little energy they possessed engaged in strike-breaking activities, preparations for the maintenance of essential supplies in the event of a general strike, and assistance for the Conservative Party in the form of stewarding its meetings and campaigning in its support during elections. There was not even a hint of radicalism from within the serried ranks of the titled aristocrats, the retired officers from the armed forces, or the wealthy eccentrics who constituted the bulk of the membership of such organisations. Rather than any desire to alter British society they considered fascism as the vigorous and independent right wing of conservatism, committed to the defence of the status quo and the preservation of established institutions, in the face of an ill-conceived threat from the red menace of international Bolshevism. Rather than having any real understanding of fascism or its aims, such organisations misused the term by applying it to what were, in effect, nothing more than anti-socialist pressure groups whose membership consisted largely of Mussolini-worshippers with a tendency towards paranoia concerning communism.

None of this motley collection of groups calling themselves fascist represents a precursor of the BUF. Their extreme conservatism offers no explanation as to the wide potential appeal of fascism as an ideology. It was within the New Party's womb that British fascism was conceived, for its development shows not only the remorseless logic with which those who sought a middle way were sucked laterally into the jaws of fascism, but it also explains the strongest element of fascism's appeal. For fascism above all else feeds upon a genuine desire for the class fighting to cease and the national reconstruction to begin. John Strachey recognised this and warned others when he wrote, with all the experience of one who himself narrowly escaped the blandishments of fascism, of how

> the path which leads to the fascist terror has a most attractive entrance. Those who have lost their way, and there are many such, in the baffling complexities of modern life, are tempted to discover in fascism an easy solution to their difficulties. They see, as I saw, the beckoning lights of social peace, economic security for all and a gradual reconstruction of society based upon a new compact between capital and labour.

But such a path warned Strachey led only to '. . . an unspeakable terror aimed at the destruction of the organs of the workers and of everything that is aspiring, merciful and intelligent in the world'.[78]

NOTES

1   A good description of *Revolution by Reason* and the economic orthodoxy which it challenged can be found in R. Skidelsky, *Oswald Mosley*, Macmillan, London 1975, pp. 133–46.
2   *Ibid.*, pp. 199–205.
3   *HC Deb*, 239, 28 May 1930, c. 1350–72.
4   *Ibid.*
5   *Daily Herald*, 24 May 1924, as quoted in Labour Research Department, *Who Backs Mosley? Fascist Promise and Fascist Performance*, LRD, London 1934, p. 5.
5   *Daily Herald*, 2 April 1924, as quoted in Labour Research Department, *op. cit.*, p. 4.
7   J. M. Keynes, *Tract for Monetary Reform*, 1923, pp. 27–30, as quoted by Skidelsky, *op. cit.*, pp. 140–1.
8   In fact Macmillan was temporarily out of parliament at this time: O. Mosley, *My Life*, Nelson, London 1968, pp. 273–5.
9   *Ibid*, p. 265.
10   *HC Deb*, 244, 29 October 1930, c. 67–81.
11   Nicolson Diaries, MS, 6 November 1930, Balliol College, Oxford.
12   W. F. Mandle, 'The New Party', *Historical Studies: Australia and New Zealand*, XII, 47, October 1966, pp. 343–5.
13   *HC Deb*, 244, 29 October 1930, c. 67–81. See also O. Mosley, 'A new national policy II: reply to criticism', *The Weekend Review*, III, 47, 31 January 1931, p. 137.
14   J. Strachey, *The Menace of Fascism*, Gollancz, London 1933, p. 159.
15   A full fifty years after Mosley's defection this legacy of bitterness was still visible amongst his few surviving Labour Party contemporaries whose memories of him tended to stress his arrogance and his pride. For Emanuel Shinwell he was a man '. . . obsessed with his own vanity. . . . Another Mussolini, that's all', E. Shinwell, interview included in C. Cross, 'Britain's Fascist Leader', BBC Radio Four, 25 January 1981. Fenner Brockway remembered him as being 'terribly arrogant', so much so that he was insulted at receiving only the Duchy of Lancaster rather than the Foreign

Office in the 1929 Labour Government. This, suggested Brockway, was at the root of his discontent within the Labour Party. F. Brockway, 'The Twentieth Century Remembered', BBC television, 28 July 1981.

16 *The Labour Magazine*, IX, 12, April 1931, pp. 534–6.

17 *Manchester Guardian*, 18 April 1931, p. 11.

18 *Ibid.*, 24 March 1931, p. 9.

19 *Ibid.*, 15 April 1931, p. 13.

20 *Ibid.*, 23 April, 1931, p. 11.

21 Young had been Mosley's political secretary in the Labour Party and defected with him to the New Party in the spring of 1931.

22 F. W. S. Craig, *British Parliamentary Election Results 1918–49*, Macmillan, London 1977, p. 69.

23 *Manchester Guardian*, 1 May 1931, p. 13.

24 A New Party employee who was with Mosley at the count later described him as '... more savage than frightened. White with rage, not fear, he showed his teeth as he smiled contemptuously out onto the crowd that was howling at him and calling him names ...', J. Jones, *Unfinished Journey*, Hamish Hamilton, London 1937, p. 259.

25 Strachey, *op. cit.*, p. 161. Mosley's own interpretation of the incident was rather different. Although he admitted the validity of the quotation he claimed that the scenes at Ashton were no more than '... a put-up show by sophisticated communists', manipulating the emotions of disappointed Labour voters. Mosley, *op. cit.*, p. 285.

26 *Manchester Guardian*, 16 May 1931, p. 13.

27 Mosley, *op. cit.*, p. 286.

28 *Manchester Guardian*, 6 March 1931, p. 12.

29 *Ibid.*, 13 March 1931, p. 6.

30 *Ibid.*, 10 March 1931, p. 12.

31 Skidelsky, *op. cit.*, p. 247.

32 *Manchester Guardian*, 18 April 1931, p. 14.

33 *Ibid.*, 21 September 1931, p. 9.

34 *Action*, 10 November 1937, p. 10. See also Skidelsky, *op. cit.*, pp. 275–6.

35 *Daily Herald*, 29 August 1931, as cited by Skidelsky, *op. cit.*, p. 257.

36 *Action*, 12 November 1931, p. 5.

37 Mosley, *op. cit.*, p. 285.

38 Nicolson Diaries, MS, 28 May 1931.

39 *Ibid.*, 25 June 1931.

40 Mosley, *op. cit.*, p. 345.

41 Letters from Mosley to Nicolson dated 16 and 17 August 1931, Nicolson Papers, Balliol College, Oxford.

42 Nicolson Diaries, MS, 3 July 1931.

43 *Action*, 26 November 1931, p. 1.

44 W. J. Brown, one of the five Labour MPs to have left the party with Mosley refused to join the New Party on the grounds that he detected signs of incipient fascism as early as March 1931. W. J. Brown, *So Far*, George Allen & Unwin, London 1943, pp. 159–60. It was also very common for those who heckled at New Party meetings to accuse the party of fascism. For example see *Manchester Guardian*, 6 March 1931, p. 12; 13 March 1931, p. 16; and 16 March 1931, p. 12.

45 Nicolson Diaries, MS, 2 June 1931. Cook was an adherent of Mosley's economic formula and had been one of the signatories of the *Mosley Manifesto*, a policy document based on the *Mosley Memorandum*, in December 1930.

46 J. Strachey, 'The progress of the New Party', *Weekend Review*, III, 67, 20 June 1931, p. 910.

47 *Ibid.*, p. 909.
48 Nicolson Diaries, MS, 17 July 1931.
49 *Ibid.*, 23 July 1931.
50 *Action*, 19 November 1931, p. 29. Nupa was not designed to reach full structural maturity until the middle of the 1930s and, therefore, much of its organisation remained at this point, if not theoretical, then certainly embryonic.
51 Letter from Nicolson to Mosley, 29 June 1932, Nicolson papers.
52 Nicolson Diaries, MS, 28 September 1931.
53 Mosley, *op. cit.*, p. 286.
54 *Action*, 15 October 1931, p. 29.
55 *Ibid.*, 8 October 1931, p. 10.
56 *Ibid.*, 31 December 1931, p. 1.
57 O. Mosley, 'Old parties or new?', *Political Quarterly*, III, 1, January–March 1932, pp. 28–9.
58 Nicolson Diaries, MS, 28 September 1931.
59 *Ibid.*, 1 October 1931.
60 *Action*, 15 October 1931, p. 3.
61 Craig, *op. cit.*, p. 69.
62 The CP polled a total of 70,844 votes spread over twenty-six constituencies: Skidelsky, *op. cit.*, p. 279.
63 *Action*, 5 November 1931, p. 2.
64 *Ibid.*, 5 November 1931, p. 1.
65 *Ibid.*, 29 October 1931, p. 1.
66 Skidelsky, *op. cit.*, p. 290.
67 *Action*'s weekly circulation plummeted from 165,000 to 20,00 between October and December 1931: *Action*, 31 December 1931, p. 4.
68 *Ibid.*, 24 December 1931, pp. 1–2.
69 Nicolson Diaries, MS, 5 January 1932.
70 *Ibid.*, 5 April 1932. See also letter to Dr Forgan dated 15 April 1932. H. Nicolson, *Diaries and Letters*, 1930–39, Collins, London 1966, p. 114.
71 *Ibid.*, 19 April 1932, p. 115.
72 The British Fascists had been founded originally as the British Fascisti in 1923 by Miss Rotha Linton Orman.
73 Skidelsky, *op. cit.*, p. 291.
74 Inevitably many of the crew would leave the vessel or be thrown overboard before the journey ended. In the case of the New Party this included not only Strachey and Young, but also Nicolson, and even Peter Cheyney.
75 In the autumn of 1931 Mosley was still undecided as to the exact shape of the instrument which he desired. The decision was made for him effectively by the total destruction of the credibility of the electoral side of the party as a result of the general election disaster.
76 *Daily Express*, 26 April 1933, p. 3.
77 *90 HL Debs*, 28 February 1934, c. 1018, as quoted by R. Benewick, *The Fascist Movement in Britain*, Penguin Press, London 1972, p. 31.
78 Strachey, *op. cit.*, pp. 165–6.

CHAPTER 2

Corporatism: the philosophy and programme of the BUF

The main object of a modern and Fascist movement is to establish the Corporate State. In our belief it is the greatest constructive conception yet devised by the mind of man.
O. Mosley, *The Greater Britain*, BUF, London 1932, p. 26

The appeal of fascism purports to be directed towards all the most noble majestic aspirations of a man. Its apparent effect is to bring out all that is most primitive and savage in a man and to make him, in the vital matters of his relations with other men, indistinguishable from the animals.
L. Birch, *Why they Join the Fascists*, People's Press, London 1937, p. 21

In me thou see'st the twilight of such day
As after sunset fadeth in the west. . . .
In me thou see'st the glowing of such fire,
That on the ashes of his youth doth lie
As the death-bed whereon it must expire,
Consumed with that which it was nourished by.
W. Shakespeare, untitled sonnet

The BUF's origin at the centre of the political spectrum was reflected within the philosophy and economic analysis which underpinned its proposed transformation of British society. Furthermore, as the BUF was a movement of the authoritarian rather than the liberal centre it contained a far greater range of elements from left and right than did other political parties.

Although it frequently dissociated itself from the traditional left and right by claiming to 'despise them equally',[1] at first sight its philosophical position appeared firmly in the tradition of the right. It stressed nation rather than class as a focus of loyalty; elitism rather than egalitarianism; and tended to analyse individual motivation in terms of irrationality rather than a more humanistic approach. But significant elements of fascist elitism were new in that they were based upon service to the party and nation rather than the mere possession of wealth, land or other relics of past plunder. Similarly, the BUF did not share entirely the right's traditional view of the innateness of human nature. For whilst rejecting humanist ideas of man as a rational organism fascism did accept, in some instances, that man's nature was a product of his environment. Also, in regard to populism, fascism was very much in the tradition of the left in seeing a mass movement as the vehicle for change, whereas the right distrusted popular action, equating it with deep-rooted fears concerning anarchy and the mob.

Thus, by temperament the BUF belonged exclusively neither to the right nor the left, but tended to combine elements of each or alternate between them. This was essential, for it allowed fascism to portray itself as a movement separate from and above the squalid squabbles of the other political parties. As Mosley wrote, 'The enemy is the 'Old Gang' of our present political system. No matter what their party label, the old parliamentarians have proved themselves to be all the same . . . their policy when elected is invariably the same. That policy is a policy of subservience to sectional interests and of national lethargy.'[2] For Mosley there was nothing illogical about a synthesis of the philosophies of right and left. Conservatism, he argued had for centuries tried to achieve stability and yet had undermined this desire by its reluctance to make necessary reforms. Alternatively, the left had sought progress but had rejected the necessary tools such as authority, loyalty and discipline because they were believed to be the inheritance of the right. The unification of these two philosophies was for Mosley the 'basis of Fascist faith and Fascist organisation' in that it could produce the ideal of a society, orderly and stable and yet unafraid to change.[3]

Alexander Raven Thomson, the primary philosopher of the BUF, developed further this idea of fascism as a higher third arising from the combination of apparent incompatibles. He gave the process a dialectical basis, arguing that Hegel's use of the dialectic was the observation of a natural process. Thesis led to anti-thesis, which in turn produced synthesis. This was a natural law of development, it was argued, which Marx had corrupted by applying it to the evolution of materialism. The Marxian belief that socialism would arise from the capitalist thesis and proletarian anti-thesis was rejected by Thomson because of the existence of an alleged corrupt alliance between capitalists and trade union leaders designed to preserve their own privileged positions within the status quo. This thesis of corrupt privilege, predicted Thomson, would lead eventually to the anti-thesis of popular reaction and this would be the prelude to the triumph of fascism, for 'irresponsible power challenged by national revolt creates the true synthesis of national authority'.[4]

Whatever the philosophical justifications advanced by Thomson, synthesis represented a method through which the BUF could attempt to reconcile some of the conflicting aims and interests of its adherents. The centrist nature of the movement made this a pressing necessity. Similarly, centrism ensured some degree of oscillation as there existed simultaneously within the movement attitudes which were directly antithetical to each other. The most striking example of this oscillation, observable in all fascist movements, was the tendency to look forwards and backwards simultaneously – to draw inspiration from the past whilst claiming to be the vanguard of the future.

The BUF promised vigorous government action to increase the total acreage of cultivated land and thereby double Britain's agricultural yield within five years of taking power.[5] This policy was justified by reference to the fascist belief in autarchy, and the perils of British dependence on foreign nations for any raw material as vital as food. The earnestness of the BUF's promise to regenerate Britain's agricultural sector also illustrated fascism's fundamental belief in the need for a society to replenish itself from '. . . the steady virile stock which is bred in the health, sanity, and natural but arduous life of the countryside'. Such a process, argued Mosley, would return to Britain the traditional yeoman upon whom her past greatness had been largely based.[6] This belief that the land was the natural repository of national values, culture and heritage involved the construction of an idealised vision of pastoral society. A. K. Chesterton condemned the growth of industrial towns which had come '. . . to sprawl over the once fair face of Britain, denying sun and air and health to generations after generations doomed to inherit them'.[7] In so doing he ignored the disease, the famine, and the premature death endemic within pre-industrial society. Others went further than Chesterton and waxed lyrically on the attributes of 'merrie' Tudor England, or mourned the passing of the English peasantry, who

> . . . were born and bred in the open country, and who, before they were driven by the blighting tyranny of modern capitalism to seek their livelihood in the sterile cities, knew the joy of working each morning in pure air to the song of the birds, or the voice of the wind in the trees, to the glow of the sun, the sting of the frost, or the soft patter of rain on the grass.[8]

In the three centuries since the English revolution had established a capitalist dictatorship, it was argued, the interests of the land (and later of industry itself) had been sacrificed to the avarice of finance capital. Consequently the nation had been reduced to a legion of spiritually nomadic city dwellers so effete that eventually they would prove incapable even of maintaining a rate of reproduction consistent with the survival of their race.[9] Thus, it was predicted darkly, 'the death of the countryside portends the death of the nation, for from the soil springs all life, physical and spiritual'.[10]

Such romantic notions of pastoral society have often been features of reactionary movements, providing a source of inspiration for those who have suffered through the process of modernisation. But rather than simply proposing a return to the pre-capitalist era, Mosley's economic programme was designed to restore prosperity to capitalism. Far from condemning science and technology as the destoyers of the past, Mosley saw them as the potential liberators of mankind, and predicted that 'not until man has mastered the machine and the machine has mastered material limitations will the soul of man be free to soar beyond the fetters of materialism'.[11] Indeed, Mosley became convinced that science had a unique and vital role to play in the establishment of a successful fascist regime. Although he subscribed to the Spenglerian analysis of European civilisations doomed from the moment of their creation to pass through evolutionary stages ending in collapse, he came to believe that science was the crucial factor overlooked by Spengler. For the first time in history, he argued, science could provide an alternative through its immense productive power which could be harnessed and used not only to improve the quality of life for many millions, but also to deny the course of destiny. Through science fascism '. . . could evolve Faustian man; a civilisation which could renew its youth in a persisting dynamism'.[12]

Fascism then could attract those whose attitude towards science and technology was nothing short of reverential as well as those who believed in the innate virtue and spirituality of the land. The tension within a movement which at once looked back to an idealised agrarian past and forward to a future of high consumption made possible by the machine, is too obvious to be laboured. It developed from fascism's centrist perspective and its inclusion of revolutionaries impatient to usher in a new and dynamic age, and reactionaries longing to return to the security of the past. Genuine fascists advocated neither the retrospective nor the progressive attitudes of fascism to the total exclusion of the other, and although the emphasis laid upon each varied for reasons of opportunism, both the forward and backward-looking aspects of fascist philosophy were retained simultaneously, and where possible synthesised. Thus, fascism could portray itself not only as the instrument which would create a humanity released from poverty and disease, in a world reborn through science, but also as the mechanism through which the world could return to those values and traditions of a bygone age which were perceived to have arisen from man's affinity with the soil.

Aspects of fascist philosophy assisted also in minimising or camouflaging the basic inconsistencies within party and ideology. The extreme nationalism of the BUF illustrated this in that it provided a basic common denominator between the nation's otherwise disparate elements and was consequently vital to all fascist movements. Class, it was argued, was essentially meaningless because through social mobility a person's class could easily change during the course of a lifetime. Nationality through birth never changed and therefore, by virtue of its greater permanence, nationality should always supersede class affiliations. The importance of this premise cannot be overemphasised. Once accepted, it allowed fascism to substitute for class conflict the idea of a nation united in its desire to destroy its own unsavoury elements regardless of their class. This internal war by the whole nation against those few traitors and wreckers lurking within its ranks could include the destruction of capitalists who placed profit before patriotism, as well as workers who sabotaged national prosperity through unfettered greed. The question, claimed Mosley, was whether Britain could '. . . recapture the union of 1914 and that rapturous dedication of the individual to a cause that transcends self and faction, or are we doomed to go down with the Empires of history in the chaos of usury and sectional greed?'[13]

Nationalism, even when defined as '. . . the idealisation of the nation as the supreme synthesis of a group of individuals with a communion of linguists and historical traditions and of regional and economic interests . . .',[14] has an inbuilt tendency to produce racism. The more extreme the nationalism then the greater is the proportional ingredient of racism within it. Therefore, inevitably, fascist movements included racism and frequently became the receptacles for racial theories and social Darwinist ideas which had emerged from the nineteenth century. The work of several British philosophers and scientists was distorted by the Nazis to this end. Similarly, Benjamin Kidd, a vigorous advocate of social Darwinism, and Houston Stewart Chamberlain, one of the most notorious of the pre-1914 racist writers, were both British.[15] Chamberlain believed implicitly in the superiority of the Aryan race, and in particular in its Teutonic or German branch. He even envisaged government control over reproduction in order to avoid random genetic mixing which weakened the race because '. . . a mongrel is frequently very clever, but never reliable; morally he is always a weed'.[16]

In the light of this rich national heritage of racial theory it is interesting to observe the BUF's reluctance to exploit it fully. It was suggested that one of the important aspects of any nation should be its 'common blood',[17] and there were half-hearted attempts to analyse history in racial terms. But when referring to the British race the party refrained from using terms such as 'Ayran', which were the common currency of racial theorists, preferring instead vague references to 'Britishness' or 'Anglo-Saxon'. Owing to the inherent superior qualities attributed to the Anglo-Saxon, of course, this represented a real form of racism nevertheless. Having established that the superior British character was racially derived, it followed naturally that this character must be protected from genetic corruption. To achieve this the measures suggested ranged from sterilisation of the unfit, to the ending of immigration and the expulsion of all foreigners (including those already naturalised) unless they were proved to be worthy British citizens. Above all the dilution of the genetic essence of Britishness through random propagation would be avoided '. . . by education and propaganda, to teach the British people what racial mixtures are bad . . . this is a matter for the teacher rather than the legislator, but if legislation was ever necessary to preserve the race, Fascism would not hesitate to introduce it'.[18]

As war approached and after it began there were attempts to create racial links between Britain and Germany by claiming that their peoples belonged to the same Nordic race. The mass murder of the finest of the race's young through war was condemned as madness which would lead to the Nordics being overwhelmed by the faster-breeding Slav or Negroid races, and would therefore amount to 'race suicide'.[19] This was the closest that the BUF ever came to emulating the racism of the pre-1914 racist writers such as Chamberlain and Gobineau. It was a far cry from the obsession with Aryan racial purity displayed by Nazis such as Streicher who warned the German nation that only a single act of intercourse was necessary between a Jew and an Aryan woman to result in the latter's blood becoming poisoned irreparably.[20] In comparison to such pronouncements, exhortations by the BUF to place British interests before those of foreigners, and even the Nordic racial nonsense of the late 1930s appear rather tame. In fact the striking feature of the BUF's pronouncements upon race is their complete lack of sophistication. They included no formal hierarchy of racial groups, and on the rare occasion that terms such as 'Nordic' or 'Aryan' were used, there was never any real attempt to define them. Indeed the BUF's racism owed far more to its extreme nationalism than to the work of the pre-1914 geneticists, even though some of the most prominent of these were British.

The explanation for this was twofold. Firstly, the inhabitants of modern Britain were obvious racial mongrels derived from genetic stock as diverse as Norse, Celt, Roman and Norman. Racial theorists such as Chamberlain had recognised this and accordingly categorised the British as inferior to the pure Aryans from north-central Europe. Such a label of inferiority was unacceptable to a movement as overtly patriotic as was the BUF. Secondly, whilst such racial theories provided Nazi Germany with a justification for seeking *lebensraum* in Eastern Europe at the expense of lesser races, they were hardly the best cement for the decrepit, multi-racial British empire. By the 1930s British imperialism sought to appear in a rather more benign and paternalistic garb as the head of a mutually supporting group of nations, rather than as masters destined to triumph over their racial inferiors through innate genetic superiority. Moreover the empire was crucial to Mosley's formula for economic recovery because it represented an economic unit large enough to insulate itself from the world economy. Thus, the empire was more than the supreme symbol of nationalism and the embodiment of glories past; it was also an integral part of BUF economics. It was too important to be undermined through the propagation of tendentious racial theories.

Another aspect of fascist philosophy which had the effect of obscuring inconsistencies was a heavy emphasis upon the leadership principle which involved discipline, loyalty, and unquestioning faith in the leader. Under the party's constitution the leader was empowered to appoint and dismiss officers at will, was able to alter the constitution as he chose, and was the party's ultimate authority on all questions of policy, organisation, administration and discipline.[21] A leadership cult was encouraged within the movement and Mosley became the object of eulogistic praise and often obsequious pandering by those around him. He was seen as a figure of omnipotence whose mystical vision of the road which lay ahead and the promised land which waited at the journey's end led to his portrayal as a '... leader among the leaders, man amongst men, dauntless and inspired crusader who shall not rest until the battle has been won'.[22]

This concept of leadership permeated the entire movement as at every level the BUF (like its predecessor, the New Party youth movement) adhered to the principle of strict discipline. For Mosley voluntary discipline and strong leadership were essential because it was only through the absolute authority which they provided that significant change could be effected. Such unquestioning discipline, whilst helping to prevent the exposure of ideological differences, also maximised scarce manpower resources and was of particular value in the stewarding of meetings. It was recognised that a highly disciplined body of men which acted in unison and whose constituent elements trusted each other implicitly could control crowds and defeat unorganised opponents, even though heavily outnumbered. BUF members were trained accordingly.

It was precisely this discipline which liberalism lacked, argued Mosley, and this shortcoming was the cause of its general inability to act decisively and its total paralysis in the face of a crisis. Obsessed with materialism and torn by class conflict, liberalism was doomed to follow the dictates of short-sighted majorities in pursuit of sectional greed. It is ironic that the BUF has been criticised retrospectively by liberal historians for being similarly obsessed by national values, pursued at the expense of the traditional freedoms of liberal democracy. It has been suggested that Mosley's conception of freedom in economic rather than political terms was an indication of the strength of the influence of the economic crisis upon his attitudes. Rather than assisting an understanding of Mosley, however, this reflects more the attitude of the liberal towards the sacrosanct freedoms of press, speech, association, and the naïve belief in equality before the law. Mosley's criticisms of liberal Britain were often sharp and accurate, retaining their validity regardless of the overall legitimacy of the corporate vision which was to supersede liberalism. Mosley recognised that a basic desire of the citizens of any society is to secure food and shelter. Those to whom these essentials for survival are not guaranteed (and there were many such in inter-war Britain) care little for the freedom of rich men to print newspapers, or the freedom to use an expensive and esoteric legal system to defend non-existent privileges. The freedom which allows a man who cannot afford food to own a newspaper or initiate a legal action is less meaningless; the society which boasts to the hungry man that he is thus free is obscene. For the hungry, concepts such as liberal freedom have always been inedible.

The BUF's unconcealed contempt for liberalism and the kind of democracy with which it was associated gave its opponents an easy target at which to aim. It felt the sting of such attacks, and its response was confused and ultimately contradictory, for it included the denunciation of democracy and the justification of dictatorship on a theoretical level whilst also claiming that fascism would end liberalism's corrupt parliamentary plutocracy and replace it with a real people's democracy. This confusion illustrates the difficulty faced by a movement attempting to justify overt dictatorship to a nation with the world's longest unbroken history of parliamentary democracy, and to a society in which many believed that such parliamentary democracy was a real and meaningful manifestation of democratic liberty. It was also indicative of the incompatible elements of fascist ideology and of the BUF's membership. For although the dictatorship principle could in some respects shield fascism's inconsistencies, in practice the attitude within the movement which reflected these inconsistencies expressed themselves frequently on the subject of dictatorship and democracy in such a way as to express these very differences. Not content with justifiable criticism of the clearly undemocratic nature of the parliamentary system and an aggressive elucidation of the merits of dictatorship, there were many within the BUF who redefined freedom in terms of economic security and service to the community as a whole through the corporate state, thus enabling them to claim that a fascist government would give its citizens a greater degree of freedom than they received under parliamentary democracy. There were also those who took this reasoning a stage further by redefining democracy to mean a system of government where the individual is given the maximum possible freedom. Having redefined freedom it could therefore be argued that dictatorship and democracy were complementary rather than contradictory concepts (as were liberty and service), as only through the former could the latter be achieved. Even for a movement as ideologically flexible as fascism, however, such a synthesis was difficult and hence the BUF's overall attitude in this area appeared inconsistent and frequently unconvincing.

Other aspects of fascist philosophy were better suited to welding together the diverse elements of the BUF, or at least could serve to disguise the conflict arising from such elements. Prominent amongst these was the concept of action. There were many within the BUF who boasted freely of fascism's lack of a '. . . long pedigree of theory like socialism, Liberalism, and Communist, and other products of the intellectual laboratory', and were proud to see it as '. . . an insurrection of feeling – a mutiny of men against the conditions of the modern world'.[23] Fascism appealed to its supporters using emotional rather than rational criteria, and they were discouraged from thinking too deeply about its internal logic. Faith was deemed more important than rational analysis. This belief in the inherent worthiness of action as opposed to reasoned thought gave rise to a deep suspicion of 'academic sterilities'.[24] The only justification for thought was when it served as a prelude to action.

This attitude in its turn encouraged a cult of struggle. Blackshirts were inspired by Mosley to believe that

> . . . the slow, soft days are behind us, perhaps for ever. Hard days and dark nights ahead, no relaxing of the muscle of mind and will. It is at once our privilege and our ordeal to live in a dynamic period in the history of man. The tents of ease are struck and the soul of man is on the march. Do we envy those who have lived in the lotus moments of the past? Do those of my generation regret their own short youth; that brief bright moment between storm and storm? No! we regret nothing, not even our own past. Those who have lived in the happy valleys of blissful, peaceful periods in the history of the world have never known our depths, but they have also never known our heights.[25]

Struggle was seen not only as the means of capturing political power but also as the noble duty of those in whom there existed innate worthiness. Rather than a means to an end, struggle became the proof of nobility as Mosley exhorted his followers to ever greater feats of sacrifice. This idealisation of the concept of struggle was concerned more with romantic notions of heroic valour than with the belief that struggle is the most effective educative medium. Nevertheless it had obvious practical advantages for the movement, not least of which was the maximisation of a small membership.

The BUF's commitment to the virtues of struggle, combined with the strict hierarchically imposed discipline, produced an organisation which often conceived of itself not as a political party but as '. . . an Order dedicated to the service of a great ideal. . . .'[26] Initiates to the order received instruction concerning '. . . the immense vision of service, of self-abnegation, even of self-sacrifice in the cause of the world'.[27] Simultaneously this desire for action and struggle encouraged the BUF's tendency to idealise the vigour of youth and the virility of the machismo man. Youth with its innocent strength and '. . . cleanness, like a white flame',[28] was conceived as the very foundation of the dawning fascist era. The virility of young males was to provide the cutting edge of fascism's advance through an effete civilisation, degenerate with rampant feminism and unchecked matriarchy.

This desire to weld together incompatible elements or to camouflage their points of conflict, which was so visible within the principle areas of the BUF's philosophy, emerged even more clearly in the blueprint of the BUF's corporate system. That this system was to be founded upon the nation state was, as already suggested, indicative of fascism's need to find a common denominator which could supersede class. Unlike the far left, which viewed the state as a means of institutionalising and maintaining the inequitable nature of non-socialist society, fascism's view was founded on the liberal concept of the state as a regulative mechanism. But whereas liberalism advocated a minimum of state interference in the affairs of its citizens, fascism sought to regulate and control almost all spheres of human existence. Therefore it would tolerate none of the inalienable rights of the individual endemic to liberalism, and demanded a total acceptance of the principle that the corporate state was superior to any of its constituent elements. The state and its needs were considered paramount and the BUF adhered to the maxim: 'All within the State: none outside the State, none against the State.'[29] The state was held in equal esteem by Mussolini, who in 1929 had declared

> It is the State which educates citizens for civic virtue, which makes them conscious of their mission, calls them to unity, harmonises their interests in justice, hands on the achievement of thought in the sciences, the arts, in law, in human solidarity. It carries men from the elementary life of the tribe to the highest human expression of power, which is Empire. . . . When the sense of the State declines, and the disintegrating tendencies of individuals and groups prevail, national societies move to their decline.[30]

This attitude illustrates fascism's tendency to move beyond the concept of the state as a machine by ascribing to it qualities of an almost mystical nature. In addition to its regulative functions the state was perceived as a repository of national culture, an expression of civilisation, and a barometer recording the health of a society. Above all fascism considered the state as an organic composition, '. . . an organism endowed with a purpose, a life, and means of action transcending those individuals, or groups of individuals, of which it is composed'.[31] Thus could the state be seen as an independent biological entity in which its citizens were cells and its institutions were internal organs of varying importance. The most frequent analogy used by the BUF, was that of the human body, where '... every member of that body acts in harmony with the purpose of the whole under the guidance and driving brain of Fascist Government'.[32] The analogy was continued through claims that the nation needed surgery rather than political reform, concluding that '... the poison of class conflict can only be countered by the drastic anti-toxin of centralised autocratic power'.[33] Just as the organs of a body each had different, but important, tasks, so also would the citizens of the corporate state have different functions. Although there would be differences of wealth and living standards, under fascism 'social class' would be eliminated. Consequently, it was argued, although '... the Managing Director of a business will perform a different function from that which the charwoman performs in sweeping out his office ... the difference will be functional and not social'.[34] The naïvety of such a view which disregarded the economic foundations of class distinction was self-evident. To what extent the charwoman or her dependants would take comfort from the knowledge that her distinction from the managing director was functional and economic but not 'social' was a subject upon which Mosley was wise not to dwell.

The concept of an organic state was not new. It had existed in some form in the work of philosophers from Aristotle and Plato, to Machiavelli and Hegel. In the nineteenth century the work of Malthus had argued the existence of inherent regulative mechanisms in human society, and Darwinism showed how the organism evolves as a result of competitive pressures in its environment. Work of this nature was used to give the idea of the corporate state a pseudo-scientific basis, as in the case of Benjamin Kidd's work on social evolution published in the late nineteenth and early twentieth centuries, which pre-empted the relationship between the individual and the fascist state. Working from the premise that an organism is more efficient than the mere sum of its parts and that natural selection leads to the evolution of more efficient organisms, Kidd argued that history, like nature, was the gradual architect of more efficient and more organic types of society. Therefore, it was natural that evolution would '... inevitably render the interests of the units subordinate to the interests of corporate life'.[35]

The BUF acknowledged little of this legacy, however,[36] preferring to portray the corporate state as a form of organisation which would facilitate the simultaneous existence of socialist planning and capitalist free enterprise, and through which class conflict could be obliterated. It was, then, a framework in which the capitalist policies of fascism would be able to operate, and was designed to fulfil two main functions. Firstly it was conceived as the necessary cure for the decadence which afflicted inter-war British society, for it was argued that '. . . decadence, an affliction of the spirit, is a collective disease exactly as bubonic plague is a collective disease'. The atomisation of society caused by democracy, and the personal self-seeking encouraged by liberalism had produced decadence, a form of mass neurosis, which resulted in the loss of spiritual values and national pride and honour. Such problems, it was predicted, indicated '. . . a strongly entrenched neurosis which is the spirit's cancer and the trumpeter of death'. The only cure lay with the disciplined order of the corporate state, for

> fascism, recognising the human necessity to serve a social purpose and the fact that in a very real sense man lives only in so far as he is related to others, provides the citizen . . . [with] . . . the corporate activity which his soul's health demands. . . . Herein is both the meaning and the mechanism of the Corporate State and Fascism – . . . the solvent of neurosis and the conqueror of decay.[37]

It was recognised that many of the ills of society, as fascism perceived them, were rooted in class conflict, but this could be eliminated, it was argued, when the corporate state fulfilled its second main function, which was to restore health to Britain's ailing economy. The prohibition of strikes and lock-outs would disarm each side of industry, and would be a prelude to the establishment of a series of interlocking corporations representing workers, employers, and consumers equally, which would replace conflict with harmony through co-operation. Issues concerning conditions of work would be settled within each industry's corporation, and as existing trades union and employers' organisations were '. . . to be woven into the fabric of the Corporate State. . . . Instead of being the general staff of opposing armies, they will become joint directors of national enterprise under the general guidance of corporate government.'[38] Whilst eliminating class conflict these corporations would also have had the task of adjusting consumption in line with demand and potential production, by raising salaries and wages uniformly in line with production increases. The establishment of minimum wage rates backed by law would prevent the raised wage levels from being undercut by domestic employers. Similarly the exclusion of all foreign goods which could be produced within Britain would ensure that wages were not undercut by '. . . sweated competition from abroad'. With the purchasing power of the British consumer thus increased in line with productive capacity, full employment and full production would be achieved, and with them a concomitant rise in living standards.[39] Under such circumstances the class war would become merely '. . . a grisly relic of the age of scarcity'.[40]

Private enterprise, the liberty to profit from the appropriation of the surplus value of the labour of others, was to be 'encouraged',[41] subject to only one proviso. The capitalist would be

> . . . required to consider the public welfare as well as his own private interest in using his property and developing his enterprise. Liberal atavism, which held that in serving his own interests the individual automatically advanced the interests of the community has been discredited long since, and we must now turn from the laws of the jungle to the laws of man.[42]

As long as such cooperation was forthcoming then the ownership of capital would remain largely outside the hands of the state. Nor was this co-operation necessarily a retrogressive step for the capitalist. Mosley's corporate vision promised him a stable and expanding market, a labour force stripped of its most important defensive weapons, and a strong government committed to '. . . protect genuine private enterprise'.[43] Thus, although it rejected *laissez-faire* economics, demanded the allegiance of property-owners and industrialists, and threatened the nationalisation of some public utilities, the corporate state was never a threat to the essence of the capitalist system.

Both in its attempt to purge the spiritual malaise of the nation and its formula for revitalising the economy, the corporate state was an attempt to achieve co-operation and harmony – if necessary, through coercion. The existence of the permanent machinery of compulsory arbitration inherent within the corporate system, backed by the government and the law, was considered sufficient to overcome any industrial problems which might arise, and thus corporatism was conceived as a means of ensuring national unity as well as precipitating economic recovery. The centrist nature of fascism was never more clearly illustrated than in its own portrayal of the corporate state as the harmonious and prosperous unification of workers '. . . by hand, or brain, or capital',[44] in short, the producers' state.

The supreme instrument of executive authority within the corporate state was to have been a small cabinet of three or four fascists under Mosley. The immense power of this government was subject only to the partial restraint of parliament or the people, who were to review its work periodically and vote to accept or reject it. In the event of rejection by either, the government would have been dismissed and would be replaced by new (and presumably fascist) ministers selected by the King.[45] Parliament, it was argued, would be in a better position to criticise government policy because, when not convened for this purpose, MPs would be responsible for carrying out the work of government in the localities, individually responsible to their superiors in strict adherence to the leadership principle. Thus, elected MPs would have a dual function. At a national level they would sit periodically as part of a bicameral assembly in which the House of Commons was to remain, although the

House of Lords was to be replaced with a Senate, or Chamber of Merit, consisting of government-appointed representatives from the corporations, or other areas of public life.[46] Most of their time, however, would be spent as local administrators. Assisted by the machinery of local government, in an advisory rather than an executive capacity, MPs at last would be free of the soporific and corrupting atmosphere of Westminster and therefore, it was claimed, would achieve a far greater affinity with the needs and aspirations of their constituents. But despite promises by Mosley that the government would submit itself for approval both to parliament and the people at '. . . regular and frequent intervals',[47] it is clear that a government with power checked only by 'yes' or 'no' appeals to the nation at interminate periods is in practice unlimited.

The primary constituents of the economic structure of the corporate state were to have been the twenty-four individual corporations, designed to include the entire adult population of the nation.[48] Each corporation was to consist of representatives of employers elected by the owners, shareholders and managers of an industry, and workers elected by the employees, together with consumer representatives appointed by the government. Each corporation would represent all of the workers, employers and consumers who fell within its category, although within them would be a number of subdivisions and subsidiary councils proportionate to their overall size. Beneath each corporation would be a complicated structure, based on indirect elections, moving upwards from local, to district, and ultimately to the zonal councils which would elect the membership of the twenty-four corporations operating at national level. Each of these was to regulate and harmonise its own industry, and its decisions were to have the force of law, subject to the approval of the National Corporation.[49] This National Corporation was conceived as the foremost economic organ of the corporate structure and was to be composed of representatives drawn from all the twenty-four lower corporations in proportion to their size and overall importance to the economy. Its task was not only to arbitrate and decide between disputes arising within corporations or between separate corporations, but also to undertake a degree of economic planning by controlling profits, hours, conditions and dividends, and in particular to adjust consumption to production through the control of wages. It was to be assisted by an Investment Board and an Import and Export Board and would receive advice from '. . . the best executive brains of industrial and professional life' in their capacity as an advisory council to the Minister of Corporations, who was to head the National Corporation and unto whom it would be ultimately responsible.[50]

All elections within the corporate state were to be based on an occupational franchise. The issues behind political decisions, it was argued, were too complex for popular comprehension and consequently elections were too often decided by meaningless slogans. Under fascism people were to vote for colleagues within their own particular trade or profession upon a platform about which they were well qualified to judge because of their working experience. By thus bringing to an end votes of ignorance a technical parliament would emerge. A serious assembly elected upon merit rather than the ability to debate cleverly or '. . . to sit up all night to obstruct the business of the nation'.[51]

This then was the corporate machinery which, it was boasted, would achieve economic progress without injury to the national interest, which was so often the case with *laissez-faire* liberalism or the bureaucratic inefficiency axiomatic with socialism. The most striking feature of the structure of the corporations, however, was that with an equal number of representatives from the employers and the workers, power would reside with the government-appointed consumer representatives. As these would presumably be loyal fascists, and as fascist parties have a tendency to affiliate closely with the orthodox right when in power, it is likely that the workers would have found themselves in a permanent minority upon the corporations and yet bound legally to accept their decisions upon pay and working conditions.

For Mosley the corporate state represented the replacement of an obsolete system of government with a system suitable for the twentieth century. A belief in a small central executive free to govern without hindrance from parliamentary opposition had been one of the major thrusts of the *Mosley Memorandum* of 1930. But the corporate structure was more than a system of strong government in that it was designed to end class conflict and provide a framework within which Mosley's solutions to the problems of the inter-war British economy could be applied. Such a definitive framework had been absent from the *Memorandum*, but the Keynesian analysis which had inspired it remained paramount to Mosley who used it to underpin the corporate state.

The failure of demand to keep pace with the power of modern science to produce goods meant that rationalisation (an inevitable part of economic progress) resulted in permanent pools of unemployment rather than increased production. Unemployment further reduced consumption and caused still greater unemployment. A vicious circle had thus been established, it was argued, consisting of four links: rationalisation, unemployment, lower purchasing power, and further unemployment. The universally conceived solution, to expand export markets by further rationalisation and enforced wage reductions, only resulted in a further drop in domestic consumption and greater unemployment.[52] Although Britain's prosperity had once been based upon its export markets the increase in the number of industrial nations able to compete with her, together with a general closure of foreign markets through tariffs and quotas, had rendered this analysis inapplicable. The problem was further aggravated by the willingness of financiers to exploit cheap labour in backward countries which would work for wages far below those demanded by white workers.[53] By cutting wages in an attempt to produce more competitively priced goods, British industry was cutting its own domestic market. The corporate state was to provide an opportunity whereby domestic purchasing power could be increased within a protected home market. This protection, however, rather than being a system of *ad hoc* committees (as had been the New Party's commodity boards) would have amounted to '. . . a permanently functioning machine of industrial self-government which continually harmonised the conflicting interests of the industrial system'.[54]

The need to prevent cheap foreign goods, the sweated products of international finance and its exploitation of backward labour, from undercutting the increased wage rates through which domestic consumption was to be raised, was paramount.[55] Whilst the corporations were designed to ensure that there was no undercutting from unpatriotic British producers, the need for protection from unscrupulous producers abroad meant that the corporate state would have to strive to achieve economic autarchy. This dream of self-sufficiency meant not only the exclusion of foreign manufactures, but also a drive to double the productivity of the agricultural sector.[56] The role of the empire in this general scheme of autarchy was crucial because it represented a large, non-industrial area from which Britain could gain the raw materials she needed, and from which a large and stable market could be carved in order to absorb British manufactured goods. 'An economic and spiritual unit insulated from the chaos and follies of the outside world.'[57] This idea of an insulated economic unit had been present in Mosley's thought long before his conversion to fascism as an essential prerequisite to any economic regeneration. On tour in the USA in the winter of 1925–6 he had seen how a large and well-insulated bloc was able to provide a stable market for mass-produced products and thereby provide the basis for unimpeded prosperity. The Ford motor factory at Detroit had illustrated this lesson vividly by producing the cheapest cars in the world whilst also paying the highest wages, thus proving Mosley's assertion that in a stable market it was rates of production rather than wage levels which determined the cost of production.[58]

It was claimed that it would be in the interests of the dominions to belong to an autarchic empire. Those who objected to the idea were the financiers who exported capital from Britain in the form of foreign loans to equip Britain's '. . . industrial competitors all over the world'. They received their interest on these loans in the form of foreign goods which entered the domestic market and thereby created unemployment. Such interests would obviously suffer from the exclusion of foreign goods, but faced with the choice between '. . . alien finance or the British producer', the BUF committed itself unequivocally to the latter.[59] Those who risked their capital by holding ordinary shares should be taxed less than those who made safe investments in bonds and debentures, it was argued, on the basis that the former was a 'producer' and the latter was a 'usurer'.[60] This hatred for the '. . . financial parasite of the world', which later was to become so inextricably entangled with anti-Semitism, became increasingly dogmatic within the BUF as international finance was blamed for producing economic instability through speculation. For '. . . the financial microbe of decadence produces a fever which may before long prove fatal. By fever the financier lives, but the body of industry perishes. . . .'[61] The roots of Mosley's contempt for international finance, like those of his belief in fascism itself, stemmed from the Keynesian concept of a community of interest between worker and capitalist against their common enemy, the *rentier*, who had profited from the maintenance of an artificially high exchange rate at the expense of the producer. The schemes of his *Memorandum* were to have been financed by raising loans in London rather than allowing that same capital to go abroad to the benefit of Britain's economic competitors.

Finally, it was accepted that between the achievement of power and the completion of the full corporate machinery, there would have to be provisions for the immediate relief of unemployment. These involved voluntary retirement for those over sixty, and the institution of a large programme of public works, including an ambitious construction programme pledged to eliminate the nation's slums within three years. This whole package of measures was drawn largely from Mosley's proposals of 1930.[62]

It is striking that so many of the salient features of the BUF's corporate blueprint, including the concept of a harmonious political machine suitable for the twentieth century, government in favour of the producer not the financier, the reflation of an insulated home market, and the role of a public works programme, belonged, at least in part, to the pre-fascist political and economic analysis of Mosley. This analysis dates from the period when Mosley was very firmly in the centre of the political spectrum, and the fact that so many of Mosley's centrist proposals could be accommodated comfortably within fascism again indicates its status as an ideology of the centre.

How radical a programme did this really represent? Its refusal to accept the status quo coupled with its belief in effecting change through struggle often gave it the appearance of radicalism. There is no doubt also that Mosley's Keynesian analysis, which underpinned British fascism, represented a real form of radicalism in so far as it challenged the sacred tenets of contemporary economic orthodoxy. But even if it had been implemented in full, would it have produced a society markedly different from that which it sought to replace?

In this respect the most obviously radical area of the BUF's programme lay in its alteration of the relationship between the citizen and the state, for the party was deeply committed to the destruction of every vestige of liberalism. The BUF stressed that individuals within the corporate state would be held more responsible for their actions than ever before, and promised that a people's court would be established to deal with those who had indulged in crimes against the people or the nation. *Rentier* wealth was a particular target. Private fortunes could be amassed only by those who gave service to the state. Families which failed to justify their riches could lose them, for the receipt of hereditary wealth was also to be a privilege rather than a right. The conscientious rural landlord who justified his position by providing local leadership (as his ancestors had done in feudal society) would be exempt from death duties, but he who neglected his obligations would be dispossessed without compensation. The urban landlord, whose rents were to be controlled whilst there remained a housing shortage, would be subject to a similar code of conduct. It was acknowledged, however, that the ownership of urban property was difficult to justify and, therefore, most would pass to the state. All were warned that '. . . the people's justice will turn with severity upon those who expect to be able to live as parasites at the national cost, and realise no obligation of service in return'.[63] It was admitted freely that such a cleansing of liberal notions would involve 'conditioning' individuals to accept new fascist values and educating the 'bourgeois mind' out of existence. This, it was suggested, would represent a real revolution – 'a revolution destroying the bourgeois concepts of monetary success and other meritricious values in order to harness the devotion of the people to the building up of a society without class barriers in which every individual instinctively harmonises his own interests within the confines of the general community interest'.[64]

But simply attacking liberalism and the duplicity of liberal regimes was not in itself sufficient to produce automatically a revolutionary perspective. Indeed, fascism is the very proof of this assertion for the BUF's programme and analysis, despite these elements of radicalism, were deeply tainted by reactionary attitudes. The most fundamental of these concerned its elitism and traditionalism. There were frequent expressions of contempt for the concept of equality which was dismissed as '. . . sentimental and unscientific . . .' on the grounds that 'the inheritance of mental and physical characteristics, the existence of insuperable differences of environment, the laws of biology and psychology make it impossible that there should exist any real equality between men'.[65] Thus, as one moved upwards through the echelons of the corporate structure, each rise would have brought a corresponding increase in privilege as well as power. Unlike the rough pyramid of liberal–democratic society, the corporate state was designed as a near perfect geometric figure held together by the authority of the party. At the summit of this human pyramid was to be that ancient symbol of institutionalised elitism: the monarch.

The sycophantic reverence with which the BUF beheld the monarchy was without limit. As well as being the embodiment of Britain's glorious heritage the crown was also considered to be the visible symbol of Britain's imperial splendour. 'He who insults the British Crown thus insults the history and achievement of the British race', it was asserted, and it was promised that a fascist government would ensure that the monarchy received the loyal support and allegiance of every subject. Therefore, all speeches by '. . . the snarling mongrels of Press, pulpit or politics',[66] which insulted or slandered the monarchy would be prohibited. This unquestioning acceptance of the institution of the monarchy went beyond a mere devotion to any individual occupant of this high office. Edward VIII was considered an ideal monarch for a fascist state, and at the time of his abdication there was even a BUF-sponsored 'Save the King' campaign which was spectacular only in its lack of impact. Despite its expressions of disapproval as to the manner in which Edward was forced to renounce his throne, the BUF was quick to pledge its complete loyalty to the brother who succeeded him and thereby assisted the junta of politicians who had forced the abdication.[67] For fascism, individuals, even kings, were dispensable but the institution of monarchy was paramount, for monarchs throughout history had personified, and thereby legitimised, societies founded upon inequality.

The only source of traditional authority (and, therefore, agent of inequality) greater than kings was that of gods. Here, too, the BUF was keen to underpin its elitist society with the blessing of that most eminent of all elitist institutions, the orthodox church. Mosley in effect admitted as much when he justified the BUF's belief in '. . . complete religious toleration' on the grounds that religion was welcome within the corporate state because it '. . . inculcates a sense of service and of spiritual values, for service and the values of the spirit are the essence of Fascism'.[68] Unlike communism, which tried to eradicate religion, fascism, it was claimed, would facilitate the fusing of the religious and secular spheres of the nation and thereby establish a 'higher harmony' between church and state. Amongst the pledges given by the BUF in this area were political representation for leading clerics within the Senate, the state maintenance of religious schools for those who demanded them, and even the assurance that 'atheism will perish under British Union; Christianity will find encouragement and security, in which it may prosper to the glory of its Creator'.[69]

Another major area of elitism within the proposed corporate state was that of education. Private and higher education were to be available for the privileged few, whilst for the majority, primary school would be followed by training in manual skills in preparation for the labour market. This brutal and wasteful system was designed '. . . to make citizens worthy of Fascist civilisation'.[70] Its numerous inequitable aspects cannot be justified by comparison with the injustices of the system which it would have replaced. The BUF's education policy, like the rest of its programme, was a theoretical document with the opportunity to shape and fashion any structure which was considered desirable. That it proposed an increase in the degree of elitism within a system already rotten with privilege gives further proof of the complete lack of egalitarianism within fascist ideology. It also illustrated the extent to which fascism feared education and logical reasoning which could expose its inconsistencies. All theory was regarded with suspicion, and those who dealt in it were considered particularly suspect as it rendered them especially vulnerable to the 'communist germ'.[71] Those intellectuals who criticised the corporate state would be considered 'diseased', as would those who spent their time 'lolling among the cushions of their own philosophy titillating themselves with the needles of refined sensation'.[72] Those thus afflicted were warned that '. . . if you be diseased . . . you cannot expect to flourish under fascism'.[73] Although from the mid-1930s onwards greater efforts were made to win the support of intellectuals, fascism remained primarily an anti-intellectual ideology.

In the sphere of international affairs elitism provided an important justification for the overt imperialism necessary for the establishment of an autarchic empire within which the party's economic policy could be implemented. Although it was often claimed that fascist imperialism would be more enlightened than that of *laissez-faire* capitalism, its ultimate justification, like that of previous generations, was based on conquest – a proof that the colonising power is more efficient in the science of mass killing than is the subject people. Like generations of past imperialists Mosley mouthed platitudes concerning the rights of the victims of the urge to colonise, whilst accepting without question that '. . . to stultify the white man's genius in order to preserve native "rights" . . . is an historical absurdity and a British tragedy. Therefore, consciously and determinedly we develop for the benefit of the British people the territory which the energy of the British people has made their own.'[74] Thus, despite promises to save the natives from the worst excesses of international capitalism and allow only British capitalism to exploit them, the BUF's conception of imperialism was almost identical to that of the reactionary right which would have concurred entirely with the BUF's belief that '. . . the people of Britain are temperamentally and spiritually fitted to assume the leadership of the nations of the earth'.[75]

Fascism was also a doctrine of profound anti-feminism, and this too illustrated another area of its reactionary traditionalism. As already suggested, fascism identified with concepts traditionally linked to male virility, such as heroism, action and struggle. Women were considered as precious objects requiring protection from white slavers, the 'Black Peril', and above all from those who, to the eternal shame of their entire sex, wished in some way to 'imitate men'.[76] At the root of this attitude to women was an attempt to demarcate clearly between the roles of each sex within society. The problem, of course, with such delineation lies in the degree of choice given to each of the groups to whom particular functions are ascribed. When the BUF advocated the training of women in spheres of life where they could best utilise their 'special gifts', and 'specific qualities as women'[77] it was referring to qualities which did not exist objectively but which were perceived to be important, usually by men. The most important and obvious of these 'special gifts' was the ability of women to become impregnated by men. Thus, when fascism declared that it would create a race of virile men and feminine women, it meant in reality a situation where men would aspire to heroism, leadership and struggle, and where women would be mothers. In an attempt to make this consignment of women to the nether regions of domesticity more palatable to its victims, its status, on paper at least, was to be raised. 'Motherhood and the joy of carrying on the race . . .' was projected as the 'fruition' of '. . . young womanhood', and it promised that within the corporate state this 'fruition' would be duly acknowledged as '. . . one of the greatest of human and racial functions, to be honoured and encouraged'.[78] Those thus persuaded to devote their lives to domesticity, which was where the 'true interest' of women was perceived to lie, would be rewarded through the recognition of the function of 'home-maker' as a 'profession'.[79] As such they would be represented politically, through their own corporation, which was referred to variously as the 'Women's Corporation', the 'Home Corporation', the 'Domestic Corporation', or 'a corporation of Motherhood', where women would '. . . vote as wives and mothers'.[80]

To those recalcitrant enough to reject this natural feminine sphere, the BUF promised the freedom to pursue any chosen career on the basis of equal pay with their male counterparts. There were also promises of maternity leave, and a legal obligation for all employers of female labour to ensure the provision of day nurseries. There was no commitment, however, to combat sexual discrimination in employment, without which existing prejudice, combined with a desire to shirk the financial burdens of maternity leave and nursery provision, would have led employers to give jobs to men rather than women. Therefore, by advocating a programme of full economic rights for employed women, without any genuine commitment to sexual equality, the BUF was proposing the mass unemployment of women. It was even admitted that many woman would be displaced from the labour market through this process, but these, it was argued, could marry and help propagate the race. Despite their enforced economic dependency upon men, married women would experience a new type of freedom based upon material comfort and security, it was claimed, as the increased wages of husbands ensured that never again would wives be forced to poverty to renounce their collective destiny of motherhood. For it was '. . . woman's birthright to be a wife and mother, not a breadwinner'.[81]

Thus the BUF's superficial advocacy of women's economic rights did not contradict its anti-feminism. After being driven from the labour market women would have found themselves subjected to increased subordination, whilst fascism received the credit for the subsequent fall in male unemployment. Thereafter, forced to fulfil a traditional male-oriented stereotype, women within a fascist Britain would have been reduced to a state of servitude greater than that which already existed.

The BUF also concurred with traditional reactionary attitudes towards permissiveness, with frequent complaints that Britain had become a den of vice and sexual exhibitionism. The press was attacked for '. . . its mendacity, trivialities and photographs more calculated to attract attention to the bodies of females than to their faces',[82] and the Sunday papers in particular were considered to '. . . revel in rape, delve into every unsavoury detail they can find, sensationalise seduction and generally flagellate their readers' imagination into a mass orgy of shady sexuality'.[83] Modern music was attacked as '. . . hot-rhythm jungle music tainted with the neurosis of the night-club',[84] and films were condemned as a collection of '. . . salacious bedroom comedies, putrescent leg shows, horrifying 'gangster' melodramas and suggestive farce. . . .'[85] Art, too, was castigated as '. . . an orgy of morbid and distorted imaginings' produced by diseased intellectuals who suffered from '. . . sexual maladjustment'.[86] The aim of these degenerates, it was claimed, was to destroy utterly the nation's moral standards by titillating the corrupt, and corrupting the innocent through luring '. . . millions of our decent English girls . . . into believing that exotic sex-appeal and so-called glamour are more desirable than motherhood and family life'.[87] Therefore the anti-social effects of obscenity were as undesirable as those of political subversion, and were to be controlled through very tight censorship of the media and the arts. The 'spiritual Bolshevism' which corroded the vital organs of the nation and excited '. . . unhealthy tastes and tendencies, . . . whereby, . . . the fairest of our girls display their allurements on films and in international dancing troupes, or "strip tease" in foreign cabarets before the multi-coloured scum of humanity',[88] would be thus destroyed, for '. . . in an age of health art must surrender deformity to the psychological clinic. . . .'[89]

In regard to trade unions the BUF also displayed a reactionary hostility. Although their preservation as an integral part of the corporate state was guaranteed, their leaders were to be purged and any political affiliations were to be prohibited. The right to strike under fascism would, of course, be unnecessary owing to the regulative and conciliatory functioning of the corporate machinery, and to the statutory rights guaranteed to all workers. Rather than weakening trade unions the BUF claimed that their position under fascism, where all workers would be required by law to belong to their appropriate union, would be stronger than that which had been achieved in liberal Britain after a century of bitter struggle.[90] But the promise that unions would become a meaningful part of the decision-making apparatus of the state was a poor exchange for the sacrifice of the only significant weapon in the armoury of the working class: the right to withdraw its labour. Similarly, the promise of a completely unionised work-force was of no value, even if honoured, if the new unions were powerless to prevent the exploitation of their members. As the BUF considered that the existing trade union movement had been penetrated by '... plotters from Moscow',[91] it would appear certain that union officials within the corporate state would have been either chosen or at least carefully vetted by the party. It is also likely that union funds would have been made vulnerable to arbitrary fines and confiscation by the government. The implications of such moves in regard to trade union independence are self-evident. Rather than destroying unions completely, the BUF planned to incorporate them within the coercive appartus of the state from where they could be used to assist in the repression of those whom they were supposed to represent, by compelling their members to accept whatever conditions the government deemed necessary to impose upon them. Under such circumstances a trade union is worse than useless. It represents a menace to its membership whom it obstructs, deradicalises, and regiments. The corporate state would have created precisely such unions.

Thus the elements of radicalism, real or superficial, within the programme of the BUF were outweighed by attitudes (especially in regard to existing institutions), which ranged from establishmentarian to reactionary. Owing to its centrist position it is less than surprising that fascism contained reactionary and radical elements simultaneously. Its support for established institutions, however, should not be seen as evidence that as an ideology it belonged to the conservative right, but rather as an illustration of fascism's readiness to utilise many aspects of the regime which it sought to overthrow in order to exploit them for its own purposes, and through them to achieve a maximum degree of continuity. It reflected also the attitudes inherent within the predominantly middle-class leadership of the BUF.

In conclusion it must be stated that the oscillation and synthesis inherent within the BUF's programme were visible not only on the formal structured level of the planned corporate state, but also within the principles and values which underpinned it. They were the products of fascism's centrism and its consequent need to bind together elements of implacable mutual hostility. Invariably, however, they served only to camouflage rather than reconcile that hostility. As such, the BUF's programme gave an illustration of both the major strength and weakness of fascism. It has been argued that the BUF's support for traditional institutions damaged its revolutionary appeal.[92] In overall terms, however, the conservative elements within the BUF programme were of great benefit precisely because they confirmed its credentials as a centrist rather than a revolutionary party. This in turn ensured that fascism had huge potential support. It was able to exploit aspects of the appeal of the left such as envy of the idle rich, the desire for a greater share of the nation's wealth, and the exposure of the faults and inhumanities of liberalism and *laissez-faire* capitalism, without necessitating its adherents to forsake the security of traditional values and institutions including patriotism, honour, monarchy, empire and the Christian church. It was not a revolutionary combination but it included many of the constituent elements of mass popularity and motivation. It is ironic that from this same combination arises fascism's most fundamental weakness: its unworkability. There was nothing within the programme of the BUF to suggest that it would have been able to overcome the intrinsic contradictions of fascism, or to have reconciled the class conflict inherent in capitalist society. Therefore the corporate state, had it been realised, would in all likelihood have amounted to nothing more than a euphemism concealing a reactionary capitalist dictatorship.

NOTES

1 *The Fascist Week*, 4–10 May 1934, p. 1.
2 O. Mosley, *The Greater Britain*, BUF, London 1932, p. 147.
3 O. Mosley, 'The philosophy of fascism', *Fascist Quarterly*, I, 1, January 1935, p. 44.
4 A. Raven Thomson: 'Fascism and the dialectic'; *BUQ*, III, 2, April–June 1939, pp. 50–8.
5 A. K. Chesterton, *Oswald Mosley: Portrait of a Leader*, Action Press, London 1937, p. 143.
6 *Action*, 24 April 1937, p. 9.
7 Chesterton, *op.cit.*, p. 138.
8 F. McEvoy, 'The disinherited of the soil', *BUQ*, III, 2, April–June 1939, p. 73.
9 W. E. D. Allen, *Fascism in Relation to British History and Character*, BUF Publications Ltd, London 1933?, p. 6. See also J. Drennan (pseud.), *B.U.F., Oswald Mosley, and British Fascism*, J. Murray, London 1934, pp. 188–90.
10 McEvoy, *BUQ*, III, 2, p. 73.
11 O. Mosley, *Blackshirt Policy*, BUF Publications Ltd, London 1934, p. 70.

12 O. Mosley, *My Life*, Nelson, London 1968, p. 325.
13 O. Mosley, *Tomorrow We Live*, 4th edn, Greater Britain Publications, London 1939, p. 76.
14 Allen, *op. cit.*, p. 2.
15 Darwin and Malthus; although the contribution of both (as was the case with many other philosophers whose work was used by the Nazis) was inadvertent. P. Hays, 'British intellectuals and the contribution to Nazism', in K. Lunn & R. C. Thurlow (eds.), *British Fascism*, Croom Helm, London 1980, pp. 173–4.
16 H. S. Chamberlain, *The Foundation of the Nineteenth Century*, London 1911, p. 261, as quoted in Lunn & Thurlow (eds.), *op. cit.*, p. 180.
17 R. Gordon-Canning, *Mind Britain's Business*, Greater Britain Publications, London 1938, p. 8.
18 O. Mosley, *Fascism: 100 Questions Asked and Answered*, BUF Publications, London 1936, Nos. 93, 94. See also W. E. D. Allen, 'The fascist idea in Britain', *Quarterly Review*, 261, October 1933, p. 226.
19 A. Reade, 'William Morris – Nordic', *BUQ*, II, 4, October–December 1938, p. 53. See also A. P. Laurie, 'Race suicide', *BUQ* IV, 1, spring 1940, pp. 46–50.
20 Streicher, *Die Sturmer* (n.d.), as quoted in *Daily Worker*, 16 March 1936, p. 4.
21 *British Union Constitution and Rules: general*, BUF, London 1936, pp. 1–5.
22 A. K. Chesterton, in the foreword to *British Union: Pictorial Record 1932–7*, BUF, London 1938.
23 Drennan (pseud.), *op. cit.*, p. 212. See also Allen, *op. cit.*, p. 2.
24 Mosley, *My Life*, pp. 305, 319. In retrospect Mosley admitted that the BUF's obsessive pursuit of action brought it disadvantages as well as advantages: *ibid*, pp. 292–3, 319.
25 *The Fascist Week*, 22–28 December 1933, p. 1.
26 C. R. Miller, 'Party-state or order-state', *FQ*, II, 3, July 1936, p. 424.
27 Drennan (pseud.), *op. cit.*, p. 281.
28 *The Fascist Week*, 19–25 January 1934, p. 8.
29 Mosley, *op. cit.*, p. 27. This principle was also enshrined within Mussolini's Charter of Labour. It was alleged by some fascists, however, that this did not mean the elevation of the state above the individual, because the state was only the sum of governed individuals within the nation. Therefore the welfare of the state and the welfare of its people were equal and synonymous. Chesterton, *op. cit.*, p. 155.
30 As quoted by H. R. Williamson, 'Democracy and Fascism', lecture delivered to the Fabian Summer School, 21 August 1939, reprinted in *BUQ*, III, 4, October–December 1939, p. 17.
31 The Italian Charter of Labour, as quoted by A. Raven Thomson, 'Why fascism', *FQ*, I, 2, April 1935, pp. 243–4.
32 O. Mosley, *Fascism in Britain* (n.d.), p. 5. Also Mosley, *Blackshirt Policy*, pp. 25–6.
33 Thomson, *FQ*, I, 2 (April 1935), p. 249. It has been suggested that because fascism attempts to heal society as a whole by appealing to potent energy sources (symbolic of the life-force) it performs a task not dissimilar to that of primitive witch-doctors, and that this may explain the importance to fascist movements of uniforms, which represent the masks of gods and demons in ancient rituals. The argument would appear to be deficient in credibility rather than originality. H. Rogger & E. Weber (eds.), *The European Right, A Historical Profile*, Weidenfield & Nicolson, London 1965, pp. 25–6.
34 Mosley, *Fascism: 100 Questions Asked and Answered*, No. 8.
35 B. Kidd, *Individualism and After*, Oxford 1905, p. 24, as quoted in Lunn & Thurlow (eds.), *op. cit.*, pp. 177–8.
36 Although there was no formal recognition or citation of the work of men like

Kidd, BUF philosophers did use similar Social-Darwinistic arguments in favour of the corporate state. For example, Alexander Raven Thomson argued that '. . . individual units do not combine into an organic form merely for their mutual benefit. By the mere fact of organic cooperation they constitute a higher entity, which must inevitably have a wider and deeper purpose than the well-being of its constituent parts.' Thomson, *FQ*, I, 2, April 1935, p. 251.

37 A. K. Chesterton, 'The problem of decadence', *FQ*, II, 1, January 1936, pp. 60–7.

38 Mosley, *op. cit.*, pp. 28–9. Also J. Beckett, 'Fascism and the trade unions', *FQ*, I, 3, July 1935, pp. 334–5; *Daily Mail*, 29 January 1934, p. 10.

39 Mosley, *Tomorrow We Live*, pp. 42–3. Also *The Fascist Week*, 8–14 December 1933, p. 5.

40 A. Raven Thomson, 'Corporate economics', *FQ*, I, 1, January 1935, p. 22.

41 Mosley, *op. cit.*, p. 27.

42 *Blackshirt*, 17 August 1934, p. 4.

43 Mosley, *My Life*, p. 332.

44 Mosley, *op. cit.*, p. 27. The phrase 'workers of hand, or brain, or capital' was a further attempt by the BUF to emphasise the idea of a natural coincidence of interest between those who produced against those who financed. For those who remained unconvinced as to the merits of the corporate state for all its alleged advantages, there was of course the familiar Mosley argument that it was the only alternative to crisis, national collapse, and the subsequent triumph of communism. *Ibid.*, p. 81.

45 Mosley's promise that the fascist government could be dismissed by a parliamentary vote of censure was contained in *The Greater Britain*, 1932 edn., p. 21. By 1934 it had been altered so that after the first general election, after fascism had achieved power, this right would have been removed, and only a direct vote of the people would have been sufficient to dismiss the government. *The Greater Britain*, 1934 edn, pp. 39–43. See also Mosley, *Tomorrow We Live*, p. 13; *Blackshirt Policy*, pp. 72–3.

46 This second chamber offers an example of the inconsistencies of detail within the BUF blueprint. Initially Mosley seems to have conceived it as synonymous with the National Corporation, *op. cit.*, pp. 31–2, but later envisaged it as an altogether separate assembly, *Blackshirt Policy*, p. 74. As a general point, where details of BUF policy appear inconsistent the works of Mosley usually have been treated as authoritative, and where the inconsistencies occur between works by Mosley the most often expressed or logical view has been taken as official BUF policy.

47 Mosley, *Tomorrow We Live*, p. 18; *Daily Mail*, 29 January 1934, p. 10.

48 Initially Raven Thomson conceived of only twenty-three corporations, but later included a separate pensioners' corporation. The twenty-four corporations divided the population into the following basic categories: Agriculture, Fishing, Mining and Fuel, Iron and Steel, Metal Trade, Engineering, Printing and Paper Trade, Shipbuilding, Textiles and Clothing, Leather and Rubber, Glass and Pottery, Chemicals, Woodworking and Furnishing, Miscellaneous Manufactures, Building, Public Utilities, Transport, Shipping and Docks, Wholesale and Retail Trades, Banking and Insurance, Civil Service, Professional, Married Women, and Pensioners. *Fascist Week*, 20–26 April 1934, p. 5; A. Raven Thomson, *The Coming Corporate State*, Greater Britain Publications Ltd, London 1935.

49 *Fascist Week*, 27 April–3 May 1934, p. 5. The National Corporation was also referred to on occasions as the National Council of Corporations. Chesterton, *op. cit.*, p. 152.

50 *Fascist Week*, 4–10 May 1934, p. 5. Also Raven Thomson, *op. cit.*, pp. 10–12, 29.

51 Mosley, *Tomorrow We Live*, p. 18; *The Greater Britain*, pp. 33–4; Chesterton, *op. cit.*, pp. 149–50; *Action*, 31 October 1936, p. 4.
52 Mosley, *Blackshirt Policy*, pp. 20–21; *Fascism in Britain*, p. 4; and *op. cit.*, pp. 52–4.
53 Mosley, *Fascism in Britain*, pp. 4–5; *Blackshirt Policy*, p. 24; and *op. cit.*, pp. 55–66.
54 Mosley, *op. cit.*, pp. 97–8.
55 Mosley, *Tomorrow We Live*, p. 28. The increase of wages was to take the form of '. . . an advance upon existing wages and salaries . . . thus retaining the element of service . . .', rather than a free hand-out to the entire population as suggested by the Douglas credit scheme promoted by the Greenshirts. To avoid inflation this advance was to be entered into the employers' costs initially, and would only gradually be shouldered by them when increased demand had increased production, and this in turn had increased prosperity and made price rises unnecessary. A. Raven Thomson, *The Economics of British Fascism*, Bonner, London 1933, pp. 7–8.
56 Mosley, *Blackshirt Policy*, pp. 32, 55–7.
57 *Fascist Week*, 15–21 December 1933, p. 5.
58 Mosley, *My Life*, pp. 185–200.
59 *Fascist Week*, 15–21 December 1933, pp. 5, 7; Mosley, *Tomorrow We Live* pp. 45–7; *Blackshirt Policy*, pp. 35–6.
60 Mosley, *op. cit.*, p. 130.
61 Mosley, *Tomorrow We Live*, p. 35.
62 Mosley, *Blackshirt Policy*, pp. 43–6.
63 *Blackshirt*, 16 October, 1937, p. 5. See also Mosley, *Tomorrow We Live* pp. 57–8; and *Blackshirt*, 29 July 1933, p. 3.
64 Chesterton, *op. cit.*, pp. 156–7.
65 W. Joyce, *Dictatorship*, BUF Publications Ltd, London 1933, pp. 2–3.
66 *Action*, 23 July 1936, p. 2; and 15 May 1937, pp. 3, 11.
67 *Blackshirt*, 28 November 1936, p. 1; 12 December, p. 1; 19 December, p. 1. See also *Manchester Guardian*, 10 December 1936, p. 6; 11 December, p. 19; and *The Times*, 5 December 1936, p. 14.
68 Mosley, *Fascism: 100 Questions Asked and Answered*, No. 10.
69 *Action*, 2 December 1937, p. 2. Also *Blackshirt*, 9 January 1937, p. 2; *Action*, 27 August 1936, p. 10; 29 October 1938, p. 7; *Fascist Week*, 9–15 February 1934, p. 5; 4–10 May, p. 7.
70 W. Joyce, *Fascist Education Policy*, BUF Press, London 1933, p. 2.
71 *Action*, 3 April, 1937, p. 6.
72 Drennan (pseud.), *The B.U.F., Sir Oswald Mosley, and British Fascism*, pp. 186–7.
73 *Fascist Week*, 5–11 January 1934, p. 8.
74 Mosley, *op. cit.*, p. 47.
75 *Blackshirt*, 26 March 1936, p. 2.
76 Reade, *BUQ*, II, 4, October–December 1938, p. 62; *Blackshirt*, 20 June 1936, p. 3.
77 A. B. Griggs, 'Reply to a letter', *FQ*, II, 1, January 1936, pp. 164–6; Reade, *BUQ*, II, 4, October–December 1938, p. 62; *Action*, 23 May 1940, p. 2.
78 Reade, *BUQ*, II, 4 October–December 1938, p. 62; Mosley, *Fascism: 100 Questions Asked and Answered*, Nos. 31–2.
79 Mosley, *Blackshirt Policy*, p. 52; A. B. Griggs, *Women and Fascism*, BUF Publications Ltd, London 1935?, p. 1.
80 These various terms are to be found respectively in the following works: Mosley, *Fascism: 100 Questions Asked and Answered*, Nos. 31–2; Griggs, *op. cit.*, p. 1; Raven Thomson, *Blackshirt*, 7 September 1934, p. 4; and Mosley, *Blackshirt Policy*, p. 52.
81 *Blackshirt*, 19 August 1933, p. 3; 7 September 1934, p. 4; 9 November 1934,

p. 9.

82 J. McEvoy, 'Marxism, the doctrine of decay', *BUQ*, II, 3, July–September 1938, p. 15.

83 *Blackshirt*, 22 July 1933, p. 1.

84 McEvoy, *BUQ*, II, 3, July–September 1938, p. 15.

85 J. Rumbold, 'The dangers of our film censorship', *BUQ*, I, 3, July–September 1937, p. 52.

86 *Fascist Week*, 5–11 January 1934, p. 8.

87 *Action*, 28 March 1940, p. 5; 16 May 1940, p. 2.

88 McEvoy, *BUQ*, II, 3, July–September 1938, pp. 17–18; Rumbold, *BUQ*, I, 3, July–September 1937, pp. 55, 65.

89 *Fascist Week*, 5–11 January 1934, p. 8.

90 W. Risdon, *Strike Action or Power Action*, Abbey Supplies Ltd, London, 193?, p. 2.

91 J. Rye, 'God save the King', *BUQ*, I, 3, July–September 1937, p. 17.

92 G. C. Lebzelter, *Political Anti-Semitism in England 1918–1939*, Macmillan Press Ltd, London 1978, p. 90.

CHAPTER 3

Shape and form: the structural evolution of the BUF

We ask those who join us to march with us in a great and hazardous adventure. We ask them to be prepared to sacrifice all, but to do so for no small and unworthy ends. We ask them to dedicate their lives to building in this country a movement of the modern age. . . .
Neither to our friends nor to the country do we make any promises; not without struggle and ordeal will the future be won. Those who march with us will certainly face abuse, misunderstanding, bitter animosity, and possibly the ferocity of struggle and of danger. In return, we can only offer to them the deep belief that they are fighting that a great land may live.

> O. Mosley, *The Greater Britain*,
> BUF, London 1932, pp. 159–60

But we, actors and critics of one play,
Of sober-witted judgement, who could see
So many roads, and chose the Spartan way,
What has popular report to say
Of us, the Thespians at Thermopylae.

> N. Cameron, from 'The Thespians at Thermopylae'

The Fascist idea is born of a secret sense of self-superiority, coupled with a lust for power, in order to indulge in the desire to dominate others.
It is distinguished by an impatience of criticism (however honest, truthful or sincere) to the point of fanaticism that borders on insanity. . . .
It lusts to 'govern' absolutely and unchallengeably, even if it means by the ruthless use of the baton, the bullet or the hangman's rope. . . .

> C. M. Dolan, *The Blackshirt Racket: Mosley Exposed*,
> n.p. 1935?, p. 5.

Structurally the BUF evolved through two distinct phases divided by a period of transition in the latter half of 1934. This resulted from the party's initial development in accordance with that same attitude which had led Mosley to nurture the New Party youth movement – his belief in the imminence of crisis, a crisis brought about by the inability of government to deal with the nation's economic problems, the effects of which would reverberate until the very foundations of British society began to crumble. In such circumstances, argued Mosley, the triumph of communism could only be prevented by opposition in the form of '. . . a real military organisation'.[1] Only when the economic problems were undeniably receding, and with them the potential for crisis, did the party reorientate itself towards electoral politics.

The first phase of the BUF's evolution from its creation in October 1932 to the summer of 1934 saw fascism enjoy a greater degree of respectability than it has found in Britain before or since. Mosley accepted invitations to elucidate his new ideology at elite establishment functions such as a Foyles Literary Luncheon. Other opportunities for publicity arose in the spring of 1933 in the form of a verbal contest in the Cambridge Union with Clement Attlee, a well-attended and much praised duel with Jimmy Maxton under the chairmanship of Lloyd George, and a debate with Megan Lloyd George sponsored and transmitted by the BBC.[2] At this level Mosley's fascism was considered more curious than disreputable.

Beneath this veneer of respectability Mosley continued to convince himself that there was every possibility of a complete breakdown of authority and proceeded accordingly to build an organisation capable of responding decisively '. . . in case we are called upon to save the nation in a condition of anarchy when the normal measures of Government have broken down'.[3] Disciplined units were required also to protect meetings, it was argued, for untrained stewards could all too easily precipitate a mass brawl, as had occurred in November 1931 at the New Party meeting in Birmingham. Even if the opposition could be subdued it would result only in a pyrrhic victory because of the adverse publicity attracted by the violence. It was vital that this be avoided. The success of meetings was essential, for they represented the party's most important channel of communication, as well as serving as an indicator of progress. Mosley believed that there existed a vast number of potential fascists in other political parties whose conversion was dependent upon the BUF being seen as an advancing force with the capability to defend itself.[4]

In response to these same pressures which had led to the formation of the New Party youth movement in April 1931, the BUF began life equipped with a 'defence force' for each of its established branches. The London Defence Force was the largest and best trained of these, and resided in the barracks of 'Black House', the BUF's national headquarters in the King's Road, Chelsea. Employed in other capacities at the headquarters by day, defence force members in the evenings would be called upon either to steward meetings or to be rushed to the aid of BUF speakers in distress. About 150 fascists were quartered permanently in Black House, although Mosley gave assurances that in the event of a national emergency accommodation could be provided for up to 5,000.[5] From the strident bugle notes announcing reveille at 7 a.m., to lights out at 11.15 p.m., the residents of Black House led a strictly regimented existence. Dressed in regulation black shirts these men were subject to military discipline and, in addition to their other duties, underwent a degree of drilling as part of the training programme designed to teach them 'to fight in organised units under clear command'.[6] The uniform was justified as a social leveller breaking down the barriers of class amongst those who wore it, a means of recognition between friend and foe amidst disorder, and as a mechanism for differentiating between fascists committed enough to proclaim their faith publicly, and those who at heart were 'shirkers'.[7] It served also, as uniforms have always served, to depersonalise and to control those who wore them, and to intimidate those who did not.

Whether the defence forces of London or the provinces were armed has been a matter of dispute. The BUF denied that its members ever carried weapons[8] although Mosley did admit that on one occasion in March 1933 at the Free Trade Hall in Manchester, some of his stewards had used lengths of rubber hose as truncheons. Since then the use of any weapons had been forbidden, he claimed.[9] Yet within three days of that Free Trade Hall meeting a Manchester Fascist was in court for using '. . . a coil of lead and rubber',[10] upon opponents at a meeting in Rochdale at which he was stewarding. There were also claims that weapons of this nature were used at meetings in Manchester and Oxford in October and November 1933. Some ex-members alleged that defence force training included instruction in the use of such weapons, and that truncheons were issued to recruits upon joining. Others, looking back, admitted that knuckle-dusters and finger rings were used freely in fights.[11]

There were those who looked at the BUF, with its armed, uniformed, and drilled members, its military discipline, its fortress-like headquarters, its fleet of 'armoured cars' and its embryonic 'airforce',[12] and concluded that Mosley was preparing for an attempted seizure of power. This seems somewhat improbable. Until the end of his life Mosley maintained that despite his frustration with the British establishment he never seriously considered any such action. 'It was out of the question. I cannot imagine the English in twentieth century going for any form of dictatorship of that sort. If we had won it would have been with the support of the people, there was no other way to win. . . .'[13] Although some of his supporters dreamed of an extra-parliamentary route to power it was never a serious proposition whilst the basic constitutional framework continued to exist. Mosley was not a democrat, but neither was he intimidated by the democratic process which he had learned to exploit with such consummate ease. There were few contemporary MPs with a more successful personal electoral record. Consequently in 1934, when it became apparent that the economic crisis was receding, and with it the likelihood of a breakdown in order, he began to think once more of building an electoral machine capable of winning power at a general election.

Even had the crisis occurred, the BUF would not have proved the most efficient instrument for the re-establishment of authority. Mosley tried to assimilate the lessons of the New Party débâcle and was committed to building the BUF 'from below gradually and not to impose construction from above'.[14] This more realistic approach was reflected by the BUF newspaper, *Blackshirt*, an austere four-page monthly launched in February 1933, and which was the very antithesis of the fat, lavish and unsuccessful *Action*, which had drained the financial life blood of the New Party with such profligacy. Nevertheless, the BUF remained always more impressive on paper than in the flesh. Outside London the party's development was geographically uneven, with areas as large as Scotland, or Devon and Cornwall, amalgamated to form single administrative blocs, each under an Area Administrative Officer.[15] In some large towns the foundations used were the remnants of the New Party, whilst in a few rural areas, notably Suffolk, the party prospered as a result of its aggressive intervention on the side of the farmers in the 1933 tithe disputes.[16] But the party's most rapid period of growth occurred from the autumn of 1933. The BUF first penetrated Scotland in October 1933 and within nine months claimed to have over twenty branches under construction. This picture was repeated in much of England and Wales. After a slow start in Yorkshire, by the summer of 1934 the BUF had established branches in Leeds, Bradford, Huddersfield, Hull, Middlesbrough, Rotherham, Sheffield, York, Holderness, Doncaster, Pontefract and Ripon. In Manchester the BUF presence had been small since the autumn of 1932. Between October 1933 and June 1934, however, eight branches were opened in the city itself, and a further ten in surrounding Lancashire towns.[17]

Other examples of the BUF's provincial development suggest this same pattern of accelerated growth between the autumn of 1933 and the summer of 1934.[18] It is not mere chance that over two-thirds of this period coincided with the aggressive championing of the BUF's cause by the Rothermere newspaper group. This Mosley–Rothermere alliance was compacted in January 1934 as Mosley, who had long realised the importance of press support in the political arena, found a patron in Lord Rothermere, a temporary supporter of many ill-fated political ventures.

The problem which was to haunt their relationship was simple but fundamental; Rothermere believed implicitly in Mosley but not in fascism. In fact Rothermere provides an excellent example of a reactionary drawn to fascism without understanding its essential nature. Like all reactionaries he desired that his country be strong and internationally prestigious, and like all reactionaries he feared popular revolution. His was a world in which the pathetic desperation of the hunger marchers was interpreted as '. . . entirely mischievous and . . . engineered by Moscow with the express intention of causing trouble'.[19] A world in which a general strike, that ultimate weapon in the class war '. . . which is the most terrible of all forms of conflict . . .', threatened at any moment to deliver the nation into the hands of its enemies. The personal charisma of Mosley, the principles of fascist foreign policy, and its complete opposition to communism, were sufficient to convince Rothermere that the BUF was '. . . Britain's only safeguard against such insanity'.[20]

In the Rothermere press, Mosley was portrayed as a protectionist Tory in the Joseph Chamberlain tradition, presenting sound Conservatism to the middle class. The economics of the corporate state were ignored, and Rothermere made commitments on behalf of the BUF rejecting anti-Semitism and promising to work within the constitution even to the extent of preserving parliament after a few 'wise reforms' had been implemented.[21] Although it was hinted that under some circumstances dictatorship was a necessity, readers were assured that Britain's '. . . new leader of genius', was '. . . too shrewd a man to believe that the British nation can ever be dragooned into any course of action against its will'.[22] The term 'fascist' was very rarely used, as the BUF was portrayed as a party of youthful idealists within which resided the true tradition of Conservatism, unsullied through contact with the National Government. As such they constituted Britain's only real hope as '. . . a well organised party of the Right . . . ready to take over control and prevent national bankruptcy and disaster'.[23]

The BUF was prepared to accept support of this nature initially, because it produced a surge of recruits sufficient to cause the Home Secretary to report that '. . . the Fascist movement has begun to attract a better class of recruits and its membership is increasing'.[24] Efforts were made to retain Rothermere's affection by compromising upon issues about which he held strong views. The incipient anti-Semitism which had become visible within the party's press towards the end of 1933 was smothered, and Mosley's attitude towards press censorship within the future corporate state became considerably more liberal. The BUF even attempted to encourage its benefactor through deception. Party members were instructed to write to Rothermere masquerading as readers previously unconnected with fascism but moved by the power of his articles to its support.[25]

The BUF's first evolutionary period ended symbolically on the evening of 8 June 1934 amid the much publicised violence of the Olympia meeting, where interrupters were ejected brutally by fascist stewards. Although Rothermere continued his support until mid-July, Olympia, and Hitler's bloody purge of the Nazi SA, combined to illustrate some of fascism's less savoury aspects. Mosley informed Rothermere, in response to his requests, that the BUF was not prepared to drop the term 'fascist' or to change the attitude towards the corporate state, its belief in dictatorship, or its increasing hostility to Jews. Rothermere replied by condemning these aspects of the party and admitting that '. . . the assistance which I have rendered you was given in the hope that you would be prepared to ally yourself with the Conservative forces to defeat Socialism at the next and succeeding elections'.[26] This frank exchange ended the relationship although the *Daily Mail* continued to treat Mosley and his followers with considerable sympathy.

The break with Rothermere illustrates perfectly the major differences between conservatism and fascism. Despite pressure Mosley was unwilling to forsake his fascist principles. Nor was he even prepared to sustain a compromise over those areas of fascist policy which Rothermere found unpalatable. By May 1934 anti-Semitism was clearly visible within the party's propaganda. There were also undisguised attacks upon the '. . . uncanny conspiracy among our friends and our enemies to regard us as the future propaganda machine for the Tory Party',[27] and reassertions of the claim to be at war with socialism and conservatism equally. The explanation of Mosley's attitude lies in the nature of the new recruits brought in by Rothermere's campaign of distortion. They were known derisively within the movement as 'Albert Hall fascists' (those attracted by the glamour of Mosley's huge public meetings and by the press coverage of Rothermere) and were remembered as '. . . the Debs of the period with Union Jacks around their lily-white shoulders . . . who probably saw just the one side of it; the patriotic side, 'Land of Hope and Glory' sort of thing and were probably very horrified when they found its socialist side as well'.[28] Certainly the nature of Rothermere's support meant that those attracted by it were primarily middle-class conservatives. They lacked ideological commitment and consequently found it difficult to sustain the sacrifices demanded of the BUF's active membership. Furthermore, their presence in the party inhibited its radical proletarian aspects, which, as already suggested, represented a vital ingredient of fascism's appeal.

Thus the Rothermere phase represents an aberration within the BUF's history rather than a high-water mark. Rothermere offered the BUF the opportunity to become a new and more active Conservative Party. After a brief flirtation Mosley spurned this poisonous embrace, though probably more because of strategy than principle. Chesterton, writing only a few years later, considered that Rothermere's intervention caused '... incalculable harm ... and the large influx of recruits which resulted proved useless almost to a man'.[29] In retrospect Mosley agreed that people who were swept in by the press '... tended to be rather unstable, and much more serious recruiting was done by our people throughout the country. We had some 400 branches with local leaders meeting serious people, talking to them seriously. They came in and really stayed with you, but the volatile elements who were usually swept in by the press might be swept out too.'[30]

The withdrawal of Rothermere's support marked the end of the BUF's first phase of development. After an initial fall, membership did begin to pick up once more in 1935 and 1936. Certainly, the BUF became a more serious party. It concentrated on the recruitment of more ideologically committed members and upon building electoral machinery, for the Rothermere experience had taught Mosley that to construct an effective fascist party something considerably more substantial was needed than a bunch of half-inspired, vaguely motivated, middle-class patriots.

Structural change designed to facilitate electoral politics occurred in 1935. It began with a package of measures introduced by Mosley in January which attempted to reduce the party's paramilitary image. Henceforth, it was proclaimed, '... the Blackshirt uniform will be a privilege reserved for those who perform conspicuous service to the Movement',[31] and all who wore it were expected to give at least two nights per week of service to the party.[32] The old defence forces were abolished as all blackshirts were expected to assist in stewarding meetings and local BUF premises were to become smaller and more akin to an office rather than to a social club or military barracks. Those who wore the black shirt were reorganised into units of five members plus a leader, in an attempt to foster a sense of fascist brotherhood. Every five units became a section and every three sections became a company. Each unit leader was exhorted to aspire to the construction of his own company.[33]

The most important of these January changes was the establishment of a 'Political Organisation' which was administratively separate from the uniformed section of the party and was to work alongside the blackshirts in building electoral machinery at constituency level. Although the blackshirts were to retain control over local headquarters, they were forbidden to undertake any political work without the permission of the local chief of the Political Organisation. In effect, Mosley was attempting to return to the structure of the New Party before October 1931, as a prelude to a return to electoral politics. Thus the new political wing of the BUF was not unsimilar to that which had existed in the New

Party, and which he had destroyed so ruthlessly after the general election disaster of October 1931. Many blackshirts felt slighted, however, and the tension and hostility between the political and paramilitary wings of the party, which had been so evident within the New Party in the summer of 1931, threatened to return and haunt Mosley once again. In May 1935 he acted to prevent a full-scale recurrence of such hostility. Uniformed members were once again given full executive control of the whole movement in all districts,[34] but all fascists were sternly reminded that they were '. . . all members of one Movement operating under the same command'.[35] To underline this point the two groups were merged and all BUF members placed in one of three new divisions. The first and second divisions consisted of those members who wore uniforms, and were organised into units, the only difference between them being that those in the first division were prepared to give more time to the party. The third division contained the non-uniformed members whose only obligation to the party was to pay a monthly subscription.[36]

Furthermore the May reforms realigned the structure of the party to coincide exactly with the electoral map of Britain. The movement was divided into districts, each of which was to correspond with a single parliamentary constituency. In time it was hoped that each district would contain a company of blackshirts operating under a district office and his staff based at the district headquarters. From such a base, units and sections were to penetrate every ward to spread propaganda and to act as a nucleus around which the mass membership of division three fascists could muster. Units were to operate from the private houses of members until they achieved company size, at which point they would be given permission to open a modest local headquarters. But such premises, it was warned, were to be workshops, not social clubs, for '. . . the social club idea is Social Democratic and is not fascist . . . the unit system is the instrument of fascist victory'.[37] The message was clear. Although the work of building up electoral machinery was to continue, it was not to be left in the hands of the non-uniformed members. The May reforms re-established the prestige of the blackshirts and gave them an active role in building the party at local level. They also sought to heal the rift opened by the structural changes of the previous January. As an example to all members to leave the comfort of their local headquarters and social clubs and re-enter the community at large it was announced that Black House was to be relinquished a year before the lease expired. In late June 1935 the party's national headquarters were moved from Chelsea to the more modest Sanctuary building in Great Smith Street, Westminster.

The unit and district system remained in essence unchanged until the movement's suppression in May 1940.[38] In 1938 the office of Area

Commander was dismantled and London was divided into districts similar to those already established in the provinces. In the same year *Blackshirt*, the BUF's oldest news publication, was regionalised into northern, southern, and east London editions.[39] It was also hoped ultimately that the party might penetrate individual streets and blocks within every ward of every constituency. Street leaders would be responsible to ward leaders who in turn would look to their district leader – a system of almost infinite elasticity, it was argued, as well as the basis of perfect electoral machinery.[40]

It was admitted that in 1934 the party had been over-confident, believing in the misconception that enthusiasm was sufficient to lead to power. The reforms of 1935 were a recognition that whilst the constitution survived, the road to power lay through the ballot box. The vehicle with which this road could be most quickly traversed was the effective political machine. It was this which Mosley attempted to create, without splitting his movement irreconcilably. Up to a point he succeeded, or at least he laid the foundations for success, and his analysis that '. . . the Movement of 1936 is . . . a very different affair from the loose, inchoate and formless association of 1933 . . .',[41] had a considerable degree of validity. The decentralisation within the BUF from 1935 onwards should not, however, be construed as an easing of the authority which emanated from National Headquarters. In the past the national leadership had removed local officials whom it deemed incompetent, and even whole branches had been summarily expelled. This degree of authority was not reduced as a result of decentralisation. National Headquarters ensured that it possessed a very clear picture of the BUF development throughout the country. The facilities existed not only to monitor the numbers and recruiting patterns of any area, but also to receive detailed reports on every meeting by its organiser and speakers, and a plethora of information concerning local finances including bank balances, existing debts and assets, and a detailed breakdown of expenditure.[42]

From 1935 onwards electoral preparations were seriously under way. Canvassing was begun, district electoral funds were established, and the first candidates were announced. At the end of 1936 Mosley confidently predicted that the BUF would win a parliamentary majority at the next but one general election.[43] He refused to be daunted by the British electoral system. Whilst acknowledging that it impeded new parties in their infancy, he drew solace from the belief that, once a breakthrough had been secured, then complete victory could quickly follow, for it was '. . . possible in Great Britain to obtain a clear majority in parliament long before you obtain a clear majority of votes at a general election'.[44] In order to capitalise upon this Mosley aimed at building a machine based upon his own pre-1931 election-winning formula. This 'ideal method' involved having one individual responsible for a few streets of every ward where they could call upon and become known to the residents.[45] It was the model responsible for the decentralisation apparent within the BUF from 1935 onwards.

Attempts to judge the BUF's efficiency as an electoral force are rendered difficult by the party's failure to contest a general election. In October 1935 it was announced that no BUF candidates would be standing in the forthcoming nation-wide elections. The decision was inescapable, for the BUF was not yet ready for electoral combat. Instead, Mosley asked for a three-week campaign around the slogan 'Fascism next time', and an acceleration of the construction of electoral machinery in all areas.[46]

The first real electoral test faced by the BUF came eighteen months later. The venue was east London. The occasion was the London County Council elections of March 1937. Two candidates were announced for each of the three constituencies of Bethnal Green (North-East), Shoreditch, and Stepney (Limehouse), in an effort to test the instrument forged for use at the next general election. The results were hailed as a triumph as the BUF polled an average of almost eighteen per cent of the total votes cast, and in Bethnal Green achieved over twenty-three per cent and beat the Liberals into third place. Labour held all three constituencies comfortably, although in two cases with a reduced vote. Critics were reminded that the BUF poll was achieved in spite of the large number of Jews living in the contested constituencies, a hostile press and that in percentage terms it compared favourably to the early electoral adventures of Mussolini and Hitler (although these were at national rather than municipal level). Therefore it was hailed as '. . . far and away the best result in any first fight of any Fascist or National Socialist Movement in the world'.[47]

Severe economies, and the realisation that local elections used resources without offering any prospect of power or prestige, even in the event of victory, meant that the party put little effort into subsequent local campaigns. Although the East-End vote held up, the results elsewhere were often very poor as candidates were expected to finance their individual campaigns unaided. In June 1937, it had been announced that the party's electoral resources were to be used only in contesting parliamentary by-elections which occurred in winnable areas. Suitable seats were not immediately forthcoming but Mosley remained unperturbed, for he predicted confidently that there would be a general election in 1939, and under such circumstances the BUF could choose those constituencies which it considered most receptive to fascism. This calculation was upset by the outbreak of war in September 1939. In desperation the BUF announced that it would stand candidates in all vacant constituencies as a means of offering the British people the chance to register a vote for peace.[48] Less altruistically this decision was also calculated to profit from the pact amongst the major political parties, compacted in the spirit of wartime co-operation, not to contest any seats held by opponents which might fall vacant. It was a miscalculation, for Labour voters in Tory constituencies were unlikely to switch their votes to such a traditional enemy as the BUF. Similarly, Tories in Labour constituencies would be more likely to abstain than to vote for a 'peace party', especially one so closely identified with the national enemy. The BUF's decision should not be criticised in such political terms, however, but rather it should be seen as the final desperate throw of a party so smeared with German Nazism that unless the war was ended promptly it faced complete and imminent annihilation.

In February 1940, under extremely unfavourable conditions, the BUF contested its first parliamentary by-election in the Labour stronghold of Silvertown won by Keir Hardie fifty years earlier. Lacking any organisation in the constituency, and unable to refute convincingly the charge that a vote for British fascism was a vote for Hitler, the result was a huge defeat. A total Labour vote of over 13,000 swamped the BUF which polled only 151 votes and had the added humiliation of finishing third, behind Harry Pollit and the Communist Party.[49] Two further efforts were made in the safe Tory seats of Leeds, North East, and Middleton and Prestwich in March and May respectively. As at Silvertown, the BUF made no impact and in each case its candidate forfeited his deposit.[50] The day after the announcement of the Middleton and Prestwich result Mosley and other leading fascists were arrested and detained. Thus an end was brought to almost a decade of struggle by the BUF to establish itself as a recognised force within British politics. Mosley's career outside the political establishment, which had begun with a decisive electoral repudiation, now ended in the same manner.

As already suggested, the BUF's membership was subject to fluctuations. Mosley admitted this but insisted that the overall trend from 1932 to 1939 was that of a steady increase.[51] Estimates of total membership figures vary greatly. Extravagant claims made by the BUF itself and by its opponents should be treated with an equal degree of caution. This applies to one of Mosley's rare pronouncements upon the subject in November 1936, when he told the German magazine *Lokelanzeiger* that the BUF was 500,000 strong.[52] In parliament in 1934 estimates ranged from 200,000 to 250,000, but were based only on hearsay.[53] Estimates for the same period by anti-fascists tended to be less high, and in May 1934 John Strachey suggested a membership figure of 17,500 and a further 100,000 'looser contacts'.[54] This was something of an exception in that it was claimed to have been computed accurately on the basis of information and internal documents sold by ex-members. But the most striking feature of contemporary membership estimates is the paucity of evidence with which they were supported. The result was often that they were wildly inaccurate.[55] There is, however, a degree of consensus in the estimates arising from those ex-members of the party who served at National Headquarters. In 1960 Robert Forgan claimed that by the autumn of 1934 BUF membership was between five and ten thousand. Four years later, Chesterton claimed, the membership of the party stood at 18,000, of whom 15,000 were inactive.[56] Another ex-member, who worked at National Headquarters throughout the 1930s, remembered that membership figures were '. . . an open secret', and that at its peak in the mid-1930s the party had around 16,000 members most of whom were active.[57] These estimates of ex-members were given further credibility in view of the Home Secretary's 1943 memorandum which estimated a paid-up membership of 8,000–10,000 at the time of the BUF's suppression.[58]

Fascism's position in the centre of the political spectrum enabled it to appeal to left and right, radical and reactionary, with equal candour. Hence, as suggested in the previous chapter, there were attempts to portray fascism as a workers' movement utterly opposed to the selfish individualism of unbridled capitalism. Equally there were appeals to the middle class in general, and in particular to the *petit bourgeoisie* whom, it was argued, were the twentieth-century equivalent to those nine-teenth-century workers who became the victims of emerging capitalism. The *petit bourgeoisie* represented '. . . a new section of the community being dispossessed this time from their shops and small businesses and being driven into the ranks of the "wage slaves" '.[59]

The BUF did not confine itself to appeals only to general class interests. It also tried to exploit the aspirations and grievances of parti-cular occupational groups and geographical areas in order to relate general fascist policy to specific local interests. Inevitably many of the occupations concentrated upon were firmly within the sphere of the *petit bourgeoisie*. Shopkeepers were offered control over the retail trade through their own corporation, and were warned that if fascism failed then the 'chain-store octopus' would bankrupt them, take over their businesses and transform them into poorly-paid employees.[60] In the autumn of 1938, a British Union Traders Group was established, although it failed to make any significant impact upon those to whom it was designed to appeal. Taxi-drivers were also singled out for special attention, as were clerks, whom it was claimed should be unionised and protected by special legislation from unscrupulous employers in the professions.[61] The 'small man', the term most frequently employed by the BUF to refer to those of *petit-bourgeois* stock, was portrayed as the very personification of the values of thrift, stability, energy and patrio-tism with which the British Empire had been built. In addition to the urban *petit-bourgeois* the BUF wooed also the small farmer, who was assured that fascist policy in regard to food and land would lead to a more

and those who believed in the achievement of social and economic harmony through impartially enforced class collaboration. The Birmingham sample revealed that the two main features given as the reason for joining were unemployment and patriotism. Although several considered both to be important, in general those members defined as working-class emphasised unemployment, whilst those from the middle class stressed patriotism.[72] It would be incorrect to read too much into these results because of the minute size of the sample of fascists interviewed. A similar impression, however, emerges from Rawnsley's study of the north of England. Here branches included prominent Tory businessmen, representatives from privileged local families, and an ex-Conservative Party agent as the Northern Senior Political Organiser; and yet contained simultaneously considerable numbers of textile workers motivated by the fear of unemployment, and several ex-communists.[73]

This dichotomy was also visible amongst the leadership of the party. Examples of those who tended to stress the socialist side of fascism included Alexander Raven Thomson, Wilfred Risdon, and possibly John Beckett and W. J. Leaper. With the exception of Thomson, who had been a member of the Communist Party, all of these prominent fascists had belonged to the Independent Labour Party, and Beckett, like Mosley, had been a Labour MP. The BUF, claimed Risdon, was '. . . the custodian of the ideals of the early Socialist pioneers',[74] and Mosley was the twentieth-century equivalent of Robert Owen. The Labour Party, it was argued, by accepting the twin capitalist values of materialism and internationalism, had betrayed its socialist supporters. Thomson shared this opinion believing Mosley to be the leader of a struggle for British socialism against the plutocratic regime of British capitalism. Even in retrospect, Thomson considered Mosley a socialist and claimed that fascism was a movement of the left, emerging not from the Marxist wing but from the tradition of syndicalist socialism.[75] Amongst the reactionaries in the leadership one finds characters such as Neil Francis-Hawkins, William Joyce, Captain Robert Gordon Canning, and Major-General J. F. C. Fuller. Both Hawkins and Joyce had been members of the ultra-reactionary British Fascists before joining the BUF, and Canning and Fuller had served long careers in the army. Hawkins it was who insisted upon military-type discipline within the party, whilst Canning, Fuller and Joyce neglected those aspects of fascism which promised a fairer distribution of the nation's wealth, in favour of railing against Jews, communists, democrats, and those who failed to take the necessary precautions to ensure the perpetuation of the British empire and Christian church.[76]

One must guard against making too much of such differences. Nevertheless it is apparent that members of these two groups received political apprenticeships which were as radically different as the features within fascist ideology which they subsequently found most attractive. Furthermore their concentration upon either the radical or reactionary side of fascism, to the virtual exclusion of the other, marked them aside from genuine fascists. They differed from those such as Mosley for whom fascism was neither a form of applied socialism within a national context, nor a disguised, reactionary dictatorship of the right, but was a doctrine of the centre through which class conflict could be reconciled by enforced class collaboration.

The rise of anti-Semitism as an integral part of BUF policy further confused these divisions. Committed anti-Semites from the left, right and centre, were united by their hatred of Jews. Indeed anti-Semitism was at the root of the BUF's only significant split, when in the spring of 1937 Joyce and Beckett left the party and founded the National Socialist League. Only a handful of BUF members defected to the new movement, but it was nevertheless a significant break. Other prominent members had resigned from the movement in the past,[77] but never before had they denounced Mosley publicly and proceeded to form a rival organisation. The split first became evident when Joyce and Beckett discovered that their salaries were amongst the casualties of Mosley's draconian cost-cutting drive of March 1937. They resigned and promptly proceeded to direct the full force of their not inconsiderable venom upon Mosley who was portrayed as an inaccessible autocrat, surrounded by flattering minions. Intrigue, corruption, the mishandling of relations with the provinces, and '. . . heel-clicking and petty militarism . . .', it was alleged, had conspired to leave the party moribund.[78] The rival National Socialist League was formed as a loose federation of local groups pre-sided over by a collective leadership with the specific intention of avoiding any repetition of these traits.

The decision to withdraw the salaries of Beckett and Joyce was not motivated solely by a desire to cut costs. Its roots lay in a revision of the party's attitude to anti-Semitism. The first hint of this was picked up by the police in the summer of 1936 when the confidential monthly report of anti-Semitic activities included the information that the BUF had '. . . given a definite warning to its speakers to refrain from attacking Jews at public meetings, it is being emphasised that arrests of its members for Jew-baiting is likely to do the Fascist movement . . . more harm than good'. The report continued with the claim that '. . . influential section of the headquarters of the BUF is opposed to this policy which they think will be regarded as a retreat and will be detrimental to party prestige, morale and discipline'.[79] Joyce was a leading figure amongst this 'influential section' and expressed his views vociferously, in his capacity as Director of Propaganda, to a meeting of the party's principal speakers in September 1936. He refused to sanction any general retreat in the BUF's attitude to Jews in the face of pressure from the authorities.

Fascist speakers, he claimed, should be prepared to go to prison for their beliefs, for he calculated that any programme of widespread arrests would increase the level of anti-Semitism in the country at large.[80]

This dispute became public at the beginning of October when Mosley contributed a front-page article to *Blackshirt* forbidding unchecked racial anti-Semitism which, he argued, made the Jews appear only '. . . as a wronged and persecuted people'. Six months later, influenced by the limited success of the LCC election results and by clear indications that the economic recovery was faltering, Mosley decided to retreat still further in the party's attitude towards the Jews. With a new slump approaching he considered it vital that no policy feature should be allowed to obscure the economic core of fascist corporatism. To this end Beckett and Joyce were sacrificed. Two days after their dismissal *Action* summarised the BUF's attitude to Jews since 1932, concluding with the reminder that

> . . . this task of repelling Jewry is a small and incidental feature of the British Union Campaign. Our task is to build a prosperous Greater Britain. From that task we shall neither deviate nor allow ourselves to be driven; and the Jews are only important in so far as they stand between us and our objective and will not be allowed to distract us from the great ends to which Mosley has called us.[81]

The role of intellectuals within the party is also of interest. As stated in the previous chapter the BUF tended to regard them with a range of emotions from suspicion to hostility. It is hardly surprising, therefore, that in the early days of its existence the party was bereft of intellectual support, although attempts were made to exploit Mosley's earlier relationship with Keynes, whom, it was claimed, had accepted the economics of fascism but not its political implications. Amongst the actual membership of the party only Raven Thomson had any claim to recognised intellectual status, and even in his case, Mosley's assertion that he was '. . . one of the leading intellectuals of his time',[82] is highly contentious. Also associated loosely with the movement in its early days were Aldous Huxley, Somerset Maugham, and George Bernard Shaw, although all were attracted by their admiration of Mosley himself, rather than any great regard for the party's fascist programme.[83]

Tentative steps were taken to try and improve this situation with the establishment of the Federation of British University Fascist Associations designed to co-ordinate the activities of fascist societies in universities all over the country. In the same vein was the January Club, which held regular dinners and was in theory a forum for general discussion, although in practice its members were mostly sympathetic to fascism.[84] The most significant attempt to curry favour with British intellectuals came in 1935 with the foundation of the periodical *Fascist Quarterly* which provided a forum for some of fascism's more theoretical aspects until 1940. Extravagant claims were made by the BUF as to the number of past British intellectuals who had been unrecognised early fascists. These claims encompassed political philosophers such as William Morris and Thomas Carlyle, as well as literary figures such as Wordsworth and Robert Burns, and were based on less than convincing evidence. But even after 1935 the number of intellectuals prepared to support openly the BUF's cause remained very low. Henry Williamson was a member of the party and made several literary contributions to *Action* in its later years. The *Quarterly* included poems by Roy Campbell, rambling and unreadable articles by Ezra Pound, and contributions from Wyndham Lewis, including a recognition that most British intellectuals sympathised with the left, and a plea for fascist toleration of such recalcitrance.[85]

This lack of support from the British intellectual establishment is explicable in terms of the party's overt anti-intellectualism which, even after 1935, remained as a clearly visible component of fascist propaganda. Whereas Marxism offered the intellectual an important role in the construction of a new rationally inspired civilisation, the BUF promised Oxford Dons '. . . a concentration camp . . . [to] . . . teach the dignity of true labour'.[86] Such sentiments, combined with the BUF's insistent emphasis upon action and self-abnegation, had the effect of repelling even those few intellectuals of the right who might otherwise have been sympathetic to the fascist cause in Britain.[87]

Similarly the BUF's anti-feminism was illustrated by the role played by women within the party. The Women's Section of the party was kept strictly segregated although it worked beside male branches. It had its own headquarters in Lower Grosvenor Place where first-aid courses and speaking classes were arranged. Recreational facilities were also available as the National Headquarters in Chelsea was rarely open to women. The Women's Section received a considerable boost in its prestige as the BUF began building election machinery because of Mosley's personal belief that at constituency level, '. . . women were absolutely invaluable in election winning, because of their persuasive abilities and more flexible daytime hours of work'.[88] Therefore, women were expected to '. . . undertake what is essentially *their* work for the Movement – that of canvassing . . . to call at the houses regularly, distributing free literature, notifying the householders of meetings in their district, and answering questions put to them'.[89] The Women's Section was reorganised along with the rest of the party on the basis of individual districts. It remained separate from the male side of the district's organisation, and although they ran parallel to each other, the two structures only coincided in that they had common officers amongst the district's leadership). They had the same three categories of membership, although at the lowest level members were divided into teams of eight plus a leader rather than the male units of five. Prominent amongst the female section were several important ex-members of the Women's Social and Political Union such as Norah Elam. Having achieved the vote for some middle-class women Emily and Christabel Pankhurst had retired genteely from the political fray leaving loyal followers like Elam longing once more to feel a part of a highly disciplined organisation which demanded complete loyalty, unquestioning obedience, and heroic self-sacrifice in the uneven struggle against the chosen enemy. Inspired by the naïve belief that communism was '. . . the negation of the natural instincts of womanhood . . . [and] . . . of every principle and practice which women value and require',[90] women like Elam replaced Pankhurst with Mosley, suffrage with the corporate state, and found in the BUF the perfect substitute for the WSPU.

Although women were expected to shoulder a disproportionate share of canvassing and secretarial work, the party maintained vigorously that women members were the equals of their male colleagues.[91] The argument used to sustain this assertion in response to overwhelming evidence to the contrary, was rooted in the notion of each sex having its own sphere, the bankruptcy of which was exposed in the previous chapter. At its most basic the argument became simply a tautological nonsense designed to perpetuate existing sexual discrimination by ensuring that those women not consigned to domesticity were confined to unrewarding and repetitive occupations, on the basis that these represented, or had become identified as, the 'female sphere'. Also, when it came to internal promotion, it appears that some fascists were more equal than others, and that the source of inequality was often gender. Despite founding the Halifax branch of the BUF, and being its most energetic participant, Nellie Driver was only appointed to the rank of women's district leader; the post of overall district leader was open only to men. She continued as the foremost member of the branch and succeeded in raising its membership to around 100,[92] but remained officially in a position of subordination to the male district leader.

The other primary purpose of the BUF's female membership was to assist in the stewarding of meetings. Mosley's own concepts of male chivalry, together with a rare example of his accurate appreciation of what would be considered acceptable by the public, combined to make him anxious to avoid the spectacle of female interrupters being ejected from his meetings by male blackshirts. Thus that which was forbidden to male fascists became automatically another sphere for female members. It was for this purpose that women stewards were at Olympia for the notoriously violent Mosley meeting of June 1934. On this occasion eyewitnesses testified to the brutality with which several women protesters were ejected. Nor were all handed over to womem stewards. Separate and often corroborating accounts described how women were assaulted and carried sometimes screaming from the arena by groups of male stewards, as well as by female fascists. On several occasions humiliation was added to violence as women were partially stripped of clothing during the ejection procedure. One unfortunate heckler was attacked initially by male stewards and was then '. . . thrown to the women Blackshirts, who hit her and clawed her as she sagged limply on the ground. They picked her up, and, with her clothes apparently torn from her, naked from the hips, they carried her screaming through the audience'.[93]

In concluding this chapter it is necessary to probe the murky area of BUF finances. No other aspect of the party has been shrouded in such mystery and secrecy, or has been the subject of such conjecture and suspicion as the question, 'how was it all paid for?'. The primary problems in examining the BUF's financial apparatus result from the elaborately constructed facades behind which the party's real financial mechanisms were obscured. Such limited liability 'front' companies were vital as, in the event of a successful legal action against the party, they could simply be wound up.

The bulk of the BUF's funds, claimed Mosley, were derived from within the party itself and consisted of subscriptions, literature sales, and canteen proceeds. Large meetings were usually self-supporting through the sale of tickets and the collection of donations, it was maintained, and all branches were expected to be financially self-sufficient with some of the wealthier areas even being taxed to help meet the high expenditure incurred by National Headquarters.[94] Other methods of meeting the high expenditure of National Headquarters consisted of appeals for donations to readers of the fascist press, and the siphoning off of some of the leader's personal fortune. This was particularly true of the later years, when Mosley was called upon to provide an increasing amount of the party's income. In retrospect he estimated that his total contribution to the BUF was less than £100,000.[95]

Also important were those donations received from some of the BUF's wealthy patrons. These extreme conservatives included Lord Rothermere, and probably also Sir E. A. Hamilton, Bt., Baron Tollemache, and that most eccentric of right-wing benefactors, Lady Houston.[96] On the whole, however, such contributions were small in number, as were those received from large business enterprises. Those large concerns alleged to have connections with the BUF included Courtaulds, Sanders-Roe and Imperial Chemical Industries, as well as the numerous enterprises of Lord Inchape and William Morris.[97] The evidence to support such charges, where it exists at all, is fragile.

Undoubtedly the most regular of all of BUF contributors was an anonymous host of small capitalists attracted by the belief that Mosley's economic programme would produce more stable conditions in which to operate, or by the realisation that under fascism they would be secure, beyond the reach of the grasping socialists who wished to dispossess them of their life's work. Throughout the 1930s Mosley maintained contact with exactly this type of producer, by his appearance as an invited guest at a vast number of lunches, dinners and similar elite gatherings of local businessmen. In some areas the links between businessmen and the party were so strong that a businessmen's section was established, affiliated to the local branch.[98] Elsewhere the relationship was less formal but equally effective. One ex-member of the Nelson branch remembered that some of the party's sympathisers were local Tory businessmen, whilst the former district leader of Hull, who as a present area official of the National Chamber of Trade frequently attends national meetings in that capacity, considers them '. . . like going to a B.U.F. reunion'.[99] Contributors of this type ranged in size from the larger regional company, to the very small local firm. These, admitted Mosley, were the saviours of National Headquarters which '. . . had a perpetual struggle to find money . . . it was always an anxiety'.[100] The manner in which the contributions were solicited was described by an ex-member who worked for many years as a fund raiser at the party's national headquarters:

> Normally we did not approach people unless they had written to H.Q., and then if they seemed of some importance, socially, financially etc., I would make a personal follow-up. Nine times out of ten it was a waste of time . . . very rarely we would approach a person who Mosley had reason to believe might put his hand in his pockets . . . Mosley did not have any really wealthy backers, it was sizeable small fry stuff, if I can put it that way.[101]

The most sensitive aspect of the party's finances concerned its receipt of contributions from foreign governments. By the end of 1935 the authorities were convinced that the BUF was being paid a monthly sum of around £3,000 by Mussolini in return for justifying the Italian invasion of Abyssinia to the British public.[102] Almost a year later this charge was first made public when the Home Secretary informed parliament that both communist and fascist funds had been supplemented from abroad.[103] Mosley denied the charge and challenged Sir John Simon to produce evidence to substantiate the claim. None was forthcoming.

Only after the party's suppression in 1940 did the authorities uncover a secret bank account in the names of several BUF members including W. E. D. Allen. Between July 1933 when the account was opened and May 1937 when it became dormant a total of over £224,000 passed through it. 'A large proportion' of the deposits were found to have been in bundles of foreign currencies such as French and Swiss francs, US dollars and German Reichmarks. Furthermore, although the deposits were largely irregular, during the first nine months of 1935 (the period of the Abyssinian crisis) the payments had been regular monthly amounts of £4,000–£5,000.[104]

During his interrogation Mosley claimed ignorance of the party's financial arrangements. When confronted with details of the bank account he suggested that it was Allen's business account which he admitted had contained some BUF funds. The foreign currency, he claimed, was a means whereby British businessmen could contribute to the party with the degree of secrecy necessary to avoid victimisation by powerful Jewish interests. As such benefactors were either anonymous or had been promised anonymity by the party, Mosley was unable to substantiate this claim.[105]

The conclusion of the Advisory Committee (which questioned Mosley closely over the issue) was that the foreign currencies were from Italy but that it was impossible to prove this contention conclusively.[106] The Home Secretary accepted this qualification as the inevitable result of the '. . . elaborate steps . . . taken to shroud the financial arrangements of the British Union in mystery'.[107]

That the government should have known of the foreign payments at least five years before the discovery of the secret bank account is indicative of the extent to which its agents had penetrated the party. A huge range of Special Branch reports to the Home Office (released to the public only in 1981) confirm this in the extent of the detailed information which they provide concerning internal party matters. Details of meetings, confidential circulars, information on individual branches, structural changes at headquarters, all were reported back to the Home Office. It was even known that Mosley and Allen had quarrelled over an outstanding debt and that Allen had threatened '. . . the disclosure to the authorities all he knew about the sources of the movement's funds' unless Mosley paid him the amount outstanding. The latter had accused him of blackmail but had nevertheless paid up.[108] The full extent of the government's intelligence concerning the movement is unknown because several important MI5 files remain closed to the public. It has been suggested, however, that Allen himself supplied some information to MI5 concerning internal party matters.[109]

For more than forty years Mosley denied the foreign subsidy charge, but always with the proviso that 'if we had had money from abroad it would not have worried me at all. If people of the same opinion . . . in a foreign country like to give you money there is no earthly reason why they should not . . .'. It was a smear by his opponents, he claimed, a set of 'wild allegations' which could not be taken seriously because of a complete lack of evidence. 'Where is your evidence?' he demanded of them, secure in the knowledge that no clear proof had ever been available to incriminate him. It was only after his death that documentary evidence was unearthed by historian David Irving in the

Italian archives. Letters between Count Grandi (the Italian ambassador in London) and Mussolini between August 1933 and January 1934 record the payment of £40,000 in mixed currencies into BUF coffers.[110] It is almost certain, therefore, that later foreign currency payments were from the same source. The passing of the Abyssinian crisis, the increasing reorientation of the party towards Berlin, the party's lack of obvious progress, and the increasing rivalry between Mosley and Grandi for the affections of Lady Alexander Metcalfe (Mosley's sister-in-law),[111] all explain why the payments ceased in 1937. This in turn explains the economies which were effected within the movement in 1937, as well as Mosley's frequent claim that 'for a considerable period before the war all contributions had been of British origin'.[112]

The existence of Italian subsidies, however, should not obscure the essentially British nature of the BUF. Both before and after the war MPs received governmental announcements concerning foreign payments without question. They wanted to believe in the concept of a British fascist party financed and controlled by a hostile nation. They wanted to believe that the BUF was an instrument of foreign fascist aggression and subversion, for it is was accepted as a genuine British movement, then its very growth and the conditions which inspired it, were hall-marks of their own failure. A failure not only of the conservative National Government to deal with the problems of inter-war Britain, but also a failure of the Labour Party to inspire belief in a socialist alterna-tive. Their readiness to believe it amounted to a form of intellectual and moral cowardice. This is not a perspective which should be perpetuated for it fetters any real appreciation of the nature of fascism in Britain. However much Italian money the BUF received, throughout its life it remained a British movement. Although at times its policy or style were influenced by fascist movements abroad, the BUF developed in response to the problems of British capitalist society.

It was precisely such sentiments which drove Mosley to deny the foreign links of his party. Despite his stubborn mendacity perhaps the final words upon the subject should rest with him in a statement he made a few months before his death. After vigourously denying the charge, claiming that even if true it was harmless, and demanding hard evidence (as yet unobtainable), he paused and said with a smile, 'none of that really matters much when you come to think of it, but it interested some people . . .'.[113]

NOTES

1   O. Mosley, *My Life,* Nelson, London 1970, p. 303. See also O. Mosley, *Fascism in Britain,* BUF Publications Ltd, London 1934?, pp. 9–10.
2   For an account of these functions see respectively: *The Times,* 22 February 1933, p. 12; *Manchester Guardian,* 25 February 1933, p. 8 and 16

March, p. 10.

3   Mosley, *Fascism in Britain,* p. 10.

4   O. Mosley, *The Greater Britain,* BUF, London 1932, pp. 152–3.

5   *Daily Telegraph,* 30 August 1933, as quoted by National Council of Labour, *Fascism: the Enemy of the People,* National Council of Labour, London 1934, p. 5.

6   Mosley, *op. cit.,* p. 301.

7   The black shirt was not compulsory amongst the ordinary rank and file of the BUF: Mosley, *Fascism in Britain,* p. 10; *op. cit.,* p. 302.

8   *Blackshirt,* 1 June 1934, p. 9.

9   *The Times,* 5 February 1936, p. 7. See also Mosley, *op. cit.,* p. 352. For an account of the meeting itself see *Manchester Guardian,* 13 March 1933, p. 9. Even in the days of the New Party, Mosley had admitted that stewards sometimes carried truncheons. *The Times,* 11 November 1931, p. 6.

10   *The Times,* 16 March 1933, p. 16.

11   C. M. Dolan, an ex-member, claimed to have been issued with a piece of hose, corked at either end and filled with lead shot. Another ex-member alleged that in the Reading branch rubber tubbing and lead piping had been used as batons. *The Times,* 6 February 1934, p. 4. See also Dolan, *The Blackshirt Racket: Mosley Exposed,* 1934?, p. 13. The idea of BUF recruits receiving truncheons is given further credence by David Pryce-Jones's assertion that upon enlisting in the women's section Unity Mitford was told that she would receive her truncheon the following day. D. Pryce-Jones, *Unity Mitford – A Quest,* W. H. Allen & Co. Ltd, London 1981, p. 92. Several of Rawnsley's sample of northern fascists admitted the use of weapons: K. Lunn & R. C. Thurlow (eds.), *British Fascism,* Croom Helm, London 1980, p. 163.

12   The armoured cars proved to be vans with wire over their windows, used to transport members of the defence force. The fascist flying corps appears to have existed more in the minds of anti-fascists than in reality although there was an air rally held under the auspices of the BUF in May 1934 in Gloucester, which was attended by 250 fascists and members of the public, and included five aircraft. *HC Debs,* 285, 31 January 1934, c. 360 – 1; 290, 11 June 1934, c. 1341–8; and 290, 14 June 1934, c. 1875–6.

13   O. Mosley, interview with author, 24 June 1980.

14   Nicolson Diaries, MS, 11 October 1933.

15   *Blackshirt,* 1 June, 1934, p. 8.

16   On one occasion fifty fascists occupied and fortified a farm near Wortham in Suffolk for sixteen days, to prevent the confiscation of farm equipment in lieu of unpaid debts. Nineteen were arrested eventually and bound over. *Fascist Week,* 30 March – 5 April 1934, p. 5.

17   The best indicators of BUF development between October 1932 and the summer of 1934 are to be found in the party's own progress reports, and in the result of a questionnaire dispatched by the Labour Party headquarters to all Divisional Labour Parties and Industrial Trades Councils, in June 1934, asking for information on fascist activities in local areas. *Blackshirt,* 1 June 1934, p. 8. See also report on replies to Fascist Questionnaire, LP/FAS/34/1, pp. 1–8, Labour Party Library.

18   It is widely accepted that the BUF's membership reached a peak in the spring and early summer of 1934. This view is confirmed by the few local studies of membership in individual branches and areas, the best of which is undoubtedly Stuart Rawnsley's excellent study of BUF membership in North-West England: S. Rawnsley, as found in Lunn & Thurlow (eds.), *op. cit.,* pp. 150–65. Whether this peak represents the highest membership figures ever achieved by the BUF is, of course, another matter.

19   *Daily Mail,* 19 January 1934, leader.

20 *Ibid.*, 25 January 1934, p. 10.
21 *Ibid.*, 20 January 1934, leader; see also 22 January, p. 13.
22 *Ibid.*, 2 May 1934, p. 12.
23 *Ibid.*, 15 January 1934, leader. The BUF was invariably referred to as 'The Blackshirts', or the 'British Blackshirt Movement'. Entire articles were written about the party in which the term 'fascist' never appeared. See *Sunday Pictorial*, 22 April 1934, p. 10; or *Daily Mail*, 22 January 1934, p. 13.
24 PRO 30/69/1/400, Ramsay MacDonald Papers: Home Office memorandum, J. Gilmour to R. MacDonald, 1 February 1934, as quoted by G. C. Lebzelter, *Political Anti-Semitism in England 1918–1939*, Macmillan Press Ltd, London 1978, p. 114.
25 *News Chronicle*, 20 January 1934, as reported in Labour Research Department, *Who Backs Mosley? Fascist Promise and Fascist Performance*, Labour Research Department, London 1934, p. 30.
26 *Daily Mail*, 19 July 1934, pp. 12–13.
27 *Fascist Week*, 4–10 May 1934, p. 1., and leader.
28 Hamm, interview, 14 April 1980.
29 A. K. Chesterton, *Oswald Mosley, Portrait of a leader*, Action Press, London 1937, p. 128.
30 Mosley, interview, 24 June 1980.
31 *Blackshirt*, 18 January 1935, p. 1. In October this idea of 'conspicuous service' was more closely defined. A member who could sell over 320 copies of *Blackshirt* in four weeks was to receive either a black shirt or a belt; selling 400 in five weeks would entitle him to a pair of trousers; 720 in nine weeks to a uniform mackintosh; and 800 in ten weeks to either a pair of breeches or a uniform greatcoat. *Blackshirt*, 11 October 1935, p. 1.
32 Those who gave two nights were entitled to wear the black shirt, whilst those who gave five nights per week could wear the newly introduced Nazi-style uniform complete with belt, greatcoat, and jackboots. *Ibid.*, 18 January 1935, p. 2.
33 *Ibid.*, 18 January 1935, p. 1. The number of sections constituting a company was later increased from three to five. *British Union Constitution and Rules,* BUF, London 1936, p. 8.
34 *Blackshirt*, 24 May 1935, p. 2.
35 *Ibid.*
36 Under the BUF constitution published in 1936 it was laid down that First Division members give two nights' service per week, and Second Division one night per month. The subscription rates were initially set as 1*s.* per month for those in employment, and 4*d* for the unemployed. *Blackshirt*, 24 May 1935, p. 2. Under the 1936 constitution, however, this sum was revised in regard to Third Division members, whose weekly subscription was assessed at 1*d* regardless of employment status. *British Union Constitution and Rules*, pp. 7, 43.
37 *Blackshirt*, 24 May 1935, p. 2.
38 At the time of its suppression, the BUF was divided into 200 geographical districts, each with a district leader. CAB 66/35, WP (43) 148, Memorandum, H. Morrison, Home Secretary, 14 April 1943.
39 It was suggested that eventually the northern and southern editions would be further subdivided to correspond with individual counties, and eventually to towns and districts. *Southern Blackshirt,* November 1938, p. 4.
40 *Blackshirt*, April 1938, p. 1.
41 *Ibid.*, 19 September 1936, p. 7.
42 *British Union Constitution and Rules,* Appendices, pp. 50–92. See also Chesterton *op. cit.*, pp. 120–1.

43 Mosley, interview given to *Berliner Lokal Anzeiger,* which appeared in the *Daily Telegraph,* 24 November 1936, as quoted by *The Liberal Magazine,* XLIV, 1936, p. 359.

44 *Action,* 13 March 1937, p. 9.

45 Mosley, interview, 24 June 1980.

46 *Blackshirt,* 25 October 1935, pp. 1–2. See also *The Times,* 28 October 1935, p. 9.

47 *Action,* 13 March 1937, p. 9. See also *Blackshirt,* 6 March 1937, p. 1.

48 *Action,* 15 February 1940, p. 1. See also 31 December 1938, p. 1.

49 *Ibid.,* 29 February 1940, p. 1; *BUQ,* IV, 1, spring 1940, 'Notes on the quarter', pp. 16–17. See also *The Times,* 24 February 1940, p. 6.

50 *Action,* 21 March 1940, p. 4; *The Times,* 15 March 1940, p. 8; 23 May, p. 3; 24 May, p. 3.

51 Mosley, *op. cit.,* p. 311.

52 *Manchester Guardian,* 23 November 1936, p. 12.

53 *HC Deb.,* 289, 16 May 1934, *c.* 1765–72; 290, 14 June 1934, *c.* 2301–4.

54 J. Strachey, 'Fascism in Great Britain', *New Republic* LXXVIII, 2 May 1934, p. 331.

55 One example of this is apparent in the Paddington South District Labour Party's 1934 estimate of the local BUF branch membership as being 3,000; Labour Party Questionnaire LP/FAS/34/1, p. 1. The BUF itself, never keen on self-denigration, claimed only just over 100 members for the same branch: *West London Regional Bulletin,* 1934, p. 5. Only four or five months separated the estimates.

56 C. Cross, *The Fascists in Britain,* Barrie & Rockcliffe, London 1961, p. 131.

57 'J.G.', correspondence with author, May 1981.

58 CAB 66/35 WP (43), Memorandum by Home Secretary, H. Morrison, 14 April 1943. This estimate was based on documents seized by the authorities at the time of the BUF's suppression. In July 1940 the Home Secretary announced that around 9,000 members had paid their last annual subscription to the BUF but a week earlier he had admitted that although the documents seized provided '. . . a nominal list of members', there were doubts as to what degree it was an accurate reflection of the party in 1939. *HC Deb,* 363, 18 July 1940, *c.* 386–7; 25 July 1940, *c.* 966.

59 W. Risdon, 'The heritage of national socialism', *BUQ,* I, 3, July–September 1937, p. 29.

60 *Blackshirt,* 11 April 1936, p. 2; F. D. Hill, '*Gainst Trust and Monopoly,* Abbey Supplies, London n.d., pp. 2–3. See also P. Heyward, *Menace of the Chain Stores,* Greater Britain Publications, London n.d.; *Shopkeepers at war 'gainst war and monopoly,* Abbey Supplies, London n.d.

61 In the summer of 1938 Mosley addressed 1,000 taxi-drivers in London: *Blackshirt,* July 1938, p. 4. For the BUF's attitude to clerks, see *Action,* 21 August 1937, p. 3, and 5 March 1935, p. 6.

62 *Daily Mail,* 15 February 1934, p. 8. For a full statement of BUF agricultural policy see J. Jenks, *The Land and the People,* Greater Britain Publications, London n.d.

63 *Blackshirt,* February 1933, p. 4.

64 *Ibid.,* 18 July 1936, p. 3, and 28 November 1936, p. 7.

65 *Yorkshire Betrayed: British Union Textile Policy (wool),* Abbey Supplies, London 1938?, p. 6.

66 *Blackshirt,* March 1938, p. 1.

67 R. Bellamy, 'Marching with Mosley', n.d., as quoted in Lunn & Thurlow (eds.), *op. cit.,* pp. 153–4, 160.

68 R. Bellamy, *op. cit.,* as quoted by Lunn & Thurlow (eds.), *op. cit.,* p. 154.

69 *West London Regional Bulletin,* April 1934?

70 J. D. Brewer, 'The British Union of Fascists, Sir Oswald Mosley and

Birmingham: An Analysis of the Content and Context of an Ideology'. MSoc Science degree, University of Birmingham, 1973, pp. 230–1. See also A. Fawcett, interview with Rawnsley, 16 July 1977, Lunn & Thurlow (eds.), *op. cit.*, p. 155.

71 W. F. Mandel, 'The leadership of the B.U.F.', *The Australian Journal of Politics and History,* XII, December 1966, pp. 361–7.

72 Brewer, *op. cit.,* pp. 16–19, 68–72.

73 Lunn & Thurlow (eds.), *op. cit.,* pp. 154–61.

74 Risdon, *op. cit., BUQ,* I, 3, July–September 1937, p. 28.

75 A. R. Thomson, 'Britain and the Continent', *BUQ,* IV, 1, spring 1940, pp. 41–5. See also letter from Thomson to D. M. Geiger, March 1951, as quoted by D. M. Geiger, 'British Fascism as revealed in British Union of Fascists' Press', PhD, New York University, 1963, p. 24.

76 For examples of the opinions held by this group see W. Joyce, *Twilight over England,* 2nd edn, Uitgevers-maatschappij 'Oceanus', The Hague 1942; *Dictatorship,* BUF Publications, London 1933; *Fascism and India,* BUF Publications, London 1935?. See also R. Gordon-Canning, *Arab or Jew?* BUF, London n.d., and *The Inward Strength of a National Socialist,* Greater Britain Publications, London n.d.

77 Dr Forgan, Mosley's veteran ILP and New Party comrade, had resigned quietly in 1934 whilst second in command of the BUF, ostensibly on the grounds of ill-health, *Blackshirt,* 12 October 1934, p. 7.

78 W. Joyce, *National Socialism Now,* National Socialist League, London 1937, pp. 7–9.

79 Report on Jew-baiting for the month of August, 9 September 1936, MEPO 2/3043.

80 Report on Jew-baiting for the month of September, 8 October 1936, *ibid.*

81 *Action,* 13 March 1937, editorial.

82 Mosley, interview, 24 June 1980. As a general point the term 'intellectual' is here being used in its broadest sense to describe not merely people of ideas, but also leading figures of literature and art.

83 The Shavian concept of the superman, so prominent in Shaw's plays, lent itself easily to the idealisation of fascist leaders including Mosley and Mussolini. See *Manchester Guardian,* 13 October 1927, 28 October 1927, as found in miscellaneous press cuttings in Labour Party Library. Mosley knew Maugham socially: Pryce Jones, *op. cit.,* p. 81. Huxley had some grasp of the BUF's economic policy but did not sustain any commitment to the party, although he did produce the mediocre novel, *Point, Counter Point,* in which he portrayed Mosley, 'J.G.', correspondence with author, April 1981.

84 F. Mullally, *Fascism inside England,* Morris Books, London 1946, pp. 62–3.

85 Wyndham Lewis 'Left wings and the C3 mind'. *BUQ,* I, 1, January–April 1937, pp. 33–4.

86 *Blackshirt,* 28 February 1936, p. 6.

87 The 1937 Gallup Poll of authors asking whether they supported Franco or the Spanish Republicans produced a large majority in favour of the latter. Amongst those prominent writers hostile to the Republican cause were Pound, Eliot, Wells, Evelyn Waugh, Edmund Blunden, Victoria Sackville-West, Alec Waugh, Seán O'Faoláin, Arthur Maclean, Geoffrey Bloss and Eleanor Smith. J. Harrison, *The Reactionaries,* Victor Golancz, London 1966, p. 35. See also *New Stateman and Nation,* XIV, 25 December 1937, p. 1094. The fact that of this group, only Pound had any formal connection with the BUF, is indicative of the party's failure to penetrate the mainstream of British intellectualism.

88 Mosley, interview, 24 June 1980.

89   *Blackshirt*, 1 June 1934. p. 3.
90   N. Elam, Fascism, women and democracy, *FQ*, I, 3, July 1935, p. 296.
91   Mosley, interview, 24 June 1980. See also *Action*, 14 January 1939, p. 14.
92   Bellamy, 'Marching with Mosley', as cited in Lunn & Thurlow (eds.), *op. cit.*, p. 156.
93   Letter to *Daily Herald*, 9 June 1934, from R. Rhys, as quoted by Vindicator (pseud.), *Fascists at Olympia*, Victor Gollancz Ltd, London 1934, p. 47. For corroboration of this incident and other examples of violent treatment of women at Olympia see statements appearing on pp. 12, 24, 43, 47.
94   Mosley, interview, 24 June 1980. See also Mosley, *op. cit.*, p. 348; *My Answer*, Mosley Publications, Ramsbury 1946, p. 6; and *Blackshirt*, 8 June 1934, p. 1.
95   Mosley, *op. cit.*, p. 348; *My Answer*, p. 7.
96   Mosley claimed that Lady Houston was going to contribute £100,000 to the party, but destroyed her cheque after an insulting reference to her had appeared in one of the BUF's newspapers, *op. cit.*, p. 347. For other alleged benefactors see Labour Research Dept, *Who Backs Mosley? Fascist Promises and Fascist Performance*, Labour Research Department, London 1934, pp. 10–12.
97   Labour Research Department, *op. cit.*, p. 10. See also A. C. Miles, *Mosley in Motley*, A. C. Miles, London 1937, pp. 8–9.
98   *Action*, 4 February 1939, p. 17.
99   Interview with Charnley, as quoted in Lunn & Thurlow (eds.), *op. cit.*, p. 161. See also N. Driver, 'From the Shadows of Exile' (unpublished autobiography, n.d.), *ibid*, p. 154.
100 Mosley, interview, 24 June 1980.
101 'J.G.', correspondence with author, May 1981.
102 FO 371/19453 No. 6483/G. Memorandum on British Political organisations in receipt of foreign funds, 14 December 1935.
103 *HC Deb.*, 317, 12 November 1936, c. 1029–30. See also *The Times*, 13 November 1936, p. 16., and *Action*, 21 November 1931, editorial.
104 HO 283/10, police details of secret account, 6 and 16 July 1940.
105 HO 283/16, Transcript of Mosley's appearance before Advisory Committee, 22 July 1940, pp. 53, 59.
106 HO 283/18, recommendation of Advisory Committee to Home Secretary, 2 August 1940, p. 20.
107 CAB 66/35 WP (43) 148, memorandum by Home Secretary, H. Morrison, 14 April 1943.
108 HO 45/24895, Special Branch report, 27 March 1940.
109 N. Mosley, *Beyond the Pale*, Secker & Warburg, London 1983, pp. 174–5.
110 *Ibid.*, pp. 30–4.
111 *Ibid.*, pp. 18, 31.
112 *Ibid.*, p. 30.
113 Mosley, interview, 24 June 1980.

Anti-Semitism and the campaign in east London

CHAPTER 4

I hate him for he is a Christian;
But more for that is low simplicity
He lends out money gratis, and brings down
The rate of usance here in Venice,
If I can catch him once upon the hip,
I will feed fat the ancient grudge I bear him.
He hates our sacred nation; and he rails,
Even there where merchants must congregate,
On me, my bargains, and my well-won thrift,
Which he calls interest. Cursed by my tribe
If I forgive him.

W. Shakespeare, *Merchant of Venice*, I, iii

Up to three years ago anti-Semitism was unknown as a strong force in Great Britain. Today, in any audience in Britain, the strongest passion that can be aroused is the passion against the corruption of Jewish power ... the Jew himself has created anti-Semitism — created it as he has always done, by letting people see him and his methods. Even Hitler was not anti-Semitic before he saw a Jew.

Mosley, Albert Hall, 22 March 1936;
Action, 26 March 1936, p. 13

The leader of a so-called political party, finding that his theories, both economic and political, were laughed out of court, and looking around for something to put in their place which would bring him notoriety if not popularity, saw across the water a party which had made the basis of its political ideology a ferocious anti-Semitism and a ghastly race hatred, and by its extravagances had gained for itself a world-wide publicity.

N. Laski, *Jewish Rights and Jewish Wrongs*,
Soncino Press, London 1939, pp. 116–17

Anti-Semitism, which had haunted human society for centuries, is not a monolithic force. A prejudice which stems from socio-religious factors differs fundamentally from that which is racially based. Both types of anti-Semitism, of course, ascribed detrimental collective characteristics to Jews but they differ in terms of their degree of mutability. Socio-religious anti-Semitism attacks Jews for what they do or for the manner in which they live, whereas the racial variant of the phenomenon displays a hatred of Jews for what they are, as defined by the immutable racial characteristics prescribed to them. The former allows the Jew an option of assimilation through the rejection of Judaism and its visible heritage. The latter does not because the essence of his Jewishness is genetically determined. The former can produce violence but it almost impossible to harness politically because of its internal diversity. The latter, linked to conspiracy theories of Jewish plans for world domination, provided the nightmare dynamic which ended in the ovens of Auschwitz and the lingering stench of burning flesh.

Both types of anti-Semitism existed in Britain long before the appearance of Mosley and the BUF.[1] In the inter-war period, however, the nature of the international Jewish conspiracy in which so many anti-Semites believed became increasingly sophisticated. The role of the Russian revolution and the high proportion of Jews amongst the leading Bolsheviks was important in this respect. Bolshevism, it seemed, was a clear manifestation of the subversive power of Judaism. Even amongst the mainstream of British politics figures such as Winston Churchill detected the scent of a Jewish conspiracy, and warned that 'this movement [Bolshevism] among the Jews is not new. From the days of Spartacus – Weishaupt to those of Karl Marx. . . . This world wide conspiracy for the overthrow of civilisation and for the reconstitution of society on the basis of arrested development, of envious malevolence, and impossible equality, has been steadily growing.'[2]

The left too had its anti-Semitic tradition based upon opposition to international finance capitalism which was sometimes conveniently personified as 'a hook-nosed Rothchild' engaged in a 'gigantic conspiracy manifold and comprehensive'.[3] These two strands of the conspiracy (the Jew as an international capitalist and as a revolutionary subversive) were brought together in the 1920s in the English translation of *The Protocols of the Learned Elders of Zion*. Concocted by the Tsarist secret police in 1905, the *Protocols* purported to be a transcript of the strategy being pursued by the leaders of international Jewry in their conspiracy against the Christian world. By using their vast economic resources and by fomenting war and revolution, Jews throughout the world would overthrow the established order and enslave their Christian enemies. Although the work was exposed as a fraud as early as 1921, it continued to enjoy a high reputation amongst committed racial anti-Semites. It was drawn upon particularly by the Britons, an obscure anti-Semitic organisation founded in 1919 by Henry Hamilton Beamish and dedicated to awaking Britain to the Jewish 'threat'. It was used also by Arnold Leese and the Imperial Fascist League. Like other fascist movements in Britain before 1932, the IFL lacked mass support and had a programme which was largely incoherent and reactionary, but the IFL did have the dubious distinction of being Britain's most overtly anti-Semitic fascist organisation. Leese was exceptional in that he was the first in Britain to place racial anti-Semitism in the framework of complete biological racism, which led him, as it was later to lead Hitler, to countenance the wholesale liquidation of Jews through the use of gas chambers.[4]

Nor were these the first organisations to attempt to organise politically upon a programme of anti-Semitism. As early as 1901 the British Brothers' League and the Londoners' League had both been founded in reaction to the influx of eastern European Jewish immigrants into London's East End. They were supported by East-End Conservative MPs through the Parliamentary Alien Legislation Committee which had been founded in 1901. By 1905 these pressure groups had withered away as a result of the withdrawal of parliamentary support, and the passing of the 1905 Alien Immigration Act.[5] The forces which had produced them, however, remained within London's East End and were rekindled thirty years later by the fire of Mosley's rhetoric.

During the 1930s it was customary for many of the elected representatives of the East End to claim that anti-Semitism was unknown in the area before the BUF's invasion. This was particularly true of those on the left, including George Lansbury, whose passionate anti-fascism lured them into self-deception.[6] Anti-Semitism was endemic within the East End, and had existed there long before Mosley entered the area. By tradition Jews in Britain had been geographically and occupationally clannish, settling in urban areas (particularly east London). The waves of eastern European Jewish immigrants towards the end of the century were drawn to these same areas. The obvious foreignness of their dress, language, and manner caused them to appear more conspicuous than were their native British co-religionists, some of whom admitted that parts of the East End '. . . had developed a ghetto-like character . . . mainly created by the immigrants themselves'.[7] Such areas were delineated by boundaries which the Jews rarely crossed, and amongst the squalid tightly-packed houses were Jewish workshops and factories, synagogues, schools where up to ninety per cent of the pupils were Jews, and shops with foreign names selling Jewish food. From Whitechapel and Aldgate the Jews pushed steadily east into Mile End where gradually whole streets, including the traditional corner shops, fell into Jewish hands.

The immigrants also provided a large pool of unskilled and un-organised labour. Sweat shops were not new to the East End nor were their proprietors uniformly Jewish. Their proponderance increased, however, towards the end of the century, and in high-density Jewish areas the sweat shop became the symbol of the Jewish entrepreneur. This industrious exploitation on the part of small Jewish capitalists made its impact upon the Gentile community either by the direct employment of its members (often with poor wages and conditions), or by undercutting its prices and wages. In either case the end result was the undermining of Gentile living standards in an area where much of the population already lived on or below the poverty line. In addition to these economic effects the heavy Jewish immigration also aggravated existing social problems especially in regard to accommodation, where the increased demand for housing led to a rise in the number of unscrupulous landlords whose single aim was the increased exploitation of the unfortunate families with whom they packed their insanitary slums.

The relationship between Jewish and Gentile communities tended to be characterised by mutal suspicion, hostility, and self-segregation.[8] On occasions these feelings spilled over into widespread violence, most notably in 1917, when anti-Semitic disorder erupted in Bethnal Green. With Britain's war casualties mounting to horrifying proportions there was resentment concerning the many Jewish immigrants who were not conscripted because technically they remained aliens of eastern Europe. They became a target of Gentile fury not merely because they were safe from the slaughter but also because it was felt that many were profiteering from the shortages caused by the war.[9] Such dramatic examples were rare, however, and although it is clear that both socio-religious and racial anti-Semitism had existed in the East End before the arrival of the BUF, it is equally clear that anti-Semitism was a force as yet unorganised and unexploited by any serious contender for political power.

The East End was a community under economic pressure and behaved as such. It struck out against innocent scapegoats and those who had contravened the unwritten moral code by engaging in enterprises which were considered exploitative. It looked back collectively to a mythical 'golden age' devoid of contemporary problems. An age when the area had not been overcrowded, and when the shops had had English names and had given their customers an honest bargain – an age before the arrival of the Jews.[10] It was into this environment that the BUF introduced itself with its anti-Semitism and its facist promises to rebuild all of the finest elements of the past in the society of the future. Given its condition and its traditions it is hardly surprising that the East End provided such fertile ground for the spores of British fascism.

On the evening of 28 October 1934, Mosley made an undeniably anti-Semitic speech at the Albert Hall. Anti-Semitism had, however, become a characteristic feature associated with Mosley's political following for some time before this. As early as the summer of 1932 some New Party members were showing inklings of anti-Semitism. In August a full-time worker and resident at the party's London headquarters was fined for illegally posting anti-Semitic handbills, causing the party to issue a disclaimer stating that the culprit had been acting entirely in a private capacity, and that '. . . anti-Jewish propaganda is neither authorised or approved by Sir Oswald Mosley'.[11] It declined to shed any light upon the origin of the handbills. In October 1932, within weeks of the BUF launch, Mosley hinted at anti-Semitism when he denounced a group of hecklers as '. . . warriors of class war – all the way from Jerusalem'.[12] By the spring of 1933 there were cases of Jews being assaulted by groups of fascists, and of fascist literature sellers being attacked by Jewish opponents.[13]

Throughout the spring and summer of 1933 there were frequent denials of anti-Semitism from Mosley personally and from the party's press. In July Mosley claimed that attacks on Jews had been strickly forbidden. 'Fascism stands for religious and racial tolerance', he maintained:

> The attacks on Jews in Germany do not rest on any Fascist principle but are manifestations of an inherent quality in the German character. It is foolish to blame Fascism for something that has its source in the mentality of a particular nation. . . . For many centuries religious and racial tolerance has been part of the British character, and I give my assurance that under Fascism that great tradition will be preserved.[14]

Yet simultaneously there were warnings that Jewish attacks upon fascists must desist, otherwise they would be met with violence, for 'there will come a time if such disgusting attacks continue, when few Englishmen would blame our men for replying in a practical form to the arguments of the attackers'.[15]

At the end of September, in an article dealing with aliens who were disloyal to the interests of Britain, *The Blackshirt* attacked 'the low type of foreign Jew . . . the men who are to the fore in every crooked financial deal', and promised that 'they will go out of the country . . . for these are the elements which the Fascist State cannot and will not absorb. They are a cancer in the body politic which requires a surgical operation.'[16] In order to avoid charges of anti-Semitism, however, the article was careful to maintain the distinction between 'good' and 'bad' Jews, and even reminded its readers that 'many Jews fought for this country, and some of their families, through years and centuries have proved themselves to be loyal citizens of Britain. Such men have nothing to fear from Fascism.'[17] A month later the BUF launched a more direct attack upon the Jews with the claim that they were attempting to embroil Britain in a war with Germany because the Nazi regime was repressing Jewish interests. It was claimed that the Conservative party was dominated by Jewish financiars and the Labour party by Jewish intellectuals, and in addition, the Jews were alleged to control the British press and cinenmas. By '. . . striving to involve Britain in war . . .', Jews were alleged to be using these instruments of public expression for the benefit of '. . . their own race . . .', and had thereby illustrated that they presented '. . . an organised interest within the State'.[18]

Two weeks later the BUF tried to back away a little from open anti-Semitism with the claim that the previous article had referred only to some rather than to all Jews. In the context of the original article such a claim was clearly absurd, and in any case it was contradicted by the party's continued insistence that 'Jewry in England must decide whether its members are of British nationality or not . . .',[19] thereby treating the entire Jewish community of Britain as a single entity. The constituent elements of anti-Semitism were all there. The attribution of common and detrimental Jewish characteristics (to the extent that those who did not possess them were exceptions and were considered more English than Jewish), the actual or potential disloyalty of the entire Jewish community because of alien allegiances and, that most common of all anti-Semitic hallmarks, the claim that Jews wielded a degree of influence and control over their host society out of all proportion to their numerical presence; all suggested that an as yet undecided variety of anti-Semitism had become official BUF policy.

During the early months of 1934 BUF anti-Semitism was submerged as a sop to Rothermere. As the ill-fated alliance foundered, however, anti-Semitism surfaced once more within the movement. At the Albert Hall in April Mosley received tumultuous applause when he declared that Jews would be expected to place Britain before the interests of Jewry,[20] whilst in May it was admitted that Jews were ineligible for BUF membership owing to the frequent Jewish attacks upon fascists, and because of the failure of the majority of Jews to end their foreign allegiances.[21] In a speech in Edinburgh in early June Mosley denounced '. . . the alien hands, which too long have had their strong grip on the life of this country, [and] dominate not only the Conservative Party but the Socialist Party as well'.[22] A few days later at the notorious Olympia meeting he made clear his view that the 'alien hands' in question were Jewish. Following the Olympia violence (for which the BUF blamed the Jews), and Rothermere's departure, the BUF's anti-Semitism became increasingly overt. In addition to anti-Jewish propaganda in *The Blackshirt* Mosley began regularly to accuse his opponents of being in the pay of Jewish financiers. During his speech at the BUF Hyde Park rally in September, Mosley claimed that 'behind the Communist and Socialist mob is the alien Jewish financier, supplying the 'palm oil' to make them yell'.[23] At Belle Vue at the end of the month, he referred to the '. . . foreign Yiddish faces . . .' within his audience, behind which was '. . . foreign Yiddish gold', and denounced his opponents as '. . . from the sweepings of Continental ghettoes financed by Jewish financiers'.[24]

This then was the background against which Mosley launched his attack upon the Jews at the Albert Hall in October 1934. It was not an aberration but rather a further stage in the development of an anti-Semitic process which had begun considerably earlier. The charges levelled against the Jews by Mosley were familiar and included the accusation that they had attacked the BUF physically and had victimised and discriminated against its members and supporters. Such attacks were motivated by the party's absolute opposition to usury, it was alleged, and because of the foreign racial allegiances of British Jews – a point further illustrated by the manner in which the Jewish-controlled press and cinema had done all in their power to encourage war between Britain and Nazi Germany. The meeting was significant, however, because of the vehemence of Mosley's attack which included the lisped mimicry of a foreign Jewish accent, and the unequivocal commitment to overcome the 'challenge' posed by the Jews. 'They have dared in their great folly to challenge the conquering force of the modern age, and tonight they will begin to have their answer! . . . We take up that challenge. They will it! They shall have it![25] In was, in effect, a declaration of war upon the Jewish community in Britain, a fact recognised in *The Blackshirt,* which carried a transcript of the speech which had '. . . marked the commencement of a new battle in British history in which the forces are arrayed – on the one hand the great cleansing spirit of Fascism, and on the other, organised Jewry representing an unclean, alien influence in our national and imperial life'.[26]

Amongst those familiar with British fascism considerable efforts have been made to rationalise and explain the rise of anti-Semitism within the BUF. There have been two main lines of approach: the traditional scapegoat theories which have cast the Jew as the innocent victim of fascist aggression, and the more revisionist analyses which have explained the conflict in terms of the interaction between fascists and Jews. In the scapegoat scenario the violence of the BUF's tactics (epitomised by the Olympia meeting) had eroded much of its support by mid-1934, and the upturn in the economy had lessened the impact and relevance of its economic proposals. These factors created the desperate need for a new dynamic to revitalise the ailing movement and, probably influenced by the success of the Nazis, anti-Semitism was chosen to fill that need.[27] Whereas the Jews were thus seen as the helpless victims of a cynical and politically-motivated campaign, the interactionist model places a share of the blame for the BUF's anti-Jewish campaign squarely upon the shoulders of the Jewish community itself, because of its attacks upon fascism. The proportion of blame attributed in this direction has varied, although Robert Skidelsky, the first recognised historian to adopt this approach, in his controversial biography of Mosley went as far as to suggest that Jews should take '. . . a large share of the blame . . .' for the BUF's anti-Semitism.[28]

The interactionist thesis, however, predates Skidelsky and those who have followed him, for in essence it is derived from the self-justifying claims of Mosley and his anti-Semitic comrades. Mosley was of the opinion that

> . . . the Jew himself created anti-Semitism; created as he has always done by letting people see him and his methods. Even Hitler was not anti-Semitic before he saw a Jew. It was when they came out into the open, when they marched to Hyde Park and tried to drag us to war with the Germany, when fear made them less cunning, when they revealed themselves to the British people. That was when anti-Semitism was born.[29]

He defended the party's attitude towards Jews in interactionist terms by claiming that the BUF was merely defending itself from Jewish attacks. The high proportion of known Jewish assailants in the first years of the BUF's existence led to a fascist investigation which in turn revealed that the Jews were involved in those areas of degenerate corruption which fascism had pledged itself to eliminate.[30] This remained the party's official line on the origins of the 'Jewish question' and was echoed even by the most rabid of Mosley's anti-Semitic supporters, although their racial anti-Semitism betrayed itself in their more exaggerated claims regarding the extent of Jewish power, which found a logical conclusion in the theories of Jewish conspiracy. Hence, in Chesterton's version of the source of BUF anti-Semitism Mosley, having examined Jewish activities in the light of their attacks upon fascism, '. . . found that there is no great financial, industrial, or commercial trust or combine which is not dominated by the Jew, whether acting in person or by proxy. . . . Every vitiating and demoralising factor in our national life was Jew-influenced where it was not Jew-controlled.'[31]

In his attempt to rehabilitate himself in the post-war era Mosley's interactionist explanation became very much more sophisticated. The idea that the Jews were in control of those areas of national life which fascism had pledged itself to reform was dropped, as was the nonsense that anti-Semitism was the natural reaction of the public following the exposure of the Jewish *modus operandi*. In their place was the assertion that the Jews assumed wrongly that British fascism would include anti-Semitism because of the example of the Nazis, and, therefore, launched pre-emptive attacks upon the BUF without any real cause. The fascists' response to such attacks, in conjunction with their opposition to Jewish attempts to foment war with Germany, caused this 'temporary fight' between the Jews and the BUF.[32] Less than ten years later came Skidelsky's interactionist analysis of the party's anti-Semitism which, although less sympathetic, was in many ways identical to Mosley's biographical exercise in retrospective self-justification. This similarity alone does not invalidate the interactionist approach, of course, but it does highlight the politically subjective nature of its origins. It is important to note that both the interactionary and the scapegoat theories were being used by contemporary supporters and opponents of the BUF respectively, long before either was adopted as an historical interpretation.

More recent attempts have been made to synthesise these two approaches. Indeed in many respects the dichotomy between interactionism and the scapegoat analysis is artificial, for the rise of anti-Semitism, regardless of the original rationale, created inevitably a degree of interaction with sections of the Jewish community. The important difference, however, is that whereas interactionist anti-Semitism concerns the relationship between a movement and its environment, the scapegoat variety involves the implementation of a conscious decision to adopt anti-Semitism for political ends. In regard to the BUF's anti-Semitism this presents a problem which is impossible to resolve conclusively. The gradual manner in which its anti-Semitism evolved suggests that a degree of interaction was at work, but proof of the mere existence of interaction is not conclusive. It can be argued with equal plausibility that the almost total suppression of ascending anti-Semitism in the Rothermere period is indicative of the degree to which it was under the strict control of the policy-makers within the party, and, therefore, its growth after the summer of 1934 was the result of a conscious decision to unleash it. A lack of documentary evidence as to how policy decisions were taken confuses the issue still further, although in this context an examination of Mosley's personal anti-Semitism is valuable for its is inconceivable that any decision could have been taken without his consent.

One must dispense at the outset with Mosley's own denials in this area.[33] Instances of his anti-Semitism are not difficult to locate, such as at Stratford town hall in 1935, when he told an East End audience that '. . . the yelling mob of Socialists and Communists [are] paid by the Jews. The big Jew finances and controls the Old Parties, both Conservative and Socialists, the little Jew sweats you in the sweat-shop.'[34] Even from such a small extract it is clear that Mosley was attempting to convince his audience that the Jew was an anti-social menace; by disregarding the class and financial status of the individual Jew, the entire Jewish community is portrayed as a single entity which dominates and exploits Gentile society. Such are the myths of anti-Semitism. Even if Mosley's claim that Jews were involved in anti-fascist violence in disproportion to their total numbers was true (as was probably the case), it provides no justification for the attribution of collective Jewish characteristics, exaggerated claims concerning their influence, and a declaration of war against them *en masse*. Mosley's memory in the post-war years proved highly selective in regard to these matters; the records of his numerous speeches, however, remain as irrefutable evidence.

Apologists for Mosley have suggested that he was not responsible for the volume and viciousness of the party's anti-Semitism, either through ignorance of its extent, or because he was a prisoner of his anti-Semitic lieutenants. Mosley himself claimed that his frequent absenses from London meant that he was not always responsible for the propaganda produced by his party, and some historians have given this claim a degree of credibility.[35] The implausibility of such a suggestion is confirmed by the testimony of those around him. Writing thirty years after his departure from the party Chesterton chided Mosley for shirking his responsibility in this sphere and concluded that 'he must have forgotten the meetings of the policy directorate over which he presided every week to read the page proofs', of the BUF's newspapers.[36] This view was confirmed by another ex-member of National Headquarters who recalled that 'Mosley vetted every issue of *Action* before it was put to bed, if he was out of London he checked it over the phone.'[37]

The idea that Mosley was the victim of influential hard-line anti-Semites within the party's leadership has greater credibility. Certainly there existed tension between Mosley and men such as Chesterton, Joyce and Beckett, who were keen to plunge the BUF ever further into the fantasy world of racial anti-Semitism. They considered the Jews as an inferior race; a tribe of 'submen' according to Joyce, who had seen amongst the anti-fascists at Olympia '. . . a mass of bestial Jewish faces contorted into hideous and obscene grimaces'.[38] The Jews were not merely embellished with widespread power and influence but were seen as the participants in a worldwide conspiracy against white civilisation. 'The Jews control and actuate alike the decadent democratic capitalism and the hideous fratricidal communism. Using both instruments they hope to prevent every white people from achieving the freedom to work out the fullness of their own economic destiny. Only through the defeat of Jewry can Britain be free.'[39] Furthermore, because the anti-Semitism of Joyce and his colleagues was racial; a series of immutable and demeaning mental, physical, and moral characteristics were ascribed to Jews, including an inability to remain diguised in white society: 'As fatal as the asp to Cleopatra is the habit of self-assertion to the Jews. Whatever mercantile cunning this race may possess, with whatever sureness of touch it may operate on the Gentile purse, it almost invariably injures its chances of operating undetected by some arrogant gesture exemplifying what we call bad taste.'[40]

Although Mosley never indulged in anti-Semitism of this nature, it is debatable as to the extent to which he was powerless to prevent it. It is conceivable that he was disturbed by the crudeness of the anti-Semitism of Joyce and Chesterton but the fear of losing the support of such people made him reluctant to take steps to curb the more extreme manifestations of racial anti-Semitism within the party. There is, however, no evidence to support Skidelsky's claim that such a move by Mosley would have damaged the party irreparably by causing '. . . both its militants and mass base . . . [to] . . . break away'.[41] Indeed, the very opposite appears true for when Mosley did check the development of full-scale racial anti-Semitism, and thereby prompted the departure of Joyce and Beckett who founded the rival National Socialist League in the spring of 1937, only a handful of BUF members defected to the new movement.

The degree to which Mosley's own anti-Semitism was sincere is unclear. Certainly there is no evidence of anti-Semitism in his pre-fascist past, although it is possible that, under pressure from the anti-Semites around him, Mosley came to believe in a form of socio-religious anti-Semitism in 1933 or 1934. It would have helped him to have rationalised his own failure. The evidence of Jewish attacks upon fascism would have assisted also in such a conversion. Other more deeply-held convictions would have played their part too, the most important of which was Mosley's traditional hatred of international finance.[42] It would have been a small step for this anonymous enemy of the state to have become synonymous with the group with which it had been connected historically – the Jews. It is also likely that Mosley's conversion would have been inspired to an extent by the traditional nature of the Jewish community itself. Its separateness not only offended Mosley's sense of extreme patriotism, but also threatened the concept of collective social harmony through synthesis which lay at the very root of fascism as a doctrine of the political centre.

During his interrogation by the authorities in 1940 Mosley did admit to such a conversion: 'I was compelled to look at the Jewish problem by their opposition to us and, having looked at the Jewish problem I developed what it called anti-Semitism.'[43] He went on to deny strongly ever subscribing to racial anti-Semitism, however. Certainly it appears significant that although capable of original and sometimes brilliant thought in a multiplicity of areas, Mosley contributed nothing to anti-Semitic theory. Arnold Leese, however, whose fascism was merely the vehicle for his obsessive racial anti-Semitism, contributed nothing to fascist theory and yet made a lasting impact in the field of anti-Semitic racism.[44] Although Mosley directed anti-Semitic propaganda from the platform and the pen, he rarely descended into the realm of crude racial abuse,[45] and although he accepted the claim that the Jews exerted pressure over national and international institutions, he was never the advocate of a full conspiracy theory involving an orchestrated attack upon European civilisation by international Jewry. When asked privately for his assessment of the *Protocols* his reply was unequivocal: 'Pure fantasy, but I wish the Jews would stop behaving as if they were genuine.'[46]

Whilst rejecting racial anti-Semitism on a personal level his failure to prevent its development within his party leads one to the conclusion that he was prepared to use it in pursuit of political gain.[47] This in no way excuses him. Indeed, he who decides to cultivate hatred and exploit personal inadequacy in such a fashion is more contemptible than he who is genuinely deluded in such matters. When Chesterton wrote an account of the manner in which the Jew seeks to compensate for his innate inferiority by dominating the world, and yet in so doing becomes excessively arrogant and draws upon himself the hostility of the honest natives, he included a revealing passage:

> To go to a swimming pool anywhere near London or the large cities is as efficacious as baptism in the Jordan; one becomes positively anointed with Semite grease. To go to the sea, especially if it be a fashionable resort, is to find the Jews in possession of almost all the hotels, swarming over the beaches, over-crowding the cafés, and always making themselves conspicuous, always drawing attention to themselves by loud clothes, loud cars, and loud behaviour.[48]

Rather than imparting any information concerning Jews, the passage indicates the nature and extent of Chesterton's personal problems. It was precisely these personal disorders that Mosley was prepared to exploit in others in his quest for political advancement.

The advantage of anti-Semitism was that it provided a more tangible target for fascist hatred than the Old Gang or the faceless purveyors of international finance. There was something of a tradition of anti-Semitism in Britain, and the Jewish community was culturally separate and identifiable, and included many foreign immigrants and their first-generation descendants. Above all anti-Semitism was perfect for a centrist movement in that it automatically alienated neither left nor right, and indeed, in some respects, could build upon traditions of anti-Semitism which had originated from both sides of the political spectrum. Unlike the stereotype image of capitalist or trade unionist (each of which draws its effectiveness from a context of class hostility), that of the Jew was almost infinitely flexible and could be used to absorb hostility from any and all parts of the political spectrum, thus providing an amalgam between the classes, and the diversion of class conflict. In the world of anti-Semitism the Jew could personify the omnipotent international financier, the unscrupulous small sweat-shop owner, the pornographer, the criminal, and even the communist thug or the bomb-throwing anarchist. In addition to this, anti-Semitism, in conjunction with the conspiracy theory, could also serve to underline the centrist position of fascism by providing a link between communism and *laissez-faire* capitalism.

Only by linking these as twin international assailants could fascism offer itself as the only real alternative form of government, and yet how but through the already established tradition of Jewish conspiracy could such diametrically opposed institutions be linked?[49] These were the advantages which Mosley wanted to derive from racial anti-Semitism.[50] His willingness to allow others to form the anti-Semitic vanguard of the party, complete with theories of Jewish conspiracy, was indicative either of his inability to subscribe to what he knew intellectually to be non-sense, or, more likely, his desire to leave open an avenue of retreat whereby he could distance himself from such a disreputable doctrine. Either way, Mosley was looking to exploit the benefits of gutter politics without soiling his own hands.

It would appear, then, that the rise of anti-Semitism was the result of internal party factors such as the pressure from hard-line anti-Semites, and the need for an alien but flexible stereotyped enemy, acting in conjunction with a genuine degree of interaction between Jews and the BUF in the form of Jewish anti-fascist activities. Mosley's decision to adopt anti-Semitism as official party policy was as politically expedient as had been the decision to suppress anti-Semitism during the Rother-mere period. It was more than a case of 'intellectual and moral careless-ness . . .'[51] on Mosley's part, but cannot be divorced from the environ-ment in which the party was operating. It is doubtful whether Mosley ever believed that anti-Semitism would lead directly to a fascist victory, but it is likely that he saw, in addition to the other attractions of anti-Semitism, a means of uniting and motivating his party until the onset of the next economic slump which he predicted for 1937. If, in the meantime, anti-Semitism did provide fascism with an impetus compara-ble to that derived by the Nazis, then so much the better.

This analysis is strengthened by the way in which the BUF's anti-Semitism developed in inverse relation to the propensity of the economy to produce crisis. Reading the party's propaganda one is struck by the degree to which anti-Semitism declined from the spring of 1937 to the end of 1938; this was the period of renewed depression which had been predicted, and throughout its duration spurious anti-Semitism gave way to the type of cogent economic analysis which had provided the *raison d'être* and the bedrock of Mosley's fascism. Even the traditional link between international finance and the Jews was no longer laboured, as in the context, the unpatriotic internationalism of 'the City of London' was singled out for blame.[52] Although throughout 1938 the party made every effort to exploit the depression, claiming that it was considerably more severe than that which had engulfed the nation between 1929 and 1933, it became increasingly apparent that it was not of sufficient severity to sweep fascism to power in Britain. Indeed by late 1938 the indications of economic recovery were undeniable, and with them came a return of anti-Semitism with articles on racial differences, and references to the 'Dusky Men of International Finance'.[53] By 1939 the conspiracy theory was being stressed once again as it was claimed that the Jews sought world domination through the twin conspiracies of international Bolshevism and international finance. Both movements were led and controlled by Jews, for in all countries '. . . the Jew is restless, homeless, discontented, the arch-plotter, the man who starts revolutions'.[54] Even Mosley stepped up his anti-Semitism with claims that international Jewish finance was aiming at world domination and the enslavement of Gentiles: 'Who benefits from the death of nations as much as the force that knows no nation? . . . International Jewish finance has ever ruled by division and break-up of civilisations from within, and . . . the sense of nation and of patriotism is the last conscious entity which it has to destroy before assuming world domination.'[55] Whether the BUF's anti-Semitism would have reached its pre-1937 heights had not the war intervened is impossible to say. It is difficult to avoid the conclusion, however, that anti-Semitism was deliberately suppressed during the 1937–8 recession, and reconstituted when it became clear that an economic recovery was under way. In addition to those reasons already mentioned, by 1939 the reintroduction of anti-Semitism had the attraction of appealing to a society which was undergoing a fresh wave of immigration by foreign Jews fleeing from Nazi persecution, as well as the ability to portray war with Germany as an alien vendetta of Jewish finance in which Britain should not become involved.

The BUF's East End campaign offers an example of the practical application of the party's anti-Semitism, but before looking at the campaign's development it is necessary to be aware of the heights reached by fascist anti-Semitism between 1934 and 1937. By 1936 all but the fascist nations were alleged to be contaminated by the Jewish world conspiracy. The democracies, in the grip of international finance, were considered as culpable as was international communism, a system inspired by that 'verminous old Hebrew', Karl Marx, in order to maintain Jewish exploitation of the Gentile worker.[56] Prominent Jewish politicians in the western democracies and the USSR were 'exposed' as proof of Jewish control, and wars and revolutions throughout the world were considered manifestations of the Jewish urge to disintegrate Christian civilisation.[57] Beneath the surface the hidden hand of Judaism was perceived to be at work: 'All is articulated yet hidden; all is planned yet obscured . . . an all-penetrating doctrine which never dies, never sleeps, never rests – its eye is forever open.'[58]

The conspiracy theories which had abounded within the party were often confused, incoherent, and either internally or mutually contradictory, especially in relation to the exact stage reached in the master plan for world domination, and the methods of control employed by its Jewish architects. This, of course, is hardly surprising, for such theories were largely the nonsensical fantasies of warped and obsessive minds. The massive exaggeration of Jewish power, however, which was a prerequisite for any variation on the conspiracy theme, was not merely applied on an international scale but was also held to be responsible for most of Britain's domestic economic problems. Nor did Jews control only the economy, for they were also alleged to be moulding public opinion to coincide with their aims, through their domination of the two major channels for the dissemination of information – the press and cinemas.[59] Politics was seen as another sphere of control ranging from the Jew-dominated city councils, to the subversion of the democratic process at national level, whereby 'International Finance, has its paid creatures standing for Parliament at every General Election, so many posing as Conservatives, so many as Liberals, so many as Labourites. International Finance, whichever party wins, selects and appoints the Ministers and they become its puppets . . . International Finance claps a hand and hey, presto! in trots little nigger slave boy Baldwin . . . .'[60] The details varied but the essence of the message was hammered home repetitively in an attempt to create the impression that '. . . in every portion of Great Britain, Jewry is stretching its tentacles like a large octopus, in order to strangle anything and everything that tries to evade its growth'.[61]

The Jews were also portrayed as cowards who had shirked their responsibility during the 1914–18 war by avoiding the fighting,[62] and as a race of criminals whose anti-social activities included the perpetration of fraud, drug-dealing, and the trafficking of women into white slavery. The risks posed to women by Jews were considered so great that within the corporate state the mere employment of white women by Jews would be strictly prohibited.[63] The Jewish sexual violation of Gentile women was presented as yet another manifestation of the general Jewish assult upon Christian civilisation, aimed particularly in this instance at that most sacred bourgeois institution – marriage.[64] This innate Jewish immorality which gave rise to such anti-social behaviour was also responsible for enabling the Jews to succeed in matters of commerce because it allowed the adoption of practices '. . . so slimy that no Englishman would stoop to do them'.[65] But even the most cunning of Jews could not avoid exposing such practices eventually because 'something in the psychology of the race seems to predestine the Jew to overreach himself and so expose his noble intentions for the shoddy and revolting shams they really are'.[66]

Those who objected to this sort of crude characterisation and who condemned it in public were viciously attacked in the columns of the party's newspapers. In January 1935 Beckett began awarding the 'Ancient Order of Synthetic Jewry' to non-Jews who took a pro-Jewish

35

stance. In December the title 'Judupe' was created and conferred upon he who

> ...attains the most exalted sense of his own humanity and goodness when he can serve the Jews against his own race ... [and who] ... readily succumbs to the obsequious and flattering attentions of the Jews ... and blindly abets them in all of their well-laid plans for getting financial, economic, and political control over his country, and of ultimately reducing the Gentiles to a condition of serfdom and servitude to the Jews.[67]

The level of racial anti-Semitism attained by the party in the mid 1930s was sufficient to draw approval from the most notorious Nazi Jew-baiter, Julius Streicher. Streicher's previously expressed contempt for the BUF had been transformed by 1935 into praise and admiration of both Mosley and the fascist struggle in Britain.[68] It would be unreasonable to assume that the alchemy responsible for this transmutation was anything other than the party's commitment to anti-Semitism.

Although the party continued to maintain that it had no argument with '... the good Jewish citizen – if such an anomaly exists ...', it was often implied that Jews in Britain would have to be treated *en masse* for, 'unfortunately, Jewry is of such virulent growth that it is useless to sever a few branches or members. The tentacles of the Jewish tenacity spread deep-rooted over all the land of his adoption. They must be totally eradicated ....'[69] What, then, was to be the fate of the Jew in a fascist Britain? The most acceptable solution appeared to be the mass deportation of Jews and their resettlement in a homeland, where they could at last '... escape the curse of no nationality',[70] and '... where their racialism can take a healthy patriotic form instead of an unhealthy parasitic form'.[71] The idea of a tract of territory being designated a Jewish homeland was not new (traditionally, anti-Semites had suggested Madagascar, because Jews could be confined more securely upon an island than elsewhere): the problem, of course, lay in the selection of the territory. Apart from denying vehemently any Jewish claims to Palestinian land, few suggestions were made in this sphere other than vague references to the establishment of a world conference to decide upon a suitable location for a homeland.

Other solutions such as sterilisation or segregation were considered, but rejected as being too difficult to implement. Extermination, which Arnold Leese had found an acceptable alternative (as long as it was humanely implemented) was only hinted at in the vaguest of terms. Occasionally, however, the holocaust mentality of racial anti-Semitism did manifest itself, as in the following passage:

> Anti-Semitism is a disease transmitted and perpetuated by the Jew himself. Exactly as the human bloodstream, infected by a poisonous bacillus, responds by mustering germ devourers to attack and eliminate the invader, so does a race-conscious community at once mobilise its forces

to fight the alien influences which instinct teaches would imperil its very existence. The fight proceeds most bitterly where infection is most intense, where provocation is most blatant.[72]

The implications of this biological analogy are murderously inexorable. It is difficult to believe that they would have been acted upon by Mosley, however, for genocide is the logical conclusion of racial anti-Semitism only in its most pure, and, therefore, in its most sincere form. Fortunately, this remains only a matter of chilling speculation.

These then were the views with which the BUF entered London's East End, to begin a campaign which had remained shrouded in myth. Anti-fascist myths which have endured for almost half a century have been added to by the more recent myths of revisionist history, which include the claim that the campaign '. . . was anti-Jewish but not anti-Semitic. It was a political campaign along ethnic lines, the basic issue being whether local power should lie with the "British" or the Jews'.[73] In addition to falling victim to anti-Semitic terminology (with the implication that a Jew cannot be simultaneously British), such a view is less than honest, for although the campaign was in part concerned with local control, this debate was conducted within a general campaign of racial anti-Semitism which, at times, employed nauseating forms of abuse.

Although the party was seen to be active in London generally, with branches as far afield as Lewisham, Hampstead and Fulham, there was almost no reported activity in the East End before the summer of 1934.[74] The first BUF branch to emerge within this area was established in Medway Road, Bow, in July 1934, the members of which '. . . expressed their determination to gain the East End of London for Fascism'.[75] Later that year a branch was established in Bethnal Green. In early 1935 the party entered Shoreditch, and in July 1936, Limehouse.[76] The significance of these dates is that they illustrate how the growth of the BUF within the East End took place after the party's clear adoption of anti-Semitism in the latter half of 1934. Having decided to adopt anti-Semitism, it would appear that the BUF's leadership sought for its application that area of Britain where such a policy would have most relevance – London's East End.

The growth of fascism within the East End was impressive. In Bethnal Green and Hackney, and parts of Poplar and Stepney, the BUF had established itself strongly by 1936 and had built a significant degree of mass support. In part this support was the result of the BUF's recognition of East London's social and economic deprivation, its overcrowding, its squalor and its neglect. This is not to suggest that the campaign was not anti-Semitic, however, for all too often such legitimate grievances were woven into the lavish conspiratorial tapestry of racial anti-Semitism. In a deliberate attempt to whip up racial hatred the East Ender's problems were projected back to a single source – his Jewish neighbour. An area of appalling poverty and recent Jewish immigration containing small capitalist sweat-shops (many of which were Jewish owned), and without a strong tradition of unionised labour, was ideally fertile ground for this approach. This portrayal of the Jew as an objectionable alien abuser of Gentile civilisation, regardless as to whether he was a capitalist or a humble employee, was the obverse of the BUF's crucial centrist claim of a community of interest between capital and labour. This community of interest could be illustrated by reference to the unity of the Jewish 'race', including both capitalist and communist malcontent, in its combined assault upon the ramparts of Gentile society, aiming at the enslavement of all Britons regardless of individual class status. Hence the residents of the East End were informed that 'today the Englishman in East London is the slave of his Jewish master, and his part of the city has become the "land of the waving palm" ', and Britons elsewhere were warned that their turn would come next. 'In the England of tomorrow one can already hear the voice of decadent Britain – "Halt Gentile – and Salute the Jew!" That will be your fate unless you follow the lead given by Mosley. . . .'[77]

The propagation of this type of odius propaganda amongst the residents of the East End was undertaken through an incessant stream of street meetings, which on occasions could exceed 200 in a single month. Often blackshirt units marched to and from such meetings and either they, or elements of the audience whom they had incited and inflamed, committed spontaneous acts of Jew-baiting. These usually took the form of the smashing of windows in Jewish shops and houses and assaults upon Jewish-looking citizens unfortunate enough to be out on the streets. Almost every month such assaults occurred and sometimes were serious enough for their victims to require hospital treatment, such as in the case of the six Jews assaulted after a BUF meeting in Limehouse in April 1939.[78] Despite the regularity of these attacks, internal police reports admitted that the assailants involved were rarely apprehended.[79]

There were also numerous examples of premeditated Jew-baiting and attacks upon Jewish property, ranging from isolated minor incidents to what amounted to a virtual pogrom in Mile End Road in October 1936. This latter incident occurred after thousands of anti-fascists had succeeded in resisting police attempts to clear a route for a large BUF march through Aldgate, culminating in the famous battle of Cable Street. A week later, whilst the anti-fascists celebrated their victory, 150 youths, shouting their support for Mosley, descended upon the Jewish proprietors of Mile End Road. Shops had their windows smashed and their contents looted, a car was ignited, and there were assaults upon bystanders including a man and young girl, who were thrown through a plate-glass window.[80] Although the BUF denied responsibility for the raid, it is difficult to avoid the conclusion that it was conducted in revenge for the party's humiliating defeat in having to abandon the Aldgate march. Although there were other instances of fascist gangs conducting orgies of window-smashing, anti-Semitic attacks were usually less dramatic though often as intimidating for those involved. Jewish market traders had their stalls overturned and were often assaulted, whilst Jewish shopkeepers, and Gentiles believed to be sympathetic to communism, had their premises attacked or picketed by fascists, and some were threatened with arson and even murder.[81] Other tactics included the prominent displaying of the severed heads of pigs, either impaled upon Union Jack-bedecked poles, or placed within the precincts of East End synagogues, as well as the more traditional methods of defacing Jewish property with fascist slogans and obscenities.

Beneath the insults and the threats lay the very real possibility that any individual, especially after dark, could be set upon by fascist thugs and given a beating. Between January and June 1936 there were over fifty complaints to the police of instances of Jew-baiting in the East End;[82] in the last six months before the outbreak of war there were still thirty-eight such complaints.[83] Because many acts of Jew-baiting were minor and went unreported the real figures were almost certainly very much higher. The figures do illustrate, however, that attacks upon the East End Jewish community were real and persistent, and that at its most vicious, the BUF campaign was concerned with acts of harassment and terrorisation. In the winter of 1936, a reporter visiting the East End wrote of the 'sullen excitement' which he sensed, and described how, 'every night from seven to eleven the East Ender can take part in political activity resembling a by-election on a national issue, and on Friday evenings he can imagine it is the eve of the poll; but no national issue is emphasised and there is no poll to put a stop to the performance'. Although the escort provided for him by National Headquarters '. . . spoke of a national policy . . . the local Blackshirts were engrossed with only one subject, anti-Semitism'.[84]

Whatever the initial reasons for the rise of anti-Semitism within the BUF, it is clear that by the mid-1930s the party in the East End had become locked into a cycle of anti-Semitic hatred, reaffirmed by anti-fascist activities amongst the Jews, which had eclipsed all other aspects of the party's programme. The response of East-End Jews was varied. Some joined movements committed to the physical opposition of fascism, such as the Communist Party of Great Britain. Others attempted to utilise the democratic channels of their society by lobbying their MPs and signing petitions such as that which was presented to the Home Secretary from 1,000 Shoreditch tradesmen in February 1936.[85] The

Jewish establishment, however, as represented by the Jewish Board of Deputies, was reluctant to involve itself in anti-fascist activities. This overwhelmingly conservative eighteenth-century institution feared populism in general, and was anxious to avoid the mobilisation of Jews in particular, for it believed that the Jew should merge into British society and avoid drawing attention to himself in any manner. Consequently its advice to the Jews was to rely upon the forces of the state for protection from fascist violence, and to ignore BUF meetings and marches, for opposition to them only served to draw unnecessary attention to the Jewish community and gave a free advertisement to fascism, thereby prolonging its artificially sustained life in Britain. As an official from the Board admitted it was a policy directed wholly '. . . towards keeping the peace in the East End'.[86]

This anxiety to avoid contributing in any way to disorder served only to underline how out of touch the sleek, rich, members of the Board had become from their less exalted constituents. Most did not live in the East End, and were unaware of the disorder which already existed there in the form of regular Jew-baiting, often unchecked and largely undetected. The inaction of the Board resulted in the emergence of the Jewish People's Council (JPC), a popular front representing almost 100 Jewish organisations ranging from trade unions to Zionist groups and synagogues, which were committed to combating fascism and anti-Semitism simultaneously, and doing so in collaboration with other anti-fascist bodies.[87] As well as applying pressure through the usual democratic channels, the JPC used street meetings to mobilise Jews and Gentiles alike in opposition to the BUF, and invariably found itself working in co-operation with left-wing anti-fascist movements.

Although roundly condemned by the Board, the emergence of the JPC forced the leaders of the Jewish community to re-examine their previously lethargic response to the anti-Semitic propaganda of the BUF. In 1936, therefore, the Board formed a co-ordinating committee to assist in the defence of the Jewish communities.[88] The defence measures undertaken were strictly non-populist in orientation for the Board continued to stress the need for order and forbade Jewish attendance at fascist meetings, and maintained its claim that its opposition to the BUF was '. . . entirely non-political . . . we are fighting the Blackshirts, not on any political grounds, but simply on the question of anti-Semitism'.[89] The Board's attitude reflected its membership – old men intoxicated with the reactionary values of the British bourgeoisie, almost as afraid of their less wealthy co-religionists as they were of the fascists. It is ironic that their refusal to head an anti-fascist offensive was of ultimate assistance to an ideology as repugnant to them as was fascism, for the communists were offering less passive lines of defence to East End Jews.

Although Mosley's personal commitment to anti-Semitism

remains something of an unknown quantity, one can conclude that, in part at least, the BUF's adoption of anti-Semitism was motivated by political expediency. This would be consistent also with the reduction of anti-Semitism during the Rothermere period, and the 1937–8 recession, as well as the timing of the East End campaign. In retrospect the decision was probably a mistake; certainly there were elements of political miscalculation within it. It had profound effects upon the party, the most striking of which was the production of the East End campaign, for it was here that, for a short period, fascism in Britain came alive and exhibited a little of the full splendour of its range of poison, viciousness, and hatred. Although the anti-Semitism within Mosley's huge Albert Hall speeches '. . . excited terrific applause from packed audiences, whom he could get fighting mad with enthusiasm'.[90] it was in the narrow streets of Bethnal Green and Stepney, where his more humble followers listened regularly in their thousands, that enthusiasm was transformed into the dynamic of action.

But the effects were far from uniformly beneficial as anti-Semitism also helped to fragment the party. This included not merely the loss of those anti-Semites whom Mosley sought to restrain, such as Joyce, but also those like Charles Wegg-Prosser, a BUF East End candidate in the 1937 L.C.C. elections, whose disillusionment led to his resignation from the party soon after the campaign. In an open letter to Mosley he denounced the BUF's anti-Semitism as

> . . . a gigantic side-tracking stunt, a smoke-screen to cloud thought and divert action with regard to our real problems . . . Hitler attacks the Jews to whip up the lukewarm and critical, you do it to get a mass support in East London and other places. I tried to interest these people in real problems, unemployment, wages, housing, and so on. I watched with dismay the mentality which said 'Get rid of the Jews, and you will automatically get rid of unemployment, slums, sweating' . . . You side-track the demand for social justice by attacking the Jew, you give the people a false answer, and unloose the lowest mob passion.[91]

An even more serious type of fragmentation occurred in the geographical and social composition of the party, however, for as the spiral of violence and increased anti-Semitism developed in the East End, it began filtering back into the party nationally a programme which was of increasing irrelevance to much of the remainder of the country. This became particularly apparent after 1937, when the decrease of the BUF's national anti-Semitic output isolated the movement in the East End to an even greater extent. A similar disintegrating trend was visible in regard to the party's class composition, as the East End campaign attracted what one ex-member described as an excess of '. . . typical East London barrow-boys . . .'.[92] Certainly the East End movement was more working-class than branches elsewhere and its radicalism often frightened middle-class supporters. An example of this can be seen in a not untypical speech by Norman Halliday at Mosley's favourite East End venue, Victoria Park Square, Bethnal Green: 'A revolution must take place in this country. I preach revolution, I am proud of it. . . . You will find that where National Socialism has penetrated there is a revolutionary movement which shows the Communist Party what a lot of hypocrites they are . . . when fascists get into power they will defend the workers against the Jews.'[93] By late 1938 the BUF in the East End was separate from the remainder of the party to such a large degree that it was given the resources necessary to publish its own editions of *The Blackshirt*. Although the peace campaigns towards the end of the decade provided a focus for party unity, the East-End movement continued to remain isolated from the party at large both in its composition and its unremitting anti-Semitism.

NOTES

1 For a full study of the development of anti-Semitism in Britain in the late nineteenth and early twentieth centuries see G. C. Lebzelter, *Political Anti-Semitism in England 1918–1939*, Macmillan Press Ltd, London 1978; C. Holmes, *Anti-Semitism in British Society 1876–1939*, Arnold, London 1979; and K. Lunn, 'Political Anti-Semitism before 1914: Fascism's Heritage', as found in K. Lunn & R. C. Thurlow (eds.), *British Fascism*, Croom Helm, London 1981.

1 W. Churchill, 'Zionism versus Bolshevism', *Illustrated Sunday Herald*, 8 February 1920, as quoted by Lebzelter, *op. cit.*, p. 18.

3 *Labour Leader*, 19 December 1891, as quoted by Holmes, *op. cit.*, pp. 83–4.

4 For details of the Britons and the IFL see Lebzelter, *op. cit.*, pp. 49–85; and Lunn & Thurlow (eds.), *op. cit.*, pp. 41–75.

5 Holmes, *op. cit.*, pp. 89–92.

6 G. Lansbury, 'Anti-Semitism in the East End', *Spectator*, CLVII, 24 July 1936, pp. 133–4. See also the testimony of the Mayor of Stepney, *Manchester Guardian*, 14 October 1936, p. 9.

7 J. Jacobs, *Out of the Ghetto*, Simon, London 1978, p. 25. See also *Jewish Chronicle*, 28 September 1888, as quoted by Holmes, *op. cit.*, p. 33.

8 Jacobs, *op. cit.*, p. 61.

9 Holmes, *op. cit.*, pp. 130–6.

10 *Ibid.*, p. 18.

11 *Manchester Guardian*, 26 August 1932, p. 7. See also 23 August, p. 16; 26 July, p. 18.

12 *The Times*, 25 October 1932, p. 16; and *Manchester Guardian*, 25 October 1932, p. 9.

13 *Manchester Guardian*, 8 May 1933, p. 9. See also *Manchester Evening News*, 29 June 1933, as cited in Lunn & Thurlow (eds.), *op. cit.*, p. 163.

14 Mosley, 'Fascism is not anti-Semitic', *Jewish Economic Forum*, I, 9, 28 July 1933, p. 3. In April it had been suggested that 'the issue of Fascism has been obscured in Germany by the irrelevant Jewish question. The early propaganda of the Nazis against the Jews has considerably complicated their accession to power and their ability to deal with the Socialist, Communist, and financial enemies of the state.' *Blackshirt*, 1 April 1933, p. 1.

15 *Blackshirt*, 22 July 1933, editorial. See also 16 May 1933, p. 2.

16 *Ibid.*, 30 September 1933, p. 1.

17 *Ibid.*
18 *Ibid.,* 4 November 1933, pp. 1, 4.
19 *Ibid.,* 18 November 1933, p. 1.
20 *Manchester Guardian,* 23 April 1934, p. 17.
21 *Fascist Week,* 4–10 May 1934, leader.
22 *The Times,* 2 June 1934, p. 7.
23 *Blackshirt,* 14 September 1934, p. 2.
24 *Manchester Guardian,* 1 October 1934, p. 11.
25 *Blackshirt,* 2 November 1934, pp. 1–2.
26 *Ibid.,* p. 1.
27 There have been many advocates of this approach. An inter-war example can be found in the *New Statesman and Nation,* XII, 10 October 1936, p. 496; and a more recent example in R. Benewick, *The Fascist Movement in Britain,* Penguin Press, London 1972, p. 18.
28 R. Skidelsky, *Oswald Mosley,* Macmillan, London 1975, p. 381.
29 *Action,* 26 March 1936, p. 13.
30 Mosley, *Tomorrow We Live,* Greater Britain Publications, London 1939, p. 63.
31 A. K. Chesterton, *Oswald Mosley, Portrait of a Leader,* Action Press, London 1937, p. 126.
32 Mosley, *My Life,* Nelson, London 1968, p. 341.
33 *Ibid.,* p. 340; interview with author, 24 June 1980; *The Times,* 31 October 1968, p. 11; and 'Sir Oswald Mosley discusses his career with James Mossman', *Listener,* LXXX, 31 October 1968, pp. 576–7.
34 *Blackshirt,* 2 August 1935, p. 5.
35 Mosley, *My Life,* p. 342. See also Lebzelter, *op. cit.,* p. 99.
36 Letter from Chesterton, *Jewish Chronicle,* 13 December 1968, p. 8.
37 'J.G.', correspondence with author, May 1981.
38 W. Joyce, *Fascism and Jewry,* BUF Publications, London n.d., p. 3.
39 *Ibid.,* p. 7.
40 *Action,* 17 September 1936, p. 2. For a full illustration of the rigidity of Joyce's racial anti-Semitism see *Twilight Over England,* NV Uitgevers-maatschappij 'Oceanus', The Hague 1942.
41 Lunn & Thurlow (eds.), *op. cit.,* p. 86.
42 For an example of Mosley's pre-anti-Semitic hostility towards international finance, see *The Greater Britain,* BUF London 1932, pp. 114–21.
43 Transcript of Mosley's appearance before the Advisory Committee, 2 July 1940, p. 36. HO 283/13.
44 Modern British racist and anti-Semitic groups have drawn inspiration from Leese and the IFL rather than from Mosley. Colin Jordan, who has been a central figure in racist politics since the 1950s, was a disciple of Leese's from whom he received a posthumous legacy to help finance the dissemination of racial hatred.
45 Even when Mosley asserted that the Jew was '. . . from the Orient and physically, mentally and spiritually . . . is more remote from [the] British character than any German or Frenchman, for they are Westerners and Jews are Orientals', he did not state directly that these Jewish characteristics were inherently undesirable or inferior, but simply that they were different, and therefore alien. Mosley, *Tomorrow We Live,* p. 65.
46 'J.G.', correspondence with author, May 1981.
47 Mosley himself admitted that he used anti-Semites in his 'temporary fight' with the Jews and saw nothing wrong in so doing, thereby establishing in principle his willingness to exploit anti-Semitism for political gain. Mosley, *My Life,* p. 341.
48 A. K. Chesterton, *Apotheosis of the Jew,* Abbey Supplies, London n.d., p. 6.
49 The link could even be used in relation to issues of foreign policy, through

the claim that the Jews were driving other countries to war with Germany because the Nazis had attacked the Jewish conspiracy.

50 As early as 1932 Mosley had contemplated denouncing an alleged plot by international Jewish bankers. Nicholson had advised him against such a move. Letter from Nicolson to Mosley, 29 June 1932, Nicolson Papers, Balliol College, Oxford.

51 Skidelsky, *op. cit.,* p. 390.

52 'Notes on the quarter', *BUQ,* II, 2, April–June 1938, p. 12.

53 A. Reade, 'William Morris – Nordic', *BUQ,* II, 4, October–December 1938, p. 62.

54 Reade, 'The defence of Western civilisation', *BUQ,* III, 3, July–September 1939, p. 22.

55 Mosley, *The British Peace and how to get it,* Sanctuary Press Ltd, London 1939?, p. 7.

56 Joyce, 'Analysis of Marxism', *FQ,* II, 4, October 1936, pp. 535–6. Communism was portrayed as yet another form of Jewish exploitation. The purpose of Marx, it was argued, was to shift the burden of guilt for the condition of the proletariat from the financier to the producer. By controlling finance and communism the Jews could continue to exploit the Gentile worker, and yet could also profit from his resentment by directing it against the honest producers – 'an ingenious swindle'. *Blackshirt,* 19 September 1936, p. 2.

57 The Jews were even held responsible for the 1914–18 war which was considered '. . . a conflict largely due to his [the Jew's] system of usury, a system which had been adopted by all Christian nations, and which unbalanced the mind, corrupted the heart and rotted the body of Western Civilisation'. Maj. Gen. J. F. C. Fuller, 'The cancer of Europe', *FQ,* I, 1, January 1935, p. 74.

58 *Ibid.,* p. 66.

59 *Blackshirt,* 7 February 1936, p. 2. See also Chesterton, *Fascism and the Press,* BUF Publications, London, n.d.

60 *Blackshirt,* 18 April 1935, p. 3.

61 *Ibid.,* 22 August 1936, p. 2.

62 During the Great War, it was claimed, the ratio of death suffered by Jews was 1:173, whilst for Gentiles it was 1:57; therefore it was concluded '. . . it was three times safer to be a Jew of military age than a gentile', *Blackshirt,* 8 August 1936, p. 1. The comparison was misleading in that it compared losses to the 46 million population of Britain and Ireland, with those sustained by the 420,000 Jews within the British Empire. This deliberate device was used both to produce a more favourable ratio and to conceal just how few Jews there were within the British Isles.

63 *Action,* 19 March 1938, p. 7. See also *Blackshirt,* 7 February 1936, p. 2; 22 August, p. 5; BUF pamphlet, *Britain and Jewry,* Abbey Supplies, London n.d., p. 5.

64 Review of L. Blum's book *Marriage,* by 'H.G.', *BUQ,* I, 3, July–September 1937, p. 105.

65 *Blackshirt,* 17 April 1937, p. 3. See also 1 March 1935, p. 2.

66 *Ibid.,* 5 September 1936, p. 5.

67 *Ibid.,* 6 December 1935, p. 4.

68 Mosley replied to Streicher's telegram for support in the following cordial manner: 'I greatly esteem your message in the midst of our hard struggle. The forces of Jewish corruption must be conquered in all great countries before the future of Europe can be secure in justice and peace . . .', *Manchester Guardian,* 11 May 1935, p. 13. Relations between the BUF and Streicher remained good and Mosley was again the object of his praise when he received a visiting deputation of twenty British fascists in Germany. *The Times,* 29 July 1937, p. 3.

69 *Blackshirt,* 1 March 1935, p. 2.
70 Mosley, *Tomorrow We Live,* p. 65.
71 *Britain and Jewry,* p. 8.
72 *Action,* 26 June 1937, p. 7.
73 Skidelsky, *op. cit.,* p. 393.
74 Report on Replies to Fascist Questionnaire, Labour Party, July 1934, pp. 1–8. LPL.
75 *Blackshirt,* 27 July 1934, p. 11. Skidelsky would appear mistaken in his belief that this branch was established '. . . in the autumn of 1934'. Skidelsky, *op. cit.,* p. 396.
76 *Action,* 6 March 1937, p. 9.
77 E. G. Clarke, *The British Union and the Jews,* Abbey Supplies, London 1938?, p. 7.
78 Special Branch report on anti-Semitism in the East End for April 1939, MEPO 2/3127. In September 1938 there was a case of marauding fascists, having attended a BUF meeting in Hackney, proceeding to Bethnal Green where they attacked several Jewish houses, smashing windows and physically assaulting at least one of the occupants. MEPO 2/3126.
79 Police reports from 'N' Division, Stoke Newington, 10 February 1936, MEPO 2/3085.
80 *Manchester Guardian,* 12 October 1936, p. 9; *Daily Herald,* 12 October 1936, pp. 1–2.
81 *HC Deb.,* 309, 5 March 1936, c. 1595–1603; 1633–4. See also *New Statesman and Nation* XII, 10 October 1936, pp. 496–7.
82 Information collated in response to confidential Home Office memorandum, 22/GEN/75(A.1).), dated 18 June 1936, MEPO 2/3042.
83 Special Branch reports on anti-Semitism in the East End, March–August 1939, MEPO 2/3127.
84 *Evening Standard,* 2 November 1936, pp. 1, 11.
85 *The Times,* 17 February 1936, p. 14.
86 *Evening Standard,* 4 November 1936, p. 13. See also *Jewish Chronicle,* 9 November 1934, pp. 24, 27.
87 Lebzelter, *op. cit.,* pp. 139–41.
88 In November 1938 it was renamed the Jewish Defence Committee. *Ibid.,* p. 143.
89 *Evening Standard,* 4 November 1936, p. 13. By 1939 the Board was prepared to admit that there was an implicit connection between the fight against anti-Semitism and the struggle against fascism. Even this concession, however, must be viewed in the light of the Board's attempts to attract the JPC which it wished to eliminate through incorporation. Lebzelter, *op. cit.,* p. 153.
90 M. I. Curzon, *In Many Rhythms: An Autobiography,* Weidenfeld & Nicolson, London 1953, p. 144.
91 C. Wegg-Prosser, *Fascism Exposed,* Jewish People's Council against Fascism and Anti-Semitism, London 1938, pp. 3–4.
92 J. Hamm, interview with author, 14 April 1980.
93 Police report on BUF meeting at Victoria Park Square, Bethnal Green, 12 March 1937, MEPO 2/3109.

CHAPTER 5

Anti-fascist opposition

Mass demonstrations must burn into the little man's soul the proud conviction that, though he is a little worm, he is nevertheless part of a great dragon.

A. Hitler, *Mein Kampf,*
as quoted by C. Cross, *The Fascists in Britain,*
Barrie & Rockcliffe, London 1961, p. 98

Nothing increases the insolence of the fascists so much as 'flabby pacifism' on the part of the workers' organisations. Nothing so destroys the confidence of the middle class in the working class as the temporising, passivity, and the absence of the will to struggle.

L. Trotsky, *Whither France,* 1934, as quoted in L. Trotsky,
Fascism, what it is and how to fight it,
Pathfinder Press Inc., New York 1972, p. 20.

Good men, the last wave by, crying how bright
Their frail deeds might have danced in a green bay,
Rage, rage against the dying of the light.
Wild men who caught and sang the sun in flight,
And learn, too late they grieved it on its way,
Do not go gentle into that good night;

D. Thomas,
'Do Not go Gentle into that Good Night'

Many, but by no means all, of those who opposed the BUF were on the political left. Some believed in direct physical confrontation, whilst others adopted a more passive approach. Amongst the former the Communist Party of Great Britain and the Independent Labour Party were particularly important, for in 1933 they formed a united front against the capitalist state and its fascist hirelings.[1] Although never numerically large,[2] the two parties made a considerable impact in the struggle against fascism by their remorseless repetition of a clear, class-oriented, anti-fascist message, and a willingness to constitute the vanguard of those who aimed at preventing the dissemination of fascist propaganda.

It was widely believed by many on the left that fascism in Britain would develop with the direct connivance of the state. This in turn was the product of the over-simplified view of fascism, whereby it was seen as a conspiracy to produce an irregular army to preserve capitalism from revolution through the brutal subjugation of the proletariat. It followed, therefore, that to rely upon the capitalist state and its apparatus of repression (including the police), was to play directly into the hands of the fascist enemy. This, of course, would be tantamount to total disaster, for the struggle against fascism was perceived as a fight to the death, involving 'a movement of organised violence whose avowed object is physically to destroy the working class movement. In this fight there can be no compromise. The examples of Germany and Italy should have taught this lesson. Fascism must be . . . . . . defeated in its early stages by the power of the mass movement, and in no other way.'[3] This refusal to distinguish between the BUF and the capitalist state provided the logic for a policy of physical confrontation from which violence inevitably arose.

The morality of this denial of free speech to political opponents was rarely considered in abstract terms. Ultimately the criterion upon which such action rested was that of effectiveness. Meetings and marches served not merely as vital propaganda channels for the fascist message, but also had an important morale-boosting function. They served as acts of confirmation for the faithful, or, as the BUF itself admitted, '. . . an outward sign of our internal faith; each is a symbol and an outward expression of our internal determination to march to power'.[4] Thus, through confrontation and disruption, the forces of active anti-fascism could damage the BUF not merely by preventing its dissemination of propaganda and by provoking it to violence which produced an unattractive public image, but also by sapping the internal morale of the party.

As previously suggested, left-wing opposition had harassed the New Party from the very beginning of its brief and feeble existence, to the extent that several of the party's meetings were marred by violence and disorder. Such attacks continued unabated after the formation of the BUF in October 1932. Later that same month a fascist meeting at the Memorial Hall, London, provided an example of the weary cycle of events which were to follow with such monotonous regularity. Mosley's speech was punctuated with interruptions, which led to the ejection of the offenders by uniformed stewards. After the meeting police intervened to prevent further violence following the outbreak of scuffles between anti-fascists and a column of blackshirts (including the stewards of the earlier meeting) who were marching back to National Headquarters.[5]

At the outset it must be stressed that often the interruptions at BUF meetings were not those of the individual heckler but of organised opponents interrupting in unison, including frequent renditions of the *Red Flag* or the *Internationale,* in a concerted effort to prevent any coherent communication between speaker and audience.[6] To an accomplished orator such as Mosley the individual heckler presented no real problems, and could even be used advantageously as a butt of ridicule, but a determined group of opponents could thoroughly disrupt even the largest of meetings. It was from this position that Mosley justified the behaviour of his stewards, arguing that '. . . among an audience of several thousand, one or two hundred men would come simply to make the speech unintelligible; just to shout you down'.[7] The remedy to this problem, ejections, was to prove inevitably violent.

Clashes continued throughout 1933 and on several occasions it is clear that fascist stewards attacked their opponents with truncheons of rubber and lead. In Manchester large meetings at the Free Trade Hall and Belle Vue were each marred by interruptions and subsequent ejections, and on the latter occasion there was fierce fighting after the meeting when anti-fascist stone-throwers ambushed a column of fascists returning to their headquarters.[8] The function of the fascist stewards, however, was beginning to be seen to stray from Mosley's original conception of them as a last resort – the components of a highly-disciplined and controlled coercive apparatus capable of acting swiftly and efficiently to preserve order. Indeed, he claimed in retrospect that fascist stewards were ordered into action only after three clear warnings had been issued from the platform informing the audience that further interruptions would not be tolerated.[9] By the end of 1933 stewards were not being used with anything like this degree of constraint, as illustrated by a Mosley meeting in Oxford, from the press reports of which two interesting points emerge.

Firstly it was reported that '. . . no sooner had the interruptions broken out than ejections from the hall began', whilst secondly, at the end of the meeting, a member of the audience refusing to stand for the national anthem was held upright by stewards.[10] The first point suggests that there was an insufficient time-lapse for three clear warnings to have been given before the ejections began, and also raises doubts as to whether the disruption caused in such a short time was sufficient to justify immediate ejections. The second point is more interesting still, for clearly the man refusing to stand for the national anthem was making a political gesture but was doing so in such a way as not to interfere directly with the progress of the meeting. In assaulting the man the stewards were not acting to preserve order nor were they defending the right of their leader to communicate with those who had gathered to listen to his message. They were imposing upon the man values to which they subscribed, but which he, presumably, rejected. Nor was this an isolated incident, as was illustrated during a meeting addressed by William Joyce at Brighton in the spring of 1933. On this occasion, during the national anthem a member of the audience, Mr W. Faulkner, bent down to pick up his eight-year-old daughter whose vision had been obscured by the throng of standing adults. His ill-considered act was construed as a mark of disrespect towards king and country by the assembled fascist stewards, four of whom communicated their disapproval to the unfortunate Mr Faulkner by beating him insensible. Whilst her husband was being rendered unconscious a fifth fascist forcibly restrained Mrs Faulkner and prevented her from interfering by assaulting her also.[11]

What such cases illustrated was the seductive simplicity of force. Rational arguments as to why a person should stand for the national anthem could be dispensed with, along with the entire tedious business of trying to convert or accommodate those determined to disagree. Force, though ugly in its full reality, invariably provides neat theoretical solutions by offering to remove (at least from sight) the unseemly, and to render malleable the intransigent. Anti-fascist opposition, irritating though it undoubtedly was, cannot be cited as the sole reason for the BUF's use of force. As suggested earlier, coercion underpinned the very essence of fascism, for it lay at the root of the BUF's centrist concept of enforced class harmony. The localised use of force at BUF meetings cannot be dissociated from this general acceptance of the principle of coercion, for both provided an easy, but deceptively superficial opportunity to produce harmony. Thus it was that force, and the violence which inevitably constitutes force, came easily to the BUF because it represented a core element of fascist ideology.

Anti-fascist activities were often fully reported in the BUF's own press although this exposed a serious dilemma. It was in the party's interests to exaggerate the idea of 'red terror', for a communist threat was vital for fascism to portray itself as the nation's saviour from chaos and bloody revolution. Besides, the simple juxtaposition of the aggressive reds attacking innocent blackshirts who dared to offer the people an alternative was in itself a valuable source of propaganda. Simultaneously, however, the BUF was anxious to avoid creating the impression that its members were weak, cowardly, or easily defeated. Hence when *The Blackshirt* gave accounts of anti-fascist victories it was stressed that they were achieved only after an heroic struggle by the vanquished fascists against impossible odds. An example of this occurred in March 1933 when a 'communist gang' of fifty was unable to attack a BUF meeting in Manchester because it was protected by eight uniformed stewards. The gang bided its time, waiting for the odds to improve, and after the meeting's conclusion pounced upon two fascists. Despite the unfavourable odds the gallant pair fought fiercely against the razors, bludgeons, and flailing boots of their attackers with nothing more than the good old English fist, until they were both knocked unconscious. To bring home the full depravity of these 'cowardly morons', it was reported that, upon reaching hospital, it had been discovered '. . . that one Fascist, amongst other injuries, had had the veins of his wrist bitten out . . .',[12] a bizarre touch more obviously at home within the pages of Bram Stoker than those of a political newspaper.

Sometimes even absurdly high odds were not sufficient for the communists to prevail, however, as in the case of their assault upon the BUF's Walworth headquarters after an alleged two-week siege of the premises. The '. . . 300 communists made an organised attack, armed with iron bars . . . Although outnumbered by over 60 to 1 the local members of the Union put up a gallant fight and the Communists . . . were repelled'.[13] But once again the appalling weapons used by the reds had taken their toll against the stalwart defenders, who were left bloody but unbowed. Such propaganda, in addition to illustrating the alleged nature of communism and the strength of its organised advocates in Britain, also served to boost the party's morale by personifying the struggle, the pain, and the heroism of fascism's march to power in the face of overwhelming but not insuperable odds.

The violence continued in 1934. In March a BUF meeting in Bristol included a display of force sufficient to leave five men requiring medical treatment. One man was ejected with such brutality that he was taken to hospital by ambulance, '. . . unconscious on a stretcher, his head swathed in bandages and covered with blood'.[14] A month later there was serious fighting at a meeting in Plymouth where three fascists were taken to hospital after chairs had been smashed and converted into weapons.[15] At the end of May the fascist press reported a battle in Newcastle where ten blackshirts drove away a thousand opponents who were attempting to disrupt their meeting, despite being '. . . assailed with broken bottles, heavy stones and every other kind of missile . . .'[16] in the communist armoury. Later the city's fascist headquarters was besieged by '. . . every hooligan in Newcastle',[17] but once again the heavily outnumbered fascists acquitted themselves honourably.

It is within this perspective of continuing fascist and anti-fascist violence that the Olympia meeting must be viewed, a meeting which became notorious for the degree of violence displayed by stewards towards those opponents with the audacity to interrupt Mosley's speech. Although eye-witness accounts vary in detail and sentiment, a general pattern of events emerges clearly. As soon as Mosley began his speech interruptions broke out amongst the audience and, without prior warnings, those responsible were ejected roughly by groups of uniformed stewards. Thereafter, throughout the evening, Mosley paused frequently in his speech whilst interrupters were manhandled from the hall. Some allowed themselves to be carried forth by the stewards, others attempted to defend themselves and some of the ensuing scuffles were illuminated by powerful spotlights.[18] In either case many of those ejected were brutally beaten either within the auditorium or in its surrounding corridors out of the public view. Whilst being carried from seat to exit by gangs of stewards many of the victims were continuously assaulted, according to eye-witness reports. Geoffrey Lloyd, Conservative MP and Parliamentary Private Secretary to Baldwin, witnessed

> . . . case after case of single interrupters being attacked by ten to twenty Fascists. Again and again, as five or six Fascists carried out an interrupter by arms and legs, several other Blackshirts were engaged in hitting and kicking his helpless body. . . . I do not think I saw a single heckler ejected from the meeting in a decent and ordinary way. On the other hand, I saw several respectable-looking people who merely rose in their places and made no struggle, treated with the unmerciful brutality that I have described.[19]

Gerald Barry, a prominent journalist, ventured into the corridors, where he found the violence was even more extreme:

> On one occasion I saw a man lying on the floor, obviously powerless and done for, being mercilessly kicked and horribly handled by a group of, certainly no fewer than eight, and possibly ten or twelve Blackshirts. On other occasion I saw a set of Blackshirts kicking and manhandling a miscreant in the stomach and all over the body more brutally than anything I have ever seen in my life short of the war. It made me feel physically sick to see.[20]

There would be little useful purpose in repeating eye-witness accounts of such brutality. It is sufficient to emphasise that a wealth of evidence exists (a considerable part of it from sources other than those on the left), which suggests that the general level of brutality on display at Olympia was horrifying. Certainly violence emanated from both sides, but as in each individual engagement the fascists appear to have outnumbered their opponents, it was the anti-fascists who invariably suffered the most. Mosley claimed that 'not only were our male Blackshirts kicked in the stomach and slashed with razors but our women Fascists were terribly assaulted . . .',[21] and a steward testified to seeing a female comrade's face slashed with an anti-fascist razor.[22] No evidence was forthcoming to substantiate these claims. Injuries sustained by anti-fascists, however, were undeniable and illustrated by the testimony of four of the doctors who helped to deal with the casualties. Each was called upon to assist with a stream of victims suffering from lacerations of the head and face and abdominal injuries. There were several cases of concussion and in some instances head wounds required stitching.[23] This impression is confirmed by the information within the register for the casualty department at St Mary Abbot's Hospital, where the most serious cases were taken after initial treatment at makeshift dressing stations in the vicinity of Olympia. Several of those registered had head injuries or concussion, and some were detained in hospital, including one with fractured ribs.[24] Independent eye-witness accounts and confidential police reports alike also suggest that violence against the protesters was such that by the time they reached the streets outside Olympia many had had their clothing torn (in some cases men had had their trousers and shoes completely removed), were bleeding from the head and in a state of semi-collapse or even unconsciousness.[25]

Why, then, was Olympia marred by such violence? Part of the answer lies in the period leading up to the meeting. As early as mid-May the CP had announced its decision to organise a demonstration against Mosley's meeting, which was portrayed as '. . . a challenge to the working class which must be taken up'.[26] Anti-fascist marches were organised from different parts of London to converge upon Olympia on the relevant evening, and those unable to march were advised to travel by underground train *en masse*, thereby making themselves eligible for the reduced fares offered to organised parties of travellers.[27] The *Daily Worker* even printed maps showing how to get to Olympia.[28] There is also evidence that at least some of the anti-fascists within the hall had armed themselves with knuckle-dusters in the expectation of trouble.[29] These preparations have been frequently commented upon, but the BUF's attitude to them has received little attention. The party was certainly aware of the possibility of trouble and boasted that those attempting to disrupt the meeting would be '. . . put outside, swiftly, efficiently, and with the minimum of noise'.[30] A *Times* correspondent at the meeting noted that interrupters were countered with a '. . . thoroughness and a uniformity of treatment which suggested a pre-scribed technique of violence'.[31] The use of the word 'prescribed' is particularly interesting for its lends further weight to the theory that the tactics adopted by the stewards had been decided upon in advance of the meeting. As in the case of their opponents, there is some evidence to suggest that some of the fascists were armed with knuckle-dusters, truncheons, and even razors.[32]

It would appear, then, that for the BUF and its opponents the Olympia meeting had taken on the appearance of a showdown long before the evening of 7 June. Both sides had perpared for a violent confrontation and then proceeded to act in such a manner as to produce it. Brutality on the part of the stewards was doubtless encouraged by anti-fascist victories scored earlier in the evening when demonstrators outside the hall had jostled, jeered at, and generally intimidated those seeking to gain entry to the meeting. Fearing that their opponents might try to rush the building BUF stewards were closely guarding the entrances and letting the audience enter the building only in a slow trickle. The combined effect of this, and the presence of the anti-fascist crowds outside, meant that much of the audience was not in place at the appropriate time, and the meeting finally began forty-five minutes late.[33] It is not unreasonable to suppose, therefore, that the 1,000 fascist stewards, whose duty it was to see that everything ran smoothly, must have been harbouring feelings of anger and frustration towards their opponents before Mosley's speech had even begun.

There is evidence, too, that the violence had a considerable degree of internal dynamism. As the long summer's evening wore on, assaults became more brutal in line with Mosley's warning from the platform that 'Interruption was getting more painful'.[34] Tempers on both sides became increasingly frayed as anti-fascists saw their comrades being savagely dealt with as the stewards struggled with only marginal success to prevent their leader's much publicised meeting degenerating into a chaotic brawl.

Finally, it is important to note that the Olympia meeting was significant not only because of its vast size, but also because amongst the audience of 10,000–12,000 there were a considerable number of representatives of the British establishment. MPs, clergymen, and prominent political commentators were amongst the many 'respectable' sections of the audience, for whom the Mosley meeting was a social occasion for which many had donned evening dress. Many of these were oblivious to the organised nature of the interruptions and were appalled at the manner in which stewards appeared to be treating ordinary hecklers. As the stewards became increasingly tired and frustrated they were probably less discriminating in their choice of victims. Certainly some of those ejected were not communists, but had risen simply to protest at the treatment meted out to previous interrupters. In an atmosphere where the slightest interjection led to swift retribution in the form of immediate and violent ejection this was inevitable, but it had the effect of increasing the impression of fascist brutality directed towards innocent and defenceless members of the public.[35]

It is probable that individually many of the assaults which occurred at Olympia were no worse than those which had been committed at several of the more violent BUF meetings before June 1934. Their sheer number, however, and the nature of the audience, meant that at Olympia they were destined to make the headlines. To suggest that the BUF used Olympia specifically to illustrate its ability to deal with 'red' opposition is, of course, nonsense, but communist determination to disrupt the meeting probably did encourage some stewards to behave with even more brutality than was usual. Despite the efforts of historians such as Skidelsky to minimise the violence at Olympia, it is beyond doubt that it was extreme, it was ugly, and that the bulk of it was perpetrated by the fascists. Mosley's speech was made and the BUF claimed a great victory, but in the light of the immediate stream of condemnations from public and private figures alike who had been present at the proceedings, it was to prove a very phyrrhic victory indeed. The Olympia violence marked the BUF for the remainder of its existence. In view of fascism's general attitude to violence this was not an inappropriate stigmatisation.

As with Olympia, so the BUF's Hyde Park rally of September 1934 became the focus of anti-fascist opposition, and, as with Olympia, the CP was in the forefront of those organising that opposition. Exhaustive publicity for the counter-demonstration hammered home the message that on 9 September British fascism must be drowned in a sea of opposition. On the day in question there was a sufficiently high turn-out to achieve this aim. Estimates as to the total number of persons in the park vary from 60,000 to 150,000. Of these, 3,000 were fascists, but many of the others were their opponents, despite police claims that anti-fascists numbered 5,600 and that the remaining 60,000 were mere spectators. Even the police, however, were forced to admit that the majority of the crowd was opposed to fascism and manifested its opposition by booing and singing throughout the fascist speeches. Within a police cordon of over 6,000 the speakers upon the BUF's five separate platforms attempted in vain to make themselves heard above the noise.[36]

Over the following two years anti-fascist disruption of meetings and its consequent violence occurred in almost all of Britain's major cities. In mid-May 1935 thirty opponents were ejected from a meeting in Birmingham,[37] and a week later in Newcastle Mosley faced such determined opposition that, following a police refusal to allow his stewards to eject interrupters, he was forced to abandon a meeting of 2,000.[38] In the autumn of that year a Mosley meeting at Paddington Baths led to ejections and eventually to a free fight during which fists and chairs were employed, and in the following spring in Warrington a meeting degenerated into similar chaos with chairs being thrown, windows smashed, and a fascist van outside the hall being overturned.[39] In March 1936 Mosley again spoke at the Albert Hall, and again there were interruptions and ejections, some of which were unnecessarily brutal. Two of the victims were carried out on stretchers (one of whom was initially placed upon the danger list at St George's Hospital), and many of the others suffered cuts and bruises. In watching the stewards at their grim work, however, one correspondent was moved to the opinion that their '. . . technique of chucking out has certainly greatly improved since the brutal knuckle-duster tactics which made the Olympia demonstration hideous'.[40]

Disorder continued throughout the summer of 1936. One of the last major indoor battles was fought at the Carfax Assembly Rooms, Oxford, in late May. In the face of continuous interruptions by the many anti-fascists amongst the audience, Mosley ordered the ejections to begin, and in so doing initiated a free fight during which chairs were again used as weapons and head injuries were sustained on each side.[41] The remainder of the summer's violence occurred at outdoor gatherings, which were becoming an increasingly common feature because of the BUF's growing difficulty in obtaining the use of halls. At the end of June anti-fascists in Manchester stoned Mosley and his followers, whilst in the following month at an open-air meeting in Hull missiles were also thrown and six stewards were knocked unconscious as they fought to prevent anti-fascists from rushing the platform. It was claimed by the fascists press that after this meeting there had been an attempt upon Mosley's life, resulting in the shattering of one of the windows of his car by a bullet.[42]

Special Branch estimates for August 1936 suggested that in the London area organised anti-fascist opposition had disrupted at least sixty per cent of the BUF's meetings.[43] Elsewhere in the country during the same month, open-air meetings were stoned and disrupted in Perth, Bristol, and Merthyr.[44] In September, Mosley's attempt to address a large open-air crowd at Leeds was made difficult by repeated volleys of stones from opponents amongst the crowd, and subsequent fighting with fascist stewards. In all, twelve people were taken to hospital, one of whom was seriously injured, and Mosley himself was struck by several stones, one of which caused a deep facial gash below his right eye.[45] Despite the violence the speech was made and a fascist victory was claimed.

Earlier in September in reviewing the tactics used against the BUF by its opponents, Joyce had suggested that the prevailing level of violence was the desperate response of those who realised that the previous tactics of silence and ridicule had failed to damage the growth of fascism. Violence would prove equally futile, predicted Joyce: 'During the next few months we shall be facing the last attack designed to prevent our propaganda . . . we shall win, because the British people are with us. Showing patience, determination and courage we shall, with the support of the people, establish beyond any future challenge, the right to be heard . . .'.[46] It was to prove a less than accurate prophecy, for within a month up to 100,000 opponents were to block the streets around Aldgate in defiance of the authorities, and prevent the BUF marching through the East End.

Before looking at the Aldgate demonstration one must be clear as to the role played by the Communist Party. Some historians have naïvely endorsed the Special Branch view that almost all active anti-fascists were organised by either the CP or its many subsidiary or 'front' organisations.[47] This erroneous approach disregards the real degree of independence exercised by many local anti-fascist groups which, even if affiliated to the CP, did not blindly follow its ordinances. It attributes also to the CP a degree of unity which in reality did not exist. The testimony of Joe Jacobs, party secretary of the CP's large and active Stepney branch, illustrates only too clearly the manner in which the party was deeply divided between those who advocated popular anti-fascism and those who believed that the party's greatest priority should be the winning of control of trade unions.[48]

Exaggerated claims made by the CP itself concerning the degree of control which it exercised over the anti-fascist forces should certainly be treated with caution. In the final analysis it could only lead those willing to follow and, therefore, had to rely upon, and indeed in some respects was the prisoner of, other anti-fascist organisations, and of the unaffiliated. Each of these constituent units of the anti-fascist mosaic could have its own ideas as to how fascism could best be combated. Hence in July 1934 the CP instructed anti-fascists to boycott a Mosley meeting in Brighton and instead attend a communist rally elsewhere. On the day, however, the rally was outnumbered by those who had chosen to protest outside the venue of Mosley's meeting. Such was the disparity in numbers that the CP simply closed its own meeting and threw its support and 'leadership' behind those already assembled in opposition to the BUF.[49]

These general points regarding the CP were illustrated by the party's attitude to the BUF's Aldgate demonstration. The events themselves are familiar enough. The BUF planned to celebrate the conclusion of its summer campaign on Sunday 4 October with a large march through east London culminating in meetings in Shoreditch, Limehouse, Bow, and Bethnal Green, each of which was to be addressed by Mosley. Throughout the morning crowds gathered in such numbers, especially at the junction of Whitechapel High Street, Commercial Road, and Leman Street, that despite police efforts, the planned route of the march from its assembly point at Royal Mint Street, up Leman Street and into the East End via Commercial Road, was no longer possible. The alternative route lay through Cable Street and it was here that the most serious fighting took place as police grappled with anti-fascists, and charged barricades, in an attempt to clear a path for the 3,000 assembled fascists. Sheer numbers prevailed, however, and at 3.40 p.m. the Commissioner of Police ordered Mosley to cancel the march. Police cordons confined the anti-fascists to the streets around Aldgate, and allowed the fascist column to make an ignominous escape westwards to the Embankment where it dispersed, having failed totally to achieve its objectives.[50]

It was a momentous victory for the forces of anti-fascism. Neither Mosley's uniformed 'troops' nor the might of the Metropolitan police had been able to circumvent the will of the masses; the fascists had been driven, albeit temporarily, from the heart of east London. But who was responsible for this anti-fascist triumph? The *Daily Worker* offered thanks on behalf of the whole labour movement 'to those who worked for the defeat of Mosley, to those masses who endured so heroically; to those organisations . . . . . . who threw their full weight into the fight . . .'.[51] The CP claimed that its role in mobilising the masses, and the leadership which it had provided, had been essential factors in the day's success. Although it was accepted that initially the party had urged the boycott of Mosley's march in favour of attendance at a Trafalgar Square rally in support of Republican Spain, it was claimed that, having decided to oppose Mosley directly, the party was responsible for the success of the counter-demonstration.

The testimony of Jacobs, however, illustrates just how great was the opportunism of the CP with regard to the Aldgate demonstration. For weeks before the march all over the East End organisations were at work preparing to confront Mosley on 4 October. Indeed, it was precisely through such action that organisations, including the Independent Labour Party, the Jewish People's Council, and the Ex-Servicemen's Movement, illustrated their independence from the Communist Party. By the end of September leaflets and printed slogans urged East End anti-fascists to unite around the slogan 'They Shall Not Pass'.[52] The CP continued to urge a boycott of the march in favour of the Trafalgar Square meeting, and Frank Lefitte, the east London communist organiser, informed Jacobs that the District Party Committee's instructions were 'If Mosley decides to march let him. Don't attempt disorder.'[53] Anti-fascist preparations to prevent the march continued regardless of the attitude of the CP. Only in the early hours of the morning of 1 October did the party's leadership realise the gravity of its misjudgement and decide that the CP must be seen to be in the forefront of the anti-fascist opposition, but it was too late to prevent that morning's edition of the *Daily Worker* continuing the call for a rally in Trafalgar Square. By the following day this error had been corrected and the newspaper was urging that the Aldgate counter-demonstration be '. . . the biggest rally against fascism that has yet been seen in Britain'.[54] For the next few days the party used its propaganda resources to build support, but there was insufficient time to produce new leaflets, so that those designed to advertise the Trafalgar Square rally were simply over-printed with brief details of the new venue. On the day itself the CP divided responsibility for different streets amongst its members, as well as establishing first-aid posts, information posts, and runners to carry messages to other sectors of 'the front'.[55] The rest, of course, is history.

The CP's initial reticence towards involvement in the Aldgate opposition was indicative of the party's increasing desire for respectability and membership of the political mainstream. Greater emphasis was placed by the leadership upon closer ties with the trade union movement and Labour Party, and with local communities, than upon the concept of populism and the mobilisation of the masses. Some party members, such as Jacobs, opposed this drift and insisted that active popular support was vital. It has proved a familiar debate for those on the left ever since. Its effect was that the CP spent less of its resources on the physical opposition of fascism in favour of working more closely with the Labour Party and serving the local community through the establishment of tenants' associations, and the organisation of local solidarity through activities such as rent strikes. Those who supported this shift of emphasis were keen to point out that it was effective in combating fascism, because it helped to deal with local problems and related them to an overall socialist perspective, thus undercutting actual and potential fascist support.[56]

Its opponents blamed the decision to allow the BUF freedom of speech for contributing to the growth of fascism. Lack of CP opposition, it was claimed, had enabled the BUF to hold successful meetings more frequently and to penetrate new areas of the East End. Large fascist meetings were held in Victoria Park Square without disruption by the communists, who were busy holding smaller meetings in the same vicinity. Fascists marched even in Whitechapel singing the Nazi *Worst Wessel* song, unmolested by the communists, and were only chased away by members of the Ex-Servicemen's Association.[57] Even large BUF marches were unopposed by the CP, which was concerned that any repetition of the Aldgate disturbances would lead to its legal prosecution for incitement to disorder.[58] It was also anxious not to endanger its growing connections with the social democratic left, through mass radical action. The reward for this loss of revolutionary perspective came in 1945 when the party increased its parliamentary representation from one to two, but by then those like Jacobs, who believed in the tactics of mass anti-fascist confrontation, had already left or had been expelled.

Opposition to the BUF continued, of course (which merely emphasises the earlier point concerning the ease with which the CP's role in anti-fascist activities can be exaggerated), although in general the anti-fascism of this period was certainly less effective than previously. At Hampstead Town Hall in October fascist stewards dealt brutally with interruptions at a meeting addressed by Joyce. An eye-witness was shocked by the violence as 'One steward full-fistedly grabbed a girl by her hair and literally tore her out of her seat. Another girl lost her shoes in the struggle and kept crying that she wanted to go out quietly. This she was not allowed to do.'[59] In the same month in Middlesbrough a crowd of 2,000 prevented an outdoor fascist meeting from being held.[60]

Meetings in Aberdeen in February and April were so well attended by anti-fascists that their ejection meant the loss of eighty per cent and seventy per cent of the respective audiences.[61]

In London the BUF concentrated its resources upon the planning of a huge demonstration for 4 July. In late June the proposed route had to be changed after the government used the powers of its newly-passed Public Order Act to ban marches in the East End, but the new route (from Kentish Town to Trafalgar Square) was deemed acceptable by the authorities. Before the march the CP conducted a thorough propaganda campaign linking it to fascism's '. . . world campaign to destroy all democratic freedom', and to substitute in its place a hideous combination of murder, war, and political and sexual oppression.[62] Interestingly, however, the CP's propaganda emphasised not the ability of the masses to prevent the march, but complained bitterly that the government ought to have banned it. Whereas the communists planned a demonstration in St Pancras and a mass rally at the end of the march in Trafalgar Square, other anti-fascist organisations, particularly the ILP, believed that the march could be prevented physically and propogandised in support of this line of action.[63] On the day in question the march was completed, although much of the route was lined with jeering opponents and there were minor skirmishes between marchers and anti-fascists, twenty-seven of whom were arrested. At Trafalgar Square the 3,500 fascists were greatly outnumbered by opponents who rendered Mosley's speech almost completely inaudible.[64] Despite this, however, the fascist press hailed the march as a triumph precisely because it had not been prevented by its opponents.[65]

In September 1937 the BUF announced the opening of its 'autumn campaign' due to culminate in a large march through Bermondsey to mark the fifth anniversary of the party's foundation. There was greater anti-fascist unity on this occasion because the leadership of the CP felt that the march could be opposed successfully. Not only was it through a working-class area (unlike much of the July 4 route), but also it could be portrayed as being more provocative than had been the July march through central London.[66] The District Party Committee felt, therefore, that the CP could be seen opposing the fascists in Bermondsey without alienating the support of those who believed in the BUF's right to freedom of speech. Once again this provides striking evidence of the party's concern regarding its image amongst liberally inclined fellow travellers. The result was a co-ordinated display of anti-fascist propaganda before the march, and on 3 October itself there was an attempt to recapture the heady success experienced at Aldgate a year previously. In this the anti-fascists were unsuccessful, although their failure was not due to a lack of courage or determination amongst those involved. Fifty thousand demonstrators packed the streets around Borough underground station and made part of the BUF's route impassable. As in Cable Street, barricades were erected and police charges to clear the area were repelled with showers of stones, and lumps of concrete. By the time that the police had broken through one barricade in Long Lane, a second had been erected, and it was decided that only by changing its route could the fascist march continue. Although the 3,400 fascists completed the revised route, the meeting scheduled to be held at West Lane had to be abandoned because of anti-fascist opposition.[67] Casualties included 113 people arrested and at least thirty injured, including two policemen.

Bermondsey was the last of the large-scale street battles which arose from BUF marches. The marches themselves continued but the CP's revised attitude towards them, together with its concentration upon events in Spain, meant that opposition was less intense. The government's permanent ban upon all marches in east London also removed some of the *raison d'être* of other anti-fascist organisations. The traditional May Day demonstration of 1938 passed off without incident as 2,000 fascists marched through Bermondsey to a rally of 50,000 which listened sympathetically to Mosley's speech.[68] A year later the BUF's last May Day march also took place without disorder.

Sporadic opposition continued at fascist meetings, however, and in October 1937 Mosley was knocked unconscious by a stone whilst addressing a crowd of 10,000 in Liverpool.[69] In March of the following year there were several ejections from an indoor meeting at Mitcham, one of whom was bleeding freely from a facial wound. Mosley expressed his regret over their departure on the grounds that '. . . it spoils the record. We have not had to put anyone out this winter'.[70] The record continued spoilt as over thirty opponents were ejected from a Mosley meeting in Stoke-on-Trent the following month after an organised attempt to drown out the speaker.[71] In September, fascists attempting to hold an outdoor meeting in Aberdeen had their lorry overturned and were showered with stones, pieces of coal, and fireworks by a hostile crowd of 6,000.[72] Having cited these examples, however, it should be added that the BUF did continue to hold peaceful meetings also, including two appearances by Mosley before a packed and largely sympathetic Free Trade Hall, Manchester, during the winter of 1938–9; and a large meeting at Earls Court in July 1939 when, less than two months before the outbreak of war, Mosley was applauded by up to 30,000 British citizens.

The above account does not purport to be in any way definitive, but merely aims at illustrating something of the nature and extent of anti-fascist disruption of BUF activities. The fascist violence generated by this opposition damaged the BUF despite Mosley's attempted justifications. The argument which had first appeared during his New Party

days concerning the importance of keeping open his primary communi-
cative channel to the public still carried some weight but failed to excuse
the frequent bouts of excessive violence perpetrated by his followers. Nor
could it be justified by lurid fascist allegations concerning communist
attacks and the fiendish weapons deployed therein. Whilst anti-fascists
undoubtedly used violence on occasions their basic aim was usually the
co-ordinated disruption of fascist propaganda. The usual BUF response
to this was one of violence, as frustration and anger amongst stewards
facing such disruptive tactics led all too frequently to acts of inexcusable
brutality against individuals who were offering no resistance. To suggest (as Mosley did) that violent political meetings were not new to
Britain[73] was no defence. The impact of blood, broken bones, and
screams of agony was little reduced by the knowledge that such horrors
had a historical precedent. Ultimately, however, the most damning
aspect of the BUF's violence lay in Mosley's refusal to condemn it even at
its most brutal. In the aftermath of Olympia Mosley did not apologise for
the conduct of his followers, which had been witnessed and condemned
by so many. This lack of condemnation helped to perpetuate the myth
that the BUF was composed wholly of sadistic thugs who enjoyed inflic-
ting pain upon their opponents.

It was for these reasons that fascist violence was counter-produc-
tive, for it made the concept of the BUF as the aggrieved party scarcely
credible. Although technically the BUF was the victim of attacks by its
opponents (occasionally these roles were reversed) it was those same
opponents who were seen to suffer at the hands of the uniformed stewards. Violence as practised by the BUF too often destroyed the party's
case, distorted its arguments, and discredited its ideology.

The point which emerges most strongly from a study of clashes
between the BUF and its opponents is the lack of simple cause and effect
relationships. No single group was solely responsible for the violence,
just as no single group was solely responsible for organising anti-fascist
activities. The bulk of such activities were organised, but often relied
also upon popular support from the unaligned masses. The motivation of
active anti-fascists ranged from those who saw themselves as one side of
an international life and death struggle between the forces of good and
evil, to those for whom anti-fascism provided a splash of colour and
diversity to lives of bleak monotony imprisoned within a drab world.
Despite this huge spectrum, however, there was a degree of common
effort towards the aim of preventing the growth of fascism. Violence, far
from being an end in itself, was simply the by-product of the attempted
achievement of this aim and of fascist attempts to deny this.

Opposition to the spread of fascism was the primary aim of all
anti-fascists, of course, but not all agreed that this could best be achieved
through tactics of physical confrontation. The bulk of these passive

anti-fascist forces comprised the Labour Party and the trade union movement. Whereas the BUF occasionally expressed a sneaking admiration for the ruthless determination and discipline of the CP, it had nothing but contempt for the Labour Party and other practitioners of social democracy, a system which it dismissed as '. . . pleasure without pain, idealism without effort, prosperity and justice without planning. No more effective form of dope for the masses could be invented'.[74] The Labour Party in particular was singled out as the very epitome of the general spinelessness of social democracy. Together with its allies within the trade union movement, the party did all that it could to live up to this image in regard to its role in the struggle against fascism. Both were prepared to propagandise against fascism but neither was willing to become associated officially with tactics which involved its physical confrontation.

The Labour Party's research department was the source of a stream of pamphlets denouncing Mosley the renegade and his fascist hordes. Fascism's wealthy patrons, its record of violence, its contempt for democracy, and Mosley's own aristocratic birthright and family wealth were all used in the fusillade of denunciation. Almost always the arguments were established within the context of the fascist regimes of Germany and Italy, which had deprived the majority of their unfortunate citizens of their living standards as well as their democratic rights and liberties.[75] It was an effective propaganda formula and one which the trade union movement also made use of, but both the TUC and Labour Party proved reluctant to go beyond this type of paper denunciation.

In 1934 it was announced that the National Council of Labour, in liaison with the General Council of the TUC, the Executive Committees of the Labour Party and the Parliamentary Labour Party, and the Co-operative movement, had agreed that the BUF should be combated by educating the public as to the true nature of fascist duplicity, whilst also seeking to ensure that the BUF was not allowed to operate outside the law. The possibility of lobbying for new legislation to curb fascist activities was not discounted.[76] The Joint Committee of the London Trades Council and London Labour Party echoed this position by initiating a campaign designed to expose the real nature of fascism through reasoned argument rather than 'mere denunciation'.[77] It was prepared to give money to aid those persecuted by foreign fascist regimes, but this, too, was only another form of paper solidarity. When it came to opposing fascism upon British streets not only did the official leadership of the labour movement disapprove, but it expressed its disapproval in the most negative manner by encouraging others to boycott such activities.

When invited by the CP to join the Olympia demonstration neither the London Trades Council nor the Labour Party bothered even to reply,[78] and in September of the same year they actually urged non-attendance at the Hyde Park anti-fascist rally. In connection with the Aldgate march in 1936 they advised 'those people who are opposed to fascism to keep away from the demonstration',[79] advice which was echoed by A. M. Wall, the secretary of the London Trades Council. A year later the party attempted to keep its followers away from the Bermondsey march by circularising its local branches and affiliated organisations, once again urging non-attendance. The main argument presented in support of this position was that fascism thrived upon opposition because of the disorder and publicity which it generated.[80] This idea, that enforced anonymity rather than confrontation represented the most effective method of combating fascism, was connected to the wider argument which interpreted fascism as a capitalist response to increased proletarian militancy. Active anti-fascism, it was argued, was a part of this militancy and, therefore, encouraged the very doctrine which it ostensibly opposed. On the simple level opposition was seen to give much needed publicity to fascism, on the more profound level the opposition itself was seen to create the very need which fascism promised to satisfy. In either case inaction was encouraged, as any direct action was conceived as advantageous to the enemy.

At the root of the labour movement's unwillingness to confront the BUF lay a refusal by its leadership to analyse fascism fully as a political ideology. There was a tendency to class all dictatorships together as a single evil system of government, regardless as to exactly who was in power, by the courtesy of whom, and ruling on whose behalf. Thus the struggle against fascism was portrayed as the struggle by democracy against dictatorship. Fascist tyranny was considered no worse than that of communism. It was the opinion of the National Council of Labour that 'If the British working class . . . toy with the idea of Dictatorship, Fascism or Communist, they will go down to servitude such as they have never suffered.'[81] This defence of bourgeois democracy reflected the Labour Party's new-found status as a major parliamentary party with aspirations of government. The trade union movement was equally committed to it, because bourgeois democracry provided the climate in which trade unionism could flourish and work for the gradual material improvement of its membership. Independent trade unions would cease to exist under any form of dictatorship, it was argued, and with their disappearance would pass the rights won by working people through a century of struggle.[82]

By supporting bourgeois democracy, however, the labour movement was also supporting the capitalist state and, unsurprisingly, this drew heavy criticism from the communists, who were particularly incensed by this simplistic vision of fascism as an aberration which had contravened the rules of civilised society. Labour Party and trade union leaders, it was complained, saw fascism 'not as the logical working out of the class struggle, but as a sudden and violent interruption of an alien force from nowhere breaking in upon the imagined "rule of reason". Therefore they call upon all to hasten to the defence of existing capitalist society against Fascism. They call for the defence of existing capitalist institutions.'[83] Owing to the prevailing communist belief as to the nature of the relationship between fascism and the state such a course was considered fatal. By restraining the masses from destroying the fascists in favour of relying upon the duplicious capitalist state for protection, the labour movement was seen to be assisting the growth of fascism and, therefore, ensuring its own destruction and that of all other parties of the left.

The CP believed that fascism could only be fought successfully through a broad anti-fascist front capable of organising '. . . active mass struggle against Fascism . . . against every legislative, executive and administrative measure of the Government leading to fascism, and against every Blackshirt provocation'.[84] Because of its size and depth of resources, the Labour Party was obviously a vital element of any such amalgamation. Owing to its interpretation of fascism, its reliance upon the forces of the state, and its distrust of the communists, however, the leadership of the Labour Party was not enthusiastic about such an arrangement. The fight against fascism, it was claimed, would not be enhanced by any such alliance with the CP, 'which, in any case, is small in membership and lacking in public influence'. Besides, the inability of the leaders of the labour movement to discriminate between different types of dictatorship caused them to detect '. . . a sinister analogy between the political theories and doctrines of Fascism and Communism'.[85]

The idea of co-operation between the CP and the Labour Party was not new. In the early 1920s the communists had called for affiliation with the Labour Party and a united front against capitalism, but its overtures had been spurned by successive Labour Party conferences. By 1928 members of the CP had been prohibited from attending Labour conferences, even in the capacity of trade-union delegates.[86] Relations between the two parties worsened after 1928 because of the Comintern's insistence that social democrats be denounced as 'social fascists'. Only gradually in the early 1930s was this line altered, thereby allowing European communist parties once again to advocate the united front. In early 1933 the Labour Party rejected a proposed united front with the CP and the ILP, and did so again in 1934. In May of that year the party's executive ruled that any united action with the CP without prior dispensation was incompatible with Labour Party membership, and at the next party conference was given powers to deal with offenders.[87] Also in 1934 the General Council of the TUC issued the infamous 'Black Circular', encouraging unions to prohibit communists from holding reponsible positions, and forcing the exclusion of communists from those trade councils which wished to be recognised formally by the TUC.[88] The basis of this hostility towards the CP lay in the past. Not only had communists infiltrated local Labour parties in the 1920s (sometimes making so many converts that the entire local party had had to be disaffiliated), but during the 'social fascist' era the CP had mercilessly denounced Labour and trade union leaders, and attacked their meetings. Leaving aside the obvious ideological differences between a revolutionary and a reformist perspective, this legacy of abuse and bitterness would in itself have been sufficient to blight any efforts towards a united front.[89]

Undeterred, however, the communists continued to call for a united anti-fascist front of 'the widest character, dominantly proletarian, but embracing also students, intellectuals and petit-bourgeois anti-fascists'.[90] In an attempt to achieve this the Committee for Co-ordinating Anti-Fascist Activity was established, the most prominent member of which was Mosley's old comrade, John Strachey. The Committee's task was to propagate the CP's analysis of fascism and to encourage the growth of, and bring a degree of centralised cohesion to, burgeoning local anti-fascist groups throughout the country. Unsurprisingly the Labour Party had little to do with the Committee. Its suspicions of the communists remained, and when it held a conference in September 1934 to consider the attitude of the labour movement to fascism, it ruled that members of the CP were ineligible to attend.[91]

The Co-ordinating Committee represented an attempt to circumvent the labour leadership's refusal to co-operate by appealing directly to local anti-fascists. The CP also demonstrated its desire for unity by throwing its support behind Labour Party candidates in most areas of the country. But despite such efforts communist affiliation was rejected by the Labour Party Conferences of 1935 and 1936, as was the formation of a united front. The concept of a united front did find increasing sympathy on the left of the Labour Party, however, especially amongst the Socialist League, which had been founded primarily by ex-ILP members, who had not left the political mainstream after the 1932 split. Under the leadership of Sir Strafford Cripps the League became increasingly autonomous within the party and produced its own propaganda in defiance of official policy. In January 1937, a 'Unity Manifesto' was issued by the Socialist League in conjunction with the CP and the ILP, and backed by a campaign demanding vigorous anti-fascism and the socialist transformation of British society. The Labour Party's leadership reacted to the threat of unity in practice, by preparing to disaffiliate those party members involved. Faced with expulsion, the Socialist League dissolved itself in May 1937.[92] At its conference in October the party once again rejected any form of united front with the communists.[93] Having been murdered in its infancy, the united front was finally laid to rest. In 1939 Cripps made a last effort to link the Labour Party with the CP and the ILP (whose alliance was breaking down in the face of communist behaviour in Spain, and attitudes towards the Moscow show-trials), and even the Liberal Party in a nation-wide campaign for a 'Popular Front'. Both he and his principal lieutenants (including Aneurin Bevan) were rewarded by the executive with explusion from the Labour Party. This decision was endorsed overwhelmingly at the party's next annual conference.

Despite prohibitions and threats by the leadership of the labour movement there was a degree of anti-fascist co-operation, especially at local level. Often the knowledge that Mosley was to visit a particular town set in motion forces which produced a united front to oppose his meeting. Indeed, it was precisely to link these local groups that the Co-ordinating Committee had been established. The groups themselves were often broadly constituted, amalgamating any number of political and religious organisations which were opposed to fascism.[94] A full story of the constitution and activities of such groups cannot be here undertaken, but their potential range can be illustrated by an example from Oxford. When it became known that Mosley was due to speak in the city a united front was organised including communists, Labour Party members, Liberals, and a few Conservatives and clergymen, and a committee was formed (reflecting these political differences) to organise an anti-fascist protest. A vigorous campaign helped to persuade the predominantly Conservative local council to rescind its permission for the BUF to use the town hall. The fascists reacted by changing the venue to a privately-owned hall and the committee then split over whether the meeting should be disrupted or boycotted. The CP and some Labour Party elements supported the former course of action and established a new committee, and it was this which organised much of the opposition that wrecked Mosley's meeting at the Carfax Assembly Rooms in May 1936.[95]

The Labour Party's co-operation with the communists was not unique to Oxford. In Hackney the Labour Party was amongst local groups which joined the CP and the ILP in a united front, and the same was true of Chiswick and Uxbridge.[96] There were doubtless many other occasions when Labour Party militants disobeyed the instructions of their leaders and allied themselves with those who were prepared to fight the BUF actively, but the official line of the labour movement continued to forbid it. The result was that the united front was prevented from expressing itself as a nation-wide campaign. Whilst it could be effective locally, it continued as a patchwork of poorly connected local organisations.

The policy-makers of the labour movement were not alone in their commitment to passive anti-fascism. As suggested in the previous chapter, the reactionary Jewish Board of Deputies projected a similar course, as did other bourgeois anti-fascist organisations. The most notable of these was the Council of Citizens of East London, founded in 1936 with the avowed aim of restoring order and good Gentile–Jewish relations to the East End. Under The Archbishop of Canterbury (whose qualifications as a 'citizen of East London' could at best be described as peripheral), the organisation also included peers, clergymen of all denominations, MPs and local mayors of diverse political persuasion, as well as employers and trade-union representatives. Whereas the analysis of fascism emanating from the left was often inadequate, that which arose from these worthies was virtually non-existent. Consequently all disturbers of the peace were condemned and appeals made to all East Enders to boycott both fascist and anti-fascist demonstrations and street-meetings.[97] It was patronising advice. Those who gave it could avoid the incessant fascist pressure and campaigning because they did not live in the East End. They avoided the poverty, squalor, and degradation of east London's slums with equal ease. For such people popular disorder of any nature was disturbing because it threatened the stability upon which was founded their prestige, wealth, and influence. One can only speculate as to how comfortable the leaders of the labour movement felt in such exalted company.

Finally the role played by the local authorities in the struggle against fascism should be mentioned. Primarily this involved the denial of halls for BUF meetings. Although it began in 1933, by 1936 it had become commonplace as the hand of local government closed like a vice around the windpipe of British fascism. *Action* denounced it as a conspiracy[98] but in truth there were several motives. Many of the premises in question were municipal property and were withheld by the political opponents of fascism; a practice obviously most frequent within areas of Labour Party jurisdiction. But even in those areas not controlled by the Labour Party, halls were frequently denied to the BUF because of anti-fascist pressure or genuine fears of damage to the property. This latter consideration was particularly important in the denial of privately-owned premises.

Even where fascist meetings were not cancelled local authorities began increasingly to impose restrictions upon them. Usually these forbade the wearing of uniforms and insisted upon the presence of police inside the hall to prevent outbreaks of violence.[99] The ban on uniforms was also extended to outdoor meetings in several areas, and in some cases the BUF was prohibited from using municipally-owned outdoor meeting sites such as parks.[100] Other tactics employed against outdoor fascist meetings included the implementation of existing by-laws against the painting or chalking of slogans, and against the use of loudspeakers. The former had often been tolerated as a traditional method of advertising political meetings and the BUF had relied upon it heavily, especially in areas such as the East End. The latter restriction was even more damaging, for it made fascist speakers vulnerable to being drowned out by relatively small groups of opponents. On occasions when it was invoked the party often recognised this reality and cancelled the meeting concerned.[101]

Each of these actions impeded the BUF's development but the denial of halls was the most irksome. Initially the party responded to this challenge with predictable bravado, claiming that such desperate measures on the part of the 'Old Gang' indicated the growing threat posed by fascism. Gradually, however, the complaints became more bitter and it was admitted that the combined effect of the lack of halls and the prohibition by the LCC of loudspeakers at outdoor meetings amounted to '. . . a severe handicap'.[102] By the end of 1938 the position was critical as almost all large halls in Britain's cities were unavailable, a fact reflected in the BUF's jubilation upon beating the blockade and hiring Earls Court in the summer of 1939. Whilst this was an individual triumph, the meeting did not reverse the general trend towards strangulation. The final blow fell with the outbreak of war when those few large halls which had remained available (such as the Free Trade Hall, Manchester, and the Victoria Hall, Leeds) were withdrawn. By the end of 1939 the position was hopeless, with not a single large hall available in any major town in England, and by the time of its suppression the party was reduced to the humiliating position of having to appeal to its members through the columns of *Action* for information as to the existence of local premises which might be available for fascist meetings.[103]

This denial of halls, together with the restrictions placed upon outdoor meetings, had the effect of rendering Mosley speechless in many areas of the country. For a movement so reliant upon the spoken word of its leader the effects were obviously serious. The denial of halls also forced the BUF to rely increasingly upon open-air meetings. In addition to being vulnerable to harassment from local by-laws the outdoor meeting had other perils, not least of which was its portrayal of the BUF as a street-party operating upon the political fringe. Whereas for its opponents on the left this was a perfectly tenable position, given their commitment to the proletariat, for the BUF's grandiose pretensions towards national regeneration through class unity it was wholly unsatisfactory. One of the party's great strengths was the breadth of its potential appeal, and it was precisely this which was damaged by the difficulty in obtaining halls. The bourgeois audiences which regularly packed the Albert Hall and local town halls elsewhere in the country, were less inclined to jostle with their social inferiors upon street corners in order to absorb the fascist message. Thus whereas the denial of the

Albert Hall to the CP was of little consequence, the denial of halls to the BUF partially severed communications with supporters and potential supporters from the middle class, and helped to disturb the delicate class balance inherent within fascist ideology.

Another significant effect of the outdoor meeting was its reduction of the power of fascist stewards. Whereas in a hall hecklers could be silenced by their removal, no such option was available in the case of street meetings where verbal opposition simply had to be suffered. It is in this context that the prohibition of amplifiers was of such importance, for if opponents could not be removed, nor the speaker rise above their interruptions through force of volume, the only remaining course of action was to abandon the meeting.

Against such tactics on the part of local councils the BUF was essentially powerless, and had to content itself with abusing those responsible from the columns of its newspapers. By 1939 the problem had become so acute, however, that the fascists attempted to apply a more practical form of pressure, and for the first time began the overt disruption of 'Old Gang' political meetings. In January of that year representatives from the Labour and Conservative parties, and church leaders, held a meeting in Limehouse Town Hall to protest against persecution in central Europe. Fascist supporters created such a disturbance amongst the audience that the speakers could not be heard, and eventually police were called to eject thirty of those responsible.[104] In the same month Sir Kingsley Wood, Minister for Air, laboured unsuccessfully to make himself heard at the same venue, and when the Conservative parliamentary candidate for Limehouse rose to speak he was rendered inaudible by fascist singing. Fighting broke out as fascists attempted to rush the platform and order was only restored when the police arrived and ejected those fascists responsible.[105] The trend continued in February, although on this occasion the victims were the Liberals who attempted to hold a meeting in York Hall, Bethnal Green, a venue denied to the BUF. The leader of the parliamentary party, Sir Archibald Sinclair, was showered with tomatoes and electric light bulbs and drowned by a chorus of singing. In all some 300 fascists were involved and once again the meeting was disfigured by fighting and ejections until the arrival of the police.[106] In March it was the turn of the left to suffer. In Shoreditch, anti-fascist Labour MP Ernest Thurtle attempted to speak in favour of the Spanish Republicans but was foiled by fascist disruption, which included the throwing of fireworks and stink-bombs.[107] Later in the month fireworks were again used at a Labour and Co-operative meeting in Hackney Town Hall, which ended with over fifty fascists having to be ejected.[108]

Although this spate of disturbances at the meetings of others was confined to the East End, it was significant because the BUF departed from its previous policy by virtually admitting responsibility for the disorder. In reply to a letter from Thurtle urging him to use his influence to end the attacks, Mosley was quick to point out that fascist meetings had been disrupted for over five years without drawing condemnation from the Labour Party. He went on to admit that his followers were no longer forbidden from attending the meetings of their opponents and were entitled to exercise '. . . the immemorial rights of the heckler at British public meetings, to the discomfiture of incompetent speakers'.[109] It was a neat redeployment of the arguments used by his opponents throughout the decade which omitted (as had they) to distinguish between the individual heckler and the organised body of opponents determined to disrupt the proceedings with the intention of making coherent speech impossible. Mosley refused to condemn the disruption which he attributed to fascist supporters voicing a protest against the denial of halls to the BUF. His advice to Thurtle was to use his '. . . influence with Labour majorities on local Councils to let public halls to all sides, and to restore the old facilities for mass meetings in public parks, rather than to address appeals to me to exert for your protection the previous discipline of our Movement . . .'.[110] In effect Mosley was offering a straightforward deal whereby he was prepared to call off the fascist interrupters in return for available public platforms; indeed it is a measure of the effectiveness of the anti-fascist tactics of local councils that he was prepared to state his terms so clearly. But even such draconian tactics on the part of the fascists failed to achieve the desired results and the iron grip of local government continued to stifle the BUF's access to the public.

Although the effectiveness of different anti-fascist tactics cannot be quantified with any real degree of precision, a general assessment is possible. Passive anti-fascism as advocated by the official labour movement was probably of little assistance in the struggle against the BUF, for its propaganda, though valuable, did not outweigh its discouragement of workers from attending anti-fascist activities. If 65,000 opposed fascism in Hyde Park in September 1934 in defiance of official labour movement policy, how many would have been present had Labour Party and trade union leaders lent the rally their support? The idea that fascism was an aberration within British society which would disappear if left unopposed was an attractive formula for inaction. It sprang from a failure to understand fascism's role as a provider of answers to the problems which beset the capitalist world. As long as the problems remained fascism would threaten the liberal democratic state and, therefore, had to be resisted rather than surrendered to.

For active anti-fascists this meant a two-pronged offensive aimed at illuminating the contradictions and weaknesses of fascism's solutions, as well as opposition to its propagation through the disruption of its meetings. It was an effective formula, for it involved the exposure of fascism as a false prophet in conjunction with the denial of facilities necessary for its growth. To those who protested that such tactics actually contributed to the growth of fascism, active anti-fascists could reply with reference to Weimar Germany where, in the face of weakness on the part of the labour movement and social democrats, the Nazis had triumphed rather than disappeared. The people of Germany were forced to pay dearly as a result.

The educative aspect of anti-fascist was straightforward and involved not simply the denunciation of fascism, but also an analysis of the source of existing social and economic grievances, and an exposition illustrating how they could be cured not by fascism, but only through the establishment of socialism. The other side of active anti-fascism (that of physical confrontation) worked upon two different levels. Obviously it denied fascism a platform on occasions and, as already suggested, for a movement so reliant upon the spoken word as a form of communication, this was of great importance. More subtly, however, such opposition provided the catalyst, which called forth displays of fascist violence, which were to prove crucial in helping to create a less than attractive image for British fascism.

It is too glib to suggest that British society was alienated by the violence which emanated from fascism, but such an assertion does contain an important element of truth. Although the physical reality of violence employed by representatives of the state differed very little from that arising from extra-legal sources, there existed a widely held perception that the former possessed a degree of legitimacy (by virtue of the mythical even-handedness of the state) which the latter did not. This absence of legitimacy was increased by the circumstances and the style of fascist violence. Several additional factors were of importance in this respect. The scale, frequency, and concomitant publicity given to fascist violence helped to foster the impression that it was unprovoked and excessive. The idea was strengthened by undoubted instances of fascist excess (as at Olympia), as well as by the tactics sometimes adopted by anti-fascist interrupters, and by the predominantly genteel nature of some audiences. In addition to this the images of fascist stewards gloating at their success amidst the bloodshed, and Mosley's refusal to condemn even the most sickening examples of their brutality, helped to lend credence to the charge that fascism revelled in violence. This was further supported by gross insensitivity on the part of other leading fascists, as exemplified by Chesterton who, when writing of the fascist tenchiques for ejecting interrupters from halls and silencing them at outdoor meetings, suggested that this side of fascism had '. . . been perhaps the most inspiring thing to witness since the War'.[111]

In so far as denying fascism the opportunity to propagate itself (as opposed to allowing it to discredit itself through the use of violence), the denial of halls and harassment of outdoor functions by local councils was probably more effective than simple physical opposition by those intent on disruption. In a sense it provided a compromise between active and passive anti-fascism, for it ensured that the BUF was denied a platform, but did so not through mass mobilisation but through boycott. Those who advocated ignoring BUF meetings were open to the charge that in so doing they were allowing fascism to spread its poisonous propaganda unopposed, just as they accused the believers in physical confrontation of giving fascism a free advertisement. Although town councils used the boycott weapon, they were not vulnerable to the former charge for the boycott was, in effect, forcibly applied to all. When a meeting was prohibited none was able to hear the fascist message. It was an ideal arrangment for the non-revolutionary left for it avoided not only fascism but also mass anti-fascist mobilisation and the disorder which accompanied it.

NOTES

1 Despite fluctuations the membership of the CP rose fairly steadily throughout the decade from 2,555 in November 1932, *Imprecorr,* Vol XII, p. 447, to 17,756 in July 1939 (Report of E.C. to 16th Congress, p. 13) as cited by K. Newton, *The Sociology of British Communism,* Allen Lane, The Penguin Press, London 1969, p. 159. When the ILP disaffiliated from the Labour Party in 1932 it had almost 17,000 members but thereafter its membership declined steadily. H. Pelling, *A Short History of the Labour Party,* 4th edn, Macmillan Press Ltd, London 1974, p. 76. This chapter's concentration upon the CP rather than the ILP reflects these antithetical trends of ascendance and decay.
2 *The Times,* 10 May 1933, p. 11.
3 R. P. Dutt, 'Notes of the month', *Labour Monthly,* XVI, 7, July 1934, p. 388.
4 *Blackshirt,* May 1938, editorial.
5 *Manchester Guardian,* 25 October 1932, p. 9; *The Times,* 25 October 1932, p. 16.
6 For example see details of Mosley's meeting in Battersea Town Hall, *The Times,* 7 December 1932, p. 11.
7 O. Mosley, interview with author, 24 June 1980.
8 *Manchester Guardian,* 16 October 1933, p. 9.
9 Mosley, interview with author.
10 *Manchester Guardian,* 3 November 1933, p. 12.
11 Three fascists were eventually charged in court with these assaults, *Manchester Guardian,* 15 March 1934, p. 14. See also *Daily Herald,* 15 March 1934, as cited by Labour Research Department, *Who Backs Mosley? Fascist Promise and Fascist Performance,* LRD, London 1934, pp. 34–5.
12 *Blackshirt,* March 1933, p. 3.
13 *Ibid.,* 17 April 1933, p. 2.
14 *Manchester Guardian,* 29 March 1934, p. 6.
15 *Ibid.,* 27 April 1934, p. 9.
16 *Fascist Week,* 25–31 May 1934, p. 5.
17 *Ibid.*

18 The ownership and purpose of the spotlights remains a matter of some dispute. Anti-fascists alledged that they were used to locate interrupters who were then seized by stewards, and to intimidate would-be interrupters by illustrating the unenviable fate of those who had preceded them. Mosley claimed that they belonged to the cinema newsreel companies, who had come to photograph the rallies, and as such were beyond his control. Certainly, in the autumn of 1933 at Mosley's Belle Vue meeting spotlights had been used to illuminate the scene of a disturbance, but whether this was to facilitate the task of the media photographers or of the stewards is unclear from the report. See *Manchester Guardian,* 16 October 1933, p. 9. See also R. Benewick, *The Fascist Movement in Britain,* The Penguin Press, London 1972, pp. 90, 170; R. Skidelsky, *Oswald Mosley,* Macmillan, London 1975, p. 376; and F. Mullally, *Fascism inside England,* Morris Books, London 1946, p. 34.

19 Reprinted from the *Yorkshire Post,* 9 June 1934, as quoted in Vindicator (pseud.), *Fascists at Olympia,* Victor Gollancz Ltd, London 1934, p. 9.

20 G. Barry, Statement broadcast on radio, 8 June 1934, as quoted in Vindicator, *op. cit.,* p. 14.

21 Mosley, radio broadcast 8 June 1934, as quoted by *Manchester Guardian,* 9 June 1934, p. 13.

22 Letters to *The Times,* 11 June 1934, p. 8.

23 Vindicator, *op. cit.,* pp. 36–8.

24 I. Montague, *Blackshirt Brutality: The Story of Olympia,* Workers Bookshop, London 1934, p. 19.

25 Independent eye-witness accounts can be found in Vindicator, *op. cit.,* and in the nation's press in the aftermath of the Olympia meeting. Police reports on the meeting are contained within MEPO 2/4319, which was opened to the public, but, owing to the sensitive nature of some of the material therein, has been once again closed by the Home Office. Several of those who examined the file before it was closed have quoted from it, however. See Skidelsky, *op. cit.,* pp. 372–3; and G. C. Lebzelter, *Political Anti-Semitism in England 1918–1939,* Macmillan Press, London 1978, pp. 105–6.

26 *Daily Worker,* 18 May 1934, p. 3.

27 *Ibid.,* 26 May 1934, p. 3.

28 *Ibid.,* 6 June 1934, p. 3; and 7 June, p. 4.

29 P. Toynbee, *Friends Apart: A memoir of Esmond Romilly and Jasper Ridley in the thirties,* Macgibbon & Kee, London 1954, p. 21.

30 *Sunday Dispatch,* 27 May 1934, as quoted in *Daily Worker,* 28 May 1934, p. 3.

31 *The Times,* 8 June 1934, p. 14.

32 At least one of those ejected had a gashed hand consistent with a razor wound, Vindicator, *op. cit.,* p. 36, and Montague, *op. cit.,* pp. 19–20; and several Olympia employees testified to having seen fascist stewards with knuckle-dusters and clubs, *Daily Worker,* 20 June 1934, p. 3, and Vindicator, *op. cit.,* pp. 47–8. On the whole, however, it would appear that the majority of the combatants on each side fought with their fists alone.

33 *Daily Worker,* 9 June 1934, p. 4. See also BUF pamphlet, *Red Violence and Blue Lies,* BUF, London 1934, pp. 15–18; and *Blackshirt,* 15 June 1934, p. 2.

34 *Daily Worker,* 9 June 1934, p. 4.

35 The effects of bourgeois accounts of fascist brutality was almost comparable to the presence of television cameras inside the hall, for they gave the stories of fascist brutality a degree of authenticity greater than that which was extended to those on the left, as well as offering a ready and reliable source of column-inches to the nation's press.

36 For police reports of the 1934 Hyde Park rally see MEPO 2/3074.
37 *The Times,* 20 May 1934, p. 8.
38 *Manchester Guardian,* 27 May 1934, p. 11.
39 *Ibid.,* 4 March 1934, p. 13.
40 *New Statesman and Nation,* XI, 28 March 1936, p. 487. See also *Daily Herald,* 23 March 1934, pp. 1–2; *Daily Worker,* 23 March 1934, p. 1; and *The Times,* 23 March 1934, p. 14.
41 *Manchester Guardian,* 26 May 1936, p. 11.
42 *Blackshirt,* 18 July 1936, p. 8. In addition to a description of the meeting there is a photograph purporting to show Mosley's car with a neat 'bullet hole' through one of its side windows. It is upon the basis of this that Skidelsky accepts that this was a 'genuine attempt' to assassinate Mosley. Skidelsky, *op. cit.,* p. 415. If this was so it seems inconceivable that it would not have commanded more publicity, if only within the context of the BUF's own propaganda material. The party's willingness to forget it so rapidly suggests that it was not as straightforward as Skidelsky had been led to believe.
43 Police report on Jew-baiting in the East End for the month of August 1936, MEPO 2/3043.
44 Skidelsky, *op. cit.,* p. 415.
45 *Manchester Guardian,* 28 September 1934, p. 9; *Daily Herald,* 28 September 1934, p. 1; and *Action,* 1 October 1934, pp. 2, 7. Estimates of crowd size vary between 25,000, 50,000 and 100,000 respectively.
46 *Blackshirt,* 12 September 1936, p. 1.
47 Skidelsky, *op. cit.,* p. 403.
48 J. Jacobs, *Out of the Ghetto,* Simon, London 1978, pp. 170, 205.
49 E. Trory, *Between the Wars: Recollections of a Communist Organiser,* Crabtree Press, Brighton 1974, p. 44.
50 Accounts of the Aldgate demonstration are too numerous to mention in full. It received coverage in all of the national press on 5 October 1936, and was given particular prominence in the *Daily Herald,* of that date, pp. 1–2. For eye-witness recollections of the eventful day see P. Piratin, *Our Flag Stays Red,* Lawrence & Wishart, London 1978, pp. 22–4; and Jacobs, *op. cit.,* pp. 254–6.
51 *Daily Worker,* 5 October 1936, editorial.
52 Jacobs, *op. cit.,* p. 238.
53 *Ibid.*
54 *Daily Worker,* 2 October 1936, p. 1.
55 Jacobs, *op. cit.,* p. 254.
56 Piratin, *op. cit.,* pp. 27–49.
57 Jacobs, *op. cit.,* pp. 263–84.
58 Statement from DPC, December 1937, as cited by Jacobs, *op. cit.,* p. 291.
59 Letter from T. Besterman, *New Statesman and Nation,* XII, 31 October 1936, p. 666.
60 *Daily Herald,* 13 October 1936, p. 2.
61 E. Kibblewhite & A. Rigby, *Fascism in Aberdeen – Street politics in the 1930s,* Aberdeen People's Press, Aberdeen 1978, p. 25; and *Blackshirt,* 10 April 1937, p. 1.
62 In addition to meetings and posters, CP propaganda material included numerous different leaflets and a four-page supplement in the *Daily Worker.* Examples of these can be found in MEPO 2/3048.
63 Jacobs, *op. cit.,* pp. 278–9. See also MEPO 2/3048.
64 Police reports on BUF's 4 July march to Trafalgar Square, MEPO 2/3048.
65 *Blackshirt,* 10 July 1937, pp. 1, 8.
66 Statement by DPC, Jacobs, *op. cit.,* pp. 291–2.
67 Bermondsey Trades Council, *Bermondsey Says 'No' to Fascism,* BTC,

London 1937, p. 5. See also police reports on the Bermondsey march, October 1937, MEPO 2/3117, and the national press for 4 October 1937, particularly *Manchester Guardian,* pp. 8–9, *The Times,* p. 14; and *Daily Herald,* pp. 1–2.

68 Police report on BUF march in Bermondsey, May 1938, MEPO 2/3117. See also *The Times,* 12 May 1938, p. 13.

69 *Manchester Guardian,* 11 October 1937, p. 9. See also *Blackshirt,* 16 October 1937, p. 1.

70 *Manchester Guardian,* 3 March 1938, p. 12.

71 *Action,* 16 April 1938, p. 3. See also *The Times,* 11 April 1938, p. 9.

72 *Manchester Guardian,* 12 September 1938, p. 11.

73 O. Mosley, *Blackshirt Policy,* BUF Publications Ltd, London 1934, p. 17. See also *My Answer,* Mosley Publications, Ramsbury 1946, p. 16.

74 J. Beckett, 'Social Democracy', *FQ,* I, 1, January 1935, p. 83. For a few of the many BUF condemnations of the Labour Party in particular, see *Action,* 17 September 1936, p. 7; 8 October 1938, p. 15; and *Blackshirt,* 12 September 1935, p. 1; and 13 February 1937, p. 1.

75 For example, see Labour Party Research Department, *Who Backs Mosley? Fascist Promise and Fascists Performance,* LRD, London 1934; *Mosley Fascism: the Man, his Policy, and Methods,* LRD, London 1935; *Fascism: Fight it Now,* LRD, London 1937.

76 TUC General Council, *United Against Fascism,* TUC General Council, London 1934, p. 27.

77 Joint Consultative Committee of the London Trades Council and the London Labour Party, 'The Labour Movement and Fascism', LPL.

78 *Daily Worker,* 5 June 1934, p. 3.

79 *Morning Post,* 1 October 1936, p. 6. See also *Daily Herald,* 3 October 1936, p. 1.

80 Circular sent from the Executive Committee to the Secretaries of all borough and divisional Labour Parties and Women's Sections; Labour mayors, MPs, and LCC members for the boroughs of Bermondsey, Lambeth and Southwark, 1937. LPL.

81 C. Cross, *The Fascists in Britain,* Barrie and Rockliff, London 1961, p. 118. See also TUC General Council, *op. cit.,* p. 1.

82 *Manchester Guardian,* 11 May 1933, p. 11.

83 R. P. Dutt, 'Notes of the Month', *Labour Monthly,* XVL, 10, October 1934, p. 587.

84 *Ibid.,* p. 594.

85 Joint Consultative Committee of London Trades Council and London Labour Party, *op. cit.,* LPL.

86 B. Pimlott, *Labour and the Left in the 1930s,* Cambridge University Press, 1977, p. 80. See also R. P. Arnot, *Twenty Years: The Policy of the C.P.G.B. from its foundation,* Lawrence & Wishart, London 1940, pp. 38–9.

87 NEC minutes, 16 May 1934, as cited by Pimlott, *op. cit.,* p. 83.

88 H. Pelling, *A History of British Trade Unionism,* 3rd edn, Penguin Books Ltd, Harmondsworth 1979, p. 198.

89 For further information on the relationship between the Labour Party and the CP in the 1920s see R. McKibben, *The Evolution of the Labour Party 1910–24,* Oxford University Press, 1974, and A. Bullock, *The Life and Times of Ernest Bevin,* vol. I, Heinemann, London 1960.

90 Dutt, 'Notes of the month', *Labour Monthly,* XVI, 7, July 1934, p. 402. See also *Daily Worker,* 12 June 1934, editorial.

91 Labour Party Economic Advisory Bureau, *Memorandum on Fascism,* Oldhams Press Ltd, London 1934?, LPL.

92 Pimlott, *op. cit.,* pp. 77–105.

93 *Daily Herald,* 6 October 1937, p. 1.

94 For references to the united front in Sheffield, see *Manchester Guardian,* 29 June 1934, p. 15; whilst for Manchester, see *ibid.,* 1 April 1935, p. 11.

95 Interview with A. Excell, member of the Oxford branch of the Communist Party of Great Britain, 21 February 1981.

96 *Daily Worker,* 31 May 1934, p. 3. See also B. Burke, *Rebels with a Cause. The history of Hackney Trades Council 1900–1975,* Hackney Trades Council and Hackney Workers' Educational Association, London 1975, p. 53.

97 Police report on Jew-baiting in the East End for October 1936, MEPO 2/3043. See also *Spectator,* CLXXX, 23 October 1936, p. 674.

98 *Action,* 31 October 1936, p. 2.

99 For example, see *Manchester Guardian,* 13 January 1935, p. 9.

100 In August 1938 the Labour Council of Southall refused to allow the BUF to hold outdoor meetings in Southall Park on the grounds that fascism, by its very nature, had forfeited its right to free speech, *Action,* 20 August 1938, p. 11.

101 *The Times,* 15 September 1937, p. 14.

102 *Action,* 3 June 1939, editorial.

103 *Ibid.,* 23 May 1940, p. 4. See also *ibid.,* 14 December 1939, pp. 1–2.

104 *Ibid.,* 21 January 1939, p. 18. See also Special Branch Report for January 1939, MEPO 2/3127.

105 *Manchester Guardian,* 1 February 1939, p. 11.

106 *Ibid.,* 17 February 1939, p. 11. See also *Action,* 25 February 1939, p. 11. Bethnal Green S. W. was the last Liberal seat held in London.

107 *Action,* 4 March 1939, p. 2.

108 *The Times,* 11 March 1939, p. 9.

109 *Blackshirt,* April 1939, p. 1.

110 *Ibid.* See also *Manchester Guardian,* 10 March 1939, p. 5.

111 A. K. Chesterton, *Oswald Mosley, Portrait of a Leader,* Action Press Ltd, London 1937, p. 121.

CHAPTER 6

Fascism and the state

It must be remembered that the essentials of . . . liberty are not only the rights of those who wish to demonstrate or protest but also the rights of the general public, who have their interests in being protected from suffering from serious and illegitimate disturbance. It must be remembered that we are not passing legislation simply for the purpose of striking at one particular section, but trying to base our legislation on a general principle. That general principle is tolerance in British public life. We should give a reasonable amount of consideration to those who wish to express views other than our own; we should give a full measure of opportunity for those who wish to gather together to demonstrate to do what they wish to do; and we should live together as people who inherit this great tradition of liberty in this country and reject foreign methods as thoroughly in our legislation as we do in our hearts. J. Simon, *HC Deb.,*
318, 7 December 1936, c. 1784

The fascist attitude is real, whilst the very nadir of unreality is reached by the old decaying democracy aping the forms of dictatorship in the vain hope of prolonging a useless life.
Notes on the Quarter, *BUQ,* I, 1, January–April 1937, p. 11

There can, nevertheless, be no doubt that we have moved definitely along the path towards the Corporate State, not only in actual legislation and methods of Government, but above all in the psychology and ideology of our rulers. . . . Coloured shirts are not necessary and are embarrassingly obvious; a special constable is much cheaper and attracts less attention. But do not let us be deluded because the signs are less obvious in this than in other countries as to the direction Britain is following . . . . S. Cripps, '*National*'
Fascism in Britain, Socialist League, London 1937, p. 8

The starting point in an analysis of the relationship between the BUF and the state lies in the attitude of the elected custodian of the machinery of state: the National Government. This in turn requires an examination of the Conservative Party for it was from this source that the National Government drew the overwhelming mass of its parliamentary support, its personnel, and its ideological influences. Certainly a number of Tory back-benchers such as Michael Beaumont (member for Aylesbury), Tom Howard (Islington South), and F. A. MacQuistan (Argyll) displayed sympathy towards Mosley's organisation, with Beaumont in particular proving himself a consistent defender of the BUF against parliamentary attacks. The basis of this support varied, although none showed any real intellectual grasp of the essentials of fascist ideology. In this sense Beaumont was ahead of his colleagues for although he denied subscribing to fascism as a doctrine, he admitted to being '. . . an avowed anti-Democrat and an avowed admirer of Fascism in other countries . . .'.[1] For most, however, the attraction of fascism lay in their own misconceptions concerning its nature. Like Rothermere, they saw Mosley as a misguided Conservative, alienated by a party which had deviated increasingly from traditional Tory values, particularly in its ambivalence towards the maintenance of the British empire. They were dismayed that such reserves of vitality and noble intentions were not being accommodated as a radical wing within their own party. Without understanding the real nature of fascism, Lieutenant-Colonel T. C. R. Moore, Conservative MP for Ayr Burghs, was moved to write that there was '. . . little, if any of the [BUF's] policy which would not be accepted by the most loyal followers of our present Conservative leaders. The majority of the essentials and many of the details are part and parcel of strict Tory doctrines.' Then, having listed those general aims of the BUF which were similar to those of Conservatism (a process which, like the blind man's description of the elephant, was inaccurate through being incomplete rather than incorrect), he mistakenly concluded that the BUF was '. . . largely derived from the Conservative Party'. Therefore he looked forward to a greater degree of unity between them, resulting in the Conservative Party becoming '. . . strengthened and rejuvenated by the spearhead of active, eager, and intelligent youth . . .'.[2]

Some MPs offered willing support to the BUF on the basis that it was striking back against those left-wing opponents who had for years disrupted Tory public meetings in every major city in the land. This view of fascism as the scourge of the Red hooligans was only a small part of a wider belief that fascism could be used by the orthodox right against its own left-wing enemies. This was a slightly different proposition from the Rothermere concept of taming fascism and incorporating it into the Conservative Party, for it recognised the independence of fascism both as a movement and as an ideology, but sought to exploit it nevertheless. It was a phenomenon more visible in Europe than in Britain and was particularly apparent in both Germany and Italy, where fascism achieved power initially only in alliance with elements of the orthodox conservative right.

The number of Conservative MPs who sympathised with the BUF for whatever reason was always small and probably declined throughout the decade as the result of the party's refusal to drop the more radical elements of its programme, and its intractable opposition to war with Germany. With Mosley offering what appeared to many as an injudicious mixture of pacifism and a treasonable allegiance to a foreign power, it proved impossible for him to tap the parliamentary reserves of right-wing Conservatism. The orthodox right in Britain was never frightened sufficiently to precipitate a major stampede towards fascism. With the economic crisis gradually receding from 1933 onwards, and the continuing weakness of the forces of the left, the spectre of communist revolution was never real enough to produce a significant realignment of Conservatism on Mosley's terms.

Thus the bulk of the Conservative parliamentary members regarded the BUF with an attitude ranging from indifference to outright hostility. Although there was some vociferous Tory support for the manner in which interrupters had been dealt with at Olympia, equally there were Conservative critics who denounced vehemently the violence which one MP described as having made his '... blood boil as an Englishman and a Tory'.[3] For many Tories the practice of politics in such a fashion was outrageous and reflected (as did the BUF's uniforms) the foreign origins of fascism. Mosley was held responsible for importing this alien doctrine, which had abused the accepted standards of British tolerance which were considered a vital ingredient of the political life of the nation. As Kingsley Griffith informed the House of Commons, 'trampling on fallen enemies, kicking unconscious men – these things are not within our British tradition'.[4] Once again it was not the violence itself but the manner in which it had occurred which was to prove so unacceptable. To those who extended the morality of a public school cricket match to the political arena (in theory at least) it was considered bad form for a gang of stewards to assault helpless or semi-conscious victims. It was simply un-British. Had Mosley apologised for the actions of his followers, maintained Griffith, '... a great deal of toleration would have been extended to him and his movement ...', his failure to do so, however, seemed to suggest that he, like his stewards, revelled in the violence.[5] In the name of honour, the honourable members felt that, where it was absolutely necessary to brutalise one's opponents, at the very least one must appear not to enjoy it.

The National Government, which was composed mainly from the

foremost ranks of the Conservative Party, also viewed the BUF with a considerable degree of hostility. In the immediate aftermath of Olympia the Colonial Secretary, Sir P. Cuncliffe-Lister, denounced the movement as a '. . . circus of foreign origin',[6] whilst his colleague William Ormsby-Gore, First Commissioner of Works, expressed his failure to comprehend why there was a need to '. . . import these foreign fashions of Blackshirts and Redshirts into this free England of ours . . .'.[7] Two years later, on the eve of the Public Order Act, the Home Secretary, Sir John Simon, expressed the view '. . . that the Fascist doctrine is as un-English and unwanted as the Communist doctrine, but the duty of the authorities is to do all they can, with complete impartiality, to maintain freedom of meeting and speech for all doctrines . . . provided that the law is not broken'.[8]

At this point it should be stressed most strongly that the National Government's disapproval of the BUF was in no way the product of any libertarian scruples. The coalition which governed from 1931 until the end of the decade under MacDonald, Baldwin, and finally Chamberlain, was dominated by the interests of the orthodox right, and its hostility towards the BUF represents a further indication of fascism's position as a movement of the centre rather than of the right. In general terms the National Government's lifetime was characterised by an increase in the secrecy and coercive power of the executive, and its more notorious legislative and procedural innovations have left a stain upon the record of British civil liberties. The Incitement to Disaffection Act and the Unemployment Act of 1934 (which reinforced the much hated Means Test which had been introduced in 1931), the greater centralisation of the police, the establishment of the Royal Defence Corps to protect the nation's vulnerable points from attacks by subversives, each reflected this trend. It was visible also in the increasing severance of government action from parliament through the use of administrative procedures (such as Orders in Council) in an overtly political fashion. All too frequently parliament was expected simply to approve a package presented to it as a whole, with little opportunity for amendments or meaningful debate.[9] This implied contempt for parliament, the theoretical font of popular sovereignty, was made all too clear by the government's persecution in 1938 of Duncan Sandys, a Conservative member of the House of Commons. Having made discreet enquiries in the form of a written parliamentary question to the Minister of War concerning government defence policy, Sandys found himself threatened with prosecution under the Official Secrets Act.[10]

There were some who saw in all of this the hand of fascism at work, covertly constructing a dictatorial corporate state within the empty shell of parliamentary democracy.[11] They were wrong in this interpretation. Such measures were symptomatic not of incipient fascism but of government fear. It was fear, often translating itself into class hostility, on the part of the orthodox right; the fear of an *ancien régime* devoid of answers in the face of the appalling problems of inter-war capitalism, which saw its own limited future reflected in the apparently successful alternatives, which had taken root in the USSR and fascist Europe. The relative stagnation of the nation's economy was manifest through declining or static living standards for large sections of the community, which meant that no longer could working-class loyalty be exchanged automatically for increased material prosperity. In short, a capitalist economy undergoing painful recession (including the permanent contraction of several of its traditional staple industries) could not afford unchecked parliamentary democracy. Thus, rather than representing a form of fascism, the National Government represented the class interests of the bourgeoisie – the orthodox right – who were frightened enough to demand strong government action in their favour, but not sufficiently terrified to flee into the centrist politics of fascism.

In the eyes of Britain's political rulers the BUF represented at best a disturber of the peace and at worst a revolutionary threat either in its own right, or as a stimulant to the growth of communism. In either case a threat was posed to the government's desire to limit popular participation in the political process. This desire – a hallmark common to all conservative regimes but entirely absent within fascist ideology – was based upon that age-old fear which has beset the masters of all inequitable societies: the fear of collective action on the part of the deprived masses. To those on the orthodox right unsolicited political activity from below was to be regarded with apprehension and suspicion.

Thus there is no evidence to support the common socialist allegation that the National Government nurtured fascism and kept it in the wings for use in some future emergency. Given the political differences between fascism and conservatism this is not surprising. One would expect to find evidence of an alliance between them only if the social and economic disintegration of a society was considerably further advanced than was the case in Britain even during the worst of the depression. Similarly, given the political perspective of the bulk of the anti-fascist movement, fascist claims that the government allied itself to the communists and the Jews in their struggle against the BUF have little credibility. From this premise, however, it would be quite wrong to conclude that the National Government occupied a position of passive neutrality. For, as will be shown, it acted to preserve its own authority and to defend the class interests of those whom it represented.

Amongst the catalogue of reactionary measures sired by the National Government, that which affected the BUF most directly was the Public Order Act, which was steered through parliament in the autumn of 1936. The act has often been portrayed as a measure designed to ban fascist uniforms and to curtail BUF marches through London's East End. In truth it represented much more than this. Its name foretold its purpose. Public order, even as an abstract concept, cannot be isolated from the class structure of a society. It has no objective existence, but is merely a euphemism for the preservation of the status quo, and the prevention of a redistribution of society's resources by the dispossessed. It was fitting that a government representing the interests of the ortho-dox right should seek to defend existing privilege by passing a statute aimed not only at fascism but capable of striking at the heart of any political movement which attempted to harness the support of the masses.

When the Public Order Act was introduced to the House of Commons in late 1936, it was as a response to the outcry which had followed the Aldgate disturbances. But the genesis of the bill lay in sources which had preceded the wild scenes at Cable Street. The first of these lay outside the fascist sphere altogether and was related to the activities of the left in the 1920s and early 1930s, and in particular to the communist-dominated National Unemployed Workers' Movement. It was the NUWM which organised the hunger marches, which became such an emotive image of the inter-war period by capturing the tragic futility of mass unemployment. Although the first march was organised as early as 1922, the bulk of the hunger marches occurred in the late 1920s and early 1930s. From 1931 the NUWM was also active in organising local demonstrations of the unemployed and by the end of that year there had been clashes between demonstrators and police in over thirty British towns and cities. The fighting continued in 1932, culminating in severe rioting in several areas in the autumn of that year.[12] In the capital, too, there was a series of violent clashes following the arrival of the NUWM's 1932 hunger march in October.[13]

The spectre of the hungry and discontented masses marching to London to demand a redress of their grievances was as disturbing to the National Government as it had been to its governmental predecessors, who had faced periodic threats of this nature since 1381. The government was shaken by the disturbances and in November 1932 a cabinet committee was established to review the legal status of marches. It was decided that new legislation was necessary to deal with marches from the provinces to London, as well as marches within London and other population centres. A draft bill to this effect was produced, giving the Home Secretary power to ban concentrations of persons outside the area of their residence, and to prohibit all marches within specific areas for a specified period should disorder be anticipated. Despite widespread support within the cabinet, the bill foundered upon the opposition of the Attorney General, Sir Thomas Inskip, and was never presented to parliament.[14]

The second source of the 1936 bill lay in the growing alarm over the BUF's development. In the first half of 1934 there was some concern in parliament in regard to the paramilitary nature of the fascist movement and to the wearing of uniforms in particular. On the former point the Home Secretary, Sir John Gilmour, assured the House that the existing law was already sufficient to prohibit paramilitary organisations.[15] On the subject of uniforms he refused to be drawn, however, other than to acknowledge '. . . the provocative effect of the wearing of uniforms', and to promise that the matter was receiving his 'serious consideration'.[16] A week later this consideration had matured into a memorandum which recognised the merits of prohibiting uniforms but, fearing parliamentary reaction to such a move, recommended further consideration before any action should be undertaken.[17] These finely balanced findings were accepted by the cabinet at the end of May but within days had been rendered obsolete by the reaction to Olympia. Many of the BUF's critics in parliament called for immediate legislation to cover the policing of meetings and there were repeated calls for the prohibition of political uniforms. From outside the chamber, too, there were cries for governmental action from journals as diverse as *The Spectator* and the *New Statesman and Nation*.[18]

Publicly Gilmour prevaricated. Within the inner sanctum of the cabinet room, however, he informed his colleagues that changes in the law were necessary.[19] In mid-July he produced another memorandum on public order. It proposed granting the police power to enter meetings if they believed that disorder was likely to occur, and the authority for chief-constables to prohibit open-air meetings if they interfered with the transaction of business by public authorities, or were considered likely to lead to disorder. Also included was the right of chief constables to prescribe the routes of processions and, taken directly from the draft legislation in regard to hunger marches, a provision empowering the Home Secretary to prevent the concentration of persons outside the area of their residence if such a concentration was thought likely to lead to a breach of the peace. Also related to the hunger marchers was a provision outlawing the possession of an offensive weapon at meetings or processions. Finally, it was proposed to make illegal the formation of any organisation of a military character through the use of drill or uniforms and that anyone who aided or abetted the leaders or members of such movements would be liable to criminal proceedings.[20] The cabinet instructed him to approach the leaders of the opposition parties with a view to ascertaining how much support would be forthcoming for such a bill. Although the Labour Party was prepared to support parts of the bill, the result of this inter-party canvass was disappointing, with the Liberals in particular unenthusiastic about supporting a statute designed to curb so many traditional freedoms.[21] In the late summer of

1934, as the controversy surrounding Olympia ebbed away with no repetition of disorder on such a scale, the Home Secretary's proposals were dropped quietly.

Calls for the banning of uniforms reappeared in parliament sporadically over the next two years, usually in connection with some recent example of disorder in which the BUF had been involved. There was also some pressure from certain sections of the press. It was not until after the Aldgate disturbances of October 1936, however, that the issue became again the subject of proposed legislation. Within a week of Cable Street, Gilmour's successor as Home Secretary, Sir John Simon, had produced a new memorandum on public order outlining the necessity of legislation. The reasons he gave in support of this opinion were interesting. They included the consistent pressure exerted upon the Home Office by MPs, mayors and other local figures in the East End, also the fear that fascist behaviour in east London was stimulating the growth of communism and driving the Jews '. . . into the arms of the Opposition', and finally a concern over the strain being placed upon the resources of the police force as a result of the disorder arising from fascist activities. As for the legislation itself, Simon believed that it should be a permanent statute rather than an emergency regulation, and that it should not be seen to be specifically anti-fascist in its orientation. Therefore a ban on uniforms should be accompanied by other changes in the law, including police powers to prohibit marches on a pre-emptive basis.[22]

Two days later the cabinet received Simon's suggestions sympathetically.[23] A cabinet committee was appointed, which, by late October, had decided on the specific ground to be covered by the new legislation. In the first week of November it presented to the cabinet a draft bill for its consideration. Having ensured that the attitude of the official opposition was 'highly satisfactory' and that there was a 'helpful attitude' in the press, the cabinet approved the bill and authorised Simon to proceed with it without further delay.[24]

The bill which was presented to parliament in November 1936 was, therefore, an amalgamation of the draft proposals of 1932 and 1934 and sought to cover a wide range of issues which had been the cause of governmental concern for up to a decade or more.[25] Sections one and two of the bill were directed towards the BUF in particular. Section one made it an offence to wear in public a uniform which signified 'association with any political organisation or with the promotion of any political object'.[26] This was a severe blow to the BUF for its uniform was important. It made those who wore it appear impressive and encouraged amongst them pride, obedience, strength, unity, and above all anonymity – a process of sublimation of oneself to the overall identity and morality of the group. Indeed it was precisely this effect which all nation states had relied upon for centuries in order to turn groups of young men into increasingly efficient liquidators of their fellow beings. The legislation on uniforms did not apply solely to the BUF, however, for there were numerous other coloured shirts in use by 1936. The most prominent of these were those of the Social Credit movement, better known as the greenshirts. These peaceful, non-provocative advocates of the economic theories of their leader, Major Douglas, found to their dismay that their distinctive green shirts were outlawed by the new act. Indeed, the most striking characteristic of section one was that it gave wide discretionary powers to the authorities. Uniforms were not defined, non-political uniforms were exempted, and no prosecution could be undertaken without the consent of the Attorney General. Thus, between them, the police, the government, and the local magistrates could decide exactly what articles of clothing were included within the new law, who should be charged with contravening it, whether a full prosecution should follow the initial charge, whether the accused was guilty, and what punishment (within the terms of the act) was suitable for an offender.

The second section dealt with quasi-military organisations and made it an offence to control or manage an association of persons organised, trained, or equipped to usurp the function of the police or armed forces, or who appeared to be prepared to use '. . . physical force in promoting any political object'.[27] Once again prosecution was dependent upon the will of the Attorney General, and once again wide discretionary powers were involved. The courts and the Attorney General were given the task of deciding whether the motivation which lay behind a particular organisation placed it within either of these rather broad categories. The prosecution had simply to show that there was 'reasonable apprehension' of such motivation and, therefore, in the hands of an unscrupulous, or frightened government, section two could provide the power to smash a wide range of legitimate opposition.

Section three of the Act dealt with public processions, and was indicative not merely of the threat posed to public order by the BUF's marches, but also that which had emanated from the agitation of the left in the early 1930s, and in particular from the hunger marches. Police chiefs were given the power to impose conditions on marches (including complete re-routing and prohibition from entering specified public places) if it was believed likely that the march would lead to a breach of the peace. If the chief officer of police was 'of opinion' that these measures would prove insufficient to prevent public disorder, however, he was empowered to apply to the local council for a complete ban upon all (or certain classes of) marches in a particular area. The ban required the Secretary of State's consent and could run for no more than three months. In the case of London the Commissioner of Police had only to apply direct to the Secretary of State for such an order.

The necessity for new legislation in this area was open to debate. It was pointed out that there were existing laws capable of dealing with BUF marches, such as the crime of unlawful assembly, which could be applied to lawful activities if there were reasonable grounds for believing that they would lead to a breach of the peace. It was also suggested that preventative action was possible under the existing law through the binding over of Mosley and other leading figures within the movement to be of good behaviour. This was a tactic used commonly by the state against those on the left, one of the most famous of its victims being Tom Mann, a leader of the hunger marchers who was imprisoned for refusing to be bound over and to provide the necessary securities as ordered by the court in December 1932.[28] It was not necessary to have been convicted of any criminal act to become the subject of a binding order. It was sufficient merely to have engaged in conduct likely to cause a breach of the peace which, in the case of Mosley, could have been interpreted as marching at the head of a fascist column.

A much quoted precedent for this was the common law case of *Wise* v. *Dunning* (1902), where Wise, a fanatical Liverpudlian protestant, had been bound over because his conduct had proved so provocative to Catholics that his meetings were characterised by scenes of grave public disorder. Wise appealed on the grounds that the precedent of *Beatty* v. *Gillbanks* (1882) had established that the organiser of a march, which was attacked by hooligans, could not be held responsible for the resulting disorder. Wise lost his case, for the appeal judges differentiated between the motives of the appellant in either case. Beatty, by leading a Salvation Army procession, was considered to be engaged in a genuine attempt to convert others through legitimate tactics when he was attacked by representatives of the gin-drinking fraternity, whereas Wise, it was argued, was intent upon mischievous and deliberately provocative conduct, which led naturally to disorder. The issue hinged, therefore, upon the state's perception of the motivation of the appellant, particularly in regard to the level of provocation, which, if sufficiently high, could legitimise the disorder consequent upon it.[29]

Any attempted application of either precedent to the BUF necessarily involved attempts to assess Mosley's exact motives, particularly in predominantly Jewish areas of the East End. It could be argued that fascism was making a legitimate appeal for support amongst the citizens of east London and that its marches were a necessary means of publicising the programme upon which it based that appeal. It could even be claimed that as its anti-Semitism was at its most effective in areas with a high proportion of Jews, it was perfectly legitimate to enter such areas preaching overt anti-Semitism. Herein lies the problem, for the very nature of the BUF, because of the centrist roots of fascism, dictated that any appeal to the majority must be linked necessarily to an attack upon a minority (for this represented a form of popular differentiation based upon a criterion other than the politics of class, which fascism claimed to reject). This was true even in areas where a minority in national terms (such as the Jews) had become locally the majority. In any case the concept of provocation is itself difficult to define satisfactorily, for it can be interpreted more subtly than simply as an act which throws one into a paroxysm of rage. Provocation can be gradual, and fury can be cold, calculated, and yet still provoked. Could not a non-fascist resident of the East End, and there were many such, feel justly provoked by months of almost incessant fascist marches along public thoroughfares, and meetings in public recreation facilities, and above all by the distorted shriek of loudspeakers penetrating windows and walls and violating even the innermost sanctity of private lives? Could not communists, socialists, liberals, libertarians, feminists, trade unionists, homosexuals, and the myriad of other minority sections of society who were fully aware of the unsavoury fate which awaited them within the corporate state, feel provoked by the propaganda of a movement which was pledged to destroy them?

Police powers to re-route processions already existed in many parts of the country through past legislation and local by-laws, but section three went beyond existing law by making such decisions unchallengable in court. For a police chief needed only to be 'of opinion' that disorder would result from a march. His opinion needed to be neither reasonable nor rational; indeed, its basis was considered completely irrelevant for its mere existence was sufficient. Obviously one could not disprove the existence of an opinion within the mind of an individual, and hence any action originating from this clause was unchallengeable in a court of law by those who were affected. The government, recognising the importance of this wording, resolutely refused all opposition attempts to amend it.[30] Thus section three provided the authorities with much more than the power to control fascist marches, for it also gave them the means to prohibit any or all demonstrations in any area of the country, thereby closing the major channel for the expression of popular discontent without rendering their actions liable to judicial examination.

Section four of the act was straightforward, and made the mere possession of an offensive weapon at a public meeting or procession an offence. As with uniforms, the term 'offensive weapon' was not defined but was left to the discretion of the courts. This section of the bill was unopposed in its passage through parliament.

Section five was also brief and made it an offence for anyone to use in a public place or meeting, '. . . threatening, abusive or insulting words or behaviour with intent to provoke a breach of the peace or whereby a breach of the peace is likely to be occasioned . . .'.[31] Its wording was lifted almost exactly from one of the clauses of the Metropolitan Police Act of 1837. Attempts to include within it a specific clause relating to the incitement of racial or religious prejudice were resisted by the government which was anxious to maintain the enormous flexibility of the charge.[32] The prosecution did not have to prove that a breach of the peace had occurred or even that the accused was trying deliberately to provoke one. It simply had to show that disorder would have been a likely consequence if the behaviour of the accused had continued unchecked. Therefore the crime could apply to a vast range of behaviour. This was illustrated by the frequency with which this charge had been used by the police in London under the Metropolitan Police Act, particularly at demonstrations and political meetings. Its flexibility and scope made it an ideal secondary charge with which the police could still obtain a conviction if their primary charge against the accused was dismissed. Whereas previously it was punishable under the Metropolitan Police Act with a fine of no more than forty shillings, however, the new act made it punishable anywhere in the country with a maximum fine of £50, and/or a prison sentence not exceeding three months.[33]

Finally, section six of the act dealt with public meetings. It strengthened the 1908 Public Meeting Act which had made it an offence to behave in a disorderly manner at any public meeting '. . . for the purpose of preventing the transaction of business for which the meeting was called together . . .', or to incite others to do so.[34] Effectively this statute had become moribund because of the difficulties in enforcing it, for although such an offence was punishable with a £5 fine or up to a month in prison, the organisers of a meeting lacked the power to arrest, detain, or even identify a person behaving in this manner. Under the terms of the 1936 act, however, it became possible for the chairman of a meeting to ask a constable to take the name and address of an offender, who, if he refused or provided false information, was liable to arrest. Essentially the provision was a compromise; an attempt to provide some help against the disturbers of political meetings, without making the police responsible for gaining a hearing for speakers. Prosecutions under the act were to remain largely in the hands of the organisers, with the police simply furnishing the necessary information to enable such prosecutions to take place. As such the act continued to discriminate (as did its 1908 predecessor) in favour of those wealthy enough to undertake civil actions, although provision was made for police to prosecute in '. . . a flagrant, outrageous case, which the police can properly regard as raising a public matter'.[35]

Many of those Tories who had suffered at the hands of interrupters were pleased with section six, and there is some evidence to suggest that the new legislation was of significant help to the BUF itself.[36] This section of the Public Order Act, however, remained more interesting for the provisions which were excluded rather than those which were adopted. The legacy of Olympia was missing, for in the aftermath of June

1934 the Home Secretary was convinced that the law regarding police rights of entry to premises wherein a public meeting was being held needed to be strengthened. In practice, by the autumn of 1936 the police, supported by the judiciary, had unlawfully acquired complete rights of entry, thus making any change in the law in this area unecessary. Furthermore, the 1936 act contained no provision for prohibiting meetings in advance, even though two years previously the Home Secretary had admitted that the police had no power over an open-air public meeting as long as it was not unlawful. He admitted privately, however, that in practice 'several Chief Constables prohibit the holding of open-air meetings on the ground that they may lead to a breach of the peace, but it is far from clear whether there is any legal justification for this practice'.[37] Despite its dubious legality, by the autumn of 1936 this action also had been upheld in court through the case of *Duncan* v. *Jones*. In both instances a change in the law by statute through the democratic process was much less convenient, than a change affected by judicial precedents of questionable legality arising from the retrospective justification of illegitimate police action.

After emerging from its committee stage the bill passed quickly through the House of Lords in mid-December, and on 18 December received the royal assent.[38] The BUF responded with its customary blend of savage bravado, denouncing the act as

> . . . a desperate and fanatical curtailment of free expression at a moment when freedom of expression becomes increasingly menacing to the corrupt financial democracy which tyrannises over the people. The British Union, accustomed for four years to obeying the law, to receiving no favours, to suffering the most odious discrimination, can not only bear this new imposition but can triumphantly rise superior to it. The National Socialist is influenced more by inner reality than outer signs and symbols. Democracy . . . and the financial democrats have accordingly made an error of classic type in supposing that their curtailment of natural rights can win for them any advantage in a struggle which each day brings them nearer to extinction.[39]

The Public Order Act became operational from the first day of 1937, and prosecutions under section one were not slow to follow. The BUF was anxious to determine what was to be considered as constituting a uniform, but a request to the Commissioner of the Metropolitan Police for advice in this matter, and possibly a test case, was rejected.[40] Meanwhile, throughout January the police took the names and addresses of those suspected of wearing a uniform. In exasperation Mosley, whilst speaking at a public meeting in Hornsey Town Hall, challenged the government to have him arrested for wearing a black shirt under his suit.[41] His generous offer was rejected, however, for the authorities preferred victims of lesser stature and more obvious guilt.

Hence, in the last week of January, William Henry Wood, a member of the BUF, was charged at Leeds Police Court with wearing a uniform. Wood admitted that on 2 January he had been wearing a cap, black shirt and tie, and badges whilst selling fascist newspapers but claimed that this represented not a political uniform but the livery of Action Press Ltd, and was not substantially different from that of other newspaper vendors. He was found guilty as charged and received a fine of forty shillings.[42]

The advantage of not defining a uniform in the statute was illustrated two days later when four fascists were found guilty of the same offence, although they had been wearing only dark navy blue pullovers with black trousers. The only items of their apparel with specific fascist connotations were belts and armlets. The four were nevertheless bound over for six months and ordered to pay a contribution to the costs of the prosecution.[43] Neither were the members of the Social Credit Party exempt, although the law was applied with perhaps a little less rigour than when dealing with the fascists. At Luton in June 1937 three greenshirts were acquitted under the act, although they were wearing green shirts, collars, ties, and armlets bearing their party's emblem. Yet only two weeks later at Lambeth a stipendiary magistrate ruled that an identical mode of dress did constitute a uniform. The accused was dealt with leniently, however, because the magistrate did not consider his to be a serious breach of the act.[44]

The first use of the new act's powers to prohibit marches came in the summer of 1937. A proposed BUF march in the first week of July through the East End to a rally in Trafalgar square led to intense anti-fascist prepartions to prevent it. Aware of these preparations, the police feared a repetition of disorder on a scale similar to that which had occurred during the Aldgate disturbances of the previous October. Accordingly the Police Commissioner asked the Home Secretary to prohibit the march. The powers of the Public Order Act were duly invoked with the effect that all marches within an area which included the boroughs of Stepney, Bethnal Green, Poplar, Bow and Bromley, Shoreditch and parts of Finsbury, Hackney, and Islington were banned for six weeks from 22 June.[45] The BUF denounced the ban as having '. . . handed over this quarter of London to Jewry, as the Jews' own territory'.[46] As far as the police were concerned, however, the ban was motivated not by a desire to protect Jewish areas but by the threat of disorder posed by the anti-fascists. Less than two months previously the BUF had been allowed to march from Limehouse to Bethnal Green – despite Jewish sensibilities – because the march had been unopposed by the left.

Initially the ban was for six weeks only but the authorities chose to retain it indefinitely. Although there was no direct threat of disorder it was renewed for a further six weeks in August, and thereafter was renewed in three-monthly cycles until the end of the decade.[47] The ease with which this was achieved gave a stark illustration of the awesome power which the act had placed in the hands of the executive.

The necessity of curbing British fascism through new legislation was arguable. The Unlawful Drilling Act of 1819 had already made quasi-military organisations illegal. The wearing of uniforms, too, had been curtailed in the years preceding the Public Order Act by local councils, which increasingly withheld permission for a BUF march or meeting unless there was a definite commitment that uniforms would not be worn. Faced with the growing difficulty of hiring halls, the BUF was forced to accept such restrictions and in many major cities it became increasingly common for fascist activities to be conducted without uniforms. Manchester City Council led the field in this respect and by the summer of 1936 had effectively banned fascist uniformed gatherings within the city.[48] By late 1936, before the passing of the Public Order Act, uniforms had been outlawed also in Cardiff and Hull, and there were signs that other cities were beginning to follow this example.[49]

The Public Order Act taken as a whole, however, represented far more than simply the banning of uniforms and quasi-military organisations. Anti-fascists fell foul of sections five and six in particular, and left-wing marches were included in the bans imposed under section three. Indeed, striking evidence of this was provided during the Harworth Colliery dispute as early as the spring of 1937. Police banned local inhabitants at certain times from specific streets of their own colliery estate; arrested pickets who had committed no crimes; and issued summonses for court appearances sometimes only twelve hours before the case was due to be heard in an attempt to deny the accused time to seek legal advice and to gather witnesses to testify in his defence. The most common charge used by the police was that of insulting words and behaviour, as laid down by the 1936 Public Order Act.[50]

It would appear then that the government used the issue of fascism and public order to place upon the statute book measures which had been coveted for many years. Certainly the government was anxious to be seen to alleviate the situation in the East End, but it is equally certain that it saw legislation upon these matters as an opportunity to increase its arsenal of repressive measures. In this context it should be noted that the government was adamant that the new legislation should be a permanent addition to constutional law. An attempt to limit the duration of the act to five years initially, followed by a period of reassessment as to its continued necessity was rejected summarily by the Home Secretary.[51] Normally a statute which embodied such reactionary measures would have been the subject of a fierce debate by many left-wing MPs, but because this particular package of legislation contained several clauses which appeared to be aimed specifically at fascism, it was accepted by them with little protest. J. R. Clynes promised the Opposition's support for the bill on this basis, and others concurred. The fiery socialist James Maxton illustrated perfectly the basic misconception which lay at the root of the left's supine acceptance of this anti-libertarian statute. Speaking on behalf of the ILP, Maxton admitted that he and his colleagues had '. . . very grave doubts and misgivings about an Act of this kind coming onto the Statute Book', but he had supported it because he wanted '. . . a crack at the Fascists . . .'. He confessed that although he had '. . . no enthusiasm for the Measure . . . I have not had the hostility towards it that I should have had if it had been presented in the abstract without the concrete position of anti-Fascism being connected with it. If it had been brought down as an abstract Measure I should have been completely hostile to it at every stage . . .'.[52] Amongst those few who could see further than a blind hatred of fascism and could discern, therefore, the dangers of the act, was the lone communist MP William Gallacher. His ideological framework and political experience led him to distrust a bill which aimed to stifle channels of popular protest and increase police powers. He feared that the bill would be used also against the labour movement.[53] Unlike so many others on the political left, he realised that the statute and its powers would remain long after the BUF had disappeared into the dark oblivion of failure.

Thus the Public Order Act was allowed to pass rapidly through the House of Commons, and became one element within a framwork of reactionary legislation whereby a right-wing government increased the power of the executive at the expense of the individual. As such it was more anti-libertarian than anti-fascist. It was a manifestation of the conservative right's desire to dampen down extra-parliamentary political activity of any description, because it threatened the stable order of society based upon privilege. In short, the Act was concerned with much more than simply the activities of the BUF and was, therefore, a high price to pay for a few morsels of anti-fascist legislation.

A full examination of the attitude towards the BUF of the police and the judiciary lies beyond the scope of this book. A few points shall, however, be made.

It was widely accepted at the time by anti-fascists that the police were biased in favour of the BUF. This view originated from several sources, not least of which was their mistaken analysis of the relationship between fascism and the capitalist state. It was the result also of careful BUF attempts to cultivate a good working relationship with the police, and of appearances. Like the fascists the police were a uniformed, disciplined body, unquestioningly obedient to an unelected hierarchy of command, who had become increasingly militarised and centralised throughout the inter-war period.[54] At BUF events it was the police who protected the fascists and appeared to be acting almost as stewards on their behalf, such as at Hyde Park in September 1934 when a total of 6,937 police officers were on duty to ensure that 3,000 or so fascists were not attacked by the hostile crowds.[55] Invariably the result was a confrontation of existing suspicions concerning the degree of collusion between the fascists and the authorities.

Some revisionist historians have suggested that there is no evidence to substantiate accusations of police partiality.[56] This is untrue. Existing police records show beyond all doubt that instances of police bias did occur. These incidents were of a random nature and arose often as a result of operational decisions taken at street level by lower or middle-ranking officers. Often such incidents were relatively minor and concerned a police failure to treat fascist and anti-fascist street meetings, hecklers or newspaper-sellers in an even handed fashion. One of the most flagrant examples of this occurred in April 1936 at Walthamstow when an outdoor meeting of the National Unemployed Workers Movement, being held on its usual site of Cleveland Park Avenue, was closed by the police and replaced with a BUF meeting. No explanation was offered as to why the police had marched the fascists under escort from their own meeting site a mile away to install them in Cleveland Park Avenue. When questioned about the matter in parliament the Home Secretary admitted that the officer in command had '. . . made an error of judgment'.[57]

Other examples of disturbing police behaviour occurred in relation to marches. After the announcement of the LCC election results in March 1937 the police allowed jubilant fascists to hold an impromptu celebratory march in Bethnal Green. At 12.45 a.m. Alexander Raven Thomson was carried shoulder-high by a joyful crowd, accompanied by a band of percussionists. Above the throb of drums and the clash of cymbals the crowd (estimated as between 400 and 2,000 strong) shouted anti-Semitic slogans. As the procession moved along Green Street a total of eighty-five police officers were engaged in supervising its passage. Some marched alongside the fascist column; others were stationed at regular intervals on either side of the street to prevent the smashing of shop windows. Despite these precautions thirteen large plate-glass windows were broken in Green Street alone, all of them belonging to shops with Jewish or foreign-sounding names. The police failed to apprehend those responsible and made only one arrest against whom their case was so weak that it was later dismissed by the magistrates.[58]

In January 1939 there was a stark contrast between police treatment of two marches in Piccadilly Circus. In mid-January a BUF procession was allowed to disrupt traffic and to engage in several violent individual assaults. Six arrests were made, two of whom were the victims of such attacks. Only seventeen days later a procession to parliament organised by the left in the hope of persuading the government to assist the dying Spanish republic was driven away by police. It later reassembled in Piccadilly Circus where it was violently attacked by police who arrested fifty-one of the marchers.[59]

There were also examples of bias arising from the decisions of senior police officers. Most usually these involved the routes sanctioned by police for proposed marches. For example, in the autumn of 1935, a BUF sandwich-board parade was allowed through London's West End, including Oxford Street and Piccadilly, although internally it was acknowledged by the police that '. . . we always deny this route to the Communists'.[60] In the following spring existing precedents were again broken when the police allowed the BUF to march along Constitution Hill past Buckingham Palace. Previously no political marches had been allowed within the vicinity of the Palace.[61] A particularly blatant example of this sort of bias occurred in relation to marches in Regent's Park in 1935. In July a BUF request to hold a meeting in Regent's Park was referred to the police by the park authorities and, as no objections were forthcoming, permission was granted. Consequently 150 fascists, preceded by twelve drummers, marched through the park, held their meeting, and then marched back to their headquarters with a police escort. Only a few days later, however, when the St Pancras anti-fascist movement requested permission to hold a small procession in the park, the police persuaded the park authorities to deny the request.[62]

Although the exact route of a march was not in itself a particularly serious matter, these examples illustrate that the police did not always regard the BUF and its opponents in the same manner. Instances of discrimination, for whatever reason, meant that the police were not upholding the law with strict impartiality. This was again highlighted in February 1937 when L. G. Byrde reported to the police that he had observed two men practising military drill outside the BUF's Hampstead headquarters in Belsize Lane. After an interview with Byrde it was adjudged that he held '. . . strong anti-fascist views',[63] and after a few days of fruitless casual observation of the premises it was decided that '. . . Mr. Byrde is probably prejudiced against the BUF. It is most unlikely that the Fascists would seriously indulge in such alleged practices.'[64] Consequently the surveillance of the headquarters was ended and the unfortunate Mr Byrde (a twenty-five year old Cambridge graduate with no police record and of unknown political affiliation) had his name and address dispatched to the Special Branch, to whom it was thought it '. . . may prove useful'.[65] A little over six months later the police received complaints from Hampstead residents about the noise of the local fascist band. It transpired that for every Sunday during 1937 the BUF's Hampstead branch had marched from Belsize Lane to

Hampstead Heath, where a meeting was held, followed by the return march. On each occasion the procession was headed by two standard-bearers and a group of percussionists, and military-style orders were given. One of the complainants also mentioned that the fascists tended to practice military drilling in Belsize Lane, as he had heard clearly the commands being shouted.[66] Yet despite this apparent corroboration of Byrde's earlier testimony, it was decided that no police action should be taken. Neither was there any revision of their earlier assessment of Byrde's sincerity nor any recommendation that his name be withdrawn from the files of the Special Branch.

It must be stressed that such behaviour was not a consistent characteristic of police policy, the main concern of which was to maintain public order. Frequently the activities of the fascists, if only through becoming the passive objects of attacks by political opponents, made the execution of this task more difficult. For some within the police, there-fore, both the BUF and their opponents were to be abhorred equally, as both seemed intent upon a needless increase in the work-load of the police. This was probably true particularly amongst the higher echelons of the force, where senior officers resented having to deploy scarce manpower resources to keep apart the supporters of rival political parties. It was for this reason that the Commissioner, Sir Philip Game, sent a minute to the Home Secretary after the Bermondsey disorder suggesting a complete and permanent ban upon all political marches.[67]

Thus whilst some police officers treated the BUF with varying degrees of sympathy, others perceived it as much as a menace to public order (and, therefore, as great an enemy of the police), as were the communists. The important point is that both of these views had one crucial common element – a deep distrust and hostility towards the left. It is in this respect that one finds consistent institutionalised bias, which, whilst not always in favour of the BUF, was always directed against its opponents.

This hostility was manifest in the banning of marches, harassment of newspaper vendors and interference with outdoor meetings through devices of dubious legality, such as the 1934 Trenchard edict, through which the Commissioner of the Metropolitan police prohibited any meet-ing within the vicinity of a labour exchange. The case of *Duncan* v. *Jones* in 1936 established a precedent whereby the police acquired the power to ban any meeting in any public place even though it might be entirely orderly and law-abiding. The victim of this case, Mrs Duncan, happened to be an affiliate of the left. Yet when the Labour-controlled Bethnal Green council (acting in response to the complaints of residents) approached the Commissioner's office with a view to prohibiting meet-ings (predominantly fascist) in Victoria Park Square they were informed that there was little that the police could do.[68]

With regard to indoor meetings police officers not infrequently displayed a similar antipathy towards those involved in anti-fascism by refusing to act even in the face of vicious attacks by fascist stewards upon members of the audience. Although there was some confusion as to the rights of the police to enter private meetings, it was accepted generally that a public meeting held upon private premises could be entered if the police believed that a breach of the peace was taking place inside. Despite the invariable attendance of plain-clothes officers inside fascist meetings, however, too often the police showed a marked reluctance to intervene. Nowhere was this more starkly illustrated than at Olympia. The Home Secretary defended the decision of the police not to intervene in the meeting by arguing that they could only have entered if they had had '. . . good reason . . .' to believe that a breach of the peace had been committed.[69] Yet the testimony of the police, both within the hall and in the streets outside, illustrates clearly that the police had every reason to suspect that this was so. A Special Branch officer inside the auditorium reported seeing

> . . . about fifty persons ejected. They were handled in a most violent manner and in some cases were punched unconscious and their clothing torn. They were then roughly dragged or carried towards the nearest exit. . . . Women were maltreated in the same manner as the men. As the evening wore on, the blackshirts grew more vicious at interruptions and as soon as a person shouted, he was pounced on by a number of fascists and felled to the ground.[70]

Another officer left the hall to observe the events outside, where he witnessed

> . . . at least thirty persons, of both sexes, ejected into the roadway. . . . Almost every person bore some mark of violence and was in a state of semi-collapse. Several men were bleeding profusely from the face and chin. . . . I saw through the open door that each person ejected was surrounded by at least twelve blackshirts, who were frog-marching, kicking and raining blows on him.[71]

Those stationed outside witnessed scenes of similar brutality. Sergeant Pocock, who was on duty at the entrance to Olympia, reported that

> at 10.43 p.m. . . . a man was thrown through the entrance by three fascists into the street. One leg of his trousers had been torn off, and the other was round his ankle. His private parts were exposed, and he was bleeding freely from a head wound. . . . At 10.47 a pair of flannel trousers were thrown over the gates into Beaconsfield Terrace. Immediately after, the gates were opened, and a man with only a shirt on was thrown by three fascists on his back in the streets where he lay with his private parts exposed. This man was bleeding from a head wound.[72]

Instinctively one might feel that the sight of semi-conscious, half-naked people, bleeding from facial wounds, being thrown into the streets by gangs of stewards, might constitute a 'good reason' to suspect that a breach of the peace or some other criminal offence was taking place within the building. Yet the police within the hall did not attempt to check the behaviour of the stewards, nor did they call for assistance, whilst their colleagues outside felt the need to make only one sortie within the building throughout the entire evening. On this solitary occasion about ten constables rescued several victims, each of whom was being 'kicked and beaten' by groups of fascist stewards. They arrested none of those responsible for administering the beatings.[73] Elsewhere, in the streets surrounding Olympia, police officers were reluctant to act against the fascists. They offered no aid or assistance to those who had been incapacitated by fascist violence, and even arrested onlookers who urged them to intervene. Ironically, many of these were subsequently charged with obstructing the police in the execution of their duty.[74]

Only two months after Olympia the police displayed considerably less reluctance in forcibly entering a left-wing meeting in Glamorgan. Although the meeting was being held on private property and no offence had been committed amongst those present, the police ignored the appeals of its organisers, who requested them to leave. This action was upheld subsequently in the high court (*Thomas* v. *Sawkins*), thereby establishing the right of the police to enter an orderly meeting in a purely preventative capacity.[75] The record of police action at BUF meetings, however, continued to provide some disturbing incidents. One such case was at a Mosley meeting in the Adelphi theatre in September 1935 (both Olympia and the Royal Covent Garden Opera House having been denied to the BUF), where over forty police officers were on duty but who had been instructed to take no action 'unless called upon by the door stewards'.[76] In effect, on this occasion, the police had become another arm of the BUF's stewarding force. Had this been generally known, it would have provided little comfort to those anti-fascists within the meeting.

Other instances of police inaction occurred at the Albert Hall in March 1936 where fascist assaults both inside and outside the hall were ignored by police witnesses, and at Victoria Park Square in June when fascist stewards hit and kicked two members of the audience under the benign gaze of those police officers present at the meeting to preserve law and order. A month later, after a brawl at the Carfax Assembly Rooms in Oxford, members of the audience who claimed that their fascist assailants could be identified were ignored by the police who took no steps to trace those responsible.[77]

The Public Order Act did not halt this trend, as illustrated by the BUF's meeting in Hornsey town hall in January 1937. Over one hundred police officers had been assigned to the meeting and Mosley had assured their commanding officer that he had '. . . no objection to police entering

the hall if you think it is necessary in the public interest for the maintenance of order'.[78] Several people were ejected, some of whom displayed
facial injuries, and yet those victims who asked police officers to accom-
pany them back into the hall in order that they could identify their
assailants were refused any such assistance. After an internal inquiry
Sir Philip Game admitted confidentially that the judgment of the officers in charge of the operation had been unwisely exercised because '. . .
there is little doubt that the Fascist stewards were somewhat out of
hand and over violent at the meeting'.[79] He qualified this criticism,
however, with an admission of his lack of sympathy for those who
attended fascist meetings in order to protest, and recommended that
there should be no public inquiry as it would only give '. . . a fictitious
importance', to the NCCL, which would use it solely 'in order to attack
the police'.[80] The Home Secretary agreed and no further action was
taken.

The police also indulged in direct forms of violence against the
opponents of fascism. Occasionally the BUF and the police worked
together, as in Bristol in June 1934 where police closed a left-wing meeting, but later allowed a BUF meeting to begin on the same site. Several
of those who objected were arrested, which led to fighting between anti-
fascists and police. The fascists entered the battle on the side of the
police and together they fought as a combined force until the arrival of
police reinforcements.[81] Another example of this was seen in Leicester
in April 1935 when fascists and police worked together to eject opponents from a BUF meeting.[82]

It was more common, however, for police violence to occur as the
result of attempts to protect the fascists or to ensure a right of way to
fascist marches. Their antipathy towards the left and their stubborn
self-perception as sole arbiters of public order meant that even in the
face of large and hostile crowds the police often attempted to bludgeon
clear a path for the fascists. The most famous example of this was at
Cable Street in 1936 when police made repeated charges in an effort to
disperse anti-fascists. Greater levels of viciousness were achieved in the
south London borough of Bermondsey in October 1937. The police,
anxious to avoid a repetition of the victory achieved by anti-fascists a
year previously, dealt brutally with those who had assembled in the
streets. Reports described how police used their batons and their fists
with little discrimination, causing injury to a number of innocent
bystanders.[83] Unlike at Cable Street, the police on this occasion outma-
noeuvered the anti-fascist forces and were able to ensure that the BUF
procession reached its predetermined destination. Police violence of this
nature could also occur even when there were no fascists in the
immediate vicinity. At an anti-fascist meeting in Thurloe Square in
March 1936 the police found it necessary to disperse the orderly crowd

with a mounted baton charge in the course of which officers lashed out indiscriminately and numerous head injuries were sustained.

The type of institutionalised anti-left bias which existed within the police was visible also within the judiciary. Here, too, on occasions it could manifest itself in the form of overt pro-fascist partiality. Notwithstanding a series of high court slander and libel actions which involved Mosley,[84] the most fundamental point of contact between the BUF and the judiciary was at the level of the courts of summary jurisdiction. These courts, which dealt with a vast number of relatively minor statutory offences, did not require the services of a jury. They were each presided over by a bench of lay magistrates with little or no legal training, the members of which had been appointed as a form of political honour. The institution was thus, by its very nature, politically partisan and invariably reflected the conservative values of the ruling class.[85]

The result was that the courts, like the Conservative Party itself, tended to project attitudes, which ranged from neutrality to overt forms of profascist bias. The neutrality was based on a mutual hostility to the BUF and its opponents, both of which were regarded as extremist elements threatening the stability of the existing order. The reactionary nature of such magistrates revealed itself through their pronouncements and their actions. When hatless women were expelled from court because they were deemed indecently dressed and only readmitted when they had, in the absence of hats, placed handkerchieves upon their heads, the magistrate responsible was defending (albeit absurdly) a series of social and political values. Similarly, when a magistrate fined a window-cleaner for contempt because he had appeared in court straight from work still dressed in his overalls[86] he expressed his own bourgeois moral code within which the clothes of a manual worker were contemptible. This attitude was encapsulated in the lament of C. Mullins, magistrate of the south-western police court: 'It is the curse of today that everyone wants to behave like people who are richer, instead of settling down comfortably, and perhaps having a family. They ape the better off, have telephones, cars, possibly cocktails, smoking and all kinds of luxuries'.[87] Such people found it difficult to sympathise with criticisms of a society which offered its citizens so much freedom for those with the wealth to enjoy it. They found it impossible to understand why the discontented felt the need to exercise their liberty so disruptively. As one London magistrate remarked when sentencing a fascist for a public order offence, 'I am tired of your processions, your slogans, and the disturbances you create.'[88] This attitude could at times override all pretence of judicial responsibility and cause cases to be decided with flagrant disregard of the available evidence. Hence in October 1938 the case against a fascist who had entered a left-wing bookshop illegally and daubed it with fascist graffiti was dismissed by Mullins who denounced the victim of the crime as vehemently as its perpetrator: 'You hate each other like poison and I shall not decide between you, but I can be rude to you. I should like to see you both get a dose of your own medicine and all of you put into concentration camps for five years. . . . Then you would form a different opinion.'[89]

There is some evidence to suggest that there existed also a degree of pro-fascist bias amongst some magistrates. Owing to the immense size and scope of the subject, and to the regional fluctuations contained therein, it is impossible here to make any direct statistical comparison concerning the treatment received in the courts by fascists and anti-fascists. Nevertheless some disturbing discrepancies are readily apparent and suggest that partiality was shown in some magistrates' courts towards the fascists. In May 1934 two fascists were each given a fifty-shilling fine in Newcastle, one for assaulting a police officer and the other for attacking two members of the public who went to the assistance of the officer.[90] Yet an assault charge, especially against the police, almost always led to imprisonment when the accused was an anti-fascist. Indeed, later that same month, a youth was given a forty-shilling fine and imprisoned for fourteen days after allegedly striking a police officer and shouting 'Down with the Blackshirts, hunger, and war', at a BUF meeting in Finsbury Park.[91] Similarly, an anti-fascist was sentenced to a £3 fine or a month's imprisonment for spitting at a BUF procession,[92] and yet the same fine constituted the heaviest sentence imposed upon three fascists who had beaten unconscious an innocent bystander at a meeting in Brighton.[93] Three months after the Brighton case two anti-fascists were condemned to a month's hard labour in London for throwing stones at a BUF member. Their victim had not been rendered unconscious, but had sustained a bruise upon one leg.[94]

Judicial partiality, where it arose, did so for two reasons. Firstly it was the result of those magistrates who saw fascism as a form of misguided but well-intentioned conservatism, whereas anti-fascists were invariably perceived as a motley collective of conspiratorial malcontents funded and directed from Moscow. This conservative misconception of fascism has already been discussed and needs no further explanation. Secondly, there was class prejudice. On the whole magistrates dealt more harshly with their social inferiors than with their middle-class brethren whose careers could be besmirched by a criminal conviction.[95] Similarly the testimony of 'respectable' witnesses was given far greater credence than that of working-class witnesses, and could often mean the difference between conviction and acquittal.[96] Such witnesses were few, however, and the vast majority of anti-fascists who came before the magistrates were from working-class backgrounds. They were not tried by their peers but by their masters, and not only did they have to labour against the class prejudice of the magistrates but also against the procedural bias of the judicial system itself. They lacked the financial resources to hire lawyers to speak on their behalf, and were often bereft of the social and educational skills necessary to articulate an effective defence. Even when the accused did manage to construct a convincing defence it was liable to be dismissed by the court as a tissue of lies. This was the case in October 1936 when, after hearing such a defence (which included the testimony of several members of the Communist Party as witnesses), a magistrate found the accused anti-fascist guilty as charged despite some rather dubious police evidence. The magistrate stated that had he heard the defendant alone he would have had doubts about the charges, but that having seen and heard those whom he had called upon to testify on his behalf, he was now entirely convinced as to the prisoner's guilt.[97]

This specimen was typical of many in that it highlighted the extremely high rate of convictions in such cases which in turn reflected the basic unwillingness of magistrates to question the motivation and testimony of the police. Between October and early November 1936, a total of 146 persons were charged with offences arising from disorder in the metropolitan area. With the exception of ten which were still pending, all but three of these cases had been found proven – a conviction rate of over ninety-seven per cent.[98] In many instances the only evidence against the accused was the testimony of the police. This reliance upon the police (which sometimes extended to the magistrate being supplied with information concerning not only the past criminal record of the accused but also the police opinion of his political views and their level of seditiousness) was rarely shaken even in the face of glaring inconsistencies in police evidence.[99] One interesting exception did occur amongst the cases of those arrested at the BUF's Hyde Park rally in September 1934. Most of the accused pleaded not guilty to the usual charges of assault and obstruction but were convicted, usually on the basis of the testimony of one or more police officers. The only acquittal was that of a middle-class man accused by two policemen of throwing a stone. Although they were quite certain that he was the culprit, two independent witnesses claimed that the missile came from elsewhere in the crowd, and the evidence of the police was eventually overruled. Unlike the accused in the other cases being dealt with, the defendant was sympathetic to fascism and admitted raising his hand not to dispatch a missile but to offer a fascist salute to Mosley.[100]

For the most part, however, judicial support for the police was unquestioning and consistent. This meant also that anti-fascist allegations of police brutality were received with very little sympathy. Some magistrates justified police action, such as in the case of an anti-fascist arrested in Stepney who was so badly beaten by police that he had to be transferred from a police cell to a hospital. The reaction of the magistrate was unsympathetic. 'When the police are dealing with cases of disorder it is obvious that . . . sometimes it is necessary to do it in a way which is not gentle.'[101] Others simply refused to entertain the possibility that such allegations were true and often prevented them from being discussed. One such magistrate told an anti-fascist who claimed that he had been 'bashed unmercifully' by the police after his arrest causing damage to several of his teeth, 'I don't believe a word you say. Not one word of it', and promptly fined him forty shillings for insulting words and behaviour.[102] In another case H. Goodrich, a local East-End Labour Party official, was rebuked severely for daring to suggest that the police had behaved with brutality towards an anti-fascist gathering in Victoria Park. The magistrate informed him that 'I have a good mind, if you say anything further, to order a prosecution for perjury.'[103]

Such attitudes too often gave the police *carte blanche* to concoct evidence and press ill-founded charges secure in the knowledge that the bias of the magistrates would be sufficient in most cases to effect the desired conviction. Thus, as with the police, the bias in the judicial system did not always operate directly in favour of the BUF, but always discriminated against its opponents.

The attitude of the police and judiciary towards anti-Semitism is also of interest. The government had rejected attempts to include the specific prohibition of racial or religious abuse within the Public Order Act on the grounds that such behaviour could be dealt with under section five of the act, which covered insulting words and behaviour. But this offence had already existed in London and several other cities before the new legislation extended it throughout the entire country, and yet it was rarely used against fascist anti-Semitism. By the mid-1930s, as the BUF's anti-Semitism reached its height, abuse of the Jews was often the most common feature of the numerous fascist speeches which were made in the grimy streets of Britain's major cities. This was particularly true of London where, despite the presence of police officers and the existence of the 1839 Metropolitan Police Act prohibiting insulting words and behaviour, rabid anti-Semitism was dispensed at street meetings without interference from the authorities.

In May 1936 the matter was raised with the Home Secretary after the police had failed to take any action against a fascist speaker at Hampstead Heath, who referred to the Jews as 'venereal-ridden vagrants who spread disease to every corner of the earth'.[104] Far from cautioning the speaker, the police who were on duty at the meeting acted as fascist stewards and ordered those members of the audience who objected to the remark to remain silent or to face arrest for insulting words and behaviour. The Home Secretary admitted that an offensive remark had been made at the meeting but claimed rather feebly that although the police had heard it they were not sure exactly who had said it.[105] Such abuse continued as a regular feature of the BUF's speeches at Hampstead Heath despite the presence of police. In Stepney a BUF speaker regaled his audience with a list of the evils perpetrated by the 'Rats and vermin from the gutters of Whitechapel. Jews are the biggest owners of prostitutes in the West End', he claimed, and it was the Jews who had stolen '. . . your jobs and houses while you were fighting in the war'.[106] The large body of police on duty at the meeting stood by impassively as the speaker warned that they would be used to eject anyone who dared to interrupt.

Even on those rare occasions when fascist speakers were prosecuted for insulting words and behaviour, the result was not such a foregone conclusion as when the accused were anti-fascists. Raven Thomson was acquitted of such a charge in September 1936 by a Liverpool Magistrate, who claimed that a speaker was at liberty to trade insults with hostile members of his audience if they were challenging his speech in a similar manner.[107]

No such problems or inhibitions afflicted the police and the judiciary in applying the insulting words and behaviour charge freely to the opponents of fascism. Of forty-six prosecutions for this offence in London during the first half of 1936, the vast majority were directed at those on the left. Like obstructing a police officer, it was a charge which was applied frequently against those involved in incidents of disorder and was used often in conjunction with a more serious offence (such as assault) to improve the likelihood of gaining a conviction. Hence it was used against many of the anti-fascist arrested in the streets around Olympia in June 1934. Its enormous versatility made it invaluable in other circumstances also. Its victims included a man prosecuted for shouting 'Fascism means hunger and war';[108] a newspaper vendor for sporting a placard which read 'André executed by Nazis'; an unemployed worker for crying out 'Give us bread' at a demonstration of the unemployed; and a pacifist, who attached an anti-war poster to a fence at Hendon Aerodrome.[109]

Yet despite this versatility the police remained unwilling to apply it widely to anti-Semitic abuse emanating from fascist street meetings. This reluctance prompted a memorandum from the Home Secretary to the Commissioner of the Metropolitan Police demanding greater efforts to suppress Jew-baiting in east London, and insisting that the police '. . . should intervene promptly if they hear grossly provocative or abusive language'.[110] The Commissioner's response was to issue his own memorandum to all ranks urging his men '. . . to err on the side of action' in all cases.[111] Yet little change was effected. E. G. Clarke, a native East-Ender and leading BUF anti-Semite, continued to make speeches condemning the '. . . hook-nosed, yellow skinned dirty Jewish swine' of east

London,[112] whilst the police continued to apply section five of the Public Order Act primarily against the left. Figures from the Home Office show that between 1 January and 31 July 1937, twenty-seven persons were charged with insulting words and behaviour in the Metropolitan police area. Of those whose political allegiances were known, fifteen had been anti-fascists and only six fascists. Of these six, four were speakers.[113] Some of the anti-fascists so charged were arrested at BUF marches or meetings, but others were seized elsewhere. One such victim was George Miles whom the police claimed was '. . . well known in Walthamstow for his Communist activities'.[114] Whilst addressing a street meeting Miles made the mistake of referring to personal criticisms of the Royal Family (such as the Queen's ugliness and the King's propensity to succumb to fits of epilepsy) in order, as he later explained, to dismiss them as irrelevant and to highlight the real importance of the monarchy, which lay in its role as a political institution. He was given no opportunity to develop his argument for the police officers present at the meeting ordered it to close. He was later summonsed on the basis of the notes of his speech taken by these officers, and charged with insulting words and behaviour. In May 1937 Miles appeared before a magistrate, who dismissed his defence and sentenced him to a month's hard labour. The police could barely contain their glee for they believed that Miles '. . . richly deserved the month's hard labour . . . . . . as . . . he has been riding for a fall for some time past . . .'.[115]

The moral, it seemed, was that anti-Semitism was a good deal more acceptable as far as the police were concerned than was republicanism. Other anti-fascist actions sufficient to secure a summons under section five included whistling, and even the blowing of one's nose whilst standing amongst the audience of a fascist meeting.[116] Yet in June 1937 Clarke was allowed to make a speech wherein he advised his audience that '. . . perhaps the best thing to do when you meet a Jew is to shoot him'.[117] Two days later Clarke was arrested and charged with insulting words and behaviour after referring to Jews as 'greasy scum', and the 'lice of the earth'.[118] Amongst his vaporous stream of anti-Semitic hatred Clarke had also found time to abuse Commissioner Game whom he referred to as 'Wobbly Willie',[119] and as 'a darned old fool who hasn't the guts of a louse'.[120] It was these 'perfectly scandalous, disgraceful', references which seemed to concern the magistrate more than the speaker's virulent anti-Semitic incitement.[121] Clarke was found guilty as charged and bound over for twelve months upon a surety of £50. It was a fate distinctly preferable to the one month's hard labour received by Miles.

The failure of the police officers who had been present at Clarke's meeting to arrest him at once prompted the Commissioner to issue a second memorandum. Referring to his earlier orders he stressed that he was 'by no means satisfied' that they were being complied with and complained of recent examples of meetings where violently abusive language had been used '. . . without any action whatever being taken by the police'.[122] Cases of police inaction persisted, however, and the manner was raised once more in the House of Commons in early 1938, after a BUF meeting in the East End on 27 February. On this occasion four anti-fascist hecklers were arrested and charged with insulting words and behaviour, yet one of the fascist speakers who indulged consistently in anti-Semitic abuse was only cautioned by police officers. Even after his warning he continued his tirade with epithets such as the 'hook-nosed unmentionables', but the police took no further action either at the time or afterwards when the transcript of his speech had been studied. At first the Home Secretary, Sir Samuel Hoare, claimed that this was because they had been unable to hear the speech owing to the incessant anti-fascist heckling amongst the crowd.[123] Later he admitted that the police had taken shorthand notes of the speech and, after examining them closely himself, he was satisfied that their decision not to prosecute the speaker had been fully justified. Requests that the notes be made publicly available so that the wisdom of the police decision could be shared by all were, however, firmly denied.[124]

There was no evidence to suggest that the record of police action improved. Between August 1936 and December 1938 the BUF held a total of 2,108 meetings in east London. Yet despite the BUF's pursuance of vigorous anti-Semitic propaganda fascist speakers were cautioned on only sixteen occasions. In all there were only seven prosecutions and three convictions.[125] This lack of action was certainly not based upon ignorance as to the nature of the language being used, for police officers were almost always present on such occasions, and from 1936 it was customary for shorthand notes to be taken of the contents of each speech. It has been suggested that the police attitude can be explained through the nature of the insulting words and behaviour charge itself, which did not proscribe words and behaviour which were merely abusive, but those which could be shown to be liable to cause a breach of the peace, and that anti-Semitic abuse, therefore, could only produce disorder at fascist meetings when Jews were present.[126] This facile reasoning echoed an argument which police officers themselves used to justify to superiors their failure to arrest fascist speakers for anti-Semitic abuse. Although the speech may have appeared offensive on paper, invariably they claimed that the audience was sympathetic to the sentiments of the speaker and, therefore, there was no risk of disorder and no need for police action. Some officers went even further than this and ejected anti-fascists hecklers from the crowd, or even arrested them for insulting words and behaviour on the pretext that their vocal objections to the speech could lead to disorder and a breach of the peace amongst the pro-fascist audience. The suggestion that words and behaviour should be judged only in their immediate context, however, was not consistently applied. In the case of *Duncan* v. *Jones,* when the meeting in question had been organised by the left, the police had argued (and the court had accepted) that a breach of the peace, although not immediately imminent, could have occurred at a later date. Nor had the presence of a sympathetic crowd been sufficient to save George Miles, the communist republican, from the savagery of official retribution. His meeting had been extremely orderly and the sympathy of the crowd had been demonstrated by the collection of twenty-eight shillings and the sale of fifty-two copies of the *Daily Worker* amongst those who had gathered to listen. But this defence had been rejected by police and magistrates alike.[127] Besides, the Commissioner had made it perfectly clear that the insulting words and behaviour charge was applicable to BUF anti-Semitic abuse, and that he wanted his officers to err on the side of action. In his second memorandum he was even more specific and stressed to his men that an absence of hecklers or a lack of resentment amongst the audience was not '. . . an excuse for inaction on the part of the police'. If such virulent abuse was left unchecked, he emphasised, then sooner or later it would lead to breaches of the peace.[128]

Why then did lower-ranking police officers fail to act against BUF speakers on so many occasions? There is no single clear answer. In some instances it may have been due to incompetence, or to a genuine confusion as to the nature of their duty, whilst in others police were intimidated by the prospect of creating disorder amongst a pro-fascist crowd by arresting the speaker. It remains inescapably self-evident, however, that in some cases police inaction was the result of some degree of sympathy for fascism, or at least for its anti-Semitic propaganda. The evidence concerning anti-Semitism within the police force is far too incomplete to give any indication as to its scale or overall distribution. But there is enough to suggest its existence. There were cases where police officers on duty at fascist meetings were reported to have been seen laughing at anti-Semitic jibes, such as at Victoria Park Square in 1937 where a BUF speaker informed his audience that 'the Jew can no more help being a parasite than a louse can being a louse'.[129] William Joyce claimed that such incidents were not uncommon, and that in general the Metropolitan police were '. . . very anti-Jewish'. He even suggested that he had been warned of his impending arrest in 1939 '. . . by friendly police officers of some rank', who advised him to reduce the volume of his anti-Semitic output.[130] Joyce's remembrances, published whilst he was residing in the Third Reich, should be treated with obvious caution; but equally damning testimony was provided by others. Eyewitnesses claimed that police officers abused an anti-fascist crowd in 1939 with shouts of 'You Jew bastards', and 'Go back to Whitechapel,

you Jewish whores.'[131] On another occasion a woman claimed that a
police inspector expressed the opinion that all London prostitutes were
Jews, that Jewish employers perpetrated acts of indecency against Gentile girls, and that Jews were a 'cancer which should be cut out'.[132]

Obviously it is impossible to assess the truth of such allegations
other than to say that it is unlikely that all were entirely fictitious.
Owing to the esoteric nature of the Jewish community it is likely that the
bulk of the Jews with whom the police came into contact were prostitutes, criminals, and anti-fascists. Certainly there is evidence that some
officers tended to treat them as a group apart. Sometimes in reports on
those arrested their religion was mentioned rather than their occupation, as was customary. Other officers suggested their belief in common
Jewish stereotypes, with claims that '. . . the foreign Jews are far more
anti-police than anti-fascist', and complaints that the leaders of the east
London Jewish community could not restrain '. . . the young and
hotheaded or the lower type of foreign Jew'.[133]

As late as the autumn of 1939 Commissioner Game was still
expressing his dissatisfaction with the attitude of his men towards the
policing of BUF meetings. By this stage, of course, events in east London
were shortly to be overshadowed by the struggle for European hege-
mony between fascist Germany and her western European enemies.
There were some indications, however, that the police and the courts
were becoming less reluctant to act against the BUF under section five of
the Public Order Act. In mid-August James Shepherd, from the BUF's
publications department, was convicted of insulting words and
behaviour in the form of an anti-Semitic speech.[134] His sentence of a £20
fine or six weeks in prison was higher than had been inflicted upon the
party in the past. Nevertheless it made an interesting comparison with
that which was passed on Jacques Kamellard who was convicted of the
same offence three months later, also at a BUF public meeting. Whereas
Shepherd had insulted the Jews, Kamellard had had the audacity to
attack the first Lord of the Admiralty, Winston Churchill, whom he
referred to as '. . . public enemy number one'. Kamellard was imprisoned
for three months.[135] Anti-Semitism, it may be supposed, remained one of
the more tolerated forms of insulting words and behaviour.

NOTES

1 *HC Deb.*, 290, 14 June 1934, c. 1938–45, M. W. Beaumont (1903–58) sat as
   Conservative MP for Aylesbury, 1929–38. T. Howard (1888–1953) served
   as Conservative MP for Islington South, 1931–5. F. A. MacQuisten
   (1870–1940) sat as Cocservative MP for Glasgow Springburn, 1918–22,
   and Argyllshire, 1924–40.
2 *Daily Mail*, 25 April 1934, p. 12.
3 *HC Deb.*, 290, 14 June 1934, 1935–8.
4 *Ibid.*, c. 1960–65.

5 *Ibid.*
6 *Manchester Guardian,* 11 June 1934, p. 9.
7 *Ibid.*
8 *The Times,* 8 October 1936, p. 7.
9 S. Cripps, *'National' Fascism in Britain,* Socialist League, London n.d., p. 7.
10 R. Kidd, *British Liberty in Danger,* Lawrence & Wishart, London 1940, pp. 102–7. See also K. Martin, *Fascism, Democracy, and the Press,* New Statesman and Nation, London 1938, pp. 6–7.
11 Amongst these were R. P. Dutt, *Fascism and Social Revolution,* Lawrence, London 1934; S. Cripps. *op. cit.,* and W. A. Rudlin, *The Growth of Fascism in Britain,* George Allen & Unwin Ltd, London 1935.
12 J. Stevenson & C. Cook, *The Slump,* Quartet Books Ltd, London 1979, pp. 167–73.
13 *Ibid.,* pp. 173–9.
14 CAB 23/73, p. 26: Cabinet Minutes, 23 November 1932, and CAB 27/497: Proceedings of Cabinet Committees, 28 November, 7 and 21 December 1932, as cited by K. Lunn & R. C. Thurlow (eds.), *British Fascism,* Croom Helm, London 1980, pp. 139–40.
15 *HC Deb.,* 285, 31 January 1934, c. 360–1.
16 *Ibid.,* 286, 20 February 1934, c. 173–4. See also 288, 9 April 1934, c. 14–15.
17 CAB 24/249, CP 144 (34), Memorandum on political uniforms by the Home Secretary, 23 May 1934. See also CAB 23/79, 22 (34)7, Cabinet Conclusions, 30 May 1934.
18 *Spectator,* CLII, 15 June 1934, p. 910; and *New Statesman and Nation* VII, 16 June 1934, p. 905.
19 CAB 23/79, 24(34)1, and Appendix I, Cabinet Conclusions, 13 June 1934. See also CAB 23/79, 25(34)7, Cabinet Conclusions, 19 June 1934.
20 CAB 23/79, 29(34)2, Cabinet Conclusions, 18 July 1934. See also CAB 24/250, CP 189(34), Memorandum by Home Secretary, 11 July 1934.
21 CAB 23/79, 31 (34)7, Cabinet Conclusions, 31 July 1934.
22 CAB 24/264, CP 261(36), Memorandum by Simon, 12 October 1936.
23 CAB 23/85, 57(36)2, Cabinet Conclusions, 14 October 1936.
24 CAB 23/86, 62(36)9, Cabinet Conclusions, 4 November 1936.
25 In his memorandum of 12 October 1936, CAB 24/264, CP 261(36), Simon refers to the recommendations which appeared in Gilmour's memorandum of July 1934, CAB 24/250, CP 189(34).
26 See text of Public Order Act, as reproduced in Appendix I of Anon., *Meetings, Uniforms and Public Order,* Jordan & Sons Ltd, London n.d.
27 *Ibid.*
28 Kidd, *op. cit.,* pp. 70–1.
29 Costin & Watson, *The Law and the Working of the Constitution,* vol. II, pp. 297–8, 315–17; as cited by R. Skidelsky, *Oswald Mosley,* Macmillian, London 1975, pp. 418–19.
30 *HC Deb.,* 318, 7 December 1936, c. 1701–27.
31 Anon., *Meetings, Uniforms etc. . . . , op. cit.*
32 *HC Deb.,* 318, 26 November 1936, 638–54.
33 *Ibid.,* c. 654–5.
34 Anon., *Meetings, Uniforms, etc. . . . , op. cit.*
35 The Home Secretary added an amendment to this effect, *HC Deb.,* 318, 7 December 1936, c. 1751–2.
36 This was the opinion of ex-communist agitator Archie Lennox, who claimed that after the 1936 act many anti-fascists in Aberdeen were forced to give their names to the police at fascist meetings, and usually ended up by being fined. Interview with A. Lennox, as cited by E. Kibblewhite & A. Rigby, *Fascism in Aberdeen – street politics in the 1930s,* Aberdeen

People's Press, Aberdeen 1978, p. 29.

37 CAB 24/250, CP 189 (34), Memorandum by Home Secretary, 11 July 1934.

38 *HC Deb.*, 319, 17 December 1936, c. 2781–4; and 18 December 1936, c. 2819.

39 'Notes on the quarter', *BUQ*, I, 1, January–April 1937, p. 11.

40 *Manchester Guardian*, 4 January 1937, p. 9.

41 *Blackshirt*, 30 January 1937, p. 5.

42 *The Times*, 28 January 1937, p. 16.

43 *Ibid.*, 30 January 1937, p. 7.

44 *Ibid.*, 17 June 1937, p. 13; See also D. Williams, *Keeping the Peace: The Police and Public Order*, Hutchinson, London 1967, p. 219.

45 *HC Deb.*, 325, 21 June 1937, c. 846–9. For the Commissioner's request see letter to Home Secretary from P. Game, 16 June 1937, MEPO 2/3048. In an effort to appear impartial the Home Office applied the ban even to the planned march of the Bethnal Green Trades Council, despite the fact that it did not consider itself a political organisation and no disorder was expected by the police. For details see MEPO 2/3113.

46 *Blackshirt*, 26 June 1937, p. 8.

47 *Action*, 7 August 1937, p. 8; and *Manchester Guardian*, 14 September 1934, p. 9.

48 For instances of bans on uniforms in Manchester, see *Manchester Guardian*, 20 July 1936, p. 11; 8 October 1936, p. 11; *The Times*, 24 December 1936, p. 14; *Blackshirt*, 18 July 1936, p. 5; and *Daily Herald*, 8 October 1936, p. 9.

49 For details of Cardiff, see *Manchester Guardian*, 27 October 1936, p. 12; and for Hull, *ibid.*, 29 July 1936, p. 5.

50 NCCL., *The Harworth Colliery Strike*, NCCL, London 1937, pp. 7–10.

51 It was argued that although a future government would probably wish to retain most of the act, section three was essentially a temporary infringement of liberty, which could be dispensed with as soon as the political situation in the East End returned to 'normal'. The Home Secretary's rejection of this argument again suggests that the act was aimed at others apart from the BUF. *HC Deb.*, 318, 26 November 1936, c. 708–9.

52 *Ibid.*, 318, 7 December 1936, c. 1763.

53 *Ibid.*, c. 1778.

54 T. Bunyan, *The History and Practice of the Political Police in Britian*, Quartet Books, London 1977, *passim*.

55 Police report on Hyde Park demonstration, 8 September 1934, MEPO 2/3074.

56 R. Skidelsky, *op. cit.*, p. 420.

57 *HC Deb.*, 312, 14 May 1936, c. 573–4.

58 Police report on BUF procession, 5 March 1937, MEPO 2/3109.

59 Kidd, *op. cit.*, pp. 136–8.

60 Mintute by A. C. A., 4 October 1935, MEPO 2/3081.

61 *HC Deb.*, 310, 30 March 1936, c. 1609–10.

62 Letter from Assistant Commissioner, P. Laurie, to the Secretary of HM Office of Public Works, 1 August 1935, MEPO 2/3079.

63 Minute by Inspector R. Roberts, S. Division, 27 March 1937, MEPO 2/3107.

64 Minute by Superintendent (signature illegible), 28 March 1937, *ibid.*

65 Minute by Roberts, 27 March 1937, *ibid.*

66 Statement taken from F. Alexander, 14 September 1937; E. W. Tickle, 16 September 1937; and M. Carrington, 17 September 1937, *ibid.*

67 Minute by Sir P. Game, 5 October 1937, CAB 24/271, CP 230(37).

68 Letters between Commissioner of the Metropolitan Police and F. A. Newsam at the Home Office, 13 and 18 September 1937, MEPO 2/3078.

69 *HC Deb.*, 290, 11 June 1934, c. 1343.

70 Statement by Sergeant Hunt, MEPO 2/4319, as quoted by G. C. Lebzelter, *Political Anti-Semitism in Engand 1918–1939,* Macmillan Press, London 1978, p. 105. This file was at one time open to the public but has since been re-closed by the Home Office.

71 Statement by Sergeant Rogers, *ibid.,* pp. 105–6.

72 Statement by Sergeant Pocock, *ibid.,* p. 106.

73 For details of this intervention, see the testimony of Inspector Carrol, MEPO 2/4319, as quoted by Skidelsky, *op. cit.,* pp. 374–5. This failure of the police to arrest any of those engaged in the violence on this particular occasion was explained inadequately by the Home Secretary, who claimed that the guilty parties had escaped into the body of the hall, *HC Deb.*, 290, 14 June 1934, c. 1965–73. When questioned about this failure by his superiors, Carrol himself reacted by altering his story and claiming that his earlier testimony had been grossly exaggerated in order to justify his own entry into the premises. Skidelsky cites this recantation as part of his attempt to underplay the level of violence which occurred at Olympia. It seems to have escaped his notice that an equally plausible explanation as to why Carrol changed his mind lay in his need to justify to his superiors his personal failure to apprehend those responsible for the incidents of thuggery, which he had initially described.

74 *HC Deb.*, 290, 13 June 1934, c. 1692–8. Only five of the thirty-six people arrested as a result of Olympia were know to be fascists. See also *New Statesman and Nation,* VII, 16 June 1934, pp. 910–11; and I. Montague, *Blackshirt Brutality: The Story of Olympia,* Workers' Bookshop, London 1934, pp. 24–5.

75 *Thomas* v. *Sawkins* 1935, 2K.B. 249, as cited by R. Benewick, *The Fascist Movement in Britain,* Allen Lane, The Penguin Press, London 1972, p. 180. See also Williams, *op. cit.,* pp. 142–8.

76 Memorandum from Deputy Assistant Commissioner's office (No. 3 District), marked 'confidential', 30 August 1935, MEPO 2/3047.

77 *The Times,* 11 July 1936, p. 15.

78 Letter from O. Mosley to the Superintendent at Hornsey police station, 18 January 1937, MEPO 2/3104.

79 Report from Commissioner Sir P. Game to the Secretary of State, 2 April 1937, *ibid.*

80 *Ibid.*

81 *Manchester Guardian,* 23 June 1934, p. 13; and *Daily Worker,* 25 June 1934, p.3.

82 *Manchester Guardian,* 15 April 1935, p. 9.

83 *Manchester Guardian,* 4 October 1937, p. 9, and 5 October, p. 10. See also *New Statesman and Nation,* XIV, 9 October 1937, p. 510; and Bermondsey Trades Council, *Bermondsey Says 'No' to Fascism,* BTC, London 1937, p. 6.

84 In November 1934 Mosley was successful in suing the *Star* newspaper for libel and was awarded £5,000 in damages. *The Times,* 7 November 1934, p. 4; *Manchester Guardian,* 7 November 1934, p. 4; and *Blackshirt,* 9 November 1934, pp. 2, 4, 7. In February 1936 he was again successful in a slander action against J. Marchbanks, General Secretary of the National Union of Railwaymen, although on this occasion it was a pyrrhic victory because Mosley was awarded only $\frac{1}{4}d$ damages, and costs were not granted. *The Times,* 4 February 1936, p. 4; and 5–8 February, p. 4. In 1937 the BUF was forced to pay £20,000 in damages as the result of an action brought by Lord Camrose, proprietor of the *Daily Telegraph,* who had been libelled by an article in *Action, The Times,* 14–16 October 1937, p. 4.

85 In his days in the ILP Mosley himself recognised that the '. . . class conscious benches of magistrates' showed their bias when dealing with working-class organisations. *HC Deb.*, 206, 17 May 1927, c. 1117. At the end of his life, however, Mosley remembered the British judiciary with 'great regard', and claimed that, for the most part, it was '. . . absolutely fair and impartial'. Mosley, interview with author, 24 June 1980.

86 For details of these examples, see Kidd, *op. cit.*, pp. 187–8.
87 *Ibid.*, p. 170.
88 *The Times,* 9 May 1939, p. 11.
89 Kidd, *op. cit.,* p. 177.
90 *Manchester Guardian,* 17 May 1934, as cited by Labour Research Department, *Who Backs Mosley? Fascist Promise and Fascist Performance,* LRD, London 1934, p. 16. See also F. Mullally, *Fascism inside England,* Morris Books, London 1946, p. 51.
91 *Daily Herald,* 30 May 1934, as cited by Mullally, *op. cit.,* p. 51.
92 *The Times,* 3 May 1938, p. 18.
93 Of the other two, one was discharged and one bound over. *Manchester Guardian,* 10 April 1934, p. 10.
94 *Manchester Guardian,* 13 July 1934, p. 8.
95 For example, see the case of E. G. Edwards, *The Times,* 21 October 1937, p. 11.
96 For example, see *Manchester Guardian,* 16 December 1937, p. 5. Also see *The Times,* 9 June 1934, p. 11.
97 J. Jacobs, *Out of the Ghetto,* Simon, London 1978, p. 253.
98 *The Times,* 12 November 1936, p. 9.
99 For cases involving inconsistencies in police evidence see *Daily Herald,* 5 October 1937, p. 7; and Jacobs, *op. cit.,* pp. 250–3.
100 *Manchester Guardian,* 11 September 1934, p. 4.
101 *East London Advertiser,* 31 July 1937, p. 1.
102 *Daily Herald,* 6 October 1936, p. 7.
103 *East End News,* 9 October 1936, as cited by Jacobs, *op. cit.,* p. 236.
104 *News Chronicle,* 21 May 1936, p. 2.
105 *The Times,* 27 May 1936, p. 11. See also police reports in MEPO 2/3088.
106 D. N. Pritt, KC (Labour Member for Hammersmith North), *HC Deb.,* 10 July 1936, c. 1547–70.
107 *Liverpool Post,* 28 September 1936, as quoted by Skidelsky, *op. cit.,* pp. 401–2.
108 *New Statesman and Nation,* 23 June 1934, as quoted by Labour Research Department, *op. cit.,* p. 15.
109 L. B. Milner, 'Fighting Fascism by Law', *Nation* (New York), 146, 15 January 1938, p. 66.
110 Memorandum by Home Secretary, Sir John Simon, 16 July 1936, MEPO 2/3043.
111 Memorandum by Metropolitan Police Commissioner Sir P. Game, 3 August 1936, MEPO 2/3043.
112 L. B. Milner, *op. cit.,* p. 65.
113 *Action,* 11 September 1937 (letter dated 18 August 1937), as cited by Benewick, *op. cit.,* p. 254.
114 Report by Superintendent, 27 April 1937, MEPO 2/3111.
115 Report by Superintendent of Walthamstow police station, 9 June 1937, *ibid.*
116 Benewick, *op. cit.,* p. 255.
117 This quotation was cited during Clarke's trial. Transcript of the proceedings at Old Street police court, 10 July 1937, p. 4, MEPO 2/3115. The police officer who was supervising this East End meeting on 23 June 1937 later justified his lack of action by claiming that he had been patrolling the perimeter of the crowd and had failed to hear any of the anti-Semitic remarks within the speech. Report by Inspector James, 12 July 1937,

MEPO 2/3115. He was later cautioned by his superiors.

118 Notes taken by Sergeant P. S. Jordan of a speech by Clarke at Victoria Park Square, Bethnal Green, 25 June 1937, MEPO 2/3115.

119 *Ibid.*

120 Transcript of the proceedings at Old Street police court, 10 July 1937, p. 5, *ibid.*

121 *Ibid.*, p. 6.

122 Memorandum by Commissioner Game, 29 June 1937, MEPO 2/3043.

123 *HC Deb.*, 332, 3 March 1938, c. 1273–4.

124 *Ibid.*, 333, 24 March 1938, c. 1393–4.

125 Skidelsky, *op. cit.*, p. 399.

126 *Ibid.*, p. 400.

127 For details of the prosecution of Miles in May 1937, see MEPO 2/3111.

128 Memorandum by Sir P. Game, 29 June 1937, MEPO 2/3043.

129 MS DCL 37.4, (NCCL): report of BUF meeting at Victoria Square, 12 March 1937, as quoted by Lebzelter, *op. cit.*, p. 122.

130 W. Joyce, *Twilight over England*, NV Uitgevers-maatschappij 'Oceanus', The Hague 1942, pp. 11, 170.

131 MS DCL 37.4 (NCCL): E. G. Watts, P. Shand to NCCL on 'Arms for Spain' demonstration, 31 January 1939, as quoted by Lebzelter, *op. cit.*, p. 122.

132 MS DCL 74.4 (NCCL): M. Battcock to NCCL, quoted in 'Disturbances in East London', 1937, as quoted by Lebzelter, *op. cit.*, p. 122.

133 Police report on Jew-baiting in the East End for September 1936; 8 October 1936, MEPO 2/3043.

134 *The Times*, 15 August 1939, p. 14.

135 *Ibid.*, 21 November 1939, p. 21.

CHAPTER 7

The BUF
and foreign policy

Material justice must be done, and the new world must be built on the sound reality of a fair economic basis. But deeper than every division of material things is the division of the spirit in modern Europe. The old world and the new world are divided and they cannot mingle. Either the new world and the old world will collide in disaster or the new world will emerge as the final system of the modern age. Therefore on the fate of Britain depends the fate of mankind.

O. Mosley, *Tomorrow We Live*,
Greater Britain Publications, London 1939, p. 75.

On Sunday, the 3rd of September 1939, the sirens heralded the first air-raid warning over Great Britain; the wail of a dying system, the 25 years armistice in the imperialist war had ended. The mad slaughter to decide which set of financiers and capitalists should dominate the markets and spheres of influence of the world had begun again. Capitalism in its desperation had set alight the conflagration that must hasten its own eventual destruction.

E. Trory, *Between the Wars:*
Recollections of a Communist Organiser,
Crabtree Press, Brighton 1974, p. 159

What passing bells for those who die as cattle?
Only the monstrous anger of the guns.
Only the stuttering rifles' rapid rattle
Can patter out their hasty orisons.
No mockeries for them from prayers or bells,
Nor any voice of mourning save the choirs, –
The shrill, demented choirs of wailing shells;
And bugles calling for them from sad shires.

W. Owen,
'Anthem for Doomed Youth'

The foreign policy advocated by the BUF is of considerable interest in that it outlined a clear and consistent alternative to that which was pursued by the British government. It illustrated also the dilemma of a party advocating extreme patriotism whilst being linked simultaneously to foreign governments with whom diplomatic relations were deteriorating.

That the BUF was a patriotic party there can be no doubt. The twin aims of its foreign policy were stated to be the primacy of British interests and the continuance of peace amongst the European powers. A passionate commitment to the British empire lay at the heart of each. As previously suggested, the empire formed an intrinsic part of Mosley's corporate blueprint, for it provided an isolated and largely autarchic economic unit. A rejuvenated empire was also considered to be the ideal medium for a restoration of much of Britain's lost international prestige. But the perpetuation of empire went beyond economic necessity and national pride, for it was considered capable of contributing greatly to world peace. Modern wars, it was argued, inevitably had economic origins such as the scramble to secure foreign markets or raw materials caused by the cut-throat competitiveness of international capitalism. Instead of this chaotic struggle of private interest, which had in the past ignited major conflicts, the BUF was proposing a system of international order based upon corporate empires, or geographical blocs, which would enable nations '. . . to discuss rationally and peacefully the allocation of raw materials and markets'.[1]

Hence it was admitted that '. . . Fascists are enthusiastic imperialists',[2] for not only was an empire a prerequisite for the full fascist development of the mother country, but also imperial expansion was beneficial to those colonised by it, and ultimately of benefit to the world at large through its considerable contribution to the cause of international peace. Furthermore, the fascist conception of empire, like its view of the state itself, was organic. Not a conglomeration of territories or nations sharing a slightly closer relationship than other states, but a living, growing unit capable of evolving in response to new pressures and, therefore, capable of long-term survival. It was inconceivable for nations to withdraw from a union of this nature, for such an action would amount to the amputation of part of a living organism. It was promised that under fascist supervision the empire would no longer be subjected to the exploitation of international finance, but freedom, in the form of an escape from the shackles of British imperial rule, could never be contemplated. '. . . True Imperialism knows nothing of disintegration', stressed William Joyce, '. . . true Imperialism knows nothing of surrender; true Imperialism knows nothing of injustice; and Fascism is true Imperialism'.[3]

In keeping with this total commitment to imperial unity the BUF refused to entertain the idea of a British withdrawal from India. Any such action, it was claimed, would damage the organic integrity of the empire and would be detrimental to Britain's economy. In particular it would have prevented the BUF's proposed reflation of the cotton industry through the destruction of Indian tariffs against the British exports, and the prohibition of Japanese textiles from entering India. Other arguments used against Indian independence included the beneficial influence of British rule, the paternal responsibility owed to India by Britain, and the charge that the internecine religious wars which would result from a British withdrawal would be of terrifying proportions and would drown Indian civilisation in an ocean of blood. Upon achieving power the BUF pledged itself to increase Britain's authority in India, which had been eroded not by genuine Indian nationalism but by a loss of respect for the British race as a result of the compromise, hesitation and cowardice of past British governments.[4] Seditious Indian nationalism would be rooted out mercilessly, it was promised, and its advocates would answer for their sedition '... with their lives .. and their property'.[5]

The party's plans for the increased economic exploitation of India were thrown badly awry by the Government of India Act which became law in 1935. The party's reaction to this meagre gesture towards Indian self-government was full of furious bravado and absurd self-deception.

> Now it is too late to beg, plead, or demand that the surrender of India should not be made; but it is not and will not be too late to recover what has been stolen from us; to establish in India a stronger British control than ever, a control that will close the Indian cotton mills to free the Indian slave, and feed the starving Lancashire household. Let our enemies tell the whole world that, if elected, we shall recapture India.[6]

Other British colonies were considered similarly with promises to protect the native populations from exploitation, being tempered with the proviso that fascism would not be sentimental in these matters. If land belonging to natives was needed for its resources then it would be taken, regardless of the rights of ownership.[7] In all matters the needs of Britain would be considered paramount. The possibility of eventual independence for dependent territories, in addition to being retarded by the fascist view of empire, was also made unlikely by the fascist concept of nationhood as a privilege not to be bestowed lightly; a privilege wholly unsuited to societies which lacked unity and corporate consciousness.[8]

Connected with the regeneration of the British empire was the BUF's attitude to foreign powers. Its view of the USSR was largely predictable, and pandered to right-wing fantasies with portrayals of an Asiatic Russian bear lurking behind the Urals, from where it eyed enviously the civilisation of Europe upon which it hoped eventually to satiate its hunger. Its evil was considered self-evident, as was the need to combat its advance upon Europe: 'Fascism is essentially European, having its roots in those ancient smiling lands which bore all the majesty and the wonder of our Latin-Gothic culture. Communism is Judaeo-Asiatic. Out of the East it comes, like a poisonous vapour from the Scythian Stepes. The Mark of the Beast is upon it, and the snarl of the submen is its choir.'[9] The signing of the Anti-Comintern Pact was greeted with joy by the BUF, which portrayed it as indicative of the resolve of the fascist nations to stand up to their mutual communist enemy. Only after the signing of the Nazi-Soviet non-aggression pact in the summer of 1939 did this hostility show and sign of abatement. It was suggested that the pact may have resulted from the USSR having rid herself of her Jewish leaders and, therefore, was the expression of a genuine desire for peace. The pact shocked fascists and communists alike, and in its confused aftermath the BUF admitted that the phenomenon had other possible explanations.[10] Within a week, however, it had been decided that the pact was simply the next stage in the diabolical plot of international communism, whereby 'Russia the wrecker' was preparing to foment war in the west (by securing Germany's eastern frontier) in order to fulfil the prophesies of Marx by conjuring forth red revolution from the embers of a shattered Europe. Only through European unity around the twin ideologies of fascism and Christianity would such a dastardly plan be foiled, it was asserted.[11]

This idea of unity was the keystone of the BUF's attitude towards the fascist nations. It was urged that Britain seek a closer relationship with Germany and Italy, which would contribute to world peace and help to provide greater security for the British empire. BUF delegations made regular visits to both Italy and Germany and, between 1932 and 1936, Mosley had several meetings with Hitler and Mussolini.[12] Both regimes were often the objects of lavish praise, and both were alleged to have the full support of their respective populations. Even the 1934 Roehm purge, the bloody destruction of the Nazi SA, was justified as an act of salvation necessary to ensure the security of the German state. Understanding was shown also for the grievances of fascist nations. In a speech in Hastings in 1936, Mosley warned his audience that

> . . . democratic Britain, holding in very feeble hands the vast Empire won by the heroism of our forefathers, is denying the right of the great and virile populations of Germany, Italy, and Japan to advance into territories where British interests are nowhere affected. . . . Sooner or later these virile nations expand or explode. Which do you want? Do you want colonial development or a world war?[13]

Hence it was suggested that the spirit of the Versailles Treaty be extirpated from Europe by returning to Germany her pre-war colonies and allowing her to expand in eastern Europe, by giving Italy the freedom to build an empire in Africa and by allowing Japan greater opportunities to exploit northern China.[14]

    This general admiration of, and desire for closer friendship with foreign fascist nations was not considered unpatriotic by the BUF, especially as it could be justified on the grounds of furthering world peace and imperial security. This had been stated as early as May 1933 after a BUF delegation to Rome, when it was claimed that 'our deep and abiding friendship with the fascist movement in Italy is based on the solid rock of our friendship between men who hold in common a vast conception and a great ideal. Such friendship raises no question of subordination, it raises only a question of common service to a common cause.'[15] But nevertheless, this question of subordination to a foreign power posed an obvious problem for a movement as patriotic as the BUF. Attempts were made to overcome it by emphasising the belief that fascism would develop differently in accordance with each country's own historical traditions. Italy, it was claimed, represented '. . . only one building in the Fascist style of architecture. It would be ridiculous to suppose that all Fascist states will be slavish copies of the Italian model.'[16] Occasionally, there was also a degree of gentle criticism levelled towards fascist regimes. The violence which had accompanied their rise to power was explained as symptomatic of how far the crisis had been allowed to develop unchecked in these particular countries before the victory of fascism. Violence, it was claimed, was not inherent to fascism, and neither was anti-Semitism which, in the case of the Nazis, was alleged initially by the BUF to be a function not of fascism but of German society.[17] Ultimately, however, such attempts as were made by the BUF to distance itself from foreign fascism were unsuccessful.

    The BUF shared the open contempt with which the fascist nations beheld the League of Nations. Many of its criticisms of the League were valid, especially those which argued that the League's failure to deter or to punish acts of international aggression had rendered it moribund. Indeed, it was true to suggest that the League was stillborn, in effect, because of its close association with the victors of 1918 and the inequitable Treaty of Versailles. It was compared to the Holy Alliance, established after the Napoleonic wars, which became an instrument for suppressing democracy which was at the time considered a revolutionary and subversive doctrine. Yet by the twentieth century, it was democracy itself which constituted the reactionary regime threatened by revolutionary change in the form of fascism.[18] This real purpose of the League had become even more apparent by the mid-1930s, it was suggested, for the withdrawal of Germany, Italy, and Japan had removed even its claim to be an international body and exposed the League as merely one side of a balance of power equation. Its foremost members, Britain and France, were those who had profited most from the Versailles settlement and in whose interests it was to maintain the status quo. The League was their creature and the inclusion of the USSR within, it was claimed, illustrated the willingness of the degenerate democracies to use even '. . . the vile and bloody instrument of world communism against the nations of European renaissance'.[19]

Even had the fascist nations stayed within the League, however, the BUF's regard for it would have been little improved. To give one vote to each member nation regardless of its size or strength contravened the elitist tenets of fascist philosophy. Real internationalism, it was argued, must be based not upon weak collectivism but upon mutual respect, strength, and a developed sense of nationalism. It must recognise that not all nations are equally advanced and, therefore, not all nations should be accorded equal status in decision-making. 'Nations which are competent to lead must give Leadership, and the constitution of the League must be revised to secure that end',[20] it was concluded, for '. . . without the principle of leadership and authority nothing can be achieved'.[21]

Although the BUF denounced the League, it expressed initially a willingness to retain British membership and to work for its reform from within.[22] Towards the end of the decade, however, international relations had become poisoned to such an extent that the party committed itself, when in government, to British withdrawal and, thereafter, to '. . . have nothing to do with a League of Nations as drawn up by the gorged and satiated victors of the Conference of Versailles'.[23] Instead it was suggested that fascist nations should establish a 'super League' of European powers consisting of a fascist Britain and France, in addition to Germany and Italy. Beneath those 'big four' would be small regional blocs representing areas such as Scandinavia, the Balkans, the Danube, and South America. Undoubtedly such a proposal recognised the problem which had bedevilled the League: strong nations tend to act in their own best interests regardless of abstract principles of international law. The solution inherent within the BUF's proposals was simple but ruthless, for the two-tier super League involved institutionalised elitism and thus gave formal recognition to the principle of the rule of the strong in the sphere of international relations. It was admitted that in such a world small and weak nations would simply have to make the best possible terms with their more powerful neighbours.[24]

Consistent with this policy the BUF advocated an increase in Britain's imperial defences and a reappraisal of strategy with particular reference to the role of air power in any future war. Accompanying this commitment was the solemn promise that British lives would be sacrificed only in the defence of British territory. The idea that '. . . every bad debt of mankind should be liquidated with a cheque signed by Britain',[25] was denounced as the principle which had governed past

British policy and which was responsible, therefore, for the unnecessary wars in which Britain had been involved.

The adoption of these principles was considered vital for the achievement of the avowed aims of BUF foreign policy: the preservation of world peace and of the British empire. If these two aims became contradictory then the latter was always to outweigh the former. Thus, Britain's role in the world was perceived as one of peaceful coexistence with other fascist powers, with international relations being conducted upon a national basis. Rearmed, and confident of her empire's security, Britain would be unwilling to become embroiled in the affairs of others, but would be willing to fight ferociously in the event of a threat to her interests. This, then, was the theoretical framework governing the party's response to international events throughout the decade.

Mosley's vision of a prosperous and insulated British empire contained echoes of the isolationism practised by the USA throughout the nineteenth century, and to which it had returned after 1918. In this respect it is interesting to note the BUF's attitude towards the USA, the most consistent aspect of which was a marked lack of hostility towards Franklin D. Roosevelt. The remnants of the affectionate personal relationship forged between Mosley and Roosevelt in 1926 undoubtedly contributed to this, as did the realisation that the New Deal was not unsimilar in its analysis or programme from the proposals made by Mosley in 1930. Consequently Roosevelt was portrayed sympathetically as 'a man of high ideals and of fine courage', striving to create a better and fairer society by adopting fascist economic measures, and yet doomed to fail '. . . because without a Fascist organisation and a Fascist administration, a Fascist Corporate State cannot be created'.[26] The absence of a fascist party had cast the impotent Roosevelt as a tragic figure who had '. . . undertaken the tasks of Hercules without acquiring the political strength of Hercules. He is a David defying ten Goliaths with no sling.'[27]

The BUF's adoption of anti-Semitism was reflected in the party's attitude towards the USA in the mid-1930s. The New Deal was considered to have failed because of Jewish opposition within important cities such as New York, within the judiciary, and within the presidential administration itself.[28] This accusation was declared proven when the Supreme Court ruled that Roosevelt's National Recovery Act (the linchpin of the New Deal legislation) was unconsitutional, after it had been challenged by a small Jewish firm from Brooklyn. Owing to its attempt to govern maximum hours and minimum wages the BUF believed the act to be 'fascist in principle', and the opportunity was not lost to reiterate Roosevelt's need for a fascist party which, had it existed, would have given him strength enough to have overridden the Supreme Court.[29] Once again emphasis was placed upon the futility of trying '. . .

to introduce mild doses of economic Fascism as curative injections into the dropsical body of the bourgeois-democratic state . . .'.[30] The dual moral to be drawn from the whole sorry exercise was that 'one cannot carry out even the pale shadow of Fascist corporate action without Fascists; just as one cannot carry out any kind of decent corporate action with the aid of Jews'.[31] In this sense, it was argued, the New Deal had rendered fascism an invaluable service.

Despite this claim, the BUF was never entirely happy with the New Deal, or clear as to how it should be portrayed. As late as 1938 it was still being conceded that amongst the democratic leaders only Roosevelt was taking action to combat the latest capitalist slump. In 1939, however, the party was still unsure as to what extent '. . . Roosevelt will permit his . . . administration to become a tool of Jewish world policy. He has an amazing number of Jews about him . . . attracted by the power vested in the New Deal bureaucracy which threatens to engulf American private enterprise in a State Capitalism as harsh as that of equally Jew-controlled Russia.'[32] This ambivalence towards the New Deal was produced by a mixture of admiration and fear. The admiration resulted from Roosevelt's ability to recognise that to which the British government was blind – that reflation of capitalist economies requires dynamic governmental action and a readiness to increase expenditure and to undertake ambitious schemes of public works. Mingled with this admiration, however, was the very real fear that if this type of Keynesian remedy could be applied successfully within a liberal—democracy, then the BUF's most powerful justification for fascism in Britain would have been removed at a stroke. It was a problem which the party failed to resolve satisfactorily, and it became yet another example of the inconsistencies within its programme.

From 1935 the BUF's foreign policy ceased to be merely a part of a theoretical programme, as events in Europe marked the increase of distrust and hostility between Britain and the fascist nations. Throughout this period the BUF conducted an almost continuous peace campaign, the intensity of which varied in accordance with the degree of crisis present in international relations at any given moment. When Italian troops invaded Abysinnia in the autumn of 1935 the British government appeared publicly to be prepared to take firm measures in support of the League of Nations, which condemned Italy's unprovoked aggression. Only in retrospect has it become clear that the government was torn between its duty to the League, and its wish to preserve Italian participation in the Stresa front against Germany, to such an extent that military intervention by Britain was never likely. At the time, the imposition of economic sanctions and a degree of sabre rattling with the British Mediterranean fleet gave the impression that war with Italy was a real possibility. The BUF reacted accordingly and demanded that, as there was no threat to the empire, Britain should remain aloof from the conflict. It was condemned as '. . . a grim reflection of the decadence of our legislators that they should be hysterically seeking to protect the negroid savage of Abyssinia . . .'.[33]

The racial overtones of the war were exploited to the utmost by the BUF in its attempt to justify Italy's aggression. It was simply an example of 'natural' racial imperialism, it was argued, for 'if an abundant and prolific European race were never to have overflowed into rich and fertile lands occupied by primitive tribes, the world would never have advanced, for better or for worse, into the modern age'.[34] In attempting to portray the war as simply another stage in Europe's development of the 'Dark Continent' it was necessary to ignore, or at least to undermine Abyssinia's status as a recognised independent nation state and member of the League of Nations. Once again the racial argument was much in evidence as Abyssinia was denounced as a primitive, slave-owning country consisting only of '. . . a black and barbarous conglomeration of tribes imbued with not one single Christian principle'.[35] As a tribute to this savagery of the Abyssinians, whose lesson in white civilisation from Italy was long overdue, ghoulish photographs were published in the fascist press purporting to show the victims of Abyssinian torture and dismemberment. Thus, even on occasions when it was conceded that Abyssinia was an independent nation, it was declared that such behaviour had placed it beyond the protection of the League. Besides, it was argued, Italy was not the first nation to have broken the League's Covenant, and yet other offenders including Japan, Poland, Lithuania, Paraguay and Bolivia had not been subjected to sanctions.[36] This last point was taken as proof of a vindictive campaign designed to victimise Italy because she was a fascist nation.

The party's response to the growing crisis was the institution of a nation-wide peace campaign based around the slogan 'Mind Britain's Business'. The campaign, which began at the end of August, aimed to expose to the public just how close to war Britain then stood, and to mobilise it in favour of peace, thereby pressurising the government into the realisation that war was not a practical possibility. Therefore, the campaign was organised in three phases; the first to arouse the public to the danger, the second to convince people that collective protest could influence government policy, and the third, which began in late September, aimed at producing '. . . concrete and tangible support for peace', in the form of a petition against war.[37] Each phase was accompanied by marches, public meetings, and the distribution of anti-war leaflets, which urged the British people not to shed precious blood in the assistance of '. . . barbaric despotism utterly alien to British character and tradition'.[38] The central message of the campaign was that either the sanctions would prove effective, in which case they would lead to war, or they would be ineffective, in which case they were mere hypocrisy. If the latter was true then Britain would be forced eventually to make an undignified retreat. If it was to be the former than Britain had to contemplate a major war, and yet successive post-war governments had cut defence expenditure to such an extent that a war was unthinkable. The Labour Party, it was observed caustically, had been the major perpetrator of this disarmament and yet was not in the vanguard of those clamouring for war.[39]

The overall impact of the 'Mind Britain's Business' campaign is impossible to assess. The central message, that Britain should not interfere in events which did not concern her, and even had it been morally right to have done so she was incapable of such an undertaking because of the cumulative effect of economies in defence expenditure, was certainly stated with remorseless repetition. This and many of the other arguments were often pertinent and clearly presented, not the least of which was Mosley's realisation that effective sanctions must entail a readiness to go to war to uphold them. Therefore, those who advocated all sanctions short of war were merely confusing the issue.[40] It was also true that Abyssinia was an extremely backward nation where the maldistribution of the little wealth that existed ensured that poverty remained endemic, and that Britain was in no position to undertake a war against Italy on her behalf. Nevertheless, the Italian aggression appeared so naked that the BUF tended to emerge from its own campaign cast not as a party of peace concerned with British interest, but as an unofficial ambassador of Mussolini, and an apologist for fascist violence. Attempts to diversify the campaign by including within it advocates of peace of other political persuasions failed to dispel the overall impression that the party was a tool in the hands of a foreign fascist power. It was to prove a recurring problem.

Throughout the campaign Mosley had suggested that Italy was being pressurised because of the large oil interests within Abyssinia. 'The greatest and most corrupt forces in the world, the international oil combines, were being challenged. Once again we could make the true and tragic statement of recent history – "Blood follows oil".'[41] There were also attempts to implicate international Jewry, although exactly in what capacity they were alleged to have been involved was never made entirely clear. In reality, however, the war highlighted the imperial instincts of fascism, and brought forth the death throes of the League of Nations. Britain's attitude illustrated the weakness of an international organisation whose primary powers had found that, in regard to a particular issue, their interests did not coincide with the interests of international law. The sanctions against Italy excluded oil specifically, and nor did Britain close the Suez Canal to Italian shipping. Although the notorious Hoare—Laval Pact, which proposed the surrender of most of Abyssinia's fertile territory to the invaders, was scrapped after a public outcry, the sanctions remained ineffective and failed to secure Abyssinian independence. After a protracted military campaign Addis Ababa fell to the Italians in May 1936, and in July the sanctions were quietly withdrawn, thus proving correct Mosley's contention that sanctions would lead either to war or to a humiliating retreat.

July 1936 also saw General Franco's army rebellion which marked the outbreak of the Spanish Civil War, which was destined to become a potent symbol of the general conflict between the forces of fascism and its opponents. As with Abyssinia the BUF's policy was consistent with its stated principles. Mosley summed up the party's attitude in a speech at Stockport, where he proclaimed his support for Franco, whom he considered was '. . . performing a good work for the whole of civilisation . . .', but also gave assurances that '. . . the whole of Spain is not worth one drop of British blood, and if we were in power we would not interfere in the quarrel in any shape or form'.[42] Neutrality was, of course, advantageous to Franco and the rebels, who were better equipped and trained than the Republican militia which opposed them.

The BUF had a high regard for the Spanish Falange whom it saw as its own equivalent, and as a true fascist party amongst the conglomeration of reactionaries and nationalists which constituted Franco's forces. But even after it had become apparent that the Falange had been swallowed up by its conservative allies and that a victory for the Nationalists would be victory for reaction rather than fascism, the BUF continued its support for Franco for he remained, if nothing else, an aggressive opponent of communism. It condemned the brave trickle of recruits from all over Europe who were prepared to make Spain their graveyard in the cause of anti-fascism. It was denied that there were regular Italian and German troops fighting for the Nationalists despite overwhelming evidence to the contrary.[43] The party's press denied reports of Nationalist atrocities even to the extent of claiming that Guernica had been destroyed not by German bombers but by the Republican government.[44]

Attempts were made to legitimise Franco's act of treason by claiming that the elected Republican Government had forfeited its right to govern because of its record of corruption and brutality. It was the same argument which had been used in reference to Abyssinia, as in both cases those in power were portrayed as barbarians, whilst those seeking to overthrow them were seen as upright patriots. Whereas in Abyssinia torture and slavery were cited as evidence of the regime's ineligibility for continued government, in Spain the Republicans were accused of crimes against the people and, in particular, against the church. Vatican figures were quoted suggesting that eleven bishops and 15,000 priests had been murdered by the Republicans,[45] and these were supported by the BUF with frequent and lurid accounts of the destruction of churches, the murder of priests and the rape of nuns, as international communism practised its declared intention to eradicate religion.[46]

The BUF linked its support of Franco with its repeated assurances that fascism cherished Christianity whereas communism was committed to its destruction. As a result the party received some ecclesiastical support. Those clergy suspected of harbouring Republican sympathies were attacked fiercely,[47] whereas those who were prepared to speak out against the 'Red terror' were commended, and the columns of the fascist press laid open for their use. Those who availed themselves of this channel tended to emphasise the complementary nature of the relationship between fascism and religion, compared to the inherent atheism of communist ideology. Fascist principles such as duty, loyalty and obedience were praised highly, whilst concepts such as pascifism were denounced as heretical.[48] These contributors were essentially reactionaries rather than fascists. Their opposition to democracy and egalitarianism was uncompromising, and they despised the toleration of liberalism, which was blamed for undermining both church and state. The atomising effect of liberalism was alleged also to have consigned the demoralised and impoverished masses to a life of spiritual and material squalor. Thus the innate unity of Christian society had been fragmented by obsessive individualism. This, however, was the closest that such contributors ever came to a clear appreciation of the corporate nature of fascism. More usually a fascist victory was looked to for the restoration of religious unity and the return of the primacy of the Catholic church based not upon the '. . . Social Democratic fallacy of Toleration', but upon the hierarchial and authoritarian principle of '. . . leadership from above . . . .'[49]

The other main attraction of fascism was its commitment to the utter destruction of communism in Britain. J. K. Heydon, a Catholic writer with no known connection to the BUF, captured this general attitude in his assertion that 'Bolshevism is the work of Satan unfurling his standard openly', whereas 'Fascism is as yet pure Patriotism, and patriotism is entirely good . . . it cannot but be God's will.'[50] Despite a degree of lip-service to fascism's planned reorganisation of industry and society through the corporate state, the central thread of Heydon's argument involved the conception of fascism

> . . . as providential in order that we may defend England against the direct assault of Satan through Communism . . . we see it as providential also that we may throw off the yoke of domination by International Finance before it is too late . . . we see it as providential also in order that England may be led back to the Corporate Church and be Merry England again.[51]

The repeated use of the term 'providential' provides the essential key to understanding this attitude amongst clerics, for they tended to see fascism as a gift of providence, which would uphold the church and reimpose those reactionary and authoritarian values which had been destroyed by liberalism and communism.

Catholics in particular tended to be drawn towards fascism for such reasons. Catholicism presented the most authoritarian, hierarchical, ritualistic, and ultimately the most corporate amongst the main branches of the Christian church. The Catholic church was more unequivocal than other brands of Christianity in its opposition to communism, its belief in the bourgeois values of family and private property, and in the anti-Semitism expounded by some of the elements within it. It is not surprising, therefore, that the ratio of Roman Catholics within the BUF was greater than that which existed within Britain's population as a whole.[52]

By championing the cause of Franco the BUF increased its prestige amongst the Catholic community and accentuated this recruiting trend. At times the party was embarrassed by the inability of the Nationalists to secure victory, and by the heroism of the Republican defence. By 1939, however, the end was in sight and the BUF was urging the diplomatic recognition of Franco's regime by Britain, in order to safeguard future relations with the new Spain.[53] By this stage, however, the war in Spain had been overshadowed by more dramatic international events which were to prove fatal for the BUF.

Before looking at the BUF's attitude to the crises which shook Europe in the final years of peace, mention should be made of the party's analysis of events in the Far East. The second phase of Japan's military expansion in China began in 1937 after a four-year lull, with the fall of Peking and a rapid drive south by the superior Japanese forces. Japan's conquests presented the BUF with something of a dilemma. Japan had moved increasingly into alignment with the fascist powers of Europe since her departure from the League of Nations in 1933; a move which heightened the common misapprehension that her regimented society and militaristic government constituted a form of fascism. Also, it was recognised by the BUF that Japan was one of the world's young and virile nations, with sufficient energy and industry to justify her desire for colonies. Japanese expansion could thus be justified with arguments identical to those used in defending the Italians in Abyssinia. Such factors should have been sufficient to have secured for Japan a degree of sympathy for her position similar to that shown to the Spanish Nationalists, if not to Germany and Italy. That sympathy of a comparable degree was not forthcoming was indicative of the two factors which differentiated Japan from the other foreign recipients of BUF support. Firstly, Japan was a non-white power. Although the BUF had never exerted itself in attempting to differentiate between the divisions alleged to exist within the Caucasian racial category, there was never any doubt that the white man was superior to all other races. The Japanese expansion in eastern Asia represented the first instance of a non-white capitalist power with the capacity to capture and develop colonies; in so doing it heralded the end of white supremacy in the region. For advocates of the British empire (which possessed more colonies in the area than did any other imperial power), this glimpse of the future was the cause of grave concern. Secondly, in addition to being an imperial competitor and the harbinger of doom in regard to white supremacy, Japan was also an economic competitor of Britain. It was the penetration of the Indian market by Japanese textiles that was held to be responsible for mass unemployment in the Lancashire cotton industry, and the BUF had long been committed to the protection of the future autarchic empire of fascist Britain from those goods produced in the 'sweat-shops' of Asia at prices against which the employers of white labour could not compete.

In view of these circumstances the BUF's policy in relation to Japanese expansion was essentially one of compromise. In return for Japanese co-operation in excluding those of their goods from India which competed with empire produce, the Japanese were to be given the freedom to colonise and exploit northern China. In the remainder of China, it was decided, there should exist equal trading rights, and any attempt by the Japanese to extend their influence south of the Yangtse river should be met with a collective European rebuff. Thus Japan would have territory into which she could expand, and yet would be tamed and kept in check by the white colonial powers. British strategic interests in the area would receive additional protection by the building of Singapore into a '. . . mighty Eastern fortress'.[54]

By the end of 1937 Japanese forces had already crossed the Yangtse and had captured Nanking. This relentless Japanese advance destroyed much of the credibility of the BUF's proposals for a compromise in China, and left Britain in a position described by Mosley as that of '. . . an impotent and humiliated spectator'.[55] This humiliation increased dramatically during the Tientsin crisis in the summer of 1939. The refusal of the British authorities to deliver into Japansse custody a number of Chinese nationals wanted on suspicion of murder led to a Japanese blockage of the British concession at Tientsin in which the suspects had taken refuge. The result was the humiliating spectacle of British men and women being bodily searched in public upon entering or leaving the concession. The BUF was furious that Britons could have been thus '. . . publicly degraded by the armed forces of a yellow race'.[56] That the British citizen could have sunk so low in the esteem of native Asians was attributed to the foreign policy blunders of the National Government and its predecessors. That respect for the white race in general could have declined to such a level as to allow a humiliation of this nature was considered to be the direct result of European disharmony.

For the BUF could never forget that the Japanese were a non-white race, and as such could only achieve parity with their racial superiors as a result of the weakness of the white colonial powers. The belief that Oriental expansion should be resisted through a collective European response illustrated the degree of racism within the party. The sympathy felt for the Japanese need to expand, and the increasing diplomatic friendship which existed between Japan and the European fascist powers, were overridden ultimately by this deep-rooted racial prejudice. Readers of the fascist press were reminded that western Europe was simply a piece of land jutting forth from the land mass of Asia. Unless the European powers could resist a fratricidal war, it was predicted, then 'our fate may be that of Athens and Sparta, Thebes and Corinth, city-states in the Greek peninsula swept away in the gigantic struggles of Macedon and Rome. These Japanese victories may be the last warning we shall receive. . . .'[57]

This idea of the essentiality of European peace was stressed with increasing vehemence as Anglo-German relations worsened throughout the second half of the decade. The influence of Italian fascism upon the party declined as Berlin superseded Rome as the source of inspiration for incipient fascist movements. Increasingly the BUF used the term 'national socialism' rather than 'fascism', and its new full uniforms, which replaced the simple black shirt, were similar to those worn by the Nazi SS. In 1936 the party's name was altered to the British Union of Fascists and National Socialists and its symbol since 1932, the *fasces* derived from imperial Rome, gave way to a flash of lightning within a circle, once again reminiscent of the SS.[58] This shift of influence marked not only the eclipse of Italy by Germany, but also the acceptance of a common northern European cultural link. The Nazis also had the additional attraction of having achieved power through the ballot box and, as already suggested, by the mid-1930s the BUF was concentrating upon preparations which would enable them to emulate this electoral success.

Given this growth in the affinity between the BUF and the Nazi Party, it is not surprising that the BUF agreed with, and encouraged, British appeasement of German territorial demands. There were three main reasons for the adoption of this approach. Firstly, there was a high degree of sympathy for the situation in which Germany found herself. Obviously this was not unconnected with Germany's position as the world's leading fascist nation, but it would be wrong to see the BUF's policy in this respect purely as the result of a slavish devotion to Berlin. Many of the German grievances were legitimate, especially those arising from the numerous unjust and short-sighted aspects of the Versailles

Treaty. Shorn of her colonies, burdened with reparations and guilt for a war she had not solely begun, and separated from millions of German-speaking people, Germany had been humiliated by her conquerors. The Versailles Treaty, a monument to those gorged upon military success and bent upon vengeance, had primed Europe with explosive charges. One need not sympathise with fascism in order to understand that Hitler's demands provided only the sparks needed to ignite these charges. The demands themselves were a response to a situation which was not of his making.

Secondly, the BUF possessed a genuine commitment to avoid British involvement in a European war. It contained a high proportion of ex-servicemen, many of whom had been in action in the Great War. For those who had come of age amid the squalor of Flanders, and had seen their comrades fall, the experience had proved unforgettable. Henry Williamson remained haunted throughout his life by the Somme, Ypres, and Passchendaele and saw 'everywhere those desolate places . . . the figures of enslaved men, the marching columns pearl-hued with chalky dust on the sweat of their heavy drab clothes; the files of carrying parties laden and staggering in the flickering moonlight of gunfire; the waves of assaulting troops lying silent and pale . . .'.[59] The lives of the survivors had been marked indelibly, for only they could know of the true horrors of modern warfare.

Thirdly, BUF members were painfully aware that a war between Britain and the fascist powers would prove fatal to their party. This had been stated openly as early as 1935,[60] and within a year there were fears that their opponents might provoke the fascist powers deliberately in order to '. . . precipitate a crisis before Fascism comes to power in Britain'.[61] By 1937 there was anxiety that the progress of the next slump could be averted by war: 'although there can be no question that war on a big scale would end depression overnight, we appeal to the sanity of the British people to choose the lesser of two evils. Surely a slump, however bad, is better than another war.'[62] By the summer of 1938 war with the fascist nations had moved even closer, and the BUF's appeals had become more desperate:

> . . . it is in the interests of International Finance to incite a further World War, as a last desperate alternative to World Depression. Undoubtedly such a war would immediately check the fall in commodity prices, equating consumption to production by sheer destruction. Undoubtedly such a war would find immediate use for the unwanted unemployed. Undoubtedly such a war would restore profits to industry. But at what costs? The probable collapse of Western Civilisation and the triumph of barbaric Communism! . . . If only war can be avoided for the next two years, the collapse of finance Capitalism and the triumph of Fascism in Britain are assured.[63]

Beneath this fear of the use of war as a means of ending the depression lay a greater fear which was not expressed. For the likely position of a British fascist patriot whose nation was at war with the European fascist powers was the stuff of which nightmares were made.

It was a combination of these factors which influenced the BUF firmly in favour of appeasement. The first instance of German expansion occurred in March 1936 when units of the German army entered the Rhineland in defiance of its status under the Versailles Treaty as a demilitarised zone. The failure of Britain and France to act decisively in response to this flagrant violation of the Treaty has usually been considered as the first example of the implementation of appeasement.[64] This verdict is somewhat harsh, for although it was a bluff on Hitler's part (his army was only a fraction of the size of that of France), it would have been unrealistic for the democracies to have gone to war merely because Hitler had marched into his own 'back yard'. The BUF's main source of embarrassment originated not from being in opposition to a general British desire for war, but from its own over-zealous defence of German intentions, for in January 1936 it had dismissed the rumour of a German reoccupation as an unfounded lie.[65] Undaunted by this its response to the events in March was a full and enthusiastic endorsement of Hitler's action by claiming that '... the resumption of full German sovereignty throughout Germany should ... be accepted by the British people as the best thing that has occurred in European affairs since the war'.[66]

In the spring of 1938, after considerable German pressure, the independent state of Austria was incorporated into the Third Reich despite the specific prohibition of such a union under the terms of the Versailles Treaty. Once again there was talk of war with Germany, and once again the BUF attempted to neutralise it by justifying the German action. The Austrian people welcomed this *Anschluss,* it was argued, and besides, should Britain consider going to war merely because 'two lots of Germans got together?'[67] By May the Austrian crisis was forgotten and the BUF was preparing the public for the next of Hitler's demands, the incorporation into Germany of the Sudetenland. There were claims that the 3,000,000 Sudeten Germans were subjected to vicious maltreatment by the Czech state, which was itself in the grip of Jewish moneylenders.[68] The hour for the correction of the myopic Czechoslovakian borders, established at the Versailles Conference, was long overdue, it was concluded, and, therefore, this large German minority trapped within an alien state should be allowed to return home. When the crisis broke in the autumn of 1938, war with Germany seemed alarmingly close. The matter was resolved at the Munich conference, where representatives from Britain, France, Germany and Italy decided upon Czechoslovakia's fate. Munich represented the height of the appeasement process as the Sudetenland, and ultimately the entire

Czech nation, were sacrificed to Hitler for the preservation of European peace. This result delighted the BUF and Chamberlain's major role in the betrayal of Czechoslovakia rendered him the object of rare BUF acclaim. 'His courage in flying to Germany and meeting Hitler face to face, his statesmanship in securing the friendship of Mussolini and using his good services at the critical moment, deserve our highest praise.'[69]

The crises of 1938 brought forth great efforts by the BUF to preserve peace. Earlier it had portrayed itself as the nation's only peace party on the grounds that its economic programme could reflate the economy without resorting to war, and its foreign policy was designed to avoid the possibility of becoming embroiled in foreign wars. 'Between the British people and the impending slaughter stands one movement and one movement alone. Indeed, the fate of the world hinges upon whether or not Mosley's advance proves rapid enough to deal with the most menacing situation ever to confront mankind.'[70] The Austrian crisis proved that the situation confronting mankind had the capacity to become even more menacing, and the BUF responded accordingly. In March 1938 the party conducted a peace campaign with numerous meetings in east London, and the invasion of the West End by hundreds of newspaper-sellers protesting against war with Germany. There were similar local drives in other regions culminating in the 'Britain First' campaign launched by Mosley at the end of June. Centred upon London, it included four large marches and nineteen meetings.[71] At its conclusion in late July, it was estimated that over 250,000 people had heard Mosley's message of peace.[72] BUF peace campaigns continued sporadically into the autumn with the national resources and speakers being concentrated upon a particular region for a short period, such as in Lancashire at the end of September where 150 meetings were held, culminating with a passionate speech by Mosley in the Free Trade Hall, Manchester.[73] The Czech crisis imbued these peace efforts with a new urgency, and prompted an ambitious BUF programme for the distribution of a vast quantity of free literature opposing war. The argument was stated clearly: 'Whether Czechoslovakia disappears or remains as an artificial state matters not one jot to the people of Britain. It can make no difference to British trade or the prosperity or the poverty of the people of Britain.'[74] Therefore, according to the tenets of BUF foreign policy, it was demanded that Britain remain uninvolved.

As with the 'Mind Britain's Business' campaign three years earlier, the BUF claimed that its almost continuous agitation against war throughout the year had mobilised the public, and had influenced the government, thus playing a crucial role in the preservation of peace. Chamberlain, it was argued, had been able to act with such courage at Munich only because of this.[75] Although it was acknowledged that the danger of war had not been removed by the Munich agreement, the BUF was optimistic for if war could be avoided in 1939, it was predicted, it would have the opportunity to contest its first general election. In his New Year's message to the party Mosley emphasised this point prophesying that 'this will be the year of decision. . . . In this year should be decided whether the desperate effort of the dark enemy to secure a world war will succeed, or whether that crime will be finally shattered on the rock of our resolution.'[76]

Early in 1939 Mosley revealed the details of a plan through which permanent peace with Germany could be established. It was based upon the underlying assumption that the interests of Britain and Germany were so diverse that there was no reason for them to conflict. The fact that both nations were in opposing armed camps, and yet were not competitors, only illustrated the confused blunders which had characterised past British foreign policy. Hitler, he argued, was concerned only with the unification of the German-speaking people of central Europe and bore no animosity towards the British empire. Indeed, he had assured Mosley personally that he considered it essential to the world, and perceived the German Reich and the British empire as the '. . . two great pillars of world peace and order'.[77] If there was no rational basis for Anglo-German competition, reasoned Mosley, conflict could only arise if Britain attempted to prevent German development; but provided that this development was not contrary to the interests of the British empire why should Britain interfere with it? Britain need not fear a developing Germany, he argued, because rearmed within the boundaries of her mighty empire Britain would be able to 'look Germany or any other nation in the eye and say we are not afraid because we are the greatest people on earth'.[78] This argument had a considerable degree of validity as the territorial ambitions of Hitler certainly lay principally to the East.[79] He considered war with the Western democracies as an inconvenience rather than an integral part of a long-term plan, and, therefore, war in the West could certainly have been postponed, and very probably avoided, had Britain and France been prepared to make further concessions in regard to Germany's eastern expansion. This was precisely what the Mosley peace plan entailed. Britain, he argued, should be prepared to fight Germany to the death in defence of her empire, but should not waste the precious lives of her subjects upon issues such as the geographical location of Germany's eastern border. Therefore Germany should be given a free hand in eastern Europe, and should have her ex-colonies restored in return for which she, and Europe's other three major powers, should commit themselves to multilateral arms reductions and peace based upon mutual respect and tolerance.[80] Britain had no vital interests in eastern Europe, it was claimed, nor did she need the mandated German colonies, which were merely an expensive irrelevance. Thus, by forsaking nothing of value, Britain could secure a just, and, therefore, more durable peace with Germany which would allow both nations to concentrate their efforts upon improving the living standards of their citizens at home and within their separate spheres of interest. 'Let Germany be strong in Eastern Europe, and Britain be strong in her world wide Empire, that together they may preserve the life of the white man from the destruction of the Orient, which the decadence of Financial Democracy invites within our gates',[81] urged Mosley, for, '. . . against this alliance of the two great Nordic peoples, no possible combination of powers could stand. There would be the guarantee of world peace. No need of conflict would arise . . . and between them they would dominate the world for peace.'[82]

In effect Mosley was proposing a form of British empire isolationism, (although he did also propose treaties with France and the USA just in case Hitler proved untrustworthy). Exactly how tenable such a position would have proved in a century when the world was shrinking and formal empires were decaying faster than at any time in history, is a matter for speculation. There is, however, every reason to suppose that German aggression towards Britain would have been avoided had such a course been followed. Mosley's peace plan, like so much of his thought, remains an intriguing paper hypothesis offering the tantalising glimpse of an alternative history for the nation he loved.

The year of decision, 1939, began ominously for the BUF, as in March the remainder of the Czechoslovakian state fell to pieces and was devoured by Germany and Hungary. The BUF claimed, with some justification, that Hitler was not responsible directly for the collapse, but this was not the general impression, as Germany was seen to profit territorially once again at the expense of her neighbour. The Munich pledge to uphold the new Czech borders, to which Germany was a signatory, had been exposed as worthless. Appeasement was over, and by the end of March Chamberlain had bound Britain to an alliance with Poland. From the spring onwards the BUF conducted a series of peace drives, mostly centred upon London, at which the pledge to defend Poland was denounced vehemently. Poland was portrayed in the fascist press as a nation containing 3,500,000 Jews, massive investment by international finance, and thousands of Germans trapped in the Polish corridor and Danzig who were the victims of fearful oppression by archaic Polish landlords.[83] 'Such is the sink of inequality called Poland to which a million British lives have been pledged. . . .' Where, demanded Mosley, were the British interests to justify such a pledge, which through '. . . any frontier incident which excites the light-headed Poles can set the world ablaze. The British Government places the lives of a million Britons in the pocket of any drunken Polish colonel.'[84]

The Polish pact was also attacked on a more logistical level. Even had it been morally sound, it was argued, it was impossible to honour it without sustaining unacceptable casualties.

> As neither British nor French troops can possibly reach Warsaw, the only means by which the Western Powers can aid Poland is by threatening to attack Germany in the West. . . . Unable to check the Eastern expansion of Germany except by an intolerable alliance with the Soviet, Chamberlain threatens to blow British and Western Civilisation sky high by a frontal attack upon the greatest military power on the Continent. This is a policy of despair, a policy of madness, a suicide pact for untold millions.'[85]

The pledge to Poland was at the centre of the party's peace efforts throughout the spring and summer of 1939, and it was these cogent arguments which Mosley put to the vast Earls Court audience in July in support of his peace plan. His two-hour speech was well received and the audience hissed and booed at references to Churchill and Baldwin, and enthused at the speaker's rejection of a 'Jewish War'.[86] Leaflets were issued urging the British people to rally around the principle that 'Britons fight for Britain only', and to reverse the country's drift into war by demanding a referendum upon the government's foreign policy. In the final weeks of peace orders were issued to intensify the campaign and there were appeals for donations to finance the increased distribution of free anti-war propaganda.[87] In his speeches Mosley attacked the government repeatedly for acting without the support of the people, and decried '. . . the shame of a British Government trotting like a tame dog at the heels of Poland, ready at the Polish command to attack anyone who threatened the interests of the financiers who rule their country'.[88]

When the Nazi-Soviet non-aggression pact became public in late August, Mosley claimed that it had rendered British intervention on behalf of Poland out of the question and concluded that the Polish pledge must be scrapped immediately, for Britain was once again in a position '. . . from which it can only withdraw with the usual humiliation'.[89] How wrong he was on this occasion. Mosley continued to lead demonstrations and make speeches urging people to 'get out on the streets and stop the war',[90] and even after the German invasion of Poland the last peacetime edition of *Action* demanded that Britain should not go to war to perpetuate and defend '. . . the inhuman living conditions of the peasants of Poland, who are sweated by alien finance to pile up the profits of usury and to undercut and destroy the western standard of life'.[91] It was all to no avail. The party's nightmare became a reality as Britain's ultimatum for the withdrawal of German forces from Poland expired, and she declared herself to be at war with the world's foremost fascist nation.

Despite an obvious bias towards Europe's fascist powers, the BUF's foreign policy was based primarily upon British patriotism. It was different from the jingoistic patriotism associated traditionally with the Conservative Party, and advocated by those such as Churchill, but it was patriotism nevertheless. Mosley's concern was that by 1939 British foreign policy had soured relationships, not merely with Germany, but with the Mediterranean powers of Italy and Spain, the Arabs in Palestine, and the Japanese in the Far East. None of these quarrels, in Mosley's opinion, had been provoked by the defence of true British interests, and yet through each of these areas ran Britain's imperial backbone, which could be severed by any of those whose enmity she had incited so unnecessarily. Thus, by 1939, Britain was stumbling ill-prepared into a war which would imperil her empire, and yet was doing so not in self-defence but in order to defend an obscure and worthless eastern European nation. It was a cogent argument. The problem for the BUF was that, since 1935, its campaign for peace and its ready understanding and advocacy of the grievances of the fascist powers had associated it too closely with those nations with whom British relations were deteriorating. When this deterioration was replaced by the official declaration of war the party's predicament worsened considerably.

The BUF refused to accept that the situation was irreparable, however, and continued its peace campaign into the autumn of 1939. There was little activity between the belligerents on the western front, and whilst the 'phoney war' atmosphere prevailed it was felt that a restoration of peace was still possible. Throughout the next two months Mosley spoke at peace meetings in London and the provinces. He re-emphasised the arguments with which he had attempted to prevent the war, stressing always that there was no clash of essential interests between Britain and Germany. Two newer lines of interpretation were also used. Firstly, in regard to Poland, it was claimed that Britain was under no obligation to honour its pledge, because the foreign policy of the government which had given it had never been endorsed by a popular vote.[92] Furthermore, Mosley was quick to point out that by the end of September the war in Poland was over, and it would be impossible for Britain to re-establish the Polish state because half of it had been annexed by the USSR. As the reason for embarking upon the war had ceased to exist it was urged that Britain should accept Hitler's offer of an armistice followed by a peace conference.[93]

Secondly, it was stated that war could not be won by Britain. The capacity of defensive warfare had increased rapidly since 1918, argued Mosley, with the result that any attack upon a modern fortified nation would lead to '. . . such crushing losses . . . that he who launches the attack is liable quickly to lose the war'.[94] By overlooking the mobility which the tank and the aircraft had restored to warfare, Mosley had mistaken the 'phoney war' for a period of deadlock similar to that which had characterised the Great War. Influenced undoubtedly by his own experience of the western front, he predicted a war of stalemate with time on Germany's side because she had to import less food and raw materials than did Britain.[95] Although he was mistaken in this, his eventual conclusions proved correct in that he envisaged Britain emerging defeated from the war. Either she would be conquered militarily and her empire destroyed, or, if she was to triumph over Germany, this could only be achieved with the assistance of the USA and the USSR. In either case Britain would no longer be a primary power in the post-war world.[96]

In addition to these arguments Mosley reiterated his four-point plan tirelessly, and urged that Britain accept an honourable peace whilst her territory and empire remained intact. There was no need to fear German aggression in the future, he argued, because the British empire with its vast population had almost unlimited strength. This potential would be realised by the party's plans to expand Britain's defence forces and revitalise the economic integrity of her empire. From such a position of secure isolationism, it was argued, British subjects could enjoy their new prosperity without fear of any aggressor.

> What a folly and what a crime for the great nations of the West to waste their energies in the mutual destruction of European civilisation, in order that the enfeebled body of Western man may fall easy prey to some of the most malignant parasites that history has witnessed. . . . We say Peace – new worlds are born of Life not Death.[97]

As with so many of Mosley's arguments, his proposals for peace were rational, coherently presented, and, to varying degrees, valid. In particular he grasped correctly the way in which war would alter the world, and Britain's place within it, irrevocably, even though the reasoning which produced this insight was in part incorrect. A nation at war is rarely an environment suitable for rational analysis and Mosley's appeals for peace on occasions provoked a violent response from his fellow countrymen. In November 1939 he was struck by missiles from an audience in Wilmslow,[98] and in May 1940 he was forced to abandon a speech in support of the BUF's candidate in the Middleton by-election. The audience booed, chanted, and threw missiles, and was only prevented from rushing the platform by a strong cordon of police. He abandoned the meeting only after the deliberate severance of the wires of his loud-speakers had rendered him inaudible. The crowd celebrated by ripping apart the platform and destroying the loudspeakers with hammers.[99] The years of patriotism with a pro-German flavour had yielded a bitter harvest. It was a sad public exit from one of Britain's last great political orators, but the final irony was yet to come. Four days later Mosley and his chief lieutenants, the fascists patriots of the British empire, were imprisoned without trial because their connections with Nazism, and their opposition to the war, were considered sufficient to threaten the security of the liberal-democratic state.

NOTES

1 *Blackshirt,* 2 September 1933, p. 1.
2 A. Raven Thomson, *The Economics of British Fascism,* Bonner, London 1933, p. 8.
3 W. Joyce, *Fascism and India,* BUF Publications, London 1935?, p. 2.
4 Joyce, 'Britain's empire shall live', *FQ,* I, 1, January 1935, p. 97.
5 *Blackshirt,* 16 June 1933, p. 4.
6 *Ibid.,* 24 May 1935, pp. 1–2.
7 O. Mosley, *The Greater Britain,* BUF, London 1932, p. 138.
8 *Blackshirt,* 16 June 1933, p. 4.
9 'Notes on the quarter', *FQ,* I, 1, January 1935, p. 5.
10 *Action,* 26 August 1939, p. 1.
11 *Ibid.,* 2 September 1939, p. 5.
12 Although struck by the differing styles of the two dictators, Mosley was impressed by each. Mosley, interview with author, 24 June 1980. When Mosley remarried in October 1936 the secret ceremony was conducted in Berlin and Hitler was amongst the guests. See Mosley, *My Life,* Nelson, London 1968, pp. 362–3.
13 *Blackshirt,* 14 February 1936, p. 5.
14 Rather than fearing the rise of Italian power in the Mediterranean, it was argued that Britain should welcome such a development, for a strong and friendly Italy would be invaluable in protecting Britain's channels of imperial communication. R. Gordon-Canning, *Mind Britain's Business,* Greater Britain Publications, London n.d., pp. 12–16.
15 *Blackshirt,* 1 May 1933, p. 1.
16 *Ibid.,* 1 June 1933, p. 4.
17 *Manchester Guardian,* 16 March 1933, p. 10. See also *Blackshirt,* 1 April 1933, p. 1.
18 *Blackshirt,* 20 September 1935, p. 4.
19 Mosley, *Tomorrow We Live,* Greater Britain Publications, London 1939, p. 69. See also *My Life,* pp. 383–4; *Action,* 29 January 1938, p. 7.
20 *Blackshirt,* 7 June 1935, p. 2.
21 O. Mosley, *Blackshirt Policy,* BUF Publications Ltd, London 1934, p. 59.
22 Mosley, *The Greater Britain,* p. 143; *Blackshirt Policy,* p. 59.
23 Gordon-Canning, *op. cit.,* pp. 6–7.
24 J. Drennan (pseud). 'Why not *Der Drang Nach Osten?' BUQ,* I, 4, October–December 1938, pp. 16–27.
25 Mosley, *The Greater Britain,* p. 144. See also Gordon-Canning, *op. cit.,* pp. 17–18.
26 *Blackshirt,* 15 March 1935, p. 1.
27 *Fascist Week,* 10–16 November 1933, p. 2.
28 *Blackshirt,* 1 February 1935, pp. 2, 10.
29 *Ibid.,* 7 June 1935, p. 5.
30 'Notes on the quarter', *FQ,* I, 3, July 1935, p. 295.
31 *Blackshirt,* 17 January 1936, p. 3.
32 *Action,* 11 February 1939, p. 5. See also 'Notes on the quarter', *BUQ,* I, 3, July–September 1938, pp. 10–11.
33 *Blackshirt,* 19 July 1935, p. 2.
34 'Notes on the quarter', *FQ,* I, 4, October 1935, p. 403.
35 *Blackshirt,* 30 August 1935, p. 6.
36 *Manchester Guardian,* 2 September 1935, p. 11.
37 *Blackshirt,* 20 September 1935, p. 1.
38 *Why Should Britain Assist Abyssinia,* BUF peace leaflet, 1935, LPL.
39 The leaders of the Labour Party were also accused of pacifism during the Great War when Britain was in peril, and yet were now demanding that

others be sent overseas to die in an alien quarrel. *Blackshirt,* 13 September 1935, p. 1.

40 This erroneous differentiation between non-military and military sanctions was frequently expressed and was included in the peace ballot of 1935. Of the 11,559, 165 people who replied to the questions posed by the ballot, the vast majority were in favour of the application of economic sanctions, but of these over three million rejected any form of military action. K. Middlemas & J. Barnes, *Baldwin,* Weidenfeld & Nicolson, London 1969, p. 835.

41 *Blackshirt,* 6 September 1935, p. 2.

42 *Manchester Guardian,* 20 April 1937, p. 11.

43 'Notes on the quarter', *BUQ,* I, 4, September–December 1937, p. 4. It has been estimated that a total of 170,000 foreign troops served with the Nationalists, most of them Italians, Germans, and Moroccans. By contrast only 40,000 fought for the Republicans, 35,000 of whom served with the International Brigades. H. Thomas, *The Spanish Civil War,* 3rd edn, Penguin Books, Harmondsworth 1977, pp. 974–85.

44 *Blackshirt,* 1 May 1937, p. 3. For an eye-witness account of the destruction see letter by R. C. Stevenson to British ambassador, Sir H. Chilton, 28 April 1937, as quoted by Thomas, *op. cit.,* pp. 986–8.

45 These figures, it was claimed, amounted to almost a half of Spain's Catholic clergy: *Action,* 13 February 1937, p. 3.

46 *Blackshirt,* 15 August 1936, p. 1. Thomas estimated that the total number of murders and executions perpetrated by the Nationalists was around 75,000, as opposed to 55,000 by the Republicans. Amongst the Republican victims were 6,832 clergy. Thomas, *op. cit.,* pp. 265, 270.

47 *Action,* 25 June 1938, p. 11. See also *Blackshirt,* 1 August 1936, p. 3; *Action,* 11 June 1936, p. 10, and 16 July 1938, p. 18.

48 *Action,* 9 July 1936, p. 7. See also 21 May 1939, p. 5; and 18 January 1940, p. 7.

49 Reverend N. E. B. Nye, 'The Religious Peace of Europe', as found in E. Turcotti (ed.), *Fascist Europe ... : an Anglo-Italian Symposium ...* published under the auspices of the National Institute of Fascist Culture of Pavia, Vol. I, 2nd edn, National Institute of Fascist Culture, Milan 1939, p. 56.

50 J. K. Heydon, *Fascism and Providence,* Sheed & Ward, London 1937, pp. 66, 129.

51 *Ibid.,* p. 136. See also Nye, *op. cit.,* p. 79.

52 For details see S. Rawnsley, 'The membership of the British Union of Fascists', as cited in K. Lunn & R. C. Thurlow (eds.), *British Fascism,* Croom Helm, London 1980, pp. 161–2.

53 *Action,* 11 February 1939, p. 4. See also 4 March, editorial.

54 Gordon-Canning, *op. cit.,* p. 15. See also Mosley, *Tomorrow We Live,* pp. 70–1, and *Action,* 5 February 1938, p. 1.

55 Mosley, *Tomorrow We Live,* p. 70.

56 *Action,* 24 June 1939, p. 1.

57 *Ibid.,* 29 October 1938, editorial.

58 The new symbol represented the flash of action within the circle of unity.

59 H. Wilkinson, *My Life's Purpose,* R. T. Cotton, Exeter 1939, p. 2.

60 Joyce, 'Collective security', *FQ,* I, 4, October 1935, p. 422.

61 'Notes on the quarter', *FQ,* II, 3, July 1936, p. 340.

62 *Action,* 16 December 1937, p. 8.

63 *Ibid.,* 11 June 1938, p. 8.

64 The reoccupation of the Rhineland has become something of a symbol, but it can be argued with equal plausibility that appeasement began with the Anglo-German naval agreement of June 1935, or even with the ineffectual response towards the Japanese invasion of Manchuria in 1931.

65 *Blackshirt,* 17 January 1936, p. 1.
66 *Ibid.,* 13 March 1936, p. 1.
67 *Action,* 19 March 1938, pp. 1, 11.
68 *Ibid.,* 28 May 1938, p. 7.
69 'Notes on the quarter', *BUQ,* II, 4, October–December 1938, p. 4.
70 'Notes on the quarter', *BUQ,* I, 3, July-September 1937, p. 13.
71 *Blackshirt,* July 1938, p. 1.
72 *Action,* 30 July 1938, p. 1.
73 *Ibid.,* 1 October 1938, p. 13. See also *Manchester Guardian,* 3 October 1938, p. 11.
74 *Action,* 3 September 1938, editorial.
75 *Ibid.,* 24 September 1938, p. 10.
76 *Ibid.,* 31 December 1938, p. 1.
77 Mosley, interview with author, 24 June 1980.
78 *The Times,* 24 March 1939, p. 8.
79 This point was made and illustrated with quotations from Hitler's *Mein Kampf* by A. Bullock in *Hitler, A Study in Tyranny,* Oldhams Books, London 1964, pp. 316–19, 337.
80 *Action,* 25 March 1939, p. 1; *Manchester Guardian,* 16 March 1939, p. 13.
81 *Action,* 25 March 1939, p. 1.
82 'Notes on the quarter', *BUQ,* III, 2, April–June 1939, p. 14.
83 *Action,* 8 April 1939, p. 1.
84 *Ibid.*
85 'Notes on the quarter', *BUQ,* III, 2, April–June 1939, p. 8.
86 *Manchester Guardian,* 17 July 1939, p. 12. See also *The Times,* 17 July 1939, p. 14.
87 *Action,* 26 August 1939, p. 20. See also 2 September, p. 1.
88 *Manchester Guardian,* 28 August 1939, p. 16.
89 *Action,* 26 August 1939, p. 1.
90 *Ibid.,* 2 September 1939, p. 1.
91 *Ibid.*
92 Mosley, *The British Peace: and how to get it?,* Sanctuary Press Ltd, London 1939?
93 *Action,* 12 October 1939, editorial. The BUF made considerable use of propaganda derived from the juxtaposition of British attitudes towards German and Soviet aggression. Whereas the justifiable German demands on Poland had led to war, the naked aggression of Russian imperialism towards Finland, Poland, and the Baltic states had gone unpunished. This, it was claimed, indicated the blatant hypocrisy of Britain's 'Jewish War'. *Action,* 7 December 1939, p. 1; *Manchester Guardian,* 20 November 1939, p. 6; and 'Notes on the quarter', *BUQ,* IV, 1, spring 1940, pp. 11–12.
94 *Action News Service,* No. 1, 30 April 1940.
95 'Notes on the quarter', *BUQ,* IV, 1, spring 1940, pp. 3–10.
96 Mosley, *My Life,* pp. 377, 392. This view that the war could not be won by Britain was shared by some MPs, amongst whom was Lloyd George, who favoured a negotiated settlement with Germany. P. Addison, 'Lloyd George and Compromise Peace in the Second World War', as found in A. J. P. Taylor (ed.), *Lloyd George,* Hamish Hamilton, London 1971, pp. 361–84.
97 Mosley, *The British Peace: and how to get it?,* p. 9.
98 *The Times,* 6 November 1939, p. 3.
99 *Manchester Guardian,* 20 May 1940, p. 9.

CHAPTER 8

The European context

I have never said that all enterprises should be socialised. On the contrary, I have maintained that we might socialise enterprises prejudicial to the interests of the nation. Unless they were so guilty, I should consider it a crime to destroy essential elements in our economic life. . . . Our National Socialist state, like the Fascist state, will safeguard both employers' and workers' interests while reserving the right of arbitration in case of dispute.

A. Hitler to O. Strasser, 1930,
J. Noakes & G. Pridham, *Nazism 1919–45,* vol. I,
University of Exeter 1983, p. 67

Neither the Right nor the Left offers a solution. The victory of either would involve the defeat and humiliation of the other. There cannot be any national life in a country split into two irreconcilable halves. . . . Fruitful coexistence is only possible in the shelter of politics which owe nothing to any party or class; which exclusively serve the supreme and integrating destiny of Spain; which, with no other aim than justice and the national interest, sort out the problems between Spaniards.
José Antonio Primo de Rivera,
Letter to a Spanish Soldier, 1936

And thus I clothe my naked villany
With odd old ends stol'n forth of holy writ,
And seem a saint when most I play the devil.
W. Shakespeare, *Richard III*

How, then, does this analysis of British fascism relate to its European counterparts? As previously suggested, the immediate characteristics of fascism: its contempt for liberal-democracy, its love of action and violence, its elitism, its populism, its championing of the cause of the little man, its nationalism, and even its corporation, all were visible before 1914. From Spain to Russia there existed a variety of movements adhering to some of the above principles. All were small and singularly unsuccessful.

Such movements were the ideological forerunners of European fascism. In the pre-1914 period they were distinguished only by their failure to make any impact within their respective societies and their inability to present a coherent programme. They were not fascist movements, for fascism as a self-conscious ideology did not exist. Nor did the preconditions for its growth. In this respect the impact of the 1914–18 war, Lenin's 'locomotive of history', was crucial. The war discredited liberalism and shattered its humanist myths of natural progress. It sanctioned violence on a massive scale. The old order was undermined and shaken, and in many parts of central and eastern Europe collapsed entirely. In all coutries the war resulted in a greater centralisation of state machinery and increased control of the individual. The needs of war overrode the ethics of *laissez-faire* economics as the state intervened in the economy on a scale hitherto unknown. The nineteenth-century trend towards economic centralisation was accelerated, causing increased pressure upon the *petit bourgeoisie*. In many countries trade unions also assumed a new and more powerful position as they were rewarded for their war-time co-operation.

The war left Europe devastated. Amidst the ruins danced the spectre of Bolshevism, as invariably the problems of the post-war world effected a sharpening of class alienation and conflict. The era of mass politics had finally come of age. It was in such an environment that fascism grew, feeding voraciously upon myths and memories of an emotional unity and integration which the war had produced in all nations. Its disparate ideas which had existed upon the margins of nineteenth-century Europe were fused to become the basis for an ideology appropriate for the age. The war did not create fascism, it simply called it forth by providing the preconditions for its prosperity.

Although in the space of only one chapter no detailed comparative analysis of fascist movements or regimes can be undertaken, it is interesting to see the extent to which foreign fascist movements validate the interpretation of fascism as an attempt to find an accommodation between capital and labour on a non-liberal, authoritarian basis.

At the outset it should be stressed that fascist movements did not exist as representatives of a monolithic or precisely delineated ideology. Some appeared more radical than others, some emphasised anti-Semitism whilst others did not, some committed themselves to the legal acquisition of power whereas others attempted its seizure. There is also some truth in the assertion that fascism in southern and western Europe tended to be a modernising force whilst similar movements elsewhere in

Europe were backward looking,[1] although this is far from being a universally valid distinction.

Such variations were entirely in keeping with fascism's avowed and genuine nationalism. Indeed it was precisely this highly developed nationalism which precluded the formation of any effective international organisation to assist and co-ordinate fascist movements. Significantly, however, one of the few attempts to create such a body (the *Comitati d'azione per l'Universalità di Roma*, established by Mussolini in 1934), whilst accepting that fascist movements must be free to develop in accordance with their own national traditions, outlined the most basic criteria of fascism as being the establishment of a strong just state which could facilitate 'agreement between social classes', and a 'co-ordinated and solid collaboration between producers', through a corporate framework.[2]

This attempt to secure an authoritarian but just class consensus within a capitalist economy was the most important common element to all of the diverse fascist movements which haunted inter-war Europe. It was this which produced the peculiar mixture of radicalism and conservatism which was so characteristic of genuine fascist movements (for although the exact proportions of each might vary, it was the fact that both could simultaneously exist which gave fascism its unmistakeable stamp) and which distinguished it from the left, right, and liberal centre, each of which it attacked with varying degrees of vehemence.

The result was that fascist movements were able to attract disaffected elements from all classes whose previous affiliations spanned the entire political spectrum. Those whose vulnerability was greatest tended to be over-represented. Thus the *petit bourgeoisie* formed the backbone of fascist movements in all countries as its insecurity was accentuated by economic crisis and political instability. But fascism also won support from alienated representatives of the upper and middle classes, and was capable of making significant inroads into the peasantry and proletariat, especially in sectors of the economy where units of production were predominantly small and union organisation weak. Studies of the growth of the Nazi party in the 1920s show clearly the manner in which it transcended the '. . . basic lines of socio-economic and religious clevage around which the German party system had been developed. By mobilising a socially and culturally amorphous electorate composed of the disaffected from virtually all strata of society, the Nazi movement of the 1920s acquired the character of a catchall party of protest.'[3]

Whilst fascism appealed to disgruntled conservatives, socialists and even communists, it could prove particularly attractive to liberals. This apparent paradox is explicable in terms of fascism's centrist appeal. As the mirror image of liberalism, it stressed unity and social and

economic integration on the basis of a harmonious and just reconciliation of class conflict. The figures in Table 1 showing the results of
the Reichstag elections between 1928 and 1933 tell their own story.[4] In
addition to the mobilisation of hitherto non-voters the Nazis gained
votes from all of the bourgeois parties, but they gained more heavily
from the centre than from the left or the right. At the last free election in
Weimar Germany the conservatives and the social democrats managed
to retain sixty per cent and sixty-nine per cent respectively of their 1928
shares of the vote. The centre, however, collapsed dramatically with the
liberals losing upwards of eighty per cent of voting strength. Of the
parties at the centre of the political spectrum only the Catholic party,
protected by the religious affiliation of its supporters, managed to avoid
decimation.

TABLE 1

Party	% of the total vote gained in general elections of:					Ratio of 1928 vote to 2nd 1932 vote (expressed as a %)
	1928	1930	1932	1932	1933	
Right						
DNVP						
(Conservative)	14·2	7·0	5·9	8·5	8·0	60
Centre						
DVP						
(right liberal)	8·7	4·85	1·2	1·8	1·1	21
DDP (left liberal)	4·8	3·45	1·0	0·95	0·8	20
Wirtschaftspartei						
(small business)	4·5	3·9	0·4	0·3	—	7
Others	9·5	10·1	2·6	2·8	0·6	29
Catholic Centre						
Party	15·4	17·6	16·7	16·2	15·0	105
Left						
SPD (Socialist)	29·8	24·5	21·6	20·4	18·3	69
KPD (Communist)	10·6	13·1	14·3	16·85	12·3	159
Fascist						
NSDAP (Nazi)	2·6	18·3	37·3	33·1	43·9	1,277

The analysis of voting patterns in German local elections have
tended to confirm this trend. Elsewhere in Europe, although the
electoral information is incomplete, there is evidence to suggest a
similar pattern attendant upon the growth of fascism. As seen in Table
2, a careful analysis of voting in Budapest in 1939 reveals a clear
correlation between the fascist and the liberal vote.[5] Those areas where

the fascist Arrow Cross party was strongest correspond with those where the liberals were weakest.

TABLE 2 % of total vote received

Arrow Cross	Social Democrats	Liberals	Government Party
35+	10–20	3–7	20–30
25–35	3–30	5–20	16–50
15–25	4–22	20–40	20–38
0–15	6–15	10–62	19–48

Liberals were too ready to see in fascism a coherent system which allowed national planning on a basis that transcended class and class interests. Indeed, one of the chief mentors in establishing the intellectual content of fascism was the Sicilian philosopher Giovanni Gentile who had split from Croce and his fellow liberals in 1921–2.[6] Claims by Mussolini that 'a new sense of justice, of seriousness, of harmony and concord guides now the destinies of all of the people and classes of Italy . . . the Italians feel themselves of one fraternity . . .'[7], were too often taken at face value with the result that prominent liberals in many countries displayed a dangerous ambivalence towards the new ideology.[8] Though objecting to its dictatorship, they were drawn towards its centrism as moths to a candle flame.

That intellectuals were as often thus deceived is not altogether surprising, for the programmes advanced by fascist movements clearly reflected the centrist nature of the ideology. The Nazi programme as first postulated in a Munich beer cellar in February 1920 consisted of twenty-five points. Amongst the aggressive nationalism, the racist anti-Semitism, and (by implication at least) the intended retention of the capitalist mode of production, almost half of the points were undoubtedly radical. These included 'the abolition of incomes unearned by work', 'the ruthless confiscation of all war profits', the nationalisation of all large trusts, profit-sharing in large industries, improved welfare and educative facilities, the abolition of ground rents, and 'the prohibition of all speculation in land'.[9] Although the programme ceased to have any real relevance to the party's leaders as they approached the threshold of power, it illustrated the origins of the ideology and highlighted the importance for fascists of the distinction between 'parasitic' finance capital and 'productive' industrial capital. The community of interest between workers and productive capitalists against their common enemy, the international financier, was stressed by Gottfried Feder, an early Nazi economist. 'Interest slavery', as opposed to the Marxian concept of wage slavery, ensnared the producers of hand, brain, and capital alike. Therefore, it was argued, a revolution was needed not against capitalism in general but against finance capital in particular. For Feder this middle course between capitalism and socialism was the true purpose of National Socialism.[10] It was for this reason that German fascism was frequently attacked in the 1920s from the conservative right as 'bolshevism in nationalist wrapping', and by the left as a form of counterfeit socialism.[11]

The same was true of fascist parties in other countries. In Belgium, Léon Degrelle's *Rexist* movement committed itself to the retention of capitalism and private property, but also attacked the 'dictatorship of super-capitalism' and called for the control of banks, the elimination of profiteering, the redistribution of land, and the unity of workers of all classes.[12] Once again the distinction between productive enterprise and parasitic finance capital was clear.

In Spain José Antonio Primo de Rivera, one of the most able of all fascist leaders, produced a twenty-six point programme for the Spanish *Falange* in November 1934. Both Marxism and capitalism were specifically rejected, the latter because it '. . . disregards the needs of the people, dehumanizes private property and transforms the workers into shapeless masses prone to misery and despair'. Whilst guaranteeing private property, the party vehemently denounced 'high finance, speculators and money lenders', and called for the nationalisation of banks and large public services, the redistribution of cultivatable land, and the appropriation of '. . . any land whose ownership has been acquired or enjoyed illicitly'.[13]

In eastern Europe the same stamp was discernible although often the denunciation of capitalism was less strident. Given that in such countries fascism was often operating within overt capitalist dictatorships this is understandable. Even so, genuine fascist organisations such as the Polish *Falanga* included in its extremely nationalistic programme calls for limitations upon private property and greater state control over the economy, resulting in class unity.[14] Fascism in Hungary from the very beginning differentiated between exploitive and creative capital and, whilst pledging itself to retain the capitalist system, sought to control it and to eradicate its most undesirable features.[15]

As suggested in the case of BUF, this attempt by fascism to encompass elements from both left and right meant that the core components of the ideology were largely incompatible. Where possible this problem was overcome by synthesis, but inevitably there was also a tendency towards oscillation whereby the same party was capable of holding contradictory positions. Attitudes towards modernity and tradition often illustrated this as clearly within European fascist movements as they did within the BUF.

The *Falange* promised increases in the standard of living for all, the restoration of Spain's position as a world power through renewed economic and military strength, and outlined impressive schemes of modernisation, especially in the agricultural sector. Yet simultaneously there was a glorification of a mythical Spain of the sixteenth century where harmony and unity were a part of the natural order. The same was true in Belgium where the *Rexists* gazed backwards to a mythical past, and in France where fascists hankered for a return to the values of the pre-1789 period. In Hungary fascism was fractured between several different movements but racist agrarian-based myths abounded and were exploited by fascists of all parties. Yet fascism also posed as a modernising force complete with promises to sweep away the feudalist relics of the past.[16]

German National Socialism, having vanquished its own radical elements and achieved power, frequently displayed a fierce hostility towards modern industrial society. It was in Germany that the racial myths and the mystical qualities of 'blood and soil' were extolled to an excessive degree. Hitler himself referred to cities as '. . . abscesses on the body of the folk, (*Volkskörper*), in which all vices, bad habits and sicknesses seem to unite. They are above all hotbeds of miscegenation and bastardisation . . .'.[17] Yet he also showed a genuine personal interest in architecture and city planning. He was obsessed with the lavishly ornate, neo-baroque Paris Opera House and, as his architect Albert Speer later admitted, the buildings which he and Hitler designed in 1939 featured '. . . excessive ornamentation, a mania for gilding, a passion for pomp, and total decadence'.[18] However popular the pastoral myths, Hitler and his followers needed the products of industrial society in order to rearm Germany and expand her frontiers, and to provide the consumer goods demanded by the German populace. Hence most Nazis 'were, in fact, fascinated by technology, and despite their hostility to industrial society, stood in awe of German industry'.[19]

It is a mistake therefore to see fascism exclusively as either a retrogressive or a modernising ideology, for it contains aspects of each. Having used elements of the modern and non-modern sectors of the economy in its struggle for power, fascism may choose, when in government, either to sacrifice the latter for reasons of opportunism such as rearmament, or attempt to synthesise the incompatible interests of the two. In Italy the second option was attempted, with the result that measures favourable to the countryside (such as the prevention of rural depopulation, protective tariffs and favourable taxation) accompanied concessions to the modern sector (including investment in industry, rearmament, and public works).[20] The dangers of such a policy are self-evident. To attempt to modernise economically without accepting the socio-political consequences of such modernisation resulted in chaos and economic failure. Far from acting as a modernising force, fascism in Italy failed to transform a society still dominated by pre-industrial values and institutions. In 1940 Italians employed in the agricultural sector continued to outnumber those in industry, and after almost two decades of fascism the proportions had hardly altered.[21] In Germany the emphasis upon rural life and agrarian values was never allowed to interfere with the continuing process of industrialisation.[22] Thus was German modernisation and rearmament achieved at the cost of shattered Nazi promises. As one author has observed:

> in 1939 the cities were larger, not smaller; the concentration of capital greater than before; the rural population reduced, not increased; women not at the fireside but in the office and the factory; the inequality of income and property distribution more not less conspicuous; industry's share of the gross national product up and agriculture's down, while industrial labour had it relatively good and small business increasingly bad.[23]

The subject of fascism in practice will be returned to later. At this juncture one needs only to emphasise the problems which arose from the irreconcilable core elements which constituted fascist centrism. Of course, many of the characteristics of fascism helped to disguise its internal contradictions. Not least of these was the *Fuhresprinzip*, or leadership principle, adhered to by every fascist party in Europe. This involved a willingness to display absolute faith in the party leader to whom was ascribed superhuman qualities of dynamism, courage, charisma and vision. Throughout the party this principle served to command absolute obedience from rank and file fascists, thereby cementing the party hierarchy and elevating faith above reason. The same was true of fascism's glorification of the cult of action which also characterised all of Europe's fascist movements.

Nationalism too was enormously important in this respect because it provided a set of criteria for collectivism which was not class-based. Indeed it was argued by fascists that nationality superseded class. Therefore it provided an ideal amalgam for bonding together the disparate elements and the incompatible economic interests which lay at the heart of fascist centrism. Hence the fierce and uncompromising nationalism of all fascist parties: indeed, in countries where there were significant national minorities it was not uncommon to find several competing fascist movements. In Belgium Flemish fascism was represented by the League of Netherlands National Solidarists established in October 1931 by Joris van Severen. In 1933 a second and more pro-German Flemish fascist party, the *Vlaamsch Nationaal Verbond,* was founded by Staf de Clercq. Both appealed exclusively to Flemish nationalist sentiment and pledged themselves to rid Flanders of the dominant Walloons. Degrelle's *Rexist* movement, founded in 1936, whilst appealing to Belgium nationalism in general, made almost all of its impact in French-speaking Walloon areas.[24]

In Czechoslovakia the position was more complex because in addition to the ruling Czech majority, sixteen per cent of the nation's population were Slovaks and twenty-five per cent were Germans. Thus in addition to several Czech-orientated fascist movements, there was a fascist Slovak Peoples' Party under Andrej Hlinka which successfully exploited Slovak nationalist sentiment, and a National Socialist movement (closely tied to the Nazis) which appealed exclusively and successfully to the German minority.[25]

The centrist nature of European fascist movements was also clearly displayed by their unfailing use of corporatism as a device whereby their much vaunted claims of national unity and class harmony could be realised. The corporate element of fascism has been too often neglected by those seeking to understand the ideology. This is partly the result of Italian fascism's failure to articulate its corporate theory until after its seizure of power (thus appearing to many to be no more than an attempt to cover the nakedness of opportunism with a few theoretical rags), and also because fascist regimes tended to ignore corporatism in practice, preferring to substitute for it the brutal exploitation of the labour movement. Despite its failures in practice, however, it is no coincidence that, whatever the regional variations, every fascist movement in Europe stressed corporatism as a fundamental element of its programme. The establishment of a corporate state was every fascist movement's ultimate goal, for it was only through such a mechanism that the opposing interests of capital and labour could be reconciled, thereby facilitating fascist dreams of synthesis and national unity.

The theoretical ancestry of fascist corporatism was both ancient and modern. In part it drew upon the concept of the crafts guilds which had governed much of the industry of medieval Europe. The Catholic church, which had always regarded society as a corporate and organic whole, was also an important source. In May 1931 Pope Pius XI's encyclical *Quadragesimo anno* condemned the injustices, crises and conflicts inherent within *laissez-faire* capitalism, and urged Catholics to support corporative associations. Fascist Italy's corporate machinery was praised accordingly for having eliminated class conflict and the threat of socialism.[26] A more modern source of corporate theory was syndicalist socialism, particularly the theories of George Sorel concerning representation through vocation.[27]

It has been suggested that fascism in advanced countries tended to use racism rather than corporatism (such as the Nazis) whereas in backward countries where fascism appeared as a modernising phenomenon the rationality of corportism was stressed.[28] The pattern, however, is insufficiently uniform for this analysis to be convincing. The racist elements of Italian fascism were certainly never as ferocious or as essential as those within German National Socialism but they undoubtedly existed especially in relation to Italian overseas conquest. As early as 1921 Mussolini referred to Italians as representatives of the Aryan race and to the Mediterranean as *more nostrum*.[29] Similarly, although racism was used extensively by the Nazis, corporate ideas also featured within their programme. The last of the twenty-five points called for '. . . the formation of Corporations based on estate and occupation'.[30] The party contained important corporate theorists such as Gottfried Feder, Walther Darré and Otto Strasser, although their ideas tended to be forgotten after the party won power in 1933.[31] In Italy the theory at least was retained even if there was little corporatism in practice.

The Nazi obsession with the *Volk* and with racial anti-Semitism was mirrored by fascist movements in Finland and Hungary. In all three nations short-lived communist republics had been established in the wake of the Russian revolution in which Jews played a leading role. This common experience assisted fascism in its attempt to build elaborate racist theories upon existing anti-Semitic foundations. But corporatism was also evident in the fascist movements of each of these countries. In Rumania the Iron Guard under Cornelius Codreanu displayed violent anti-Semitism and spoke mystically of purifying the race, yet the movement also contained Mikail Manoilescu, one of the greatest corporate theorists of the 1930s.[32] In Britain, the most industrially advanced of all European nations, the BUF stressed the rationality of its corporate framework and yet also indulged in vaguely defined racism and anti-Semitism.

Thus, fascist movements, rather than using either racism or corporatism, tended to contain elements of each. Certainly one might be emphasised more fully than the other, but no fascist party abandoned either entirely before its accession to power. This difference of emphasis is explicable in terms of fascism's desire to accommodate national traditions. Hence, in countries where there was little evidence of racism and anti-Semitism but where there was a strong syndicalist and Catholic tradition (such as Spain or Italy), corporatism took precedence over racism. In those nations where racism and anti-Semitism were already firmly rooted (such as Germany, Rumania and Hungary) it is understandable that native fascist movements should have sought to exploit them. The important point, however, is that both corporatism and racism served the same function of providing a basis for social unity and integration – the *raison d'être* of fascist ideology. That one should seek to provide it on the basis of a nationally conceived harmonising mechanism, and the other through the irrational medium of common blood and genes, does not negate this observation. The fact that fascism was capable of containing each simultaneously merely underlines its contradictory nature.

Before leaving the subject of corporatism it is necessary to differentiate between fascist corporate theory which was distinctly centrist, and those conservative governments which cynically appropriated corporate trappings in an attempt to bolster the popularity of their traditional authoritarian regimes and undercut the appeal of fascism.

A clear instance of this occurred in Austria where, by the early 1930s, Chancellor Dollfuss and his ruling Christian Social Party were coming under increasing pressure from both socialists and fascists. The latter were represented by two organisations. The *Heimwehr,* under Prince Staremberg, had originated amongst the paramilitary formations which had protected Austria from chaos and revolution in the aftermath of the 1918 defeat, and had gone on to evolve a full fascist programme with particular emphasis upon the achievement of a corporate state. Its fascist rival was the small but vociferous National Socialist Party – the NSDAP. Whereas the *Heimwehr* looked to Italy for its inspiration and support, the NSDAP became increasingly dominated by its namesake in Germany. Dollfuss responded to the pressure by suspending parliament, suppressing the socialists and the NSDAP, and by incorporating the *Heimwehr* into a 'Fatherland Front' which preached the virtues of corporate organisation. It was only after considerable prodding from Mussolini and Staremburg, however, that Dollfuss saw fit to embody this new-found belief in corporatism in a new constitution framed in May 1934. Seven corporations were established to organise the nation's economic and cultural activities, and some of the new governmental advisory bodies were given theoretical corporate characteristics. In reality, however, corporatism remained entirely theoretical under both Dollfuss (who was assassinated in an attempted NSDAP putsch in July 1934) and his successor, Schuschnigg.[33] Both resisted all *Heimwehr* efforts to give flesh and blood reality to the paper corporatism. Eventually in 1936 Staremburg was dropped from the government and the *Heimwehr* dissolved.[34] The sham corporatism of the regime continued with Schuschnigg reiterating his belief in the 'corporate articulation of the populace', and claiming that the regime represented 'the united solid front of all of our people, no matter to what rank or class they may belong'.[35] Increasingly such statements were devoid of all credibility. The bourgeois conservatism of the Fatherland Front found itself unable to compete with the fascist potency of the NSDAP, which continued to grow and recruit ex-*Heimwehr* members until 1938 when it played a key role in destroying the Schuschnigg regime by achieving a union between Austria and the Third Reich.

The same was true in Hungary where the reactionary head of state Admiral Horthy appointed Gyula Gömbös as prime minister in 1932. Although Gömbös had racist and fascist credentials and paid lip service to the corporate notion of a 'unitary Hungarian nation with no class distinctions', he made no attempt to create a corporate state, although the conservative regime did acquire some corporate ornamentation.[36] Genuine Hungarian fascism asserted itself through Zoltán Boszormeny's Nazi-inspired and fiercely anti-Semitic Scythe Cross movement, and the more classically fascist Arrow Cross Party founded by Ferencz Szálasi in 1935. The Arrow Cross programme incorporated extreme nationalism with the demand for a corporate state where class conflict could be reconciled on the basis of justice for all. It grew rapidly, attracting support from the disaffected of all classes.[37] Despite the imprisonment of its leaders and government attempts to undercut its appeal through the enactment of anti-Semitic legislation, by 1939 it had a membership of 250,000 and polled twenty-five per cent of the vote in the May elections.[38]

In Rumania King Carol II, fearful of the advances of Codreanu's fascist Iron Guard in the elections of December 1937, established his own dictatorship and dressed it in Guardist corporate trappings. He responded to the fury of the Iron Guard by prohibiting it and having its leaders (including Codreanu) brutally murdered. Nevertheless the Guard continued to grow as an underground movement, implacably hostile to the sham fascists of the Carol regime.[39]

In the Iberian pensisular also, old-fashioned reactionary conservatism stole some of the corporate characteristics of the genuine native fascisms which it destroyed. Salazar's right-wing regime never seriously sought a mechanism for class collaboration despite its superficial expropriation of the corporate aspects of Rolão Preto's genuinely fascist National Syndicalist party which was suppressed by the authorities in 1935.[40] In Spain the pattern was repeated when the sophisticated fascism of the Falange was forcibly amalgamated with reactionary elements (such as the pro-monarchy Carlists) into a monolithic and arch conservative party dominated by Franco, the right-wing militarist. It is ironic that even from his Republican prison cell the Falange's leader José Antonio Primo de Rivera forbade the party to make alliances with either the conservatives or the army. Such alliances, he believed, would never produce the Falange goal of a national syndicalist state. Indeed, one of his greatest fears was the development of '. . . a false conservative Fascism without revolutionary courage and young blood'.[41] Within six months of his execution by the Republicans, Jose Antonio's movement had been swallowed up and neutralised by Franco's conservatism. After the Nationalists' victory corporate trappings were adopted in Spain and Rivera's martydom was ruthlessly exploited for propaganda purposes. What José Antonio feared had come to pass, for Franco's Spain, like Salazar's Portugal, represented not fascism but a traditional conservative military dictatorship.

It was suggested in the introduction that the centrist appeal of fascism represents its chief source of strength but also its foremost weakness, for it ensures that the ideology is rent with internal contradictions and, therefore, is ultimately unworkable. The examples of Germany and Italy, the only two nations where fascism achieved power without external intervention, demonstrate the validity of this hypothesis.

Despite Mussolini's boasts of unity and national synthesis it is clear that the corporate state in Italy was an ornate and bureaucratic façade. Plans to shift political representation towards an occupational basis were afoot as early as 1928, but as the government closely controlled the official list of candidates (all of whom would be elected) and controlled the national organisations which put forward names for the list, in reality it functioned as a straightforward dictatorship. Its economic functions followed a similar pattern. In 1926 trade unions were incorporated into single category syndicates with power to draw up collective labour contracts, strikes and lockouts were prohibited, and a ministry of corporations was established to co-ordinate the syndicates. In 1930 the ministry spawned a body known as the national council of corporations which consisted of representatives from government, party, the ministries, employers and workers. Its functions were to advise the ministry and to regulate economic relations between the various categories of production. It was redundant from its very inception, however, and soon after the twenty-two corporations were finally created in 1934 it ceased to convene altogether. Each corporation was governed by a body composed of representtives from the party and government, employers and workers. In all cases the government decided upon appointees.[42]

The corporations were bureaucratic, expensive, corrupt in that they provided jobs for the party hacks, and out of touch with ordinary Italian citizens.[43] They were also denied any real authority over their own spheres of the economy and were weakened by the proliferation of public organs which ran parallel to them but over which they had no control.[44] In any case, as the representatives of capital were given a far greater degree of freedom than were those of labour, those corporations which functioned to any degree at all were dominated by the business community.

Real control of production lay not with the corporations but with producers' cartels. Increasing capitalist rationalisation and centralisation (encouraged by the government) led to the formation of a growing number of voluntary consortia to regulate production, control prices and curb competition. Although theoretically accountable to government, in practice they often had a completely free hand.[45] As the cartels themselves were dominated by the largest producers it meant that an enormous amount of unaccountable power lay in the hands of a small number of capitalists whose primary motivation was not the economic well-being of the nation but the level of their own profits. Controls, where they existed, were either ignored with impunity or else evaded through the skilful manipulation of the law. Restrictions on industrial expansion, for instance, were manipulated by large concerns in order to gain exemption for themselves but not for their competitors. The larger a concern the more successful it was for it had greater clout.[46]

In short, the Italian corporate state, far from achieving harmonious class collaboration, provided only a dictatorial framework within which labour was exploited and the forces of capital given a free hand to increase profits through monopolistic and oligopolistic methods of production. A dictatorial framework within which chaos reigned supreme as the state unnecessarily duplicated administrative functions, and where powerful capitalists pursued selfish aims without regard to the interests of the community. Ill-conceived fascist economic policies, such as the struggle for autarchy or the revaluation of the lira for reasons of prestige, added to the dismal picture. Even the much vaunted public works schemes involving land reclamation were successes of propaganda rather than economics, for only ten per cent of land upon which reclamation was begun actually showed any increase in productivity.[47] Nor did the corporate state facilitate economic planning to any real degree, for amidst the chaos there was little opportunity for coherent vision.

Far from increasing unity, fascism increased the divisions within Italy and thus failed to achieve its most basic end. As the few made huge profits the many found that their wages were reduced. In the wake of the world depression per capita consumption actually fell in the 1930s.[48] Yet although the state demanded complete control over the lives of its citizens the welfare services which it offered in return were poor and fragmentary. The economic gulf between north and south remained as wide as ever, with more than ninety per cent of all engineering, metallurgical and textile workers continuing to be based in the north.[49] Italian unity remained as mythical as ever: conflicts were not harmonised but simply covered with the thin veneer of fascist bombast and state authority. Fascism failed also in its other ends. Italy was not significantly strengthened economically or militarily. Modernisation was not achieved, but then nor was the conflicting aim of returning Italians to the land as smallholders from whence they could enjoy the physical and moral health of the countryside. The *petit bourgeois* capitalist, far from being specifically protected, was often left at the mercy of the large capitalist enterprises which exercised unchecked power over much of the Italian economy. Fascism in practice was a cruel parody of its own theoretical pronouncements.

In Germany in May 1933, just six weeks after the Enabling Act had been passed to destroy the Weimar constitution and give the Nazis complete power, the trade unions were dissolved and their leaders arrested. They were replaced by the German Labour Front, '. . . a misshapen child to hectic improvisation',[50] which included all industrial workers and employers in common organisations. The purpose of the Front was to preserve industrial peace and to promote welfare schemes, but from the outset the fears of the employers were soothed by its leader, Robert Ley, who assured them that it would not interfere in matters of material interest to the workers. Thus, despite propaganda concerning 'factory communities' and the existence in factories of 'councils of trust' (initally chosen jointly by workers and employers, but after 1935 simply appointed by the latter) to liaise with management and harmonise industrial relations, corporatism in Germany was stillborn. The councils of trust were specifically forbidden from making complaints to the Labour Front for it was deemed desirable that each plant should manage its own affairs without external interference. Only in regard to making work superficially more attractive did the Labour Front have any real impact. Its Beauty of Work department forced some employers to improve workers' amenities, and its Strength through Joy campaign increased worker access to subsidised cultural and recreational activities.[51]

As previously suggested the Nazis were more than willing to sacrifice theory in order to appease German industrialists whose co-operation they required if rearmament was to be swiftly and smoothly achieved. Within weeks of the Enabling Act Hitler had reiterated to representatives of industry and banking his assurances that private enterprise was to remain the basis of the regime.[52] The immediate victims of the co-operation between government and industry were the anti-capitalist sections of the Nazi party such as the handicraft and factory cell organisations, and the SA whose populist anti-industrial tendencies were a matter of concern to many within the business community.[53]

Free from any fear of organised labour German capitalists enjoyed the economic boom inspired by government expenditure, and were relieved of the necessity of planning or the use of cartels to restrict output and maintain prices. Whatever collective interest had existed in the past was replaced by the short-term greed of individual firms. This was clearly illustrated by the response of employers to the increasing labour shortage which began to manifest itself in the Third Reich from the mid-1930s. As firms producing for government contracts had their costs already covered they could afford to raise wages with impunity. The effects of this uneven wages explosion was a flood of workers moving from export-orientated industries (which were trying to keep costs low in order to remain internationally competitive) to the construction and metallurgical industries where government contracts were fattest. It led also to firms poaching workers with the relevant skills from their competitors through increased wage inducements; rural depopulation; an erosion of discipline amongst those workers who knew that even if sacked they could easily find new employment; and a deep resentment by those not in the boom sectors of the economy and whose pay was not spiralling.[54] Although some measures were taken to control labour in those areas where the shortages were most acute, the government was reluctant to be seen acting overtly against the interests of workers and consumers. It was also realised that by conspiring together employers and workers could easily circumvent state controls, for capitalists were willing to disguise pay rises in the form of free accommodation or other job related perks. Not until 1938–9, as war approached, did the government introduce comprehensive controls which included the fixing of maximum wage levels, and moves towards the militarisation of labour through restrictions on freedom of movement and industrial conscription.

Thus there was as little economic unity within the economy of Nazi Germany as within that of fascist Italy. The regime pandered not only to industry and to the consumers (as late as 1942, as the tide of war turned against him, Hitler was adamant that military expenditure should not squeeze the production of consumer goods)[55] but also tried from the mid-1930s to buy the loyalty of the proletariat. Bribery became a substitute for the failure to achieve national integration. This disunity was displayed also in the internal bickering which characterised Nazi rule. To existing German conflicts (such as that between the interests of agriculture and industry) there were added new structural disputes involving the overlapping bureauracies of party and state. There were quarrels between the *Gauleiter* and central government; between the party and the *Wehrmacht* and civil service; between the SS and the SA;[56] and between individual government ministries each jealously defending its own sphere of activity. As in Italy the result was confusion, duplication, inefficiency and a failure to undertake any effective economic planning. As the rearmament drive increased industrial concentration, collective relations with government were replaced by individual firms negotiating directly with the state in pursuit of short-term profits, oblivious to the overall welfare of the national economy.[57] General Keitel summarised the socio-economic structure in 1938 as 'a war of all against all'.[58] It was a war which was simply being conducted in silence. It was, as one recent author has described it, a system where 'the constantly invoked 'national community' of the propaganda concealed a reality in which the only acknowledged conformism was the cynical prosecution of one's own material interests . . .'.[59]

Both Italy and Germany used parades, propaganda, pomp and

ceremony to create and reinforce the image of an organic society: a unified people harmoniously living and working together as one, and offering collective support to their respective fascist governments. It was style rather than substance. Beneath the façade, amongst the institutionalised chaos there lived populations who, robbed of their rights and representative institutions, consisted of atomised and often deeply alienated human beings. Speer, who witnessed it first hand, confessed to being astonished by the gulf between fascist promises and reality. Far from producing the community of the people (*Volksgemeinschaft*) as promised, the Nazi system '. . . had the effect of stamping out the promised integration, or at any rate of greatly hindering it. What eventually developed was a society of totally isolated individuals.'[60]

In conclusion, it appears that corporatism, whether cynically appropriated by reactionary regimes to undercut the appeal of native fascism, or as constituting the centrist core of genuine fascist movements, in practice represented no more than a dictatorial framework within which capitalist exploitation could proceed unhindered. As a harmonising force it was unworkable: its unworkability lay in the illusory nature of authoritarian centrism itself. In the BUF's carefully constructed corporate blueprint there was nothing to suggest that this essential paradox could have been overcome.

Before leaving the subject of the European context within which the BUF existed, it is worth pausing to consider the conditions which assisted the growth of fascism. The degree to which a society is traumatised is the obvious starting point here. The trauma can originate as a result of the impact of modernisation (hence the growth of fascism in relatively underdeveloped societies) or because of the onset of economic depression in an advanced capitalist society. War too can be a contributory factor. As already suggested the 1914–18 war was crucial to the development of fascism in several respects. It undermined the old order, accelerated the rise of communism, militarised the belligerent societies and gave them the illusion of unity which rapidly evaporated in its aftermath, and caused a degree of frustrated nationalism in those nations which suffered territorial loss from the reshaping of Europe by its victors. In countries such as Germany and Hungary which were humiliated and deprived of vast tracts of territory, native fascist movements had the perfect context for the extreme nationalism which was so vital in sustaining their centrist approach. This was the case also with Italy, for although technically it was on the winning side it was not rewarded with those areas of enemy territory which were coveted. Hence there grew up the myth of the 'mutilated peace' whereby Italy had been deprived of the spoils commensurate with great power status, thus adding a diplomatic humiliation to the pain of unfulfilled expectations. In victor countries such as Britain, or neutrals such as Sweden,

Denmark, Norway or Switzerland, fascism struggled to make headway in the absence of such a legacy.

The existence of trauma within a society, whatever its source, helped to create and sustain a climate of disintegration proportionate to its severity. This disintegration provided fertile soil for fascism's appeal to organic unity and national synthesis on the basis of enforced class collaboration. The existence of trauma, therefore, when sufficiently deep, provided the potential for fascist growth. This potential was most easily realised in societies whose four other characteristics were also present. Foremost amongst these was an inadequate level of integration predating the onset of crisis. It is no coincidence that both Germany and Italy achieved political unification only towards the end of the nineteenth century. Even then their unity was superficial, for the new states were unevenly developed economically, prone to strong regionalism (and in Germany's case religious disunity), and with populations apt to forge bonds of loyalty to sub-communities and groups.[61] The effect of crisis upon these societies was to intensify rapidly the deep divisions which already existed, thus making them particularly receptive to the blandishments of fascism.

The second important characteristic was the extent to which the ruling regime was discredited. Once again Italy and Germany provided excellent examples of this. In the decades after unification both experienced forms of parliamentary democracy which by 1914 had become seriously discredited. In Italy there were theoretical groupings of left and right but in reality there was little difference between them. Politicians frequently bargained without regard to party affiliation in order to cling leech-like to office. Parliament, therefore, was an amorphous mass of deputies led by a government whose composition shifted on the basis of individual self-seeking. The response of the populace was apathy laced with cynicism. In Bismarckian Germany sham constitutionalism produced much the same effect, for although a legislature existed it lacked effective control over the government. Executive power until 1918 lay exclusively in the hands of the Kaiser and his appointed chancellors. In neither country was there a genuine attempt to institute liberal democracy, and when such an attempt was made it was done so with dramatic speed and in a post-war climate of humiliation and, in Germany's case, defeat. What had taken countries such as Britain and France centuries to evolve was attempted overnight in the worst possible conditions. The result was that far from increasing the levels of German and Italian national integration, liberal democracy intensified the deep existing divisions by making them more visible. In effect they were institutionalised. Thus, parliamentary government which had appeared corrupt and ineffective in the pre-war period was attacked after 1918 as divisive and unstable. The proliferation of small parties and the unstable coalition governments which characterised both countries in the post-war period helped to reinforce this growing hostility towards liberal democracy.[62]

The third factor related to the success of a fascist movement concerns the concept of political space. Fascism flourished more fully in societies where the liberal centre was discredited and sagging beneath attacks from the far left and the conservative right. In both Germany and Italy communism was growing rapidly until the triumph of fascism. In both countries, also, social democracy presented itself in a revolutionary rather than a reformist guise. In Germany the moderately socialist SPD frequently appeared to be a vehicle for Marxism as in its slogans and aspects of its organisation it maintained the façade of a revolutionary party.[63] In Italy the socialists campaigned in the November 1919 general election under the slogan 'all power to the proletariat', polled one third of the total vote, and trebled the number of deputies returned to parliament.[64] Where the centre remained strong (as in Britain, where it was bolstered by the National Government albeit with a heavy conservative gloss), or where right-wing authoritarian regimes neutralised any real threat from the left (as in much of eastern Europe) fascism struggled to find the political space whereby it could exploit the potential breadth of its appeal.

The final characteristic concerned the degree of political violence within a society, for this affected the potency of the fascist centrist appeal, particularly in respect to its impact upon the middle class. In Italy the years between 1918 and Mussolini's seizure of power in 1922 were marked by a consistently increasing level of political violence. Factory occupations by workers were commonplace. In the autumn of 1920 280 factories were occupied in Milan alone, and another 200 in Turin. Protective units of paramilitary 'red guards' were organised by the controlling workers' committees. Clashes with the fascists were common, as were fascist attacks upon a range of labour movement targets. In the first six months of 1921 the fascists destroyed eighty-five agrarian co-operatives, fifty-nine chambers of labour, forty-three unions of agricultural workers, twenty-five peoples' centres, and innumerate left-wing printing presses.[65] In the course of such attacks opponents were systematically beaten, humiliated, and not infrequently murdered. Rarely, however, were the perpetrators brought to justice for the authorities tended to turn a blind eye to such outrages, and on occasions the police and army even assisted the fascists. The Liberal prime minister Giolitti, faced with large-scale socialist gains in the May 1921 elections, formed a national bloc which included fascists and nationalists. Not only did he ensure that the fascists were not persecuted by the authorities, but he also assisted Mussolini with gifts of money and arms.[66] This response was in keeping with that of the Italian middle class as a whole, for as the level of lawlessness and perceived socialist threat increased, so also did bourgeois contributions to the fascist party's coffers.

Germany too provided an example of the same paradox whereby fascism fed upon its own violence, by helping to create an atmosphere of lawlessness and then exploiting it by posing as the defender of the established order and the only viable alternative to the destructive tide of communism. Although the breakdown of law was never as complete as that which preceded the fascist triumph in Italy, the right-wing Bavarian state government co-operated fully with the Nazis from the very beginning. Here the Nazis found a haven safe from persecution by the national government, whilst the army in Bavaria offered a valuable source of recruits and arms.[67] Even the attempted Nazi *putsch* in Munich in November 1923 was dealt with by the Bavarian judiciary with considerable lenience. As in Italy, political lawlessness spread in Weimar Germany as the crisis deepened, resulting in an increasing number of representatives of the establishment coming to see the Nazis as a force capable of restoring order and averting the communist threat. Barons of industry such as Fritz Thyssen lent their support and made heavy financial donations to the party.[68] This type of support became especially common after the conclusion of a pact between the Nazis and the DNVP, Germany's large *Junker*-based conservative party. This influx of money, middle-class respectability, and establishment connections accelerated Nazi growth.[69]

Thus, in both Germany and Italy the support of the traditional right was essential in the fascist rise to power. Indeed both Hitler and Mussolini first took office in conservative coalition governments containing only a minority of fascists. Skilful political manipulation was necessary before either assumed unchecked authority. In countries where such leadership was absent, as in Spain, the result could be disastrous for fascism. The election of the vociferously left-wing Popular Front government in May 1936, coinciding with increasing political violence, provoked a sufficient degree of middle-class fear to cause an influx of right-wing members into the Spanish *Falange*. Leaderless (José Antonio had been imprisoned by the government in March and was executed in November), the party was engulfed by conservatism, and powerless to prevent its forcible incorporation into Franco's conservative coalition.

This question of political skill on the part of the leadership touches upon the final set of criteria for the success of fascism: those elements relating to the fascist party itself. Assuming all of the characteristics which can assist its advance are present in a society, they still have to be exploited skilfully if fascism is to be successful. Given the fascist leadership-principle, therefore, the style and quality of a fascist leader is crucial to the movement's fortunes. Not merely must such a figure be charismatic and mystical, but also politically adroit enough to defeat his opponents and to harmonise the feuding factions which exist within all fascist movements. Hitler, of course, was an undisputed genius in this respect. By 1922 he had amalgamated the NSDAP with its rivals and had established himself as the dictatorial head of the party. He then proceeded to win power by outmanoeuvering opponents whilst continuing to hold together the contradictory elements of his own party. Mussolini also showed a considerable degree of political cunning in defeating rivals within his party and opponents outside it. In Spain José Antonio managed to merge his *Falange* with the *Juntas de Offensiva Nacional Sindicalista,* Spain's original fascist party, and quickly assumed the leadership of the new movement. Had his premature death not robbed Europe of one of fascism's most able leaders it would have been fascinating to have observed how he might have dealt with the reactionary conservatism represented by Franco and the army rebellion.

Mussolini and Hitler also had an advantage in that they originated from humble origins and could, therefore, speak the language of the masses. Most other fascist leaders, including Degrelle, Codreanu, Sźálasi, Mussert and Quisling came from professional backgrounds. Some, like José Antonio and Mosley, were from the ranks of the aristocracy and, despite their intellectual and oratorical skills, they suffered from a lack of credibility in projecting themselves as men of the people. For an ideology as overtly populist as fascism this was a serious failing.

The quality of leadership also affected the degree to which fascism was tailored to suit the traditions of a particular nation. Owing to the extreme nationalism inherent within the ideology it was of vital importance, particularly after 1933, that native fascisms were not perceived either as foreign imports or subservient creatures of a foreign power. Speer remembered that Hitler considered many of Europe's fascist leaders (including Mosley) as 'mere copyists who had no original or new ideas', and who would come to nothing. In every country, he argued, 'you had to start from different premises and change your methods accordingly'.[70] Certainly many, if not all, of Europe's fascist movements aped the successful fascist regimes too closely in a world where international relationships were rapidly deteriorating. Ironically Hitler was pleased with the failure of fascist movements abroad for he recognised that fascist success in a country would result in a strengthening of its nationalist resolve which could only be detrimental to the interests of Germany.[71] Whereas Mussolini made financial donations to many foreign fascist movements and, as suggested, toyed with the idea of establishing a fascist international; Hitler would have none of it. His support of foreign fascist parties was very rare and occurred only if they advocated pan-Germanism, and therefore fitted into his expansionist foreign policy. Significantly, in both Rumania and Hungary Hitler supported the stable right-wing authoritarian regimes of Carol and Horthy rather than the more radical manifestations of native fascism. When Carol's regime fell in 1940 it was replaced by Iron-Guard fascism with attendant chaos and destruction as old scores were settled. In January 1941 the German occupying forces supported a conservative coup led by Marshal Ion Antonescu to restore order.[72] It was a dramatic confirmation that the interests of the Third Reich came above those of international fascism.

The extent to which Britain has ever experienced the preconditions for fascist growth is examined in the concluding chapter. At this juncture it need only be stressed that the centrist and therefore contradictory nature of fascism leads to serious internal problems within both the ideology and those movements which adhere to it. But it is also this centrism which enables fascism to project itself as a unifying and harmonising force – a negation of politics – which provides the chief source of its wide potential appeal. Given the conditions outlined above, fascism is capable of spectacular growth. Germany and Italy provided the requisite conditions; other countries provided them in part. Britain, as will be shown, displayed fewer of them than many other nations and consequently the BUF struggled to make any significant headway.

The great irony of fascism remains, however, that even when the preconditions for its growth were ideal and it was able to exploit the breadth of its appeal to the full, its centrist solution to the problems of capitalism was unworkable. Thus, wherever fascism succeeded to power, the regime it produced was characterised not by harmonious centrism, but by increased capitalist exploitation within a framework of conservative dictatorship and individual isolation.

NOTES

1   For an example of this argument see A. Cassels, 'Janus: The Two Faces of Fascism' in H. A. Turner, *Reappraisals of Fascism,* New Viewpoint, New York 1975, pp. 69–92.
2   Comitati d'azione per la universalità di Roma, *Reunion de Montreux,* 16–17 Decembre, 1934, XII, Rome 1935, pp. 40, 87, as cited by M. A. Ledeen, *Universal Fascism,* Howard Fertig, New York 1972, pp. 116, 122.
3   T. Childers, 'The social basis of the national socialist vote', *Journal of Contemporary History,* II, 1976, p. 25.
4   S. Lipset, *Political Man,* Heinemann, London 1963, p. 141.
5   G. Ránki, 'The Fascist Vote in Budapest in 1939', as found in S. U. Larsen, B. Hagtvet & J. P. Myklebust (eds.), *Who Were the Fascists?,* Bergen-Oslo-Fromsø 1980, p. 404.
6   D. Mack Smith, *Italy. A Modern History,* University of Michigan 1959, p. 412.
7   B. Mussolini, *My Autobiography* (trans. R. W. Child), Hurst & Blackett, 1936, p. 224; as quoted in H. R. Kedward, *Fascism in Western Europe, 1900–45* New York University Press 1971, p. 111.
8   See, for example, the support given to Mussolini by the famous US liberal Henry Croly in the *New Republic,* a traditional bastion of liberalism. J. P. Diggins, *Mussolini and Fascism. The View from America,* New Jersey

1972, pp. 227–33.

9   The full programme can be found in J. Noakes & G. Pridham (eds.), *Nazism 1919–45,* vol. I, University of Exeter 1983, pp. 14–15.

10 *Völkischer Beobachter,* 12 June 1920; 2 March and 26 April 1923; as edited by M. H. Kele, *Nazis and Workers,* Chapel Hill 1972, pp. 42–3.

11 Childers, *op. cit.,* p. 26.

12 F. L. Carsten, *The Rise of Fascism,* Methuen London 1970, p. 214. See also Kedward, *op. cit.,* p. 215.

13 For the complete programme see H. Thomas (ed.), *José Antonio Primo de Rivera: Selected Writings,* Jonathan Cape, London 1972, pp. 132–7.

14 P. S. Wandyez, 'Fascism in Poland: 1918–39' as found in P. J. Sugar (ed.), *Native Fascism in the Successor States 1918–45,* California 1971, p. 96.

15 G. Ránki, 'The Problem of Fascism in Hungary', Sugar, *op. cit.,* p. 67.

16 Carsten, *op. cit.,* p. 175.

17 G. L. Weinberg (ed.), *Hitler's Zweites Buch,* Stuttgart 1961, p. 61(f), as cited by Turner, *op. cit.,* p. 136(f).

18 A. Speer, *Inside the Third Reich,* Sphere Books, London 1971, p. 232; see also pp. 122, 247, 253.

19 Turner, *op. cit.,* p. 126.

20 A. F. K. Organski, 'Fascism and Modernisation', as found in S. J. Woolf, (ed.) *The Nature of Fascism,* Weidenfeld and Nicolson, London 1968, pp. 31–3.

21 Instituto Centrale di Statistica, Compendio statistico italianno, vol. 14, Rome, 1940, p. 41, as cited by E. R. Tannenbaum, *Fascism in Italy, Society and Culture 1922–45,* Allen Lane, London 1972, p. 115.

22 W. Carr, *Arms, Autarchy and Aggression,* Edward Arnold, London 1972, p. 19.

23 D. Schoenbaum, *Hitler's Social Revolution: Class and Status in Nazi Germany 1933–39,* New York 1966, p. 285; as quoted by Childers, *op. cit.,* p. 37 (f.46).

24 Carsten, *op. cit.,* pp. 204–18.

25 J. Havronek, 'Fascism in Czechoslovakia'; as found in Sugar, *op. cit.,* pp. 49–55.

26 Tannenbaum, *op. cit.,* pp. 233–4.

27 Cassels; Turner, *op. cit.,* p. 74.

28 *Ibid.,* pp. 69–92.

29 0016/105–6 (8 January 1921), 159, 239, 300–1 (3 May 1921), as cited by D. Mack Smith, *Mussolini,* Weidenfeld & Nicolson, London 1981, p. 43.

30 Noakes & Pridham (eds.), *op. cit.,* p. 16.

31 Cassels; Turner, *op. cit.,* p. 74.

32 *Ibid.,* pp. 80–1.

33 R. J. Roth & C. Schum, 'The Dollfuss – Schuschnigg Regime: Fascist or Authoritarian?', as found in Larsen *et al., op. cit.,* p. 253. See also Carsten, *op. cit.,* p. 228.

34 R. J. Roth, 'Authoritarian Austria', as found in Sugar (ed.), *op. cit.,* p. 26.

35 The *Reichspost* (Vienna), 25 February 1938; pp. 1–6; as quoted by Roth, *ibid.,* p. 24.

36 Carsten, *op. cit.,* p. 173. See also G. Ránki, 'The Problem of Fascism in Hungary', as found in Sugar (ed.), *op. cit.,* p. 68.

37 Ránki; Larsen *et. al., op. cit.,* p. 416.

38 Ránki; Sugar (ed.), *op. cit.,* p. 71.

39 S. Fischer-Galati, 'Fascism in Rumania', as found in Sugar (ed.), *op. cit.,* pp. 114–20.

40 S. Payne, Introduction to 'The Diffusion of Fascism in Southern and Western Europe' as found in Larsen *et al., op. cit.,* p. 421.

41 Letter of 12 July 1936, quoted by B. Nellessen, *José Antonio Primo de Rivera,* Stuttgart 1965, p. 23; as quoted by Carsten, *op. cit.,* p. 201.

42 For an excellent description of Italy's corporate structure see A. Aquarone, 'Italy: the crisis and corporate economy', in *Journal of Contempory History*, IV, 4, October 1969, pp. 37–50.

43 Mack Smith, *Italy. A Modern History*, p. 395.

44 Aquarone, *op. cit.*, p. 50.

45 *Ibid.*, pp. 52–4.

46 P. Capoferri, *Venti anni col fascismo e con syndicati*, Milan 1937, p. 109. *Ibid.*, p. 55.

47 Mario Bandini, *Cento anni di storia agraria italiannia*, 2nd edn, Rome 5 Lune 1963, p. 161; as cited by Tannenbaum, *op. cit.*, pp. 107–9.

48 Giovanni Demaria, '*Il problema industriale italianno*', Giornale degli economisti e rivista di statistica', 3, September–October 1941, p. 533, as cited by Tannenbaum, *op. cit.*, p. 115.

49 Aquarone, *op. cit.*, p. 57.

50 T. Mason, 'Labour in the Third Reich', *Past and Present*, 33, April 1969, p. 114.

51 *Ibid.*, pp. 115–23.

52 Carr, *op. cit.*, p. 51.

53 T.W. Mason, 'The Primacy of Politics – Politics and economics in National Socialist Germany', as found in Woolf, *op. cit.*, p. 176.

54 Mason, 'Labour in the Third Reich', *op. cit.*, p. 128.

55 Speer, *op. cit.*, p. 310.

56 Mason, 'The Primacy of Politics . . .', *op. cit.*, p. 190.

57 *Ibid.*, pp. 184–5.

58 'Kampf alles Bedarfsträger um menschliche Arbeitskräfte, Rohstoffe und Geld' minutes of meeting of Reich Defence Committee, 15 December 1938, *Bundesarchiv Koblenz*, Wil F5, vol. 560/2, p. 5(f), as quoted by Mason, *ibid.*, p. 190.

59 *Ibid.*

60 Speer, *op. cit.*, p. 67.

61 W. S. Allen, 'The Appeal of Fascism and the Problem of National Disintegration', as found in Turner, *op. cit.*, p. 53.

62 A clear impression of this can be gained from the 1928 general election results in Germany. Even at the peak of its popularity over twenty-five per cent of voters supported parties dedicated to the destruction of its constitution. Carsten, *op. cit.*, p. 132.

63 W. S. Allen, *The Nazi Seizure of Power*, Eyre & Spottiswoode, London 1966, p. 275.

64 Carsten, *op. cit.*, p. 53.

65 *Ibid.*, p. 58.

66 *Ibid.*, p. 57.

67 *Ibid.*, p. 109.

68 Kedward, *op. cit.*, p. 208.

69 Allen, *op. cit.*, pp. 133–4.

70 Speer, *op. cit.*, p. 182.

71 *Ibid.*

72 Fischer-Galati; Sugar (ed.), *op. cit.*, pp. 118–20.

CHAPTER 9

The aftermath

. . . Would I have broke this happy dream,
It was a theme
For reason, much too strong for fantasy,
Therefore thou wak'd'st me wisely; yet
My dream thou brok'st not, but continued'st it.

J. Donne, 'The Dream'

Each venture
Is a new beginning, a raid on the inarticulate
With shabby equipment always deteriorating
In the general mess of imprecision of feeling.

T. S. Eliot, 'East Coker'

What is it that touches off a chord in the instincts of the people to whom we seek to appeal? It can often be the most simple and primitive thing. Rather than a speech or printed article it may just be a flag; it may be the sound of a drum; it may be a marching column; it may be a banner or it may just be the impression of a crowd. None of these things contain in themselves one single argument, one single piece of logic. . . . They are recognised as being among the things that appeal to the hidden forces of the human soul.

J. Tyndall, as quoted in
M. Walker, *The National Front*,
Collins, London 1978, p. 145

Shortly before the outbreak of war the government had armed itself with the Emergency Powers Act, which allowed it to pass emergency regulations free of the time-consuming parliamentary process. Thereafter a stream of regulations emerged designed to prevent the incitement or spread of disaffection, and to ensure that the free-born citizens of Britain did not question the wisdom of their leaders who were exhorting them to suffer and die in the struggle against Germany. As one Conservative MP was later moved to comment, the government had equipped itself with '. . . powers which would make Himmler absolutely green with envy'.[1] One element of this draconian legislation was Regulation 18B, which abrogated the ancient right of *habeas corpus* by allowing the Home Secretary to detain any person suspected of hostile origin or association, or of having committed acts prejudicial to the safety of the realm.

Throughout the winter of 1939–40 there were few detentions. In the spring of 1940 came the hugely successful German offensive against western Europe. Denmark, Norway and the Low Countries were over-run, and by late May German tanks had smashed through the Allied lines and reached the English channel. By the end of May the evacuation of the British Expeditionary Force from Dunkirk had begun, and the fall of Paris was imminent. The shock of such military reverses and the fear of invasion provoked elaborate and sometimes comical measures of home defence in Britain. Amongst the least amusing of these was the treatment of those whose loyalty was considered suspect through birth or association.

Space precludes any full examination of wartime detentions. This sordid chapter of clumsy state coercion, of mistakes, mismanagement and mendacity, of casual careless injustices committed against the innocent and then concealed beneath a velvet curtain of secrecy and crude wartime patriotism, provides scope enough for a book in its own right – a book which would expose the myriad of personal tragedies which lay behind bureaucratic errors and indifference.[2] False information or a mistaken identity was enough to cause some victims to languish in prison for an indeterminate period; charged with no offence, with access to no judicial review of their cases. 'Hostile origins' caused many of the 75,000 Germans and Austrians in Britain (the vast majority of whom were anti-fascists who had sought refuge there before 1939) to be locked up as a threat to national security.

Detainees were sometimes deported to Canada or Australia, some being robbed, beaten or even killed *en route*.[3] At best the mass imprisonment was administered with an alarming absence of common humanity. Some of the victims were mere infants, others as old as seventy. Many of the British detainees had fought in the Great War (some even in the Boer War), their scars bearing testament to their loyalty to King and country. Bonds of love were torn asunder, and families shattered, sometimes irrevocably. Some of those detained were disabled before their ordeal; many became so in mind or body as a result of the privations inflicted upon them. Some received premature release through death; the youngest to die in confinement being an infant of eleven months who was born to an interned mother in Holloway prison in January 1941 and who died in a detention camp on the Isle of Man in November of that same year. The entire duration of the child's brief existence was spent within the confines of a British prison. Its only crime had been to be born in the midst of a war which was not of its making, to a German mother who had married and settled in England some years previously.

Unsurprisingly, amongst those of British origin who were detained many were members or associates of the BUF. At a cabinet meeting on 22 May 1940 it had been decided to '... cripple the organisation,' by arresting its leaders. But as Mosley was 'too clever' to commit any overt act of disloyalty, it was deemed necessary to amend 18B accordingly.[4] Later that same day Regulation 18B(1A) was announced, giving the Home Secretary the power to hold indefinitely (subject only to an appearance before an Advisory Committee) any member or associate of any group which was either subject to foreign influences and control, or which had had associations or sympathies with persons in the government of countries with which Britain was now at war. Its sweeping retroactive powers were applicable to members and sympathisers of organisations as diverse as the Communist Party and the Boy Scout movement, but were aimed primarily at the BUF, all of whose members and associates became vulnerable to immediate arrest.

The first wave of arrests occurred on the following day. Mosley, Raven Thomson, Francis-Hawkins, and several other senior officers were detained, and files and documents kept at the party's headquarters were scrutinised for three days.[5] More arrests followed in the ensuing weeks until by late July over 500 members of the BUF were in custody.[6] In the same month the Home Office, having already wound up the BUF's propaganda outlets and publishing concerns, used Regulation 18AA (designed to control hostile organisations) to liquidate what little remained of Britain's largest fascist movement.[7] By the beginning of November the number of internees with BUF connections had risen to 700, but thereafter the total fell gradually until by the autumn of 1944 only a handful remained.[8] The common perception of the BUF as a potential, if not active, nest of traitors had little real foundation. The party's pre-war foreign policy, whilst accepting a degree of common interest between fascist nations, had never involved disloyalty to Britain or subservience to foreign fascist influences. As suggested in chapter 7, the BUF advocated armed isolationism from within a strong, self-contained empire, and had always expressed a willingness to fight any power which threatened British interests. Central to this belief was the idea that Britain and an expanding Germany could coexist peacefully with neither posing a threat to the other's security. This doctrine of isolationism from a position of strength was preached throughout the decade, usually with a high degree of logical coherence and based upon a rational foundation of genuine patriotism. Before September 1939 the

BUF had gone to considerable lengths to convince the public that war was unnecessary; after the outbreak of war these efforts continued, but the party also attempted to differentiate between opposition to the war and support for the enemy. The former had a heritage which read like the roll-call of respectable British radicalism and included Chatham, Burke, Fox, Cobden, Bright, Lloyd George, Keir Hardie, and MacDonald; whilst the latter clearly amounted to treason. It was in pursuance of this end that the BUF published an unequivocal message in the first wartime edition of *Action* from Mosley to his supporters: 'Our country is involved in war. Therefore I ask you to do nothing to injure our country or to help any other Power. Our members should do what the law requires of them and if they are members of the Forces or Services of the Crown, they should obey their orders and, in every particular, obey the rules of their Service.'[9] All connections with William Joyce (who had begun a broadcasting career which was to lead him to the gallows) since March 1937 were correctly denied, and the party went to great lengths to disclaim the receipt of any foreign funds.[10] With the military situation deteriorating rapidly in early May 1940, Mosley promised that in the event of an invasion of Britain '. . . every member of British Union would be at the disposal of the nation. Every one of us would resist the foreign invader with all that is in us. . . .'[11]

Would the BUF's members have reacted in such a manner? Certainly it would have been consistent with their unquestionable patriotism, but there is little evidence to provide even the basis for informed speculation. It is interesting, however, to note that there were few instances of seditious or treasonable activity involving current members of the BUF either before or after its suppression. Similarly there is no evidence to support the view that Mosley was a potential Quisling waiting in the wings for a foreign army to establish him as the ruler of his defeated nation. To the end of his life Mosley himself had been adamant as to how he would have reacted to a German invasion. 'I would have gone straight back into the professional army and put on a uniform again and fought against the Germans. I would have been killed or, if the country had collapsed, taken prisoner, but I would have certainly done nothing to help the invader.'[12] It is difficult to conceive of Mosley as the puppet of a foreign power. His arrogance as much as his patriotism would surely have prevented it. But then it is also difficult to imagine him spurning the offer of power if the conditions were acceptable. By 1940 he had spent the best part of a decade locked in a struggle with a government and a system which he had come to despise, and in so doing he had sacrificed a promising political career. By leaving the Labour Party he had thrown away the prospect of achieving high office; would his will-power have proved sufficiently strong to have done so for a second time in 1940? Could Caesar have once again passed up a crown on offer?

Could such an offer by the Nazis have been made sufficiently tempting by including within it the possibility of real power? Would Mosley have been allowed to fall alive into enemy hands? These are all intriguing if unaswerable questions.

The depth of Mosley's sincerity in this, as in so many other areas, will never be known. The state spurned his pleas to join the army or to live under house arrest upon his farm where he could be 'useful' rather than 'a nuisance to my country',[13] preferring instead to keep him in prison. He appealed in the name of honour for the opportunity to answer publicly the charges against him,[14] but from a Home Secretary whose intellectual mediocrity he had been in conflict with since the days when they were both in the Labour Party he received an unsympathtic hearing. When the matter was finally discussed by the war cabinet in April 1943, Morrison took refuge in an insistence upon the internationalist nature of fascism. He concluded, therefore, that 'the success of British Union was bound up with the success of the Axis Powers', and remained convinced that 'by breaking up the British Union we smashed an incipient Fifth Column'.[15]

Initially the conditions under which the internees were remanded were appalling. They were later moderated to the extent whereby they became simply unpleasant. In theory the prisoners were to be treated as though on remand, but in practice few such privileges were available to ameliorate the cold, cramped, unhygenic conditions of their detention.

In May 1941 the bulk of the remaining detainees were moved to the Isle of Man where a male and female internment camp had each been established. No married quarters existed and, therefore, married couples held in detention remained forcibly separated. Conditions were harsh and the only alternative to enforced tedium was menial labour within the camp or on neighbouring farms where the renumeration for an eight-hour day was between sixpence and a shilling.[16]

Senior members of the BUF were retained in Brixton in order to prevent them influencing their followers. Here, too, conditions improved gradually as the regulations were relaxed to allow a considerable degree of free association. Mosley spent much of his time reading avidly (although he had access only to those books which were considered suitable by the authorities) and learning German. From February 1941 those prisoners whose wives had been detained also were allowed to visit them once a fortnight in Holloway. Eleven months later most of the fifteen married couples still in detention were allowed to live together. For the Mosleys this meant the establishment of a home within a disused wing of Holloway prison. Here they had facilities for cooking, could buy food from outside, and employ other prisoners as servants. In his new surroundings Mosley received visits from former political comrades, including Maxton, Boothby, and Harold Nicolson, as well as from his son,

Nicolas, who was a frequent guest, who often stayed late and had to be smuggled out of a side entrance.[17]

The one supposed safeguard against the arbitrary power of the Home Secretary was the right of the accused to appear before an Advisory Committee, the workings of which were hardly a tribute to British justice. Under Star Chamber conditions, which flouted completely the rules of evidence established within the judicial system and weighted the procedure heavily in favour of the authorities, the prisoner was interviewed. He was often given little notice of his appearance, and no specific charges, witnesses or evidence were produced against him. He was denied legal representation and access to information pertinent to his case. On the basis of one such meeting the committee made a recommendation to the Home Secretary as to whether the victim should continue in detention. Even in the unlikely event of an internee managing to convince the Advisory Committee that he was not a threat to national security he was still a very long way from securing his release. The purpose of the committee was to make recommendations only, and it had no power to force the Home Secretary to accept its findings. By July 1941 Morrison had overruled the committee on 132 occasions: in 126 of these the result was that the individuals concerned were detained in custody by Morrison in direct contradiction to the specific advice of the committee which had examined them.[18]

The panic of May 1940, induced by military catastrophe, was understandable as a catalyst for the 18B detentions. But the Luftwaffe's failure to gain air superiority over Britain, followed in June 1941 by the German invasion of the USSR ensured that there would be no serious attempt to launch an invasion of Britain in the foreseeable future. There was little scope therefore, for effective fifth columnist activities, which meant that the continued detention of the internees took on the unmistakeable air of being punitive rather than simply preventative. Some of the more obvious punitive aspects sprang from the initial lack of resources or from bureaucratic pettiness and the over-zealous adherence to regulations. On a general level this included primitive washing and hygiene facilities and the confiscation of personal effects, such as watches and even toothbrushes. On an individual level bureaucratic insensitivity produced needless suffering, as in the case of one detainee who was refused permission to visit his dying mother, and was not even informed of her death until four days after the event.[19]

Some of the punitive aspects of detention were also orchestrated by Morrison, who admitted that the unseemly delays between the receipt of a recommendation from the Advisory Committee and his final decision regarding an individual case were in part the result of a deliberate policy. Morrison's judgement was coloured by his loathing of the BUF and by a bond of hatred between he and Mosley which had matured poisonously for almost two decades.[20] He was also influenced by a genuine desire to avoid provoking public disquiet and opposition from the left of the Labour Party by being seen to be lenient towards British fascists.

Mosley's eventual release in November 1943 was the result of his declining health. Several doctors were convinced that the thrombophlebitis from which he was suffering could damage his health permanently, or even prove fatal, if his detention was continued. Wishing to avoid his martydom, and perhaps moved by some degree of genuine compassion, the cabinet decided that he could be liberated on condition that his geographical whereabouts remained strictly regulated and that he made no public statements nor engaged in any kind of political activity.[21] There was a storm of protest from the left, particularly from the Communist Party, whose hatred of their pre-war arch enemy had not been diminished by his years of imprisonment. Immediately a campaign was launched to get Mosley re-interned. It petered out eventually and the Mosleys were able to settle quietly in the country and enjoy a comfortable existence for the remainder of the war. Many less exalted members of the BUF, who did not have aristocratic family connections with the Churchills and other members of the ruling class, were less fortunate. Some remained in prison, including those who were ill but unable to afford the fees of a royal physician to testify to the state of their health. Others found that the stigma of internment followed them into civilian life and that a release from detention did not result in freedom. Frequently their identity cards were endorsed to indicate they had been in custody, which caused difficulties in finding employment after their release. Some were refused unemployment benefit, and amongst those lucky enough to find work there was at least one instance of the police visiting an employer to inform him of his employee's detention.[22] The result was that for many of those unable to draw upon social and financial resources comparable to those possessed by Mosley, life after internment involved hardship and prejudice.

In retrospect Mosley claimed to feel no great bitterness against those responsible for his confinement, which he used for intensive intellectual study, uninterrupted by the demands of active politics. As though unable to admit the extent of the 'Old Gang's' triumph he rationalised the pain and humiliation of his own defeat: 'Plato used to say that a man in the middle of his life should withdraw from life for a few years and go back to university. Well I would never have done it, of course, but prison gave me that chance . . . intellectually it was an immense advantage to me – not intended by my opponents. It greatly strengthened me.'[23] His main objection was one of principle to the loss of individual liberties, and especially the right of *habeas corpus*. Given his own fascist philosophy and programme, however, one cannot help feeling that such a complaint involved at least an element of transcendental morality, if not flagrant hypocrisy.

The post-war world into which Mosley and his followers emerged was hardly the most conducive environment within which to sustain a revival of fascism. Even after the state's wartime restraints on political activity were lifted, there remained fascism's appalling legacy, in the shape of shattered continents and the images and appartus of industrial genocide. Fascism, it seemed, would have to be rebuilt upon a foundation of corpses.

Initially Mosley's supporters were scattered amongst numerous, semi-autonomous book clubs and discussion groups. The most dedicated of his followers had already begun to revive pre-war activities in the East End in the form of the British League of Ex-Servicemen, under Jeffrey Hamm. To begin with, Mosley refrained from active involvement. He founded a publishing corporation and attempted a justification of his opposition to the war by reprinting *Tomorrow We Live,* and by producing *My Answer.* He also distributed a regular newsletter to keep in touch with his scattered followers. His return to politics began in the autumn of 1947 with the publication of his new vision: *The Alternative.* This statement of the post-war creed was followed by a meeting in Memorial Hall to explain his new ideas. In February 1948 his return to the political fray was confirmed with the official launch of the Union Movement.

The policy of the new movement was based upon that which had been outlined in *The Alternative.* Much was similar to the BUF's pre-war programme, including the concept of a strong executive intervening in the nation's economy in order to secure class co-operation, which, as suggested, represents the essence of fascist ideology. The same twin enemies of international finance and communism were attacked; the same appeals were made to 'assert the right and will of the whole British people above every faction', and 'to create a new sense of service and a new morality in the State'.[24] But there were important differences also. Corporatism was dispensed with on the grounds that it was too bureaucratic. Government was to exercise control over the economy through a wage-price mechanism: a form of compulsory incomes policy, within a tightly insulated economic sphere where production and consumption could be raised scientifically and kept in perfect equilibrium, where profits could be guaranteed, and class harmony achieved. Within this framework capitalist free enterprise would be allowed to operate with minimal interference from the state,[25] and the elimination of restrictive and expensive bureaucracy would result in vast tax reductions for workers and employers alike.

It was a programme which reflected the centrist, underconsumptionist analysis at which Mosley had arrived in the 1920s and which he had maintained throughout his fascist years. It involved the same mixture of dynamic, productive capitalism, with a dash of radicalism in the form of hostility towards finance capital, restrictions on inherited wealth, and the replacement of state-owned nationalised industries by a form of workers' participatory 'guild socialism' whereby each would receive '. . . a personal share in the results of his own endeavours'.[26] But it represented also a shift back towards a more voluntary form of class collaboration than had been aimed at in the 1930s. This shift was visible also in the new party's oft-stated commitment to the sacrosant nature of democratic liberties, and its pledge to win power 'by the vote of the people'.[27] Given the legacy of the war this rejection of overt authoritarianism was essential if the movement was to stand any chance of popular growth. Beneath the surface, however, lurked state compulsion as the final arbiter in all matters. Trade unions, for instance, were invited to play an important role with employers' federations in administering the welfare state (which was to be restructured on a more contributory basis) as well as in the economy in general. But any resistance towards government control of wages, they were warned, would result in a violent showdown with the full force of the state.[28] For as Mosley had explained so often in his years as a fascist, governments must have the authority and the power to implement their chosen programmes.

The most strikingly original feature of the Union Movement's programme was the replacement of nationalism with pan-Europeanism. This was not considered a form of internationalism, which the party continued to eschew, but rather an extension of patriotism through the realistic recognition that an impoverished Britain, stripped of empire, could not hope to compete alone in a world divided between two superpowers. The only hope for independence lay in unity with Europe, for only a united Europe would have sufficient strength to stand outside the power blocs of East and West. Europe, together with approximately one-third of Africa (primarily the south and east) was to replace the empire in forming the insulated unit so central to Mosley's economic analysis. The remaining African land mass was to be given over to black independence. Thus, rather than having apartheid within Africa, the continent as a whole was to be partitioned into strictly preserved white and black areas. The great global power blocs would each, therefore, have its own sphere of interest (Europe and Africa; the USSR and Asia; and USA and the Americas) within which the others would refrain from interfering. Immediately the United Nations Organisation would become redundant and would be replaced by direct negotiations between the great powers: the method of conducting international relations preferred by the BUF.

Even if the commitments to liberal rights and the democratic process are taken at face value, the programme smacked of fascism. It was typical of Mosley's inventiveness and mental agility, however, that it should have been a form of fascism amended to take account of the post-war world rather than a simple restatement of past beliefs. For Mosley it represented an ideology which went 'far beyond Fascism and Democracy'.[29] Some past BUF pamphlets were still sold, however, and occasionally the fascist lineage was shyly acknowledged. Fascism, it was suggested, had been an unsuccessful nationally-associated attempt to break free from a crisis-ridden system of international finance. When the crisis inevitably returned, it was predicted, Europe as a whole, led by dedicated men from all nations, would shatter its fetters and succeed where fascism had failed. Fascism, it was boasted, '. . . in the national sense may be dead; but a new Movement is uniting these elements in defence of Europe, which have fought for a generation against the Soviet menace, and once in a disunited Europe engaged in internicine strife flung the Red Army back 600 miles into the Russian Steppes'.[30]

Aside from such oblique references to the Nazi war effort there were other indicators of the Union Movement's pre-war ancestry. The party newspaper, *Union,* openly admitted to having incorporated *Action,* and used the same format, style and even the BUF's flash and circle motif. Through its columns it blasted away at favourite pre-war targets. The USSR was perennially popular in this respect and was portrayed as a brutal army of occupation within eastern Europe and, aided and abetted by its hireling communist parties of the West, as a formidable threat to Western civilisation. During the Berlin blockade Mosley wrote demanding that before 'oriental communism is ready to strike', the West should insist upon Russia's withdrawal from Europe and disarmament subject to Western verification. 'If the Bolsheviks refuse to accept this ultimatum, they should be assailed with the atom bomb and with all other weapons of modern science which the Western nations possess, but which the Soviets do not yet possess.'[31] The 'Old Gang', of course, were belaboured in the usual fashion, particularly the Labour Party. There were some hostile references to Jews also, but nothing which approached either the venom or the scope of the pre-war anti-Semitic verbiage.

The new movement resembled the structure of the BUF although it was less centralised and less overtly militaristic. Old faces predominated, the most prominent of whom was Alexander Raven Thomson, party secretary until his death in 1955, when he was succeeded by Hamm.[32] Old quarrels resurfaced too, especially in the East End, where organised opposition to Union Movement meetings and marches led to renewed violence and a new banning order by the Home Secretary which covered much of north-east London. Predictably, the party was outraged and complained that '. . . a large part of London is now scheduled as a Jewish protected area in which English men and women are to be deprived of their civil rights, because the exercise of those rights is provocative to an alien minority'.[33] Amidst a welter of claims, counter-claims and bitter recriminations concerning civil rights and provocation, it appeared to be just like old times. But appearances were deceptive. The scale of the Union Movement's operation was tiny in comparison to that of the BUF, for even at its height in the late 1950s it probably never exceeded 1,500 members. Assured by Mosley of the imminence of crisis, his minute band of adherents struggled on in the face of an undesirable wartime legacy, full employment and growing prosperity, and competition for membership from other quarters.

The most serious source of competition initially came from the League of Empire Loyalists established in 1954 by A. K. Chesterton, an erstwhile BUF member. The LEL was a reactionary rather than a fascist organisation. Amongst its Tory membership, however, it did offer a home to some of the nationalists, racists and anti-Semites who had previously been associated with the BUF. Its programme included a stalwart defence of the British Empire and British sovereignty, hostility towards international finance, and opposition to the steady trickle of non-white immigrants into Britain and to the power of international Judaism. The implacable belief in an international Jewish conspiracy bent on world domination shared by Chesterton and many others within the movement was more in the tradition of Arnold Leese than Oswald Mosley. Through skilfully organised stunts the party achieved a degree of publicity disproportionate to its actual size. Even at its peak it remained small, probably failing to exceed 3,000 members,[34] for Chesterton preferred to use it as a flamboyant, elitist Conservative Party pressure group, rather than attempt to build a genuine mass movement.

The LEL contracted rapidly from the late 1950s, wrecked by financial problems and internal splits. Its significance in terms of post-war fascism, however, lay in its provision of a stamping ground for almost all of the new generation of British fascist and neo-fascist leaders. Martin Webster, John Tyndall, John Bean, and Colin Jordan were all members of the LEL in the mid-1950s. Jordan, in particular, was an obsessive anti-Semite, a self-confessed racist and admirer of Hitler, and the spiritual heir of Arnold Leese with whom he had been in close contact since 1946.[35] It was these figures who, towards the end of the 1950s, began to flex their administrative muscles independently in an attept to create organisations more closely tailored to their own needs than was Chesterton's Tory ginger group. The year 1958 saw the establishment of Jordan's White Defence League, and also of the National Labour Party with Andrew Fountaine as its titular head and Bean and Tyndall as founder members. Rather than presenting a coherent fascist programme in the style of Mosley, both organisations preferred to exist within a farrago of white racism and anti-Semitic fantasies of an international Jewish conspiracy designed to destroy the 'Nordic race' and with it the British nation.

The growth of these organisations coincided with the rise of immigration as a public issue, and an increasing number of racial disturbances in those areas where black immigrants had settled. This trend culminated in the Notting Hill race riots of September 1958. Like all immigrants they tended for reasons of security (both pyschological and material) to live in close proximity of each other in well-defined areas of the major cities. This, together with the real acceleration of non-white immigration as the economic boom of the late 1950s[36] hungrily demanded new sources of cheap labour, often created the impression that immigrants were more numerous than was in fact the case. All too often this impression was heightened by the different lifestyles, customs, diet, language and culture of the immigrants. It was a similar cycle, producing similar patterns as had been caused by Jewish immigration in the late nineteenth and early twentieth centuries. Unsurprisingly it became a new source of inspiration to post-war British fascists.

The Union Movement had expressed its hostility towards non-white immigration since the early 1950s. The immigrants were seen as bewildered victims torn from their natural environment to satiate the greed of finance capital which was importing them in order to undercut domestic wage rates. But they were portrayed also as dark racial stereotypes; unclean, violent, and sexually threatening. Miscegenation was condemned as unnatural and highly undesirable. References were made to the high illegitimacy rates '. . . in the crowded, sweltering tenements of the "black belts" of our big cities',[37] where, it was claimed, '. . . decent married women are afraid to go out alone at nights'.[38]

Since 1951 Mosley had been living mainly abroad in France and Ireland learning to be a true European and waiting with millenial faith for the crisis which would create the necessary preconditions for the revival of his moribund party. The growth of immigration as a public issue and the riots of 1958 lured him home to full-time active politics. The area he chose to concentrate upon was North Kensington, which encompassed Notting Hill, scene of the worst disturbances. Inevitably Mosley denied any intention to inflame the situation further, but with a general election imminent he felt duty-bound to give the electors '. . . the opportunity to express legally and peacefully by their votes what they felt about the issues involved . . .'.[39] It was an appeal for votes, not violence, he stressed repeatedly, but was unwilling to acknowledge that, as in the East End two decades previously, the two could not always be separated.

Even before his candidature was officially announced the Union Movement was active in North Kensington preparing the ground with meetings and provocatively racist speeches. In March Jeffrey Hamm protested over the prison sentences imposed upon a gang of Teddy boys convicted of racial violence during the previous year's riots. Armed with iron bars they had set out on what was afterwards admitted to be a 'nigger-hunting' expedition, which involved a series of random attacks upon innocent black bystanders. Holding aloft a picture of the convicted criminals culled from the press, Hamm declared them to be '. . . some of the finest faces you could wish to see in Britain'.[40] In April Mosley's candidature was announced at a well-attended public meeting; within a week, in the same area, a white gang had beaten three blacks and stabbed one in the back.[41] Before the end of May the first fatality had occurred when Kelso Benjamin Cochrane, a young black carpenter engaged to be married, was stabbed to death by a white gang in a North Kensington street on Whit Sunday.[42]

It is true that Mosley advocated the full Union Movement programme, complete with class harmony, economic dynamism and European unity. It is true also, however, that the racial element of the programme (including the compulsory repatriation of immigrants and the prohibition of mixed marriages) assumed a disproportionate degree of prominence. It was this which drew thunderous applause from his audiences and which dominated their questions to the platform.[43] Mosley, as has been emphasised by his apologists, was careful not to endorse violence against black people, and on occasions actually condemned it. They were the victims of ruthless exploitation, it was explained, whereby they were driven by unemployment and starvation from the West Indies to the slums of Britain where they were forced to work long hours for poor wages. Their repatriation would be humanely conducted, with passages paid for by the state and new government investment in the West Indies to ensure that jobs and decent homes could be provided for them upon their return. Yet behind this elegant verbal façade Mosley was not averse to employing the racist language and sentiments of the gutter on those occasions where he thought he could get away with it. Inner-city problems such as poor public amenities or the acute housing shortage were equated directly with the presence of immigrants whom, it was suggested, considered Britain 'a spongers' paradise'.[44] From the platform of his numerous street meetings Mosley entertained his audiences with lurid tales of teenage white girls kept as slaves by gangs of black men, or explanations as to how black workers could undercut white wage rates because of their ability to survive on a tin of cat food.[45]

As with anti-Semitism Mosley wished to exploit the appeal of racism without besmirching himself with its odium: to fish in a cesspool without smelling of excrement. As with anti-Semitism Mosley's hypocrisy and sheer, cold-blooded cynicism damn him more finally than any of the deluded creatures who genuinely believed the racial nonsense which he helped to peddle. At North Kensington he proved once again that no vehicle was too low for him to stoop to if he felt that it could be exploited to his advantage.

By polling day in October, Mosley and his canvassers had managed to convince each other that their months of labour would be rewarded with a narrow victory. In the event, however, he finished bottom of the poll with 2,821 votes,[46] a derisory eight per cent of the total. For the first time in his life Mosley had lost his deposit and suffered public humiliation at the hands of a returning officer. His response was to retreat once again to France where he would spend increasingly lengthy periods between his sporadic bouts of active politics in Britain.

Others too had been peddling the poison of racial hatred in areas of heavy immigration such as Notting Hill in the late 1950s. A representative of Jordan's White Defence League stated unashamedly that 'I loathe Blacks. We are fighting a war to get them out of Britain. They spread disease and vice . . . and the whole future of the British race is in danger.'[47] The WDL worked closely with the National Labour Party to promote vicious anti-Semitism and white 'Nordic' racism. The Welfare State was attacked on the grounds thut it gave child benefits to blacks '. . . for the coffee coloured monstrosities they father . . . material rewards are given to enable semi-savages to mate with the women of one of the leading civilised nations of the world'.[48] This close relationship between the WDL and the NLP was cemented in 1960 by their amalgamation to form the British National Party, with Fountaine as its president and the widow of Arnold Leese as vice-president. The nation was under threat from Jewish controlled international finance and communism, and from racial mongrelisation, it was suggested, the only road to salvation lay through the establishment of 'a Racial-Nationalist Folk State'.[49]

But all was not well within the party for there were elements, particularly those around Jordan such as his elite Spearhead corps, which continued to display overtly Nazi paramilitary tendencies. Not unreasonably there were many in the party who considered this a liability for a supposedly British movement. This was a rift which was to run throughout post-war British fascism. It was never a clear ideological split, but rather a difference of presentation between those who wished to concentrate primarily upon the issue of white racism and present it within a British tradition, and those like Jordan who wanted to give anti-Semitism its rightful position of prominence and to glory openly in the Nazi tradition. In each case there was a marked difference with the Union Movement which was prepared to use racism but never to the same uncompromising degree. It was denounced by Jordan as a party which '. . . is not and never has been a genuine racialist organisation'.[50]

The political differences between Bean and Jordan were

aggravated by personal hostility, with the result that Jordan, Tyndall and Webster split from the movement in 1962 and, on the seventy-third anniversary of Hitler's birth, inaugurated the National Socialist Movement. This tiny sect was proud of its Nazi heritage and boasted of its belief in 'orthodox national socialism' and its intention to organise itself '. . . on the system in Germany between 1933–45'.[51] It displayed an obsessive concern with Aryan blood which was perceived as the source of past and future British greatness. Therefore, it was claimed, 'it is the first duty of the state to protect and improve this blood'.[52] The diabolically clever Jew was portrayed as bent upon destroying this sacred British treasure through mongrelisation, communist subversion, and the propagation of alcohol, narcotics, tobacco, pornography, rock and roll music, and a host of other indulgences whereby the body's strength could be sapped and its blood adulterated.[53] The solution proposed by the NSM was an authoritarian, puritanical, capitalist state organised upon the fascist leadership principle.

At every opportunity Tyndall and Jordan trumpeted their anti-Semitism. Nazi genocide was denied as a Jewish lie,[54] the discredited *Protocols* were cited as evidence of a world conspiracy, and pre-war IFL pamphlets were openly sold by the party. At a rally in Trafalgar Square in 1962 the press reported that 'the outpourings of hate for the Jews were perhaps the vilest speeches made in Trafalgar Square since the 1930s'.[55] These outpourings included Tyndall's memorable claim that 'In our democratic society, the Jew is like a poisonous maggot feeding off a body in an advanced state of decay.'[56] The meeting ended in a riot as outrageous opponents attacked the platform. Both Tyndall and Jordan received short prison sentences for the provocative nature of their speeches, and longer terms at the end of the year on charges connected with the training and equipment of a paramilitary force.

After the disappointment of the 1959 election Mosley's political commitment had become rather spasmodic. There were still some well-attended indoor meetings (although halls had once again become difficult to hire) and rallies in Trafalgar Square, and some unsuccessful electoral forays. The movement continued to pledge itself to repatriation and to condemn intermarriage on the grounds that it would produce 'a country of mongrels'.[57] Mosley, however, spent an increasing amount of his time abroad, aloof from the daily grind of party activity. Some of this time he spent renewing the fascist and neo-fascist contacts he had made in Europe, Argentina and South Africa shortly after the war. It was from amongst this unsavoury residue that a conference was organised in Venice in 1962 which, after some debate, accepted Mosley's vision of European unity. Europe was to have a common parliament with a strong executive, although national parliaments were to retain authority over domestic affairs. Within this new bloc, free from the military presence of the USSR and the USA, and from entanglement within the United Nations Organisation, prosperity and harmony would be ensured through the wage-price mechanism, selective workers' control, and integration with white Africa.[58]

It was, of course, no more than a paper agreement; a declaration of intent signed by men who lacked the power even to begin moving towards its objectives. Besides, the old thorn of nationalism proved too deeply embedded in such men to be so easily dispensed with, and attempts to create a common European movement foundered accordingly. Even within the Union Movement old-style fascist nationalism reared its ugly head with increasing frequency. In 1963 the government was castigated for standing idly by whilst, as a result of civil unrest in south-east Asia, the British flag was 'insulted', an embassy sacked, and Britons were beaten and their property stolen. Fear of the Chinese was no reason for British governmental inertia, it was claimed, for 'the Chinese have no nuclear weapons to use against us . . . this gives us in Asia a hand free from nuclear fear. We should use it quite ruthlessly to restore the British name and to salvage British interests.'[59] Yet according to the party's oft-stated spheres of influence Britain had neither motive nor right to make such an intervention in Asia. Other aspects, too, of pre-war fascism resurfaced within the movement, not least its clear affirmation of the leadership-principle, and the hint of old-style corporatism in the commitment to change the electoral system in favour of an occupational franchise which would lead to 'a truer democracy'.[60] In the light of such trends it is difficult to avoid the conclusion that the grandiose ideas of European unity and the pledges to individual freedoms were nothing more than economic and political expedients forming a façade which, whilst recognising the realities of the post-war world, obscured a fascist perspective which remained basically unaltered.

Despite Mosley's paper alliances, the reality of life for his party was increasingly bleak in the early 1960s. Waiting for the economic crisis to sweep it into power there was little to be done in the interim period other than to declaim bitterly against the degeneracy of contemporary society. An attempt at renewed activity in the wake of the Venice Declaration and the NSM's violent Trafalgar Square rally led to an escalation in the level of violent opposition encountered by Mosley. In July and August 1962 Union Movement meetings and marches were broken up by hostile crowds in several parts of the country, and Mosley was felled physically on two occasions. Eventually he recognised his defeat and called off his speaking tour, trying to salvage some pride by claiming that the growth of television had rendered the traditional political meeting obsolete. Mosley also tried to distance himself from the Jordan—Leese strain of 'crackpot' fascism, whose doctrines he denounced as alient to Britain and based on the fundamental misapprehension that the Nazis had achieved power through anti-Semitism, whereas in fact they had risen on a wave of economic crisis.[61] He condemned utterly the Nazi extermination programme, and of Jordan's Hitler-worshipping tendencies wrote caustically that 'there is always something tragically comic in the spectacle of live dwarves posturing in the clothes of dead giants'.[62]

Despite such efforts, however, the publicity created by the NSM together with old scores and pre-war regulations, created a surge of anti-fascist activity which swept Mosley from the streets for the last time. His organisation no longer had the resources or the will to resist. From 1963 the Union Movement declined terminally. With Mosely abroad *Action* became thin, irregular, and subject to a seemingly permanent financial crisis until it was wound up finally in May 1964. The party lacked the resources to participate in the 1964 general election, a decision defended weakly on the grounds of not wishing to split those votes in favour of Britain's independent nuclear deterrent, without which, it was claimed, the nation would be reduced to colonial status. Until the bitter end the movement was claiming to '. . . put country before party. Patriotism before division.'[63] A last spasm of activity occurred during the 1966 general election when Mosley stood as a candidate for Shoreditch and Finsbury where he polled a derisory 1,600 votes: 4·6 per cent of the total.[64] This was his last defeat. Now seventy years old, he turned over the party's leadership to a five-member directory and detached himself from active politics '. . . in order to advocate a policy and action which is beyond party'.[65]

The party became a dwindling band of old retainers dedicated to preserving the memory of Mosley. The leader lived out his remaining days in France, exploiting the rare instances of coverage given to him by the British media to the full. His views remained essentially unaltered, with economic reconstruction through a 'consensus of the nation'[66] as his primary objective, to be achieved by a government of 'national union, drawn from all that is best and most vital in the nation'.[67] A government of limited duration (for eventually Britain would unite with Europe) which, whilst being subject to the will of the people, would have the independence of action and the authority to 'make Britain strong and fit again'.[68] The views were frequently expressed with all the old power and capacity, but few now listened, for the forces of British fascism lay in other hands. His peaceful death in Orsay in December 1980 went largely unnoticed other than by those who chose to use it as an illustration of the calamitous consequences of political impetuousity.

In the mid-1960s, without the influence of Mosley, the fascist and racist groups within Britain began to move steadily towards a new unity. Jordan's overt Nazism continued to isolate him from this process and to frustrate many of those around him. In 1964 Tyndall, Webster and the more realistic elements of the NSM abandoned him amid a welter of recriminations, accusations, and mutal expulsions, to form the Greater Britain Movement. Its programme, although allegedly less Nazi-oriented, was unapologetically rascist and aimed at establishing an authoritarian National Socialist government in Britain which would shoulder its responsibility for the preservation of the race through the prohibition of marriage between Britons and non-Aryans, the sterilisation of defectives, and the removal of Jews from Britain.[69] Jordan ignored the split and maintained his obsession with Hitler, but even he by 1967 had come to recognise the propaganda value of home-grown rather than foreign ideological roots (if only in appearance) and changed the NSM's name accordingly to the British Movement. His following remained small and isolated, however, although frequently the BM, through its vicious propaganda and its violence, attracted a degree of publicity beyond that warranted by its size. But it was amongst Jordan's erstwhile colleagues that a new alignment took place which produced a greater degree of unity within British fascism than had been achieved at any time since the 1930s.

The National Front was established in 1967 under the leadership of Chesterton, after months of delicate inter-party negotiations. At its inception it included around 1,500 members and was an amalgamation of the League of Empire Loyalists, the British National Party, and the Racial Preservation Society (an independent white racist pressure group). Despite attempts by the more conservative elements of the LEL to exclude known Nazis, Tyndall, Webster, and the bulk of the membership of the Greater Britain Movement soon joined the new party. For the next decade the NF was to dominate the twilight world of racist and fascist politics.

The authoritarian centrism so characteristic of fascism was clearly visible within the NF's political analysis and its programme. It presented itself as a supra-class, supra-party mass movement capable of restoring national unity through the elimination of '. . . the insidious disease of class warfare'.[70] Whereas the traditional parties were the representatives of class interests, and therefore incapable of reconciling class conflicts, the NF projected itself as '. . . a new party of the character that can capture a majority following from both sides of the present political spectrum'.[71] This centrist approach would enable the reconciliation of class hostility through synthesis, it was claimed, thereby restoring the social and economic harmony of Tudor England, which had been the foundation of past English greatness. As with the BUF the party's centrism was of an authoritarian nature, although this, like the label 'fascism', was frequently denied by those who wished to minimise those aspects of the pre-war legacy which would handicap the new movement's growth. Commitments were made to the preservation of individual rights and the parliamentary system, yet the party also pledged itself to drive political opponents out of public life and to replace degenerate liberalism and its sham democracy with strong leadership. In the past fascism 'may well have gone too far' in its quest for order at the expense of personal freedom, but liberalism had most certainly offended in the opposite direction.[72] Therefore, it was suggested, a synthesis of these two ideologies was required to produce '. . . a revolution of ideas within the British people which will lead to the abandonment of liberal softness and to the recapture of *National Pride, Willpower,* sense of *Destiny* and awareness of *Race*'.[73]

This attempt to achieve class collaboration through compulsion meant that the programme of the NF, like that of the BUF, was a peculiar amalgam of left and right. There was no clear blueprint for unity (as in the manner of Mosley's corporate structure) for the NF's economic programme was too vaguely stated. The preservation of capitalism was, of course, guaranteed, but domestic capital was to be guided by the state in order to serve the best interests of the nation as a whole, and strict control was to be exercised over the money supply. Protection from the vagaries of international capital could be assured through the construction of an autarchic seige-economy, secure behind ramparts of tariff barriers and import quotas. This would be a true producers' state, it was claimed, encompassing the most attractive elements of right and left. Key sectors of the economy would be nationalised or, like banks, threatened with nationalisation in order to coerce them into patterns of patriotic behaviour.[74] The union movement would be rationalised in a corporate direction whereby there would be one union per industry which would include employers as well as employees. Through this apparatus the workers were to be included within the decision-making process and would be given a share in the profits of their industry.[75]

It was a similar if less sophisticated version of the BUF's economic proposals. The contradictions contained within it caused the NF to engage in similar feats of synthesis and instances of oscillation as had the BUF before it. Whilst guaranteeing the continued existence of capitalism it was admitted that 'we take from socialism the principle that business has an underlying social duty over and above the pursuit of profit'.[76] The same party could align itself with the traditional right in calling for curbs on union power and the regulation of their internal affairs, and yet also join workers on picket lines and offer vociferous support for the miners in their dispute with the Heath government.[77] Calls for greater defence spending, a more selective educational system, and cuts in the Welfare State to encourage greater self-reliance, could coexist with demands for minimum wage rates, improved working conditions, and workers' participation in both the control and the profits of industry.[78] Where possible such contradictory aspects were presented in unison in order to maximise the movement's centrist appeal. Where the contradictions were too great for synthesis, however, the radical or reactionary aspects of the programme were brought to the fore on the basis of opportunism. Thus, during the general elections of 1974, NF candidates from a broad cross-section of social backgrounds showed, in their presentation of party policy, widely diverging attitudes towards capitalism, anti-Semitism, the EEC, Northern Ireland, and other key issues raised in the course of the campaigns.[79]

Where the NF departed radically from the ideological mould created by the BUF was in regard to racism. Like the BUF before it, the NF's fascist centrism caused it to emphasise the community of interest between the productive capitalist and worker, and to vent its spleen upon the forces of finance capital. This parasitic enemy, however, was personified and mystified to a far greater extent than had been usual within the BUF. The bankers did not merely rule the world behind the façade of governments but were inbued with superhuman characteristics. 'The men of whom we are speaking are silent and invisible. . . . But do not imagine that these men of immense power, because they are unseen, do not exist; their invisibility is their greatest protection'.[80] Furthermore, such men were undeniably Jewish, it was alleged, and their activities represented an important element in a Jewish plot to dominate the world. This all-embracing silent conspiracy, worthy of Arnold Leese at his most obsessive, included amongst its agencies almost all international creeds and organisations. Finance capital, liberalism, communism, the UNO, the EEC, all were perceived as sapping the independence of nations by pressure from without or subversion from within. Black immigration fell into this latter category. The immigrants themselves were no more than helpless tools of the Jews who used them to attack the nation from within by mongrelising its racial purity, as part of their bid for world control. 'If separate races can be eradicated by the process of miscegenation and the whole of humanity submerged into a single slant-eyed khaki-coloured lumpen, then racial differences will have disappeared – along with any sense of national identity – and a world governmental system will be much easier to impose.'[81]

The NF's horror of miscegenation was founded upon a passionate belief in biological determinism. Not only were character traits such as intelligence, male virility and female passivity genetically determined, but so it was for all human instincts, even the urge towards collectivism, for otherwise the phenomenon of self-sacrifice was inexplicable. Although some complex racial hierarchies were constructed by the party, in general it preferred the simplicity of white and black racial categories, each having its own gene pool which promoted different, and immutable patterns of behaviour and levels of intelligence.[82] History and science both proved that the white race was superior to the black, and the British race (forged from Angles, Saxons, Norsemen, Celts, Jutes, and other white Europeans) was a particularly superior branch of the white race. Superior races needed room to expand, good quality leaders, and the careful preservation of their racial stocks. Fascism promised to satisfy these needs by the white reconquest of Africa and other lost imperial possessions, and the implementation of the leadership principle. In regard to protecting racial purity the party proposed the deportation of non-whites; the removal and destruction of degenerate genes from the gene pool (murderess Myra Hindley was cited as a candidate for such action); the discouragement of birth control and abortion in respect of healthy genes; and the inculcation of eugenic consciousness within the masses whereby the selective mating of the 'best types' could be achieved.[83]

Thus, although black immigration was frequently attacked on the grounds of white access to jobs, housing, education and social services, or in terms of race relations and crime, its importance to NF theorists lay in its relationship to a much older and wider racial life and death struggle with the forces of international Jewry. In this deadly duel the blacks were seen as units of exploited labour, the recepticles of disease, the passive victims of forces which they could neither comprehend nor control. Even the muggers and rapists who were over-represented amongst them were victims of their genetically programmed blood-lust instincts. It was the Jews, as ever, who were the real perpetrators and the real enemy.[84]

The NF's programme was undoubtedly fascist, complete with resonant, if unacknowledged, echoes of the BUF. Its commitment to individual rights and democracy was probably no more sincere than was that of Mosley in the post-war period. The scars of war necessitated the use of cosmetics. But the party's fascism was distorted by its acute racism, its eugenics, and its subscription to an obsessional belief in the Jewish world conspiracy which placed it more fully in the Hitler-Leese tradition than that of Mosley even at his most cynical. The differences between Keynesianism and the *Protocols* was the gulf between sanity and a form of madness. In public the NF's policy was swamped by anti-black racism. The centrist appeal of fascism was never adequately exploited, and too often it was submerged to the extent that the party appeared to be no more than a vociferous and somewhat disreputable anti-immigration pressure group operating upon the political fringe. In the face of governmental willingness to restrict immigration (and its consequent decline as an issue of public concern), and a united, broadly-based and popular campaign against NF activities organised in the late 1970s, the movement struggled to make consistent headway and finally fragmented into political oblivion.

All fascist movements are prone to schisms and ruptures. The leadership principle itself encourages pettiness of rank and internal empire building, and all of the distrust and betrayal consequent upon such administrative patterns. The NF, lacking a single leader of the status of Mosley, found itself particularly stricken in this respect. The 3·6 per cent of the poll scored in the 1970 general election[85] was a great disappointment to the party which had been receiving encouraging signals from local elections in the previous year. In some instances it had taken an eighteen per cent share of the poll.[86] In the wake of this failure, Chesterton, who was considered insufficiently populist in sentiment, was brutally ousted and replaced by John O'Brien in 1971. Attempts to purge the party of Tyndall and Webster (owing to their continued links with the European neo-Nazi movement) led to months of bitter internecine warfare before O'Brien acd his supporters abandoned the movement and defected to the National Independence Party, which closely resembled the NF in all matters of major policy.[87] By skillfully outmanoeuvring the rebels Tyndall prevented too great an exodus in their favour, and quickly replaced O'Brien as party leader. Almost immediately the party's fortunes were boosted by the arrival of thousands of Ugandan Asians expelled by Idi Amin. Not since the early days, in the aftermath of Enoch Powell's infamous 'rivers of blood' speech and the influx of Kenyan Asians, had the movement shown signs of such vitality. Recruitment accelerated and there were encouraging results from local elections and particularly from the West Norwich by-election in May 1973 where Webster polled sixteen per cent of the vote and saved his deposit.[88]

Again local trends did not stand up to the severe test of a general election. In February 1974 the NF put forward fifty-four candidates and in October this figure was increased to ninety, making the NF the fourth largest party. But the results were once again disappointing, with all candidates forfeiting their deposits, and only a handful managing to exceed even six per cent of the votes cast. The party's overall share of the vote, taken equally from all three major parties, remained in the region of three per cent.[89] As in 1970, electoral failure proved the catalyst for internal change. Tyndall was replaced as chairman by John Kingsley Read in a move which instituted a new era of factional fighting, the attempted expulsion of Tyndall and subsequent legal actions. Eventually Tyndall again outmanoeuvred his enemies and it was Read who resigned in December 1975 to form his own National Party, taking with him a little more than one quarter of the NF's membership.

Tyndall re-established control over the party, but despite the rise of racial passions with the arrival of Asians from Malawi, the NF failed to exploit the situation fully. The loss of valuable personnel had weakened the movement, and great efforts were channelled into ensuring that remaining branches stayed loyal and did not defect to the National Party.[90] Local election results continued to show some promise, and Tyndall tightened his iron grip on the party by pushing through constitutional changes which made it more difficult for him to be challenged for the leadership. But rifts continued to open, especially as the movement began to display symptoms of decline in the late 1970s. In 1979 Tyndall beat off a challenge from Fountaine who was expelled and responded by establishing a rival National Front Constitutional Movement, claiming to have taken with him 2,000 NF members.[91] The Leicester branch of NF seceded to form an independent British Peoples' Party (until it was realised that the name had already been used, whereupon it became the British Democratic Party).[92] In January 1980 Tyndall tried once more to consolidate his position by seizing dictatorial power within the party, but was resisted. In response he resigned and created the New National Front.[93] He was replaced as NF chairman by Andrew Brons.

This process of terminal fragmentation of the NF shattered the unity which had existed within British fascism for more than a decade. The enormous pressures generated within a party of the authoritarian centre had been intensified by the unsavoury wartime legacy of fascism and resulted eventually in disintegration, apathy and disillusionment. Tiny splinters continue to exist. Pathetic alliances of the maladjusted, these remnants of British fascism continue to haunt the ruins. Lacking the strength for parades or impressive meetings, all too often they have resorted to squalid acts of random violence. A stabbing on the football terraces or the murder of an Asian family through an arson attack: these have become the hallmarks of those who carry forward the grandiose ideas of British fascism.

NOTES

1 *HC Deb.*, 381, 21 July 1942, c. 1428–30.
2 For an attempt at such a book see R. Stent, *A Bespattered Page?*, Andre Deutsch, London 1980.
3 *Ibid.*, pp. 102–5; 117–26.
4 CAB 65, 133 (40) 10, Cabinet Conclusions, 22 May 1940.
5 *Manchester Guardian,* 24 May 1940, p. 5; *Action,* 30 May 1940, p. 1. Not all of those detained during this period were members of the BUF. Some were connected to the various pro-German movements which had existed in the 1930s, amongst whom the most prominent were the obsessive anti-Semite, Admiral Sir Barry Domvile, founder of the Link which was designed to foment closer ties between Britain and Nazi Germany, and the Conservative MP for Midlothian and Peebles, Captain A. H. Ramsey, founder of the Right Book Club.
6 *HC Deb.*, 363, 25 July 1940, c. 966, 991–2. A word of caution should be expressed as regards the figures for those interned. The Home Secretary's pronouncements in parliament were not always clear, and in some cases appear to contradict previous statements.
7 Order Number 1273, 10 July 1940. Separate orders (nos. 767–774) had been

made under 18AA on 26 May for eight companies connected to the party. LPL.

8   *HC Deb.*, 365, 7 November 1940, c. 1424–5; 403 (26 September 1944), c. 43.
9   *Action,* 16 September 1939, p. 2.
10   *Ibid.,* 14 March 1940, p. 8; 25 April 1940, p. 1.
11   *Ibid.,* 9 May 1940, p. 5.
12   Mosley, interview with author, 24 June 1980.
13   Transcript of Mosley's appearance before the Advisory Committee, 22 July 1940, p. 116, HO 283/16.
14   CAB 66/36, WP (43) 148, written statement from Mosley to Prime Minister, October 1942. Considered by Cabinet 21 April 1943.
15   CAB/65/34, 60 (43), Appendix I, Cabinet Conclusions. Memorandum by Home Secretary, circulated at cabinet meeting on 28 April 1943.
16   CAB 66/20, WP (41) 279, memorandum by Home Secretary, 21 November 1941. See also *HC Deb.,* 380, 11 June 1942, c. 1221.
17   Mosley, interview with author, 24 June 1980. See also *My Life,* Nelson, London 1968, pp. 406–10. Mosley believed that his move to Holloway was prompted by the persuasive efforts on his behalf of his brother-in-law, Tom Mitford, who had lunched at Downing Street shortly before the move was announced. See also *HC Debs.,* 368, 13 February 1941, c. 1532; and 377, 8 January 1943, c. 6–8.
18   *HC Deb.,* 373, 23 July 1941, c. 989.
19   *Ibid.,* 371, 8 May 1941, c. 987–8. Sir Barry Domvile, *From Admiral to Cabin Boy,* The Boswell Publishing Co. Ltd, London 1947, pp. 129–30.
20   Mosley, *My Life,* p. 235. See also B. Donoughue & G. W. Jones, *Herbert Morrison: Portrait of a Politician,* Weidenfeld & Nicolson, London 1973, pp. 96–7, 158.
21   CAB 65/36, 156(43)4, Cabinet Conclusions, report on Cabinet meeting, 17 November 1943. See also *HC Debs.,* 393, 23 November 1943, c. 1428–36; and 395, 1 December 1943, c. 395–478.
22   The 18B Publicity Council, *The Case of Mr. G. R. Merriman,* 18B Publicity Council, London n.d., pp. 5–6. See also *HC Deb.,* 376, 4 December 1941, c. 1238–40.
23   Mosley, interview with author, 24 June 1980.
24   *Union,* 14 February 1948, p. 2.
25   Mosley, *My Life,* pp. 488–91.
26   *Union,* 18 December 1948, p. 3.
27   *Ibid.,* 14 February 1948, p. 2.
28   Mosley, *op. cit.,* p. 497.
29   *Union,* 21 February 1948, editorial.
30   *Ibid.,* 7 January 1950, editorial. See also 13 May, editorial.
31   *Ibid.,* 3 July 1948, p. 1.
32   R. Skidelsky, *Oswald Mosley,* Macmillan, London 1975, p. 490.
33   *Union,* 3 July 1948, p. 1.
34   N. Nugent, 'Post-war Fascism?', as found in Lunn & Thurlow (eds.), *British Fascism,* Croom Helm, London 1980, p. 213.
35   M. Walker, *The National Front,* Fontana/Collins, London 1978, p. 27.
36   The number of non-whites in Britain in 1954 was approximately 74,000; this figure had risen to 336,000 by 1961; 924,000 by 1966; and 1,500,000 by 1971. N. Nugent, 'The anti-immigration groups', *New Community,* V, 3, autumn 1976, p. 302.
37   *Union,* 16 July 1957, p. 3.
38   *Ibid.,* p. 4.
39   Mosley, *op. cit.,* p. 449.
40   *Shepherds Bush Gazette,* 13 March 1959, p. 3. Teddy boys were prominent amongst the Union Movement. Mosley defended them as 'fine types', and

suggested that their creed was '. . . vital and . . . also virile, which is what youth should be'. *European,* October 1958, as quoted by Skidelsky, *op. cit.,* p. 511.

41 *Kensington Post,* 17 April 1959, p. 1; 10 April, p. 1.
42 *Ibid.,* 22 May 1959, p. 1.
43 *Ibid.,* 10 April 1959, p. 1.
44 *Action,* 4 July 1959, p. 8.
45 Mosley's eldest son Nicolas witnessed one such meeting. N. Mosley, *Beyond the Pale,* Secker & Warburg, London 1983, p. 307. See also D. E. Butler & R. Rose, *The British General Election of 1959,* p. 179, as cited by Skidelsky, *op. cit.,* p. 513.
46 Skidelsky, *op. cit.,* p. 514.
47 *Reynolds News,* 14 June 1959, p. 1.
48 Walker, *op. cit.,* pp. 33–4.
49 Nugent; Lunn & Thurlow (eds.), *op. cit.,* p. 215.
50 Skidelsky, *op. cit.,* p. 491 (f). Certainly Jordan's fanatical belief in the international Jewish conspiracy was in marked contrast to the Union Movement's stated policy whereby the 'Jewish question' was considered relatively minor; 'we consider that there are far more important matters . . . than the status and influence of a small racial minority in our midst, which may be capable of causing intense social irritation but cannot ultimately alter the destiny of nations . . .', *Union,* 27 March 1948, editorial.
51 *Guardian,* 19 June 1962, as quoted by Nugent, *op. cit.,* p. 215.
52 C. Jordan, *Britain Reborn: The Will and Purpose of the National Socialist Movement,* NSM, London n.d., as quoted by Nugent, *op. cit.,* p. 215.
53 J. Tyndall, *The Authoritarian State,* NSM, London 1962, p. 15.
54 *Guardian,* 19 June 1962, p. 3.
55 *Ibid.,* 2 July 1962, as quoted by Nugent, *New Community,* V, 3, autumn 1976, p. 304.
56 Walker, *op. cit.,* p. 39.
57 *Action and the European,* 25 October 1963, p. 1. See also 13 April, p. 5.
58 Mosley, *op. cit.,* pp. 435–7. See also *Action,* 1 May 1964, p. 3.
59 *Action and the European,* 4 October 1963, p. 6.
60 *Ibid.,* 13 March 1964, p. 6.
61 *Ibid.,* 5 April 1963, p. 6.
62 *National European,* August 1965, as quoted by Skidelsky, *op. cit.,* p. 491 (f).
63 *Action and the European,* 1 May 1964, p. 1.
64 Mosley, *op. cit.,* p. 461. See also Skidelsky, *op. cit.,* p. 516.
65 Mosley, *op. cit.,* p. 462.
66 *Ibid.*
67 *Ibid.,* p. 500.
68 *Ibid.*
69 *Official Programme of the Greater Britain Movement,* Albion Press Ltd, London n.d., as cited by Nugent, *op. cit.,* p. 216. See also Walker, *op. cit.,* pp. 46–7.
70 J. Tyndall, *Six Principles of British Nationalism,* 1970, as quoted by Walker, *op. cit.,* p. 79.
71 *Ibid.,* p. 82.
72 *Spearhead,* November 1978, as quoted by Nugent, *op. cit.,* p. 220.
73 *Spearhead,* March 1977, p. 13, *ibid.,* p. 219. See also S. Taylor, *The National Front in English Politics,* Macmillan, London 1982, pp. 70–6.
74 J. Tyndall, *Beyond Capitalism and Socialism,* p. 3., as cited by Taylor, *op. cit.,* p. 75.
75 *Ibid.,* see also *Spearhead,* June 1977, as cited by Nugent, *op. cit.,* p. 230.
76 Tyndall, *op. cit.,* p. 17, as quoted by S. Eyres, *The National Front is a Socialist Front,* Aims for Freedom and Enterprise Production, 1977, p. 14.

77 *Spearhead,* 106, June 1977, as cited by D. Edgar, 'Racism, Fascism and the Politics of the National Front', *Race and Class,* XIX, 2, autumn 1977, p. 126. See also Walker, *op. cit.,* pp. 146–7, 230.
78 Edgar, *op. cit.,* p. 126; Eyres, *op. cit., p. 15.*
79 M. J. De Locke, 'The National Front and the general elections of 1974', *New Community,* V, 3, autumn 1976, p. 299.
80 C. Macdonald, *The Money Manufacturers,* NF, London n.d., p. 10, as quoted by Nugent, *op. cit.,* p. 217.
81 *Spearhead,* April 1971, as quoted by Edgar, *op. cit.,* p. 119.
82 *Spearhead,* 122, 113; as cited by Taylor, *op. cit.,* pp. 65–6.
83 *Spearhead,* 107, 120, 124, *It's our Country,* p. 60, as cited by Taylor, *op. cit.,* p. 73.
84 Edgar, *op. cit.,* p. 128.
85 De Locke, *op. cit.,* p. 292.
86 Walker, *op. cit.,* pp. 90–1.
87 *Ibid.,* 91–107.
88 *Ibid.,* 133–142.
89 De Locke, *op. cit.,* p. 292. See also Walker, *op. cit.,* pp. 174–5, and Nugent, *op. cit.,* p. 307.
90 Walker, *op. cit.,* pp. 195–202.
91 Taylor, *op. cit.,* p. 91.
92 *Ibid.*
93 *NF News,* 20, 1980, as cited by Taylor, *op. cit.,* p. 91.

Conclusion

O, I have pass'd a miserable night,
So full of ugly sights, of ghastly dreams,
That, as I am a Christian faithful man,
I would not spend another such a night
Though 'twere to deny a world of happy days,
So full of dismal terror was the time!

W. Shakespeare, *Richard III*

The system that gives people what they desire must prevail. If Fascism does not succeed in delivering at least this minimum demand, then sooner or later it will die a natural death. If it declines to do so naturally, there are many who will see that it dies unnaturally, and they will be justified. No system can live, or has the right to live unless it is a success.

W. J. Leaper, *Fascism for the Million*,
BUF Publications Ltd, London 1936, p. 9

What we call the beginning is often the end
And to make an end is to make a beginning.
The end is where we start from.

T. S. Eliot, 'East Coker'

Before looking at the overall impact of the BUF upon the environment in which it operated, it is as well to underline several of the most important features of fascism, which were illustrated clearly by the nature of the party's development.

The most fundamental point is that the growth of the BUF from its embryonic stage to its emergence as a fully-fledged political movement illustrated the quintessential centrism of fascism. It was conceived as the result of an attempt by Mosley to appeal to the political centre. He tried unsuccessfully to achieve this initially by the realignment of parliamentary politics, and thereafter, in the country at large, through the formation of the New Party. The significance of the political centre towards which Mosley struggled was its theoretical embodiment of neutrality. It was a political El Dorado within which a neutral regime could operate; a regime controlled by the sectional interests of neither right nor left, but based upon a common desire to reconstruct the ailing British economy. To those with the foresight to realise it, it had become apparent in post-war Britain that there could be no return to the simple *laissez-faire* capitalism so dear to the heart of nineteenth-century liberalism. The alternative to economic stagnation and concomitant social decay (with the related spectre of communist revolution) was, therefore, a new capitalist order reconstructed upon a rational scientific basis. No longer could 'the invisible hand' be trusted to regulate the complex economic machinery of a vast empire.

In order to begin this reconstruction, and to maximise the improvements of the new economic order once it had been attained, it was essential that class war be eliminated. But the guns of the opposing industrial armies could only be silenced through firm action from a strong, independent, and impartial government, which was unafraid to use direct coercion in pursuit of what it regarded as the welfare of the nation as a whole. The representative institutions of capital and labour and the weapons at their disposal (including the strike and the lock-out), had to be destroyed and replaced by a new industrial unity based upon communication and co-operation as facilitated by economic corporatism. In order to control these new corporate institutions (which were expanded to cover the political as well as well as the economic sphere of the new order), and to provide the central government with a general transmission mechanism for the realisation of its own authority, there was the need for a very special kind of political party. A party not merely capable of mobilising nationwide political support for electoral purposes, but one which would provide the new society with a spinal column and a central nervous system; a highly centralised and powerful party with the internal discipline to ensure that decisions emanating from its leaders would be acted upon without question. The nature of the party was also determined by Mosley's belief that a major crisis was approaching British society which would involve widespread social disintegration and possible left-wing insurrection. Under such circumstances the party needed to be capable of seizing the reins of government and restoring authority.

The New Party attempted to meet these needs but as its programme became increasingly fascist, the need for an orthodox fascist party increased. The foundations of this were provided by the New Party's youth movement, but it was the formation of the BUF as a more disciplined, centralised, and authoritarian organisation which satisfied this requirement fully. It dealt still in the politics of the centre but its form and political philosophy were more in keeping with Mosley's corporatism and his belief in the crisis. (Indeed, Mosley's vision of catastrophe was so strong that it was not until the mid-1930s, when increasing prosperity reduced the likelihood of a crisis, that the BUF was decentralised in an effort to build the electoral machinery at constituency level, which was necessary if power was to be pursued through the ballot box).

Mosley perceived the BUF as a carefully honed precision tool; a scalpel with which national surgery could be performed, as well as a scientific instrument which would regulate the new order. The party's position at the centre of the political spectrum meant that it had a vast breadth of potential appeal, to both right and left, to the bourgeois capitalist and the manual worker alike. Although this was a source of great potential strength it also presented problems, for it lay at the root of many of the contradictions inherent within fascist ideology. Too often its programme oscillated between the conflicting interests of right and left or creaked and groaned under the strain of attempting to synthesise demands, which were in essence incompatible. An attempt was made to come to terms with these conflicts through the design of the complex mediatory machinery embodied within the corporate state, and through a heavy emphasis upon concepts such as patriotism, unquestioning obedience, and the inherent worthiness of action, all of which helped to camouflage the cracks and ideological flaws.

Anti-Semitism was also useful in this respect although in the case of the BUF its development must be seen also in the context of other internal party pressures as well as the party's external environment. Jews were as ideal target for fascism because they could engender hostility, which was classless. They could be portrayed as the common enemies of all patriotic Britons, whether rich or poor. Thus, like the concept of patriotism itself, they could be used by fascism as an amalgam to help hold together supporters drawn from different parts of the political spectrum, the fundamental interests of whom were often diametrically opposed. Given Britain's distribution of Jews, however, the BUF's anti-Semitism was not sufficiently relevant to the nation at large to produce this result. Its effect upon the party was nevertheless profound for it provided the dynamism of the campaign in east London. This proved to be the only area of the country where fascism acquired a significant mass base. In so doing the East End consumed a disproportionate amount of the party's resources, distorted its national policy, and altered the social composition of the movement. The result was that by 1939 a dangerous gulf had opened between the BUF's branches in east London and those elsewhere in the country.

Despite the great potential popular appeal of fascism, after almost a decade of unremitting struggle, Mosley and his followers had made very little impact upon British society. Assessments as to the state of the party in 1939 are difficult, but it seems probable that it had a small but ideologically committed membership, and the basis of electoral machinery in some areas of the country. But despite its support in the East End and Mosley's continued ability to draw large and enthusiastic audiences, by 1939 an air of stagnation pervaded the movement. In retrospect Mosley claimed that his defeat was due to the untimely intervention of the war, which created a climate in which the party could no longer operate.[1] In a sense this was true, for the war did administer the *coup de grâce* to the BUF by creating the opportunity for the government to extinguish it formally. It is true on a more obtuse level also in that it was only through wartime mobilisation that the depression, which had afflicted the capitalist world in the 1930s, was finally banished. It can be argued that the government lacked the will and the wisdom to have adopted any other reflationary strategy and, therefore, war was the only means by which a further depression (upon which the BUF was relying to increase its support) could have been avoided. But even had there been no war and the BUF had been able to fight a general election in 1939 or 1940 it is difficult to visualise any large-scale fascist success, especially as, since 1937, rearmament had prevented the British economy from returning to the depths to which it had plunged in 1932.[2]

Even if one accepts that the party was lying dormant in the late 1930s, however, and was ready to make rapid advances in the event of its environment becoming favourable to fascist growth, the long-term impact of the BUF upon British society is questionable, not least because of its failure to leave a discernible fascist legacy. Anti-Semitism remained in the East End after 1940 but then it had existed there long before the arrival of the BUF. Elsewhere one looks in vain for visible evidence of lasting fascist penetration. Mosley's post-war career at the head of the remnants of his party was a fiasco, for he failed to revive any significant proportion of the popular support which he had enjoyed throughout his career until 1940. Even amongst those bizarre and teratogenic figures on the current political fringe involved in racist and authoritarian movements, allegiance is owed not to Mosley but to German National Socialism. The most important British inter-war figure in this unsavoury lineage was probably Arnold Leese whose copious work on racism in general, and anti-Semitism in particular, remains important reading for the exotic creatures who inhabit this bleak and unforgiving political landscape.

The BUF's apparent failure to make a lasting impression upon its host society is obviously connected to its brief duration. As such, therefore, it is a part of the wider question concerning the party's failure to make greater headway in its quest for political power. Why did fascism fail in Britain? There is no simple answer to such a question, of course, but it is as well to dispense at the outset with the popular myth that fascism was eliminated by the moderation and tolerance of the British character, or culture. In reality neither nations nor races have inherent common traits of character. Nor even is there such an entity as a single national culture. Nations are no more than arbitrary lines drawn upon maps containing individuals and groups of individuals with competing interests and incompatible needs and aspirations. Certainly there were differences in the historical development of individual nations, but to suggest that there were any unique elements within British society, which made it immune to the threat of fascism, is to illustrate an extraordinary complacency founded upon misplaced arrogance.

This smug chauvinism was not uncommon amongst those on the centre and right of the political spectrum. Their myth of the free-born Englishman, honest, just, and infinitely reasonable, has been perpetuated by some historians of British fascism who have suggested that the 'respect for the rights and dignity of the individual'[3] inherent within British democracy made Britain immune from fascist ideas. Individuals, condemned by the ruling class to fight its wars and to manufacture its profits from the sweat of their ill-rewarded labour, received scant respect for their rights to life, liberty and self-fulfilment. Whilst for those whose lives were spent in poverty, squalor, and fear, who were exploited when their services were needed, only later to be cast aside workless to watch impotently whilst their families starved, there was little dignity of the individual.

The left was not as prone to these errors of complacency and, consequently, was more alive to the dangers of fascist advances.[4] This may have been due in part to the mistaken belief that fascism was a well-orchestrated capitalist conspiracy, but was also the result of its more sophisticated analysis of industrial society. It recalled that brutality, ruthlessness, and authoritarianism were not absent trends even in recent British history. In the twentieth century alone, state-sanctioned violence had been employed against political opponents and protesting workers with sickening regularity. National minorities had been persecuted within Britain[5] and atrocities had been committed within the empire. The ideals of justice, tolerance, and fair play were not always the sentiments which governed British activities. Those who had experienced persecution directly, as had many on the left, knew this all too well.

Fascism was not alien to Britain. Both as a movement and as an ideology fascism incorporated aspects of its style from abroad but as a whole it was not a foreign import. It developed from British roots to fulfil British needs. In some areas, notably in its economic theory, its analysis went far beyond that of the fascist parties of Europe. Its foreign policy was based not upon subservience to foreign fascist nations but upon the maintenance of a strong, independent, and autarchic empire: isolationism from a position of strength. As such it was a rational and patriotic programme. A different form of patriotism to that displayed by Churchill, but patriotism nevertheless.

The failure of the BUF was not, then, preordained by the intrinsic nature of British society nor by fascism's innate foreignness. The reasons for its lack of success can be divided broadly into three categories. The first of these concerns those problems which arose within the party itself, the most debilitating of which concerned Mosley's leadership. Although his wealth, status, oratory and general charisma were immensely beneficial to the party, he also brought with him a tendency to make serious errors of judgement, particularly with regard to his sense of timing.[6] This is an issue which will be further examined when looking at the necessary preconditions for fascist growth. At this point, rather than looking at his tactical misjudgements, it is sufficient to illustrate the flaws within the BUF which Mosley not only failed to eliminate but, to an extent, was actually the cause of. His overweening arrogance and self-confidence, resulting largely from the astonishing success of his early political career, led him to dominate his party with the autocracy of a strong medieval monarch. But as with monarchs this elevated position encouraged power struggles amongst those immediately below him. An essential part of such factional manoeuvring involved attempts to curry favour with the leader, which in practice meant the obsequious idolatry of Mosley by his lieutenants. A particularly ironic example of this came from the pen of A. K. Chesterton, who seemed completely unabashed by his own overblown prose in praise of his leader's 'majestic endowments', which included '. . . his tall athletic frame with its dynamic force and immense reserves of strength; his unconquerable spirit, with its grandeur of courage and resolve', all of which underlined Mosley's position as '. . . an outstanding leader of men'.[7] It proved ironic because, having left the party, Chesterton later felt compelled to reassess Mosley's leadership qualities. 'I have been amazed that a man so dynamic on the platform should prove so unimaginative, so timid, so lacking in initiative and resolve', he claimed, and suggested that Mosley had surrounded himself with a clique of grasping incompetents led by Neil Francis Hawkins.

> I have never known him give a decision against his favourites or fail to come to their help when they have been embarrassed, or maintain any semblance of a judicial attitude where their interests were involved. Clearly they are very important to him: he finds them comfortable men shielding him from the impact of every reality, subjecting him to no heart searching, no self-analysis, no stress or turmoil of intellectual conflict. . . .[8]

Joyce and Beckett had pointed to similar traits a year earlier, denouncing in particular Mosley's over-inflated ego and '. . . the petty malicious intrigue with which the organisation is riddled'.[9]

Such behaviour on Mosley's part would not have been irrational. Faced with failure and the unpalatable belief that for all his talents and energy the prophet was not to be called by his people, it is possible that he retreated to the warmth and security of those amongst whom his status was little short of divine. It would have been a more attractive option for an egotist as great as Mosley than the acceptance of the bitter cup of personal failure and the agonies of self-doubt, which must surely have accompanied it.

Another internal flaw which retarded the party's progress was its inability to rid itself of its essentially middle-class image. Its claim to be a union of patriots above the sordid squabbles of the class war was essential to its centrist programme and philosophy. Yet its claim lacked credibility because in too many areas of the country its image remained that of a vehicle for a retired army officer or the wealthy eccentric. This was in part due to effective anti-fascist propaganda, as well as to the prevailing aspects of the BUF's own philosophy. It was also the result of Mosley's readiness to incorporate into the BUF many of the tiny right-wing fascist groups already in existence in 1932, many of the members of which were indeed ex-officers and middle-class eccentrics. With the exception of the East End where the party was truly rooted in the working class, the BUF appeared generally as a less credible vehicle for left-wing traditions than for those of the right. For a movement which relied upon the support of both sides for success, this was a very serious fault. Despite repeated policy statements which stressed that fascism was allied to neither the right nor the left, it was a problem which was never resolved by the party and consequently its potential appeal was reduced.

The issue of Mosley's incapacity as a politician was, as already suggested, connected to his timing of the BUF's launch. This involves looking at the second general area relevant to fascism's failure, that which concerns the nature of the preconditions associated with fascist growth. As suggested in chapter 8 the existence of crisis and the disinte-grating consequences attendant upon it were essential in creating a need for fascist centrism. The ideology's growth could be accelerated by an absence of long-term integration within a society, a discredited ruling regime, increasing political disorder, and the existence of political space at the centre of the spectrum. Weimar Germany was, of course, the archetypal example of a society which displayed precisely these symp-toms. In Britain, with its relatively homogeneous society and its stable institutions, there was an almost complete absence of these accelerating factors. An economic crisis, however, did exist in the early 1930s. Industrial production plummeted by 15% between 1929 and 1932, with a

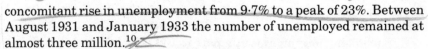

concomitant rise in unemployment from 9·7% to a peak of 23%. Between August 1931 and January 1933 the number of unemployed remained at almost three million.[10]

The impression created by such statistics can be misleading, however. In Britain the onset of the depression was very much more gradual than elsewhere. The British economy had never recovered its pre-war position and during the 1920s remained relatively stagnant, with a permanent pool of over a million unemployed. Although the situation worsened after 1929, it lacked the air of a sudden and dramatic crisis. Secondly, and more importantly, the effects of the depression were not uniform. Northern Ireland, Scotland, Wales, and northern England bore the brunt of the deprivation, especially in those areas dependent upon the traditional export industries. In Jarrow and Merthyr the situation had reached horrifying proportions by 1935 with the percentage of unemployed workers standing at 67·8% and 61·9% respectively. Yet comparable figures of 8·6% for London and 5·1% for Coventry illustrate that south-east England and the Midlands escaped relatively lightly. Indeed, many prospered amid the hardship. Imports became cheaper and new opportunities for investment presented themselves. For those in work stable wage rates and falling prices increased real wages significantly. There was a boom in private housing, motor vehicles, and other new consumer industries. The result was that those who lived outside the depressed areas and who continued in employment remained largely immune to the ravages of the slump.[11]

Finally, Britain's recovery from the depression was more rapid than that of the USA, Canada, or many of her capitalist neighbours in Europe. The abandonment of the gold standard in 1931 effectively devalued Britain's currency, thereby giving her an advantage over her competitors, and removing a major obstacle to economic recovery. Impoverished primary producers had no alternative but to accept the devalued sterling. The terms of trade continued to move in Britain's favour. Furthermore, despite the government's expressed wishes, based upon narrow-minded economic orthodoxy, much of the population translated its higher real wages into consumption rather than savings. As the Keynesian model predicted, increased spending generated further wealth and employment, which fuelled Britain's steady recovery from early 1933 to 1937. It was a haphazard rather than a planned solution. It was sufficient, however, to ensure that the worst of the depression was relatively short-lived in most of Britain.

In the words of one historian, 'Recovery, despaired of in 1931, was in the air by 1933, obvious by 1935.'[12] Thus, not only was the economic depression unsatisfactory from the BUF's point of view in terms of its undramatic onset and lack of uniformity, but for most of the party's life the depression itself was receding visibly. In short, the BUF had been launched much too late to take advantage of the slump in Britain. In retrospect Mosley accepted this, claiming the BUF's success in the face of such adversity proved that it would have triumphed had the conditions beem more favourable.[13] At the time, however, the party was reluctant to make any such admission, and preferred to see its struggle made easier by the timing of its launch. Whereas 'the Italians – and for a time the Germans – struggled in the dark to leap into the dawn . . . we have entered it in the noonday sun of Fascism'.[14] Although it was later admitted grudgingly that there had been some degree of economic improvement since the early 1930s, Mosley pinned his hopes upon the onset of a new cycle of depression. In late 1937 the trend towards recovery stammered and unemployment began to rise once again. The BUF looked forward to making significant gains but it was not to be. The new depression proved to be only a temporary fluctuation. The government's expenditure on rearmament unintentionally instituted the kind of Keynesian reflationary programme which Mosley had been advocating for years. The result was that, despite sometimes hysterical fascist claims to the contrary, the new depression was shallow and short-lived. It is more than a little ironic that preparations for the destruction of fascism abroad prevented a return of the conditions which could have led to its success at home.

Finally, the third group of factors working against the BUF involved areas of anti-fascist opposition. The most active opposition came from the left, and in particular from the Communist Party. But although the CP was prominent, it did not control all of the numerous unaffiliated individuals and radical groups which opposed the BUF upon the streets, and which together constituted the anti-fascist movement. They disrupted the spread of BUF propaganda, and helped to create an unfavourable public image for fascism. In some areas, most notably the East End, the memory of such activities became popular community myths. Some live on still, such as how, on a warm October Sunday, the common people of east London broke the back of British fascism when they defeated Mosley and his police escort at the battle of Cable Street. In reality, although the anti-fascist movement produced individual acts of great heroism, it was but one of several sources of opposition which retarded the BUF's growth. The official leadership of the labour movement did little to oppose fascism and even injured the cause by preventing the formation of a united anti-fascist front. But many of its members worked more constructively in an individual capacity. MP's raised the issue of fascism in parliament. Other party members joined local anti-fascist organisations, or worked through their local councils to deny fascist speakers the use of municipal property. Although not offi-cially orchestrated from above, these tactics (particularly the denial of halls) restricted the BUF considerably, and were probably as effective, albeit not as dramatic, as the violent confrontation of fascism upon the streets.

Another important source of opposition orginated from the National Government and was channelled via the state. On one level the government opposed the BUF by upholding the law and its own authority. Despite some sympathy within the police and the judiciary the government acted in the interests of its conservative supporters by attempting to ensure that the BUF was met with official hostility. Both fascism and the left were seen as subversive, rabble-rousing disturbers of the peace. Neither was allowed to create an atmosphere of political lawlessness, as had developed in Weimar Germany. It damaged the BUF on a more obtuse level also be stealing its thunder concerning the need for a national consensus. For although the National Government was in reality a Conservative administration, since being elected in 1931 it had maintained the garb of a national coalition concerned with the welfare of the nation as a whole, and standing above the petty wranglings of party rivalry. As such it was offering a consensus of the centre not unlike that which underpinned the appeal of fascism. Furthermore, it was a more secure form of centrism, for it wore the familiar guise of liberal-demo-cracy and was peopled by established and experienced political leaders. This erroneous impression of the government's classless consensus of the centre was strengthened by the 521 seats which it held after the 1931 election. The Labour Party, the main party of opposition, had been reduced to a meagre fifty-two representatives, many of whom lacked parliamentary experience.[15]

Thus, regardless of its actions, the mere existence of the National Government was a hindrance to the BUF's progress for it denied fascism the political space which it requires if it is to maximise the breadth of its centrist appeal. The democratic centre did not collapse as in Weimar Germany for the National Government conveyed the unmistakable impression of solidity. Through a mixture of undemocratic procedures and repressive legislation it eroded individual liberties, but in so doing it maintained order and an air of normality. There was no serious disinte-gration in social fabric or the political institutions of Britain. The government had only to uphold the law and wait for the depression to run its course. As the economy began to improve (despite, rather than because of government strategy), the problems of the government receded.

This economic recovery was absolutely vital, for had it not occurred the National Government could, in time, have become as discredited as the leaders of the Weimar Republic. Indeed, there may have followed an increasing disillusionment with the process of parliamentary democracy itself. In such an event the political centre could have become vulnerable to the fascist challenge on the basis of a new, non-liberal government of national consensus. A failure to oversee some form of economic recovery could have led also to a growth of the left. This may have taken the form of a regalvanised Labour Party prised from the reformist grip of men such as Morrison and Attlee. Alternatively it may have produced a rise in those parties situated to the left of Labour. In either case the result would have been to provoke right-wing defections from orthodox Conservatism. The alternative for those who felt that Conservatism could not be relied upon to deal with this rise of a left-wing menace would have been fascism. The simultaneous growth of the left and the BUF would have increased street fighting and public disorder, which would have further discredited the government and cause further defections; a downward spiral of disorder, discredit, defection, and further disorder, undermining the liberal centre, swelling the ranks and coffers of fascism and its opponents, and providing the important accelerating factors required for fascist growth.

Each of these three groups of reasons alluded to were important in preventing the success of fascism in Britain. The nature of the preconditions, the anti-fascists and the government, and the internal flaws within the party itself – each played its part. All had one important feature in common: they denied the BUF the sort of wide political appeal upon which fascism thrived. The party was despised and attacked by the left and, aided by its own internal flaws, became perceived widely as a party of the authoritarian right. Had it achieved power it would probably have become this in any case, because its attempts at genuine impartial mediation would have been impossible to realise. But in its early stages it was vital for the BUF to draw support from the left and the right in order to maximise the full potential of its centrist appeal, and it was in this that it was most frustrated. As a party of the right the BUF was redundant, for the interests of conservatives were being adequately catered for by the National Government, which retained its credibility because of the economic recovery from 1933 onwards. The result was that the BUF failed to make an impact commensurate with the breadth of its potential appeal, and found itself adrift within an increasingly hostile environment attracting the feckless, the inadequate, and the eccentric.

The development of fascism in British society, illustrated the intrinsic strength of the ideology in the form of its appeal to a national consensus based upon a classless spiritual and patriotic unity for the restoration of a properous, but humane and controlled capitalist system. Although unobtainable in reality, it could prove a powerful platform capable of marshalling sufficient popular support for the achievement of power. It is ironic, therefore, that the party's evolution and failure should prove that this same intrinsic strength was also a source of grave fascist weakness. For unless the prevailing conditions had rotted the bonds of traditional class and political allegiance, thus facilitating an inter-class appeal to the extremism of the centre, fascism was destined to struggle against the odds. It was this which was illustrated by Britain's inter-war fascists. Although Mosley was loath to admit it, the 'Old Gang' had triumphed yet again. The established political leaders remained firmly at the nation's helm. They did so not because they were the best qualified to do so, nor even because they had any of the necessary answers, but because they had exploited the compelling appeal of a non-partisan coalition government of the centre. As such it was the twentieth century British response to wartime emergencies applied to a peacetime crisis. That its claim to be a coalition was entirely fraudulent was irrelevant, for by 1935 when it was once again called before its electors the signs of economic recovery were undeniable. It was returned to power and, thereafter, there were no further general elections for a decade. Treaties were signed, pledges were given, and a long and bloody war was fought. The people of Britain were called upon to make great sacrifices and they did so with a touching but alarming degree of obedience. Leaders came and went as those who retired were replaced by others of a similar ilk. The system, however, remained largely intact. It emerged into a brave new post-war world of Marshall aid, cold-war politics, Keynesian economics, and the Welfare State.

That fascism has been unable to regenerate itself in this climate is unsurprising. Although non-white immigration offered the possibility of a popular cause, the preconditions for fascist growth simply have not existed in anything like the required strength. In addition to dealing with the common problems thrown up by authoritarian centrism and internal division, fascist movements have had to cope also with the appalling legacy of Nazi Germany and its atrocities. Opposition has been more unified, intense and effective than in the inter-war period because the bloody reality of the ideology in practice has become common knowledge.

British fascism should not be written off, however. Ideologies do not die. They evolve in shape and form and they wait. A serious fascist revival would require a deep and sustained economic crisis, growing political violence and a credible threat from the left, and a serious disillusionment with the liberal centre and the parliamentary process. As the manufacturing basis of the British economy presently dwindles, unemployment rises and political polarisation increases, foolhardy indeed would be he who would assert that such preconditions could never arise.

NOTES

1   O. Mosley, interview with author, 24 June 1980.
2   A word of caution should be exercised here, for it should be remembered that the onset of economic recession in Germany thrust the Nazis to power with

dramatic speed in the early 1930s. Had there been no war and no public spending on rearmament, it is possible that a 1939 or 1940 election could have been fought against the background of a renewed slump of comparable severity to that of 1931. Under such circumstances the result would have been uncertain and the BUF could have achieved dramatic success as the beneficiaries of political disillusionment and despair.

3   D. M. Geiger, 'British Fascism as revealed in the British Union of Fascists' Press'. PhD, New York University, 1963, p. 315. See also R. Benewick, *The Fascist Movement in Britain,* Penguin Press, London 1972, p. 13.

4   For instance, see R. P. Dutt, *Fascism and Social Revolution,* Lawrence, London 1934, p. 242. See also E. Wilkinson & E. Conze, *Why Fascism?,* Selwyn & Blount, London 1934, pp. 232–3.

5   For examples of such persecution, see K. Lunn & R. C. Thurlow (eds.), *British Fascism,* Croom Helm, London 1980, p. 126.

6   Even Skidelsky, Mosley's sympathetic biographer, has admitted in retrospect that he did not sufficiently condemn Mosley's '. . . incapacity as a politician'. Lunn & Thurlow (eds.), *op. cit.,* p. 83.

7   A. K. Chesterton, *Oswald Mosley: Portrait of a Leader,* Action Press, London 1937, p. 164. See also the foreword by Chesterton in *British Union Pictorial Record 1932–37,* BUF, London 1938.

8   A. K. Chesterton, *Why I Left Mosley,* National Socialist League, London 1938, p. 4.

9   Foreword by J. Beckett in W. Joyce, *National Socialism Now,* National Socialist League, London 1937, p. 7.

10 C. L. Mowat, *Britain between the wars 1918–1940*, Methuen & Co. Ltd, London 1966, p. 432.

11 *Ibid.,* pp. 433–4, 463–70.

12 *Ibid.,* p. 432.

13 O. Mosley, *My Life,* Nelson, London 1968, p. 310.

14 *Blackshirt,* 8 February 1935, p. 6.

15 All but one of the Labour Party's former cabinet ministers lost their seats. A. J. P. Taylor, *English History 1914–45,* Penguin Books, London 1977, p. 406.

Primary sources

A. Interviews, private papers and memoirs

There are few known collections of private papers which relate directly to the development of the BUF. Many of the party's own internal records were seized by the authorities in 1940 and their whereabouts since that date have been something of a mystery. Others have been lost or destroyed since the movement's suppression, or are in the hands of ex-members who are not pre-pared to make them public. Mosley retained few of his private papers, and neither he nor any of the leading members of the BUF kept a diary during the 1930s. Similarly, interviews are hard to come by for over half a century has elapsed since the beginning of the fascist struggle and many of the participants are now dead. This problem is compounded in the case of fascist veterans by their reluctance to admit to a past political affiliation which has since become utterly disreputable.

Fortunately, however, personal reminiscences by both Mosley and some of his leading opponents do exist in the form of published political memoirs or autobio-graphies. I was also able to meet Mosley in person on several occasions, and conducted a lengthy interview with him. For details of this, and other interviews, see below.

(i) INTERVIEWS

Excell, A., interviewed 21 February 1981, Oxford. Excell was a lifelong member of the CP and had been active in opposing the BUF in the Oxford area.

'J.G.', correspondence with author, March–May 1981, Devon. 'J.G.', whose identity I promised not to reveal, was an anti-fascist infiltrator who pene-trated the BUF. Throughout much of its existence he worked in the fund-raising department at National Headquarters.

Hamm, J., interviewed 14 April and 12 June 1980, London. Hamm, who is in charge of the remnants of Mosley's post-war political party, was a member of the BUF before the war.

Mosley, O. E., interviewed 24 June 1980, London. This interview was conducted with Mosley when he was over eighty-three years old and, as one would expect, had fallen victim to some of the mental and physical frailties attendant upon old age. Despite this, however, he was coherent and spoke at length about the development of the BUF, its policies, and its rela-tionship with aspects and institutions of inter-war British society. He also expressed some forceful opinions upon current political issues. A little over five months later, on 3 December 1980, he died peacefully in his sleep at his home near Paris.

Various informal conversations with residents of London's East End.

(ii) PRIVATE PAPERS

Excell, A., unpublished autobiography, Oxford.

Mosley Secretariat, London; collection of press cuttings and pamphlets pertaining to Mosley and the BUF.

Nicolson Papers, Balliol College, Oxford. This collection consists of the diaries of Harold Nicolson for the years 1930 to 1964, and also includes miscellaneous letters, some of which are from Mosley. As such it is the single most important primary source on the evolution of the New Party and its youth movement, and provides a valuable insight into Mosley's increasing acceptance of overt fascism.

(iii) MEMOIRS

Brown, W. J., *So Far,* George Allen & Unwin Ltd, London 1943.

Clayton, C. F., *The Wall is Strong,* Long, London 1958.

Curzon, M. I., 2nd Baroness Ravensdale, *In Many Rhythms: an autobiography,* Weidenfeld & Nicolson, London 1953.

Dalton, E. H. J. N., *The Fateful Years: Memoirs 1931–45,* Frederick Muller Ltd, London 1957.

Domvile, Sir B., *From Admiral to Cabin Boy,* The Boswell Publishing Co. Ltd, London 1947.

Hannington, W., *Unemployed Struggles 1919–1936,* Lawrence & Wishart, London 1977.

Hyde, D., *I Believed: The Autobiography of a former British Communist,* Heinemann, London 1951.

Jacobs, J., *Out of the Ghetto,* Simon, London 1978.

Jerrold, D., *Georgian Adventures,* Collins, London 1937.

Jones, J., *Unfinished Journey,* Hamilton, London 1937.

Litvinoff, E., *Journey Through a Small Planet,* Penguin Books, Harmondsworth 1976.

Mosley, O., *My Life,* Nelson, London 1968. This autobiography began the gradual process of Mosley's post-war rehabilitation, which was still in progress at the time of his death. It provides a lucid and interesting account of his entire political career, and illustrates the development of his centrist philosophy, which was to lead him into fascism. At times, however, as one would expect, Mosley's memory can be very selective. As an exercise in retrospective self-justification, the book lay the foundations for the post-war revisionist interpretations of British fascism (especially in regard to anti-Semitism) to which Robert Skidelsky later gave historical credence.

Mosley, N., *Rules of the Game,* Secker & Warburg, London 1982.

—— *Beyond the Pale,* Secker & Warburg, London 1983.

Nicolson, H., *Diaries and Letters 1930–39,* ed. Nigel Nicolson, Collins, London 1966.

Paynter, W. *My Generation,* Allen & Unwin, London 1972.

Piratin, P., *Our Flag Stays Red,* Lawrence & Wishart, London 1980.

Speer, A., *Inside the Third Reich,* Sphere Books Ltd, London 1978.

Toynbee, P., *Friends Apart: A Memoir of Esmond Romilly and Jasper Ridley,* MacGibben & Kee, London 1954.

Trory, E., *Between the Wars: Recollections of a Communist Organiser,* Crabtree Press, Brighton 1974.

Williamson, H., *My Life's Purpose,* R. T. Cotton, Exeter 1939?

B. BOOKS AND PAMPHLETS

The works below are subdivided generally according to political affiliation. The most numerous are those produced by fascists and fascist movements. The most important general exposition of inter-war British fascism can be found in the works of Mosley, particularly *The Greater Britain, Blackshirt Policy, Fascism: 100 Questions Asked and Answered* and *Tomorrow We Live*. These chart the chronological development of the party's programme throughout the decade.

Anti-fascist publications arising from conservative, liberal, Jewish, or anonymous sources have been separated also, as have those which were produced specifically by the Labour and trade union movement, or by the ILP and CP.

The final miscellaneous subdivision includes selections from the writings of the French racist philosopher Gobineau, publications of the British People's Party (which included many ex-members of the BUF), and of the 18B Publicity Council, which agitated against the injustices inherent in the wartime internments, as well as a few of the major theoretical works relating to European fascist movements.

(i) FASCIST

Allen, W. E. D., *B.U.F., Oswald Mosley and British Fascism,* Murray, London 1934. Written under the pseudonym James Drennan.

—— *Fascism in relation to British History and Character*, BUF Publications Ltd, London 1933?

British Union of Fascists, *Appeal to Dockers,* n.p.

—— *A.R.P., Be Prepared,* Greater Britain Publications Ltd, London 1938?

—— *Bowie's Annual,* Action Press, London n.d., WL.

—— *Britain and Jewry,* Abbey Supplies, London 1938?, BL.

—— *The British Union and the Transport Workers,* n.p., 1938?, LPL.

—— *British Union Constitution and Rules,* BUF, London 1936, WL.

—— *British Union: Pictorial Record 1932–37,* BUF, London 1938.

—— *The British Union stands for Trade Unionism,* n.p., LPL.

—— *Britons You are Pledged to Die for Poles . . .,* n.p.

—— *A Guide to Constituency Organisation,* BUF Publications Ltd, London 1935?, LSE.

—— *Is Lancashire Doomed?,* Abbey Supplies, London n.d.

—— *Labour Means War: Stop the War Mongers,* n.p. 1938?

—— *Lancashire Betrayed: cotton: British Union Textile Policy,* Abbey Supplies, London n.d.

—— *The Miners' Only Hope,* BUF Publications Ltd, London n.d.

—— *Pharmacy and British Union,* Abbey Supplies, London n.d., BL.

—— *Red Violence and Blue Lies,* BUF, London 1934.

—— *Shot and Shell: extracts from Blackshirt,* Abbey Supplies, London 1936.

—— *Stop War,* n.p., 1939?

—— *Trade Unionists! You are the Victims,* n.p., 1938, LPL.

—— *Yorkshire Betrayed: wool: British Union Textile Policy,* Abbey Supplies, London n.d.

—— *Why Should Britain Assist Abyssinia?*, n.p., 1935?

Chambers-Hunter, W. K. A., *British Union and Social Credit,* n.p.

Chesterton, A. K., *Apotheosis of the Jew,* Abbey Supplies, London n.d.

—— *Fascism and the Press,* BUF Publications Ltd, London n.d., WL.

—— *Oswald Mosley, Portrait of a Leader*, Action Press, London 1937.

—— *Why I Left Mosley,* National Socialist League, London 1938. ——

Clarke, E. G., *The British Union and the Jews,* Abbey Supplies, London n.d., BL.

Drennan, J., see under Allen, W. E. D.

Fuller, J. F. C., *Towards Armageddon: the Defence Problem and its solution,* Lovet Dickson, London 1937.

Gordon-Canning, R., *The Holy Land: Arab or Jew,* BUF, London 1938, BL.

—— *The Inward Strength of a National Socialist,* Greater Britain Publications, London 1938, BL.

—— *Mind Britain's Business,* Greater Britain Publications Ltd, London 1938?

Goulding, M., *Peace Betrayed: Labour's Peace Policy through British Union eyes,* Greater Britain Publications Ltd, London 1939?

Griggs, A. B., *Women and Fascism: 10 Important Points,* BUF Publications, London 1935?, LPL.

Heyward, P., *Menace of the Chain Store: British Union Policy for the distributive trades,* Greater Britain Publications, London n.d.

—— *Shopkeepers at War: 'gainst war and monopoly,* Abbey Supplies, London n.d.

Hill, R. D., *'Gainst Trust and Monopoly: commercial travellers and shopkeepers action,* Abbey Supplies, London n.d., BL.

Imperial Fascist League, *Bolshevism is Jewish,* IFL, London 1939.

—— *Jewish Press Control,* IFL, London 1939, WL.

Jenks, J., *The Land and the People: British Union Policy for agriculture,* Greater Britain Publications Ltd, London n.d.

Joyce, W., *Dictatorship,* BUF Publications Ltd, London 1933, LSE.

—— *Fascism and Jewry,* BUF Publications Ltd, London 1936?

—— *Fascism and India,* BUF Publications Ltd, London 1935?

—— *Fascist Education Policy,* BUF Publications Ltd, London 1933, BL.

—— *National Socialism Now,* National Socialist League, London 1937.

—— *Twilight over England,* NV Uitgevers-maatschappij 'Oceanus', The Hague 1942.

Leaper, W. J., *Fascism for the Million,* BUF Publications Ltd, London 1936.

Leese, A., *Devilry in the Holy Land,* IFL, London n.d.

—— *My Irrelevant Defence,* IFL, London 1938.

Mosley, O., *The Alternative,* Mosley Publications, Ramsbury 1947.

—— *Blackshirt Policy,* BUF Publications Ltd, London 1934, LSE.

—— *The British Peace and how to get it,* Sanctuary Press Ltd, London 1940?, LPL.

—— *British Union Policy: 10 Points,* n.p., LPL.

—— *Fascism in Britain,* BUF Publications Ltd, London 1934?, LSE.

—— *Fascism: 100 Questions Asked and Answered,* BUF Publications Ltd, London 1936.

—— *The Greater Britain,* BUF, London 1932. Further editions of this important work were published in 1934 and 1939. I have used the 1932 edition in both the text and footnotes except where otherwise stated.

—— *Mosley: Right or Wrong?* Lion Books, London 1961, BL.

—— *Mosley: What they say, What they said, What he is,* Raven Books, London 1947.

—— *My Answer,* Mosley Publications, Ramsbury 1946.

—— *10 Points of Fascism,* BUF Publications Ltd, London 1934?

—— *Tomorrow We Live,* 4th edn, Greater Britain Publications, London 1939. Editions 1–3 were published in 1938, 4–6 in 1939, and 7–8 in 1946. Except where otherwise stated, edition 4 has been used in the text and footnotes.

Raven Thomson, A., *Big Fish and Little Fish: Finance, Democracy, and the Shopkeepers,* BUF Publications Ltd, London 1936.

—— *The Coming Corporate State,* Greater Britain Publications Ltd, London 1935.

—— *The Economics of British Fascism,* Bonner, London 1933.

Risden, W., *Strike Action or Power Action,* Abbey Supplies Ltd, London n.d., LPL.

Tyndall, J., *The Authoritarian State,* NSM, London 1962.

—— *The Case for Economic Nationalism,* NF Policy Committee, 1975.

(ii) ANTI-FASCIST

All-British Anti-Fascist Committee, *All About Sir Oswald Mosley,* (A-B A-FC, Sheffield, 1937), LPL.

Britain's Fifth Column; a plain warning, Anchor Press Ltd, Tiptree 1940, WL.

The B.U.F. by the B.U.F., Anchor Press Ltd, Tiptree 1938?, LSE.

Dolan, C. M., *Mosley Exposed: the Blackshirt Racket,* n.p., 1935?, LPL.

Jewish Labour Council Workers' Circle, *Sir Oswald Mosley and the Jews,* JLCWC, London 1935, LPL.

Laski, N., *Jewish Rights and Jewish Wrongs,* Soncino Press, London 1939.

Melville, C. F., *The Truth about the New Party: and much else besides concerning Sir Oswald Mosley's political aims, the Nazi movement of Herr Adolf Hitler and the adventure in political philosophy of Mr. Wyndam Lewis,* Wishart, London 1931.

Miles, A. C., *Mosley in Motley,* A. C. Miles, London 1937.

Montague, I., *Blackshirt Brutality: the Story of Olympia,* Workers' Bookshop, London 1934.

National Constitution Defence Movement, *Fascist Fallacies,* NCDM, London n.d., WL.

National Council for Civil Liberties, *The Harworth Colliery Strike . . .,* NCCL, London 1936, LSE.

—— *Report of a Commission of Inquiry into certain disturbances at Thurloe Square South Kensington on March 22nd, 1936,* NCCL, London 1936.

—— *Sir Oswald Mosley's Albert Hall meeting, March 22nd, 1936: extracts from statements of eye-witnesses,* NCCL, London 1936.

Rudlin, W. A., *The Growth of Fascism in Great Britain,* Allen & Unwin, London 1935.

True Blue Patriots of the B.U.F., Lane, London 1940?

Vindicator, (pseud.), *Fascists at Olympia. A record of eye-witnesses and victims,* Victor Gollancz Ltd, London 1934.

Wegg-Prosser, C. F., *Fascism Exposed,* Jewish People's Council against Fascism and Anti-Semitism, London 1938.

Youth Anti-Fascist Committee, *British Fascism Explained,* Union of Democratic Control, London 1935, LPL.

(iii) LABOUR PARTY AND TRADE UNION MOVEMENT

Bermondsey Trades Council, *Bermondsey Says 'No' to Fascism: United against Mosley*, BTC, London 1937.

Cripps, S., *'National' Fascism in Britain*, Socialist League, London n.d., LSE.

Joint Consultative Committee of the London Trades Council and the London Labour Party, *The Labour Movement and Fascism*, n.p., 1934?, LPL.

Labour Party (Economic Advisory Bureau), *Memo on Fascism*, Oldhams Press Ltd, London 1934.

Labour Research Department, *Fascism: Fight it Now*, Labour Research Department, London 1937, BL.

—— *Mosley Fascism: The Man, his Policy and Methods*, LRD, London 1935, WL.

—— *Who Backs Mosley? Fascist promise and Fascist performance*, LRD, London 1934, LSE.

Lansbury, G., *Anti-Semitism in the East End*, Woburn Press, London 1936.

Martin, K., *Fascism, Democracy and the Press*, New Statesman & Nation, London 1938.

National Amalgamation of Shop Assistants, Warehousemen and Clerks, *Fascism or Freedom. Which?* n.p., 1934?, LPL.

National Council of Labour, *Fascism: The Enemy of the People*, NCL, London 1934, BL.

—— *What is this Fascism?* NCL, London 1934?, LSE.

Trade Union Congress, General Council, *United Against Fascism*, TUC, London 1934, LPL.

Wall, A. M., & Morrison, H., *The Labour Movement and Fascism: a special memorandum*, Joint Consultative Council of the London Trades Council and London Labour Party, London 1934, LPL.

(iv) THE COMMUNIST PARTY OF GREAT BRITAIN AND THE INDEPENDENT LABOUR PARTY

CPGB, *Drowned in a Sea of Working Class Activity, September 9th*, CPGB, London 1934.

—— *Put Mosley Back in Prison*, CPGB, London 1943, WL.

Douglas, J. L., *Spotlight on Fascism*, CPGB, London 1934, LSE.

Dutt, R. P., *Fascism and Social Revolution*, Martin Lawrence Ltd, London 1934. A second edition was printed in 1974.

ILP, *They Did Not Pass: 300,000 Workers Say Not to Mosley: A souvenir of the East London workers' victory over Fascism*, ILP, London 1936, LSE.

Pollitt, H., *Selected Articles and Speeches, vol. I, 1919–36*, Lawrence & Wishart, London 1953.

Rust, W., *Mosley and Lancashire*, Labour Monthly, London 1935, LPL.

Strachey, J., *The Menace of Fascism*, Victor Gollancz, London 1933.

Young Communist League, *10 Points Against Fascism*, YCL, London 1934.

(v) OTHERS

Biddiss, M. (ed.), *Gobineau: Selected Political Writings,* Jonathan Cape, London 1971.

British People's Party, *La Verité Cette Guerre,* BPP, London 1940, WL.

18B Publicity Council, *The Case of G. R. Merriman,* 18B Publicity Council, London n.d., WL.

—— *18B: In Search of Justice,* 18B Publicity Council, London n.d., WL.

Nilus, *Protocols of the Learned Elders of Zion,* The Britons Publishing Society, London 1931. Translated from the Russian by V. E. Marsden.

Noakes, J. & Pridham, G. (eds.), *Nazism 1919–45,* University of Exeter 1983.

Seton Hutchinson, G., *The National Workers' Party,* National Socialist Workers' Party of Great Britain, London 1936, WL.

Thomas, H. (ed.), *José Antonio Primo de Rivera: Selected Writings,* Jonathan Cape, London 1972.

C. NEWSPAPERS   ~~British Library~~ ?

Action, Vol. I., nos. 1–13, October–December 1931. This weekly newspaper of the New Party was edited by H. Nicolson. It was lavishly produced and attempted to cater for a wide variety of tastes by covering an extensive range of cultural pursuits and hobbies outside the sphere of national politics. Its circulation fell rapidly throughout its existence and at the end of the year it was terminated by Mosley in an effort to preserve party funds.

Action, February 1936–June 1940. From 1936 until its suppression in 1940, *Action* was the NUF's leading weekly news-journal. Its appearance resembled that of a national daily newspaper, with pages devoted to foreign affairs, women's issues, sport, reviews and even a weekly short story. In addition to this there was coverage of home affairs, and news concerning the development of the party and its programme. Most leading members of the movement contributed articles, including Mosley, Raven Thomson, Chesterton, Joyce, Beckett, and Gordon-Canning.

Action News Service, 30 April–24 May 1940. Issued during the final weeks of the party's life, this weekly newsletter was a supplement to *Action.* Given the deteriorating military situation in Europe, unsurprisingly it concentrated upon the futility of the war with Germany and included articles by Mosley calling for the negotiation of an honourable peace whilst Britain was still in a position of strength.

Action, 1957–64. (Became *Action and the European.*)

The Blackshirt, February 1933–August 1938. *The Blackshirt* was the party's first newspaper and began as an austere four-page monthly, concentrating solely upon politics and the BUF's programme for Britain. Soon it became a weekly publication and grew in size, receiving contributions from most leading fascists, including Mosley. Between January and June 1934 it was relegated to the position of an internal news bulletin for party members only, and was replaced on the news-stands by *The Fascist Week.* In June 1934 it emerged from its obscurity, swallowed up *The Fascist Week* and became once again the party's premier news organ. It lost its exalted position in 1936, however, through the launch of *Action,* which was larger, more diverse in its coverage and, with a cover price of 2*d,* was twice as expensive. *The Blackshirt* remained devoted to overtly political issues, and to those which concerned the development of the party directly. From the beginning of February 1938 it became the victim of financial economies and was reduced to a monthly. From September 1938 it was divided regionally into northern, southern, and east London editions. *Southern Blackshirt,* September 1938–March 1939, *East London Blackshirt,* April–May 1939.

Combat, August 1958–March 1968.
The Daily Express, 1933.
The Daily Herald, 1933–7.
The Daily Mail, 1933–7.
The Daily Telegraph, 1932–46.
The Daily Worker, 1933–39.
The East London Advertiser, 1937.
The Evening Standard, 1936.
The Fascist, 1934. The monthly national newspaper of the IFL, edited by Arnold Leese.
The Fascist Week, November 1933–May 1934. This short-lived BUF publication replaced *The Blackshirt* during the first half of 1934. It adopted the same format and included articles by the leading members of the BUF. In June 1934 it was incorporated into *The Blackshirt.*
The Guardian, 1962.
The Jewish Chronicle, 1933–68.
The Kensington Post, 1959.
The Manchester Guardian, 1929–40.
The Morning Post, 1936–7.
National Front News, 1976.
The News Chronicle, 1936–7.
Reynolds News, June 1959.
The St Pancras Gazette, 1938
The Shepherds Bush Gazette, 1959.
Spearhead, 1964.
The Sunday Pictorial, 1934.
The Times, 1931–68.
Union, 1948–57.
The Yorkshire Post, 1940.

D. PERIODICALS

British Union Quarterly, I–IV (January 1937–Spring 1940). This periodical succeeded the *Fascist Quarterly* as the BUF's forum for the more theoretical and intellectual aspects of fascism. Each edition included poetry, book reviews, and coverage of the arts, as well as several articles on politics or economics. Contributors included Mosley and most of the leading members of the party, and some fellow travelling intellectuals including Wyndham Lewis, Ezra Pound and Roy Campbell, LSE.
Fascist Quarterly, I–II (January 1935–December 1936). The forerunner of the

BUQ, it used the same format and included contributions from similar sources. BL.

Green Band, II, 46–52, (August–September 1934). The official organ of the New World Fellowship, an anti-fascist organisation which flourished in the early 1930s.

Jewish Economic Forum, I (28 July 1933).

Labour Magazine, IX (April 1931).

Labour Monthly, XIII–XVI (1931–34). Journal of the CPGB, it included articles on fascism by R. P. Dutt and J. Strachey.

Left Book News, VII (November 1936).

Liberal Magazine, XLIV (1936).

The Listener, LXXX (31 October 1968). Interview with Mosley.

Nation (New York), CXLVI (15 January 1938).

New Republic, LXXVIII–LXXX (May–August 1934).

New Statesman and Nation, V–XIV (1933–7).

Political Quarterly, III–V (January 1932–April 1934).

Quarterly Review, CCLXI (October 1933).

Review of Reviews, LXXXI, 494 (March 1931).

Round Table, XXIV (June 1934).

The Saturday Review, CLVII–CLVIII (May–December 1934).

Searchlight, 1965–7; 1975–

The Spectator, CLII–CLVIII (June–October 1936).

The Weekend Review, III, 46 (January–June 1931).

West London Regional Bulletin, no. 1? (1934?). A fortnightly news-sheet produced by the Paddington Branch of the BUF. WL.

Weiner Library Bulletin, 1947–

E. PUBLIC RECORDS OFFICE

Since 1981 numerous documents relating to the BUF have been released by the authorities, including the lengthy transcript of Mosley's interrogation in 1940.

Cabinet Papers, 1934–45.

Foreign Office papers, 1935.

Metropolitan Police and Special Branch files, Series 2, 1934–40.

F. GOVERNMENT PUBLICATIONS AND ANNUAL REPORTS

Board of Deputies of British Jews, *Annual Report*, 1938 (BoD, London 1939).

HC Debs, 5th series, vols. 133–423, October 1920–June 1946.

National Council for Civil Liberties, *Annual Report and Balance Sheet* (1938–9), NCCL, London 1939.

Commissioner of Police of the Metropolis, *Report of the Commissioner of Police of the Metropolis for the year 1936*, HMSO, London 1937.

G. MISCELLANEOUS PRIMARY SOURCES

Circular sent to the secretaries of all Borough and Divisional Labour Parties and Women's Sections, Labour mayors, MPs, and LCC members for the boroughs of Bermondsey, Lambeth, and Southwark; 1937. LPL. A document urging non-attendance at the BUF's march through Bermondsey on 3 October 1937.

Correspondence in files on anti-fascism re: a women's international congress against war and fascism, July 1934. LPL.

Defence Regulation 18AA, copies of orders made by Home Secretary relating to prescribed organisations, nos. 767–774, 26 May 1940; and no. 1273, 10 July 1940. LPL.

'Labour Democracy and Fascism', from the proceedings of the 54th Annual Convention of the American Federation of Labour, San Francisco, 1934. LPL. Speech by W. Citrine condemning fascism.

Labour Party, National Joint Council, Research Document n. 269, Quotations taken from *The Blackshirt* and *The Fascist Week,* 25 June 1934. LPL.

Miscellaneous press cuttings, Wiener Library, London.

Payne, W., *A London Busman Reports on Fascism,* European Workers' Anti-Fascist Congress – British Delegation Committee (n.p. 1933?).

Replies to fascist questionnaire, 27 July 1934, L.P./FAS/34/1. LPL. This questionnaire was circulated to the secretaries of all Divisional Labour Parties, Industrial Trades Councils, and party agents on 12 June 1934. Its purpose was to monitor the regional strength of the BUF, but often the information received was too vague or too general to give an accurate picture of fascist development.

Turcotti, E, (ed.), *Fascist Europe. ... An Anglo-Italian symposium ... published under the auspices of the National Institute of Fascist Culture of Pavia,* vol. 1, 2nd edn, National Institute of Fascist Culture, Milan, 1939. LSE. British contributors sympathetic to fascism and the BUF included the Revd. H. E. B. Nye, Rear-Admiral W. E. R. Martin, and E. G. Mandeville Roe.

Selective secondary literature

Allen, A. S., *The Nazi Seizure of Power,* Eyre & Spottiswoode, London 1966.

Arendt, H., *The Origins of Totalitarianism,* George Allen & Unwin, London 1958.

Arnot, R. P., *The Policy of the Communist Party of Great Britain from its foundation,* Lawrence & Wishart, London 1940.

Aquarone, A., 'Italy: the crisis and corporate economy', *Journal of Contemporary History,* IV, 4 (October 1969).

Benewick, R. & Smith, T. (eds.), *Direct Action and Democratic Politics,* Allen & Unwin, London 1972.

Benewick, R., *The Fascist Movement in Britain,* Allen Lane, The Penguin Press, London 1972. This detailed account of the development of British fascism concerns itself primarily with the BUF and the threat posed by it to public order. It is marred by a liberal's failure to comprehend fully either the nature of interwar capitalism, which spawned fascism, or the attractiveness of the ideology itself.

—— 'Interpretations of British fascism', *Political Studies,* XXIV, 3, September 1976.

Billig, M., *Fascists,* Harcourt Brace Jovanovich, London 1978.

Birch, J. E. L., *Why they Joined the Fascists,* People's Press, London 1937.

Bosworth, R. J. B., 'The British Press, the Conservatives, and Mussolini 1920–34', *Journal of Contemporary History,* V, 2, 1970.

Brady, R. A., *The Spirit and Structure of German Fascism,* Victor Gollancz Ltd, London 1937.

Brewer, J. D., 'The British Union of Fascists, Sir Oswald Mosley and Birmingham: An analysis of the Content and Context of an Ideology', MSoc Science degree, University of Birmingham, 1975.

Brozat, M., *The Hitler State,* Longman, New York 1981.

Bullock, A., *Hitler. A Study in Tyranny,* Oldhams Books, London 1964.

—— *The Life and Times of Ernest Bevin, vol. I. Trade Union Leader: 1881–1940,* Heinemann, London 1960.

Bunyan, T., *The History and Practice of the Political Police in Britain,* Quartet Books, London 1977.

Burke, B., *Rebels with a Cause: The History of Hackney Trades Council 1900–1975,* Hackney Trades Council and Hackney Workers Educational Association, London 1975.

Cammett, J. M., 'Communist Theories of Fascism 1920–35', *Science and Society,* XXI, 2, spring 1967.

Carpenter, L. P., 'Corporatism in Britain 1930–45', *Journal of Contemporary History* II, 1976.

Carr, W., *Arms Autarchy and Aggression,* Edward Arnold, London 1978.

Carsten, F. L., *The Rise of Fascism,* Methuen & Co. Ltd, London 1978.

Catlin, Sir G. E. G., 'Fascist stirrings in Great Britain', *Current History,* XXXXIX, February 1934.

Childers, T., 'The Social Basis of the National Socialist vote', *Journal of Contemporary History,* II, 1976.

Chorley, R. S. T., *The Threat of Civil Liberty,* Haldane Society, London n.d.

Cole, G. D. H., *A History of the Labour Party from 1914,* Routledge & Kegan Paul, London 1948.

—— *The People's Front,* Victor Gollancz, London 1937.

Cole, J. A., *Lord Haw Haw – and William Joyce: the full story,* Faber & Faber, London 1964.

Craig, F. W. S., *British Parliamentary Election results 1918–49,* Macmillan Press Ltd, London 1977.

Cross, C., *Adolf Hitler,* Coronet Books, London 1974.

—— *The Fascists in Britain,* Barrie & Rockcliffe, London 1961. A much respected history of British fascism, concentrating upon Mosley and the BUF. It gives the impression of seeking to enquire rather than attempting to justify or condemn.

De Locke, M. J., 'The National Front and the General Election of 1974', *New Community,* V, 3, autumn 1976.

De Felice, R., *Fascism: An Informal Introduction to its Theory and Practice,* Transaction Books, New Jersey 1976.

Diggins, J. P., *Mussolini and Fascism. The view from America,* New Jersey

1972.

Donoghue, B. & Jones, G. W., *Herbert Morrison: Portrait of a Politician*, Weidenfeld & Nicolson, London 1973.

Edgar, D., 'Racism, fascism and the politics of the National Front', *Race and Class,* XIX, 2, autumn 1976.

Edwards, J., *The British Government and the Spanish Civil War,* Macmillan, London 1979.

Falk, R., 'Local Elections', *Spectator,* CC, 18 April 1958.

Fielding, N., *The National Front,* Collins, London 1981.

Foot, M., *Aneurin Bevan: a biography. vol. I. 1897–1945,* McGibbon & Kee, London 1962.

Geiger, D. M., 'British Fascism as revealed in the British Union of Fascists' Press'. PhD thesis, New York University, 1963. This piece of work is distinguished by a startling degree of naivety. Its conclusions concerning both British society and the BUF are often banal.

Goldman, A. L., 'Defence Regulation 18B: emergency internment of aliens and political dissenters in Great Britain during World War II', *The Journal of British Studies,* XII, 2, May 1973.

Guerin, D., *Fascism and Big Business,* Monad Press, New York 1979.

Hamilton, A., *The Appeal of Fascism: A study of intellectuals and fascism 1919–1945,* Blond, London 1971.

Harrison, J., *The Reactionaries,* Victor Gollancz Ltd, London 1966.

Harrison, M., *Peter Cheyney Prince of Hokum,* Neville Spearman, London 1954.

Hayes, P. M., *Fascism,* George Allen & Unwin Ltd, London 1973.

Heydon, H. K., *Fascism and Providence,* Sheed & Ward, London 1937.

Hibbert, H., *Benito Mussolini,* Penguin, Harmondsworth 1975.

Holmes, C., *Anti-Semitism in British Society 1876–1939,* Arnold, London 1979.

——— *Immigrants and Minorities in British Society,* Allen & Unwin, London 1978.

Janus, pseudonym, *Spectator,* CLXXVI, 14 June 1946.

Kedward, H. R., *Fascism in Western Europe 1900–45,* Blackie, Glasgow 1973.

Kele, M. H., *Nazis and Workers,* Chapel Hill 1972.

Kenyon, R., *Fascism and Christianity,* The Industrial Fellowship, London 1935.

Kibblewhite, E. & Rigby, A., *Fascism in Aberdeen – street politics in the 1930s,* Aberdeen People's Press, Aberdeen 1978.

Kidd, R., *British Liberty in Danger: an introduction to the study of civil rights,* Lawrence & Wishart, London 1940.

Koss, S., 'One of the lost boys', *New Statesman and Nation,* LXXXIX, 29 March 1975.

Laqueur, W. (ed.), *Fascism: A Reader's Guide,* Penguin Books Ltd, Harmondsworth 1979.

Larsen, S. U., Hagtvet, R. & Myklebust, J. P. (eds.), *Who were the Fascists?,* Bergen/Oslo/Tromso 1980.

Lebzelter, G. C., *Political Anti-Semitism in England 1918–39,* The Macmillan Press Ltd, London 1978. This survey of anti-Semitic groups in inter-war Britain includes a considerable amount of useful information on the BUF and succeeds in establishing it within the limited context of British anti-Semitism. It is less successful in analysing the essence of the BUF, which lay in the party's fascism rather than in its anti-Semitism.

Ledeen, M. A., *Universal Fascism,* Howard Fertig, New York 1972.

Lee, E. G., *Christianity in Chains*, Longmans, Green & Co, London 1939.

Lipset, S., *Political Man*, Heinemann, London 1960.

—— *Social Stratification and 'Right Wing Extremism . . .'*, University of California 1960.

Littlejohn, D., *The Patriotic Traitors*, Heinemann, London 1972.

Lloyd, R., *Revolutionary Religion, Christianity, Fascism and Communism*, Student Christian Movement Press, London 1938.

Longmate, N., *If Britain had Fallen*, BBC and Arrow Books, London 1972.

Lunn, K. & Thurlow, R. C. (eds.), *British Fascism*, Croom Helm, London 1980. This collection of individual essays upon various aspects of British fascism, with particular reference to the BUF, varies in quality. Amongst the best is that by Stuart Rawnsley dealing with the party's membership in north-west England.

McKibben, R., *The Evolution of the Labour Party 1910–24*, Oxford University Press 1974.

Mack Smith, D., *Italy. A Modern History*, University of Michigan 1959.

Mack Smith, D., *Mussolini*, Weidenfeld & Nicolson, London 1981.

Mandle, *Anti-Semitism and the British Union of Fascists*, Longmans, Green & Co. Ltd, London 1968.

—— 'The leadership of the British Union of Fascists', *The Australian Journal of Politics and History*, XII, December 1966.

—— 'The New Party', *Historical Studies: Australia and New Zealand*, XII, 47, October 1966.

Mason, T., 'Labour in the Third Reich', *Past and Present*, 33, April 1969.

Martin, K., 'The prophecies of doom', *New Statesman and Nation*, LXXVI, 25 October 1968.

Meetings, Uniforms, and Public Order, Jordan & Sons Ltd, London 1937?. WL.

Middlemas, K. & Barnes, J., *Baldwin. A Biography*, The Macmillan Company, London 1970.

Milward, A. S., 'French labour and the German economy 1942–45', *Economic History Review*, 23, 1970.

Mosse, G. (ed.), *International Fascism: New Thoughts and New Approaches*, Sage Publications Ltd, London 1979.

Mowat, C. L., *Britain Between the Wars, 1918–1940*, Methuen & Co. Ltd, London 1976.

Mullally, F., *Fascism inside England*, Morris Books, London 1946. An interesting study of Mosley and the BUF by Frederic Mullally, an anti-fascist journalist. Today, although much of it remains valid, it appears rather dated and a little too simple.

Nearing, S., *Fascism*, n.p., 1934?, LPL.

Newton, K., *The Sociology of British Communism*, Allen Lane, The Penguin Press, London 1969.

Nolte, E., *The Three Faces of Fascism. Action Francais. Italian fascism, National Socialism*, Weidenfeld & Nicolson, London 1965.

Nugent, N., 'The anti-immigration groups', *New Community*, V, 3, autumn 1976.

Nugent, N. & King, R. (eds.), *The British Right: Conservative and right wing politics in Britain*, Saxon House, Farnborough 1977.

Pelling, H., *The British Communist Party*, Adam & Charles Black, London 1975.

—— *A History of British Trade Unionism,* Penguin Books Ltd, Harmondsworth 1979.

—— *A Short History of the Labour Party,* 4th edn, The Macmillan Press Ltd, London 1974.

Pimlott, B., *Labour and the Left in the 1930s,* Cambridge University Press 1966.

Pinder, J., *50 years of Political and Economic Planning,* Heinemann, London 1981.

Pryce-Jones, D., *Unity Mitford: A Quest,* Weidenfeld & Nicolson, London 1976.

Randall, L., *An Economic History of Argentina in the Twentieth Century,* Columbia University Press, New York 1978.

Raymond, J. (ed.), *The Balwin Age,* Eyre & Spottiswoode, London 1960.

Rees, P. (ed.), *Facism in Britain. An annotated bibliography,* The Harvester Press, Sussex, 1979. As a bibliography this piece of work is reasonably comprehensive and extremely valuable to students of British fascism. The editor's own contribution to the debate, however, in the form of an essay at the beginning of the volume, leaves much to be desired.

Reich, W., *The Mass Psychology of Fascism,* 3rd edn, Orgone Institute Press, New York 1946. Translated from the German by T. P. Wolfe.

Ridley, F. A., *Fascism: What is it?,* Freedom Press, London 1941.

—— *The Papacy and Fascism,* Martin, Secker & Warburg Ltd, London 1937.

Rogger, H. & Weber, E. (eds.), *The European Right: A Historical Profile,* University of California Press, Berkeley 1965.

Rose, L. S., *Fascism in Britain,* n.p., London 1948. LPL.

Sharf, A., *Nazi Racialism and the British Press, 1933–45,* The World Jewish Congress, London 1964?

Skidelsky, R., *Oswald Mosley,* Macmillan, London 1975. Although well-written and scholarly, the book suggests that Skidelsky's judgment was warped by his obvious sympathy and admiration for his subject. Consequently, as a biography it neglects the unsavoury details of Mosley's personal life and refuses to condemn sufficiently his political failings. As a history of the BUF its considerable sympathy for the party tends to detract from some of the author's more legitimate analysis.

—— *Politicians and the Slump: the Labour Government of 1929–31,* Macmillan, London 1967.

—— 'The Problem of Mosley: why a fascist failed', *Encounter,* XXXIII, September 1969.

—— 'The return of Mosley – a reply', *Wiener Library Bulletin,* XXX, 43/44, 1977.

Sparks, C., 'Fascism in Britain', *International Socialism,* IXXI, September 1974.

Spengler, O., *The Decline of the West,* 2 vols., George Allen & Unwin, London 1926–9.

Stent, R., *A Bespattered Page?,* Andre Deutsch, London 1980.

Stern, J. P., *The Führer and the People,* Fontana/Collins, London 1978.

Stevenson, J. & Cook, C., *The Slump,* Quartet Books Ltd, London 1979.

'The Story of Regulation 18B: freedom's defence against subversion', *Wiener Library Bulletin,* IX, 5/6, September/December 1955.

Strachey, J., *The Theory and Practice of Socialism,* Victor Gollancz, London 1936.

Sugar, P. F. (ed.), *Native Fascism in the Successor States, 1918–45,* California 1971.

Tannenbaum, E. R., *Fascism in Italy. Society and Culture, 1922–45,* Allen Lane, London 1972.

Taylor, A. J. P., *English History 1914–45,* Pelican Books, London 1977.

—— (ed.), *Lloyd George,* Hamilton, London 1971.

Taylor, S., *The National Front in English Politics,* Macmillan, London 1982.

Thomas, H., *The Spanish Civil War,* 3rd edn, Penguin Books, Harmondsworth 1977.

Thompson, E., *Fascist Threat to Britain,* Communist Party of Great Britain, London 1947.

Thurlow, R. C., 'Political Witchcraft: the roots of Fascism', *Patterns of Prejudice,* XI, May–June 1977.

Toland, J., *Adolf Hitler,* Doubleday, New York 1976.

Trotsky, L., *Fascism: What it is and how to fight it,* Pathfinder Press Inc, New York 1969.

Trythall, A. J., *'Boney' Fuller: the Intellectual General 1878–1966,* Cassell, London 1977.

Turner, H. A. (ed.), *Reappraisals of Fascism,* New Viewpoints, New York 1975.

Vajda, M., *Fascism as a Mass Movement,* Allison & Busby, London 1976.

Walker, M., *The National Front,* Fontana/Collins, London 1978.

Weber, E., *Varieties of Fascism: Doctrines of Revolution in the Twentieth Century,* Van Nostrand, Princeton 1964.

Wilkinson, E. C. & Conze, E., *Why Fascism,* Selwyn & Blount, London 1934.

Williams, D. G. T., *Keeping the Peace: the Police and Public Order,* Hutchinson, London 1967.

Wood, N., *Communism and the British Intellectuals,* Gollancz, London 1959.

Woolfe, S. J. (ed.), *The Nature of Fascism,* Weidenfeld & Nicolson, London 1968.

—— (ed.), *Fascism in Europe,* Methuen & Co. Ltd, London 1981.